Spring 88

ENVIRONMENTAL DISASTERS AND COLLECTIVE TRAUMA

A JOURNAL OF
ARCHETYPE
AND
CULTURE

Winter 2012

SPRING JOURNAL
New Orleans, Louisiana

SPRING: A JOURNAL OF ARCHETYPE AND CULTURE

Nancy Cater, Editor-in-chief
Stephen Foster, Guest Co-editor

Jungiana Editor: Riccardo Bernardini   Film Review Editor: Helena Bassil-Morozow
Book Review Editor: Emilija Kiehl

Spring is the oldest Jungian psychology journal in the world. Published twice a year, each issue explores from the perspective of depth psychology a theme of contemporary relevance and contains articles as well as book and film reviews by a wide range of authors from Jungian psychology, the humanities, and other interrelated disciplines.

Founded in 1941 by the Analytical Psychology Club of New York, *Spring* was edited by Jane Pratt until 1969. With the 1970 issue, James Hillman became the editor of *Spring* and moved it to Zürich. When Hillman left Zürich and became the Dean of Graduate Studies at the University of Dallas in 1978, he transferred the editing and publishing of *Spring* there. It was edited in Dallas until 1988 when Hillman and *Spring* moved to Connecticut. Hillman retired as Publisher and Senior Editor of the journal in 1997. From 1997 until 2004 *Spring* remained in Connecticut and was edited by Charles Boer. *Spring* moved its offices to New Orleans, Louisiana in 2004 and has been edited by Nancy Cater there since.

Cover Image:
"Escape from Eden" 2006 © Rolland Golden. Watercolor 30" x 22". Reprinted by permission. All rights reserved. Courtesy of Mr. & Mrs. Manuel Zepeda.

Song Lyrics:
"We Take Care Of Our Own" by Bruce Springsteen. Copyright © 2012 Bruce Springsteen (ASCAP). Reprinted by permission. International copyright secured. All rights reserved.

Editorial and production assistance:
Drummond Books, drummondbooks@gmail.com
Cover design, typography, and layout:
Northern Graphic Design & Publishing, info@ncarto.com

Spring is a member of the Council of Editors of Learned Journals.

Spring Journal™, Spring: A Journal of Archetype and Culture™, Spring Books™,
Spring Journal Books,™ Spring Journal and Books™, and Spring Journal Publications™
are all trademarks of Spring Journal Incorporated. All Rights Reserved.

CONTENTS

Environmental Disasters and Collective Trauma

JUNGIANA

ABOUT THE COVER ARTIST

The painting on our front cover, "Escape from Eden," is by Louisiana artist Rolland Golden, who in 2005 rode out Hurricane Katrina in his home near New Orleans. In his book *Katrina: Days of Terror, Months of Anguish*, he writes:

> The paintings I produced on Hurricane Katrina were my attempt to express what I experienced, what I saw and what I didn't see but could mentally visualize. Along with my wife, daughter, and brother, we weathered Hurricane Katrina in our home near Folsom, Louisiana, fifty miles north of New Orleans. We spent a harrowing night with violent winds and rain; then the tornadoes came and toppled huge trees like they were toothpicks, landing on our house and cars, completely blocking all roads, and literally covering the ground and trapping us on our property.

> After four days without electricity or communication in grueling 96 degree heat, the roads were cleared by neighbors, enough for us to weave our way out and escape to Jackson, Mississippi.

> It's my hope that the paintings I produced on Katrina will help those who see them better understand what occurred and that the area continues to suffer long after Katrina died. It will happen again somewhere; let's hope we will be better prepared.

> —excerpt from *Katrina: Days of Terror, Months of Anguish*, exhibition catalog, New Orleans Museum of Art, 2007.

Rolland Harve Golden was born in New Orleans, Louisiana, on November 8, 1931. He graduated from the John McCrady Art School in New Orleans and opened his first gallery in June 1957 on Royal Street, in the French Quarter. He resides in Folsom, Louisiana, and Natchez, Mississippi. A nationally recognized artist, Golden's work has been published in numerous art books and magazines, including *Rolland Golden: The Journeys of a Southern Artist*; *Katrina: Days of Terror, Months of Anguish*; *The World of Rolland Golden*; and the July 7, 2007 cover of *Harper's Magazine*. Among other awards, Golden is a two-time recipient of the Thomas Hart Benton Purchase Award, a three-time recipient of the National Arts Club First Place Award, and a winner of the Winslow Homer Memorial Award. He has had more than one hundred one-man exhibitions, some of them touring nationally and internationally, notably in the former USSR in 1976–1977. Golden's works are found in many private, museum, and corporate collections, including the New Orleans Museum of Art, the Pushkin Museum of Fine Arts, Moscow, and the Ogden Museum of Southern Art.

ENVIRONMENTAL DISASTERS AND COLLECTIVE TRAUMA

A NOTE FROM THE EDITOR

NANCY CATER

Spring is delighted to have environmental scientist and Jungian analyst, Stephen Foster, Ph.D., serve as the guest co-editor of this issue. Steve has a B.S. degree in chemistry from Sussex University, and a Master's and Ph.D. in organic chemistry from Imperial College, London. He has completed post-doctoral fellowships at the University of Wisconsin in biochemistry and toxicology, and at Harvard University in cancer research, and worked as an environmental consultant in hazardous waste for over 28 years. Steve also has a Master's degree in counseling psychology from Regis University, and graduated as a Jungian analyst from the Inter-Regional Society of Jungian Analysts in 2009. His book, *Risky Business: A Jungian View of Environmental Disasters and the Nature Archetype*, expands on the archetypal aspects of environmental psychology and shadow.

Steve has prepared risk assessments and explained human health hazards to the public for thirty years and authored more than one hundred risk assessments. Some of the high-profile environmental problems he has worked on include the 2000 cyanide spill near Baia Mare, Romania, by a gold mining company into the Somes River where waters polluted with cyanide and heavy metal eventually reached the Tisza and Danube Rivers, killing large numbers of fish in Hungary and Yugoslavia; the Chuquicamata copper mine and smelter in Chile, where workers were exposed to arsenic contamination; and the Selebi-Phikwe copper mine and smelter in Botswana, where drinking water was contaminated with heavy metals.

In the United States, he has worked at numerous sites, including the Milltown Reservoir Sediments Superfund Site and Clark Fork River, Montana; the BP/Amoco refinery property closures in Wyoming; and the Rocky Flats Plant, a nuclear weapons facility in Colorado. He is also a national expert on vapor intrusion into homes.

As an environmental consultant and Jungian analyst he works with individuals and groups who have been exposed to environmental and emotional trauma and is interested in exploring our connections to our roots in nature, seeking to gain a deeper understanding and appreciation of the damage we cause the earth and ourselves.

Spring extends a huge thanks to Steve for all his work in putting this issue of the journal together.

In addition to introducing Steve Foster to our readers, *Spring* would also like to take this opportunity introduce the following new members of our editorial staff:

Film Review Editor: Helena Bassil-Morozow

Helena Bassil-Morozow is a cultural philosopher and film scholar. She grew up in Russia and holds degrees in literature and linguistics, with a Ph.D. in English, but her principal research interest is the dynamic between individual personality and sociocultural systems in industrialized and postindustrial societies. She is an honorary research fellow of the Research Institute for Media Art and Design, University of Bedfordshire. Her books include *Tim Burton: The Monster and the Crowd: A Post-Jungian Perspective,* discussing the themes of creativity, identity, nonconformity, and individualism in terms of postmodern alienation and plurality of the subject, and *The Trickster in Contemporary Film,* examining the role of the trickster in cinematic narratives against the cultural imperatives of modernity and postmodernity and arguing that cinematic tricksters invariably reflect cultural shifts and upheavals. She is currently working on two new projects, *Jungian Film Studies: The Essential Guide*, coauthored with Luke Hockley, and *The Trickster in Society and Culture* (both forthcoming from Routledge).

Jungiana Editor: Riccardo Bernardini

Riccardo Bernardini, Ph.D., Psy.D., is a historian of analytical psychology, serving as scientific advisor at the Eranos Foundation in Ascona, Switzerland. He previously taught analytical psychology and educational psychology in Italy at the University of Turin, and he maintains a private practice in Turin. His research interests are focused on the history of the Eranos phenomenon. His writings include *Carl Gustav Jung a Eranos 1933–1952*, with Gian Piero Quaglino and Augusto Romano (the English edition, *Carl Gustav Jung at Eranos, 1933–1952*, is forthcoming); *The Spirit of Eranos*, with John van Praag; and *Jung a Eranos: Il progetto della psicologia complessa* (the English edition, *Jung at Eranos: The Complex Psychology Project*, forthcoming). Current projects include editing C. G. Jung's Eranos seminar on *Opicinus de Canistris*, together with Gian Piero Quaglino and Augusto Romano; *James Hillman at Eranos, 1964–1988*; and an edition of Emma Hélène von Pelet-Narbonne's analytic diaries. He is coeditor of the *Eranos Yearbooks* (Eranos Foundation/Daimon Verlag). He also serves as Editor-in-Chief of the *Eranos Series* (Eranos Foundation/Spring Journal Books).

Book Review Editor: Emilija Kiehl

Emilija Kiehl, MSc, is a Jungian analyst trained at the British Association of Psychotherapists, London, in psychodrama and systemic family therapy. She works with individuals and couples. She has translated a number of books and and has contributed book reviews and interviews to cultural and informative publications in the former Yugoslavia. Since 2008, she has been the editor of the newsletter and online newssheet for the International Association for Analytical Psychology (IAAP). She has a private practice and works at the St. Marylebone Healing and Counselling Centre in London.

Spring warmly welcomes Helena, Emilija, and Riccardo to our editorial team and looks forward to the new perspectives and insights they will bring to the journal.

Nancy Cater, J.D., Ph.D., Editor
Spring: A Journal of Archetype and Culture
New Orleans, Louisiana

GUEST CO-EDITOR'S INTRODUCTION

Environmental disaster is a difficult topic. For those who have been in the path of a hurricane or tornado or lived through an earthquake or forest fire, it is a life-changing experience. This year Hurricane Sandy wrecked the New York–New Jersey shore and fires scorched the Rocky Mountains, raging through mountain communities and filling the air with smoke that was visible many miles away. In 2005 Hurricane Katrina and the failure of the levies destroyed much of New Orleans. And it is impossible to conceive of the devastation caused by the magnitude 9.0 earthquake and tsunami off the coast of Japan in March 2011 that led to the subsequent nuclear accident at the Fukushima Daiichi power plant, and the earthquakes in China in 2008 and 2012 that claimed almost 100,000 lives. One earthquake seems to follow on heels of another. It appears that the historical 100-year flood high-water marks are no longer improbable events (with a one percent chance of occurring) and that these flood events are starting to occur more frequently, requiring many low-lying towns to rethink flood protection and evacuation planning.

Many of us passively look on as these disasters unfold, secure on unshakable high ground, perhaps worried about friends and family, but unable to change the fate of those in the eye of the storm. We see televised images of the rubble left by storms, tsunamis, and earthquakes, with people sleeping rough in the cold streets, but we are less aware of the fact that repairing the damage may take decades. When seen through a psychological lens, in a natural disaster the natural world crashes into the personal psyche with the force of an unmediated archetype, and lives are forever changed as individuals struggle to hold the tension of safety and survival in response to the event.

Human-made environmental disasters are no less powerful. Devastating chemical contamination in communities goes unreported until health problems reach unprecedented levels; then we take notice. The human-made disaster is often a slowly unfolding series of unrecognized events causing destruction of unknown and unseen proportion. These events rarely make the news, while the more dramatic results of human error, such as Chernobyl or Fukushima, pass out of the media's attention and fall into shadowy legend long before even one half-life of the deadly radioactive nuclear materials has passed.

The highly charged nature of the topics addressed in this issue of *Spring* makes them difficult to write about. I respect and thank all those who took on this task and whose works are published here. For many authors it takes time, determination, and courage—the act of writing put some of the contributors back into their own painful experiences of trauma induced by direct exposure to environmental catastrophes, back into chaotic feelings and emotional states and loaded archetypal fields, where further traumatization awaited them. The overwhelming nature of the story can make it hard to keep a particular perspective. By reliving the event in the mind, its connection to other archetypal stories may take a dominant role, leading away from personal feeling states into the refuge of the archetypal. This issue also contains essays from those who work closely with affected communities, where resilience and resolve are required to hear individual stories of lost loved ones, trauma, and destruction over and over again. This crucial work demands the ability to attend to and hold the question of why and the ever-present search for meaning in such insolvable situations.

It is becoming increasingly obvious that our relationship with nature has changed. While our ability to predict natural events has increased, our collective illusions of control are being eroded by global communications that confront us with detailed information and images of the damage wrought by such events, leaving us to recognize how fragile our communities really are. The intrusion of natural disasters into the human psyche stimulates an age-old anxiety about our place on the earth and activates our fear of catastrophic change. It is my hope that the articles in this issue will stimulate discussion about environmental disasters and our relationship with the earth and how this is changing. I hope it will stimulate more professionals to work with impacted communities or, at a minimum, promote some new approaches to anxiety management. With more than seven billion humans on the earth and global climate change affecting food production, weather, and natural cycles, change is inevitable. In response to these shifts our state of consciousness must expand to meet new environmental challenges.

SOLASTALGIA
WHEN HOME IS NO LONGER HOME

DON FREDERICKSEN

I n the process of having students in a new film ecocriticism seminar introduce themselves, I vividly remember one student who told of his family's disheartened response to the changes taking place in his small Connecticut town, once a New England version of the biblical land of "milk and honey." In the 1990s the newly rich from New York City began to move in. In place of the small older homes on lots filled with trees hundreds of years old, which they bought up, they built mammoth new homes, tearing down the small houses and chopping down the old trees. Rather quickly, the entire town began to experience frequent flooding and a discernible increase in summer temperatures and insects. The village stores, owned by local families for generations, held no attraction for the newcomers; like invasive weeds, upscale franchises moved in, and the town's idiosyncratic coloring went dull. The newcomers, lacking any sense of deep time, saw only the change and called it progress. The town's longtime residents, including the student's family, entered a period of mourning from which they could see no means of escape.

Don Fredericksen is professor of film in the Department of Performing and Media Arts at Cornell University and a psychotherapist in the tradition of C. G. Jung. He currently serves as chairman of the executive committee of the International Association for Jungian Studies.

In the next session the student made an excited entrance and announced that the reading assigned the day before had given a name to his town's dis-ease, calling it solastalgia. He had phoned his parents to tell them that they now had at least a name for what ailed them and, moreover, that serious attention was being given this increasingly noticeable, and worldwide, affliction of the soul.

Australian environmental philosopher Glenn Albrecht coined the word *solastalgia* in 2003 in reference to the psychological condition of persons near the university where he taught who were contending with the degradation and devastation of their environment as a result of massive strip-mining of coal, against which they had no recourse.

> I developed the concept of solastalgia to describe the pain or sickness caused by the inability to derive solace from the present state of one's home environment. It is the lived experience of negatively perceived environmental change to one's sense of place and existential well-being. It is closely linked to feelings of powerlessness and a loss of hope about the future. In summary, it is the melancholia or homesickness experienced while you are still at home and your home environment is being gradually desolated. . . . That which once gave you solace is now giving you solastalgia.[1]

This condition is predicated on the sometimes overt, sometimes subtle, direct relationship between place and psyche, and it shows the influence of the concept of ecosystem distress syndrome, coined by the ecosystem health spokesman David Rapport.[2]

Solastalgia is distinct from the sense of nostalgia that refers to homesickness occurring when one is away from home; moreover, it differs from the nostalgia of yearning for a lost past and a lost home. By way of illustration, we might propose that in the history of the United States the indigenous population first experienced a period of devastating solastalgia, then a much longer period of nostalgia as they were moved onto reservations, and—if their current homes are surrounded by environmental degradation, and many are—then a contemporary confounding of a memory of historical solastalgia, unredeemed nostalgia, and present-day solastalgia. The current suicide rate and alcoholism among Native Americans on tribal lands testifies to the magnitude of this triple blow to the psyche.

Solastalgia occurs in different scales and registers—local, regional, global, urban, and rural—for which examples come easily to mind: the BP oil spill in the Gulf of Mexico, the negative effects of fracking in Canada and the United States, urban sprawl, the devastation of New Orleans by Hurricane Katrina, and climate change. These examples reveal that solastalgia may occur as the result of both man-made and natural events. Virtual solastalgia can occur in films such as *Avatar*, where viewers can identify with the Navi and their home as it is assaulted by militaristic materialism's quest for unobtainium. Aural solastalgia is now a common experience as the sounds of the natural world are drowned out by what Bernie Krause calls "anthrophony"—the total soundscape produced by human societies—whose worst offense is "technophony," the noises produced by human technology, including the "cacophony of our air conditioners, road and air traffic. . . . and the digital roar inside the earphones."[3]

Solastalgia can also occur in dreams, a fact to which I can attest. I grew up on a farm in the coastal range of Oregon, an area whose economy until recently was driven by clear-cut logging. As a child I perceived this logging as normal and took pride in my father's ability to cut roads through heretofore untouched stands of old-growth Douglas fir. I readily, and thankfully, joined other college students with summer jobs in the nearby lumber mill. Then, on a summer visit home after college, I drove alone one evening up into a stand of old-growth trees and sat quietly and listened to the sounds as the slanting rays of the setting sun spread through a garden of ferns under the trees. The forest possessed me that evening, and I knew that I was a guest at a quiet, diurnal, and sacred ceremony, whose sounds reminded me of the opening flute melody of Aaron Copland's *Appalachian Spring*. It was a gift that permanently etched itself onto my psyche. Years later, during a period of psychological analysis, I had the following dream, which I understand now as solastalgic in its feeling and sensation:

> *I am driving an old VW bus of the kind iconic of the West Coast*
> *wanderers of the late 1960s and early 1970s. My path takes me*
> *north along Oregon Coast Highway 101, one of the world's most*
> *beautiful roads. On the right side of the road, opposite the ocean,*
> *there still remain stands of old-growth Douglas fir and cedar. In*
> *the dream I have been given, or created for myself, a painful task*

*of solidarity with these endangered stands of trees. The task consists
first of finding out the plans of the logging companies—precise dates
and forest sections—for the clear-cutting in the near future, then
of moving ahead of these operations by some short period of time to
those sections as their turn comes for destruction. There I speak to
the trees to tell them what is coming and what will happen to them.
I try to calm their fears. Together we pray. Then I must move on to
the next stand, and the next, and the next.*

II

Albrecht places solastalgia on the list of what he calls
"psychoterratic" diseases. The phrase implies dis-ease that occurs when
the relations between the psyche and the earth becomes somehow
psychologically toxic. He proposes six such "land-based sicknesses": eco-
anxiety, nature deficit disorder, eco-paralysis, eco-nostalgia, global dread,
and solastalgia.[4] Without going into detail about the symptoms of all
of these psychoterratic diseases, I note that for those of us trying now
to flesh out the parameters of a Jungian ecocriticism of the arts or a
Jungian ecopsychology, this list appears to have both diagnostic and
hermeneutic utilities. They could serve well in a Jungian or
ecopsychologically based version of the DSM, that is, the *Diagnostic
and Statistical Manual.*

Eco-anxiety is defined as the first response to stressors in natural
and man-made environments. Nature deficit disorder is defined by its
partner, artifact overload disorder, which is familiar to anyone who has
spent time in those stores in the shopping malls that sell artificial flowers
of highly saturated colors, displayed under harsh fluorescent lighting.
Eco-paralysis occurs when there is an overload of negative ecological
information against which persons can do nothing sufficiently positive.
Eco-nostalgia is the homesickness that afflicts one who is forced away
from home in time or space as a result of environmental causes, in
tandem with the obsessive desire to return home. Global dread occurs
when the "news is all bad," unredeemable.[5]

Albrecht suggests this list of diseases because there is currently a
paucity of words for thinking through the dysfunctional relationships
that occur among natural environments, human psychological
conditions, and man-made environments generally and within
psychology and ecocriticism of the arts, including film.

Critical discussion of the status of solastalgia as a mental illness has brought out the suggestion, along the line of argument in Thomas Szasz's writing, that solastalgia is more accurately described as a "problem of living."[6] Solastalgia may not be a mental illness where evidence of physical lesions is a necessary criterion, but it is most certainly a disease of the soul. From the perspective of Jung's typology one can envision it as a debilitating attack upon the feeling function by sensations whose toxicity is increased by intuitions and thoughts nested in fear and anxiety.

One thing is clear: as a land- and place-based dis-ease, solastalgia is a disease of the soul that ultimately forces our attention to move out of the reflective space of the therapy room and into the register of social and political activism. In this regard, the consequences of engaging solastalgia are similar to those evoked by ecocriticism of the arts. The armchair begins to reveal its own deficiency.

Albrecht's suggested antidote to solastalgia is what he calls soliphilia, namely, a "love of the totality of our place-relationships, and a willingness to accept, in solidarity and affiliation with others, the political responsibility for the health of the earth, our home."[7] After interviewing scientists directly engaged in the creation of nuclear and atomic bombs, as well as survivors of the Hiroshima bombing, psychiatrist Robert Jay Lifton suggested our collective need for "species consciousness," an expanded scale of community, and a "species-self," described as an "active sense of self inseparable from all other humans in sharing with them the ultimate questions of life and death."[8] Albrecht's soliphilia appears to entail the addition of a "place-self." This has implications for how we as Jungians conceive and seek the personal completeness we call individuation. We temper our introverted vector in analysis with Jung's reminder that we cannot individuate while isolated on a mountaintop. We are now in the position of having to worry that the admonition is moot, as mountaintops are denuded by clear-cut logging and leveled by strip-mining.

The heartbreaking activist documentary *The Last Mountain* (2011) shows us this, along with the resulting solastalgia of the people of West Virginia.[9] In the film the people of West Virginia are shown fighting the titanic company Massey Coal, the immediate culprit, but, as one of the residents bluntly states, we are all implicated by our insatiable demand for the myriad products of coal. The West Virginia struggle is ongoing, without guarantees that it will save the few mountaintops that remain untouched.

Sometimes the factors bringing about solastalgia simply overwhelm those that nurture soliphilia. This danger is present and growing for all of us now, in large part because television, as Marshall McLuhan pointed out in the 1960s, acts as an extended and global nervous system, especially when transmitting images of disaster in real time and immediate replay, and because climate change has the real potential to bring on eco-paralysis and global dread. Globally ubiquitous social media only exacerbate the danger. We do not yet know if the human capacity to withstand psychoterratic diseases will follow a linear path or a nonlinear one, but if their spread follows a nonlinear one, as environmental scientists tell us climate change itself will likely do, then we must surely worry that the tipping point in the climate's change will trigger a negative tipping point in our capacity to navigate our collective and global way through eco-anxiety, solastalgia, eco-paralysis, and global dread. Like Albrecht, I deeply fear the distinct possibility of a psychoterratic disease pandemic in our lifetime. An antidote to counter such an outbreak does not exist, nor am I aware of any planning for one by media practitioners or theorists.

A modern, more localized parallel to such psychic numbing—to borrow Lifton's phrase—occurred in the Nazis' death camps. Persons who lost their capacity to withstand the toxicity of their inescapable environment were immediately recognizable by their demeanor. Called musselmen, they were avoided by other inmates who feared psychic infection. No longer capable or willing to work, they were routinely gathered up and sent to the gas chambers. Lifton found a similar condition among survivors of the Hiroshima bombing, *akirame,* described as a profound resignation and passivity in the face of the great forces of destiny.[10] Lifton suggests that there exists in our global unconscious an *"akirame* complex" whose central archetypal image is an image of the end of human life, fed not just by traumatic memories, but by the fear that we are exterminating ourselves with our technological progress.[11] In relation to place- and land-based diseases, the *akirame* complex evokes images not of environmental crises, but of the very death of the environment and of doubts that we can stop it. As a species we have not arrived at this point yet, but if we do not have the moral courage to imagine this terminally dark outcome, we may lack the angry and compassionate energy necessary to stop it from occurring.

III

The English director Nicolas Roeg made the film *Walkabout* in Australia in 1971. It narrates the story of a white brother and sister abandoned by their father in the outback, and their rescue by a young aboriginal man on his walkabout, his rite of passage into adulthood. The film provides an example of a deeply moving fictionalized narrative of aboriginal solastalgia and of a white girl's possible eco-nostalgia.[12] The solastalgia ends with a gesture of hopelessness that is both shocking and mysterious to those of us outside aboriginal culture; the possible eco-nostalgia may or may not signal the girl's awareness of the significance of the journey she went through with the young aboriginal man on his walkabout. Roeg and his Marxist screenwriter Edward Bond do not appear sanguine, choosing, as they do, to end the film with the poignant poem "Land of Lost Content" by the English poet A. E. Housman, which indicates there will be no return to a happier time when place gave solace.

Although the film appears to foreclose on a return to solace in the outback for the two white children and definitely leaves the aboriginal boy in a cul-de-sac of Western culture's making, the unexplained disappearance of the white boy at the film's end leaves open the possibility that when he experienced the gratuitous killing of a buffalo by white sport hunters, something of its tragic nature imprinted on his mind to good purpose—but we will never know.

IV

Solastalgia must be a land-based disease with a long history; indeed, it quite conceivably has afflicted, and is still afflicting, other animals, including elephants, whales, and the higher primates. We can attribute its visibility to us to the fact that it is now happening to us, and to the realization that a solastalgic pandemic with unforeseeable consequences for our survival is a possibility that must be contemplated and acted upon. Solastalgia and the other psychoterratic diseases present those working in the Jungian tradition with challenges in terrain not well traveled, several of which I will attempt now to describe.

First, while we cannot control the climate, we need to acquire a better understanding of the persons and institutions whose actions have brought us to where we are. Righteous moralism may have its place, but not if it replaces the primacy of psychological insight. Some readers may be familiar with the Canadian documentary *The Corporation* (2003), which takes the clever and subversive tack of suggesting that since the U.S. Supreme Court has ruled that corporations have the same constitutional status as individuals, they might be fitting subjects for psychological diagnosis. Perhaps not surprisingly, the filmmakers arrive at the conclusion, based on corporate behavior, that corporations are psychopathic individuals that display the following symptoms from the diagnostic checklist of the ICD-10 and the DSM-IV:

1. callous concern for the feeling of others;
2. incapacity to maintain enduring relationships;
3. reckless disregard for the safety of others;
4. deceitfulness, repeated lying, and conning others for profit;
5. incapacity to experience guilt;
6. failure to conform to social norms with respect to lawful behaviors.[13]

We would contribute little to the therapy of corporations if, as Jungians, we simply clucked our tongues knowingly at this conclusion. One necessary starting point for reflection vis-à-vis this diagnosis might well be Jung's description of evil in the modern world, which is a salutary venue for soul-searching:

> The individual who wishes to have an answer to the problem of evil, as it is posed today, has need, first and foremost, of *self-knowledge,* that is, the utmost possible knowledge of his own wholeness. He must know relentlessly how much good he can do, and what crimes he is capable of, and must beware of regarding the one as real and the other as illusion. . . .

> In general, however, most people [including Jungians] are hopelessly ill equipped for living on this level, . . .

> Today we need psychology for reasons that involve our very existence. . . . We stand face to face with the terrible question of evil and do not even know what is before us . . . . With glorious

> naïveté a statesman comes out with the proud declaration that
> he has no "imagination for evil." Quite right: *we* have no
> imagination for evil, but evil *has us in its grip.* . . . Evil today has
> become a visible Great Power. . . . [We sicken] from the lack of a
> myth commensurate with the situation. . . .
>
> [W]e are shaken by secret shudders and dark forebodings; but
> we know no way out, and very few persons . . . draw the
> conclusion that this time the issue is the long-since-forgotten
> *soul of man.*[14]

I hear in those words the admonition to move closer to evil than we
are comfortable doing and the unsavory claim that we will meet it both
within and outside ourselves, and further, that upon our capacity to
generate a "myth" commensurate with our situation rests our very
existence and the long-forgotten issue of the soul of humankind.

By way of putting these thoughts into an area germane to the
factors underlying the psychoterratic diseases, including solastalgia,
I want to return to a relatively unattended area of Jungian
psychology and cultural analysis written about by Venezuelan
analyst Rafael Lopez-Pedraza and a few others, including American
philosopher Lee Bailey: the register of the psyche resident to titanic
energies and vectors.[15] Lopez-Pedraza characterizes titanic
psychology as simultaneously empty and excessive, and he speculates
reasonably that its excessiveness arises out of its emptiness.[16] Paul
Diel describes it as brutal, rebellious, ambitious, and with an
unmistakable tendency toward dominance and tyranny. Lest we
imagine that we have nothing ourselves to do with *this* energy, Diel
observes that the titanic is all the more to be feared because it can
also be hidden under "an obsessive ambition to make the world a
better place, found in the civil service and technocracy."[17] He
provides an intriguing image for their activity by suggesting that
they are subject to "moral ague"—defined as a kind of fever (literally,
material; metaphorically, moral in character)—that is attended by
paroxysms at regular intervals. What is puzzling is how little
awareness we have of the ubiquitous presence of titanic psychology
in ourselves and in our cultural history. Lee Bailey has drawn our
attention to the titanic nature of utopianism, an observation that
takes us uncomfortably from forms we might wish to distance

ourselves from—the "new man" and "new world" sought by totalitarian
social engineering, five-year plans, and cultural revolutions—to forms
given positive, albeit variable allegiance by contemporary culture: the
Enlightenment's valorization of the powers of human reason and the
resulting developments in science and technology, and the putative
merits of capitalistic economic globalization.[18]

Titanism shows up in what Lifton calls totalistic urges.[19] Nicholas
Gier writes about spiritual titanism as an extreme form of humanism,
in which humans take on divine attributes and prerogatives, including
a Gnostic titanism in which humans contend they have perfect
knowledge.[20] Isaiah Berlin reminds us that romanticism has its darker
side: "Worship not merely of the painter or composer or the poet, but
the more sinister artists whose material are men—the destroyers of old
societies and the creator of new ones—*no matter at what human cost.*"[21]

The titanic side of romanticism shares this blindness of human
costs with technological and economic titanism. This fact brings us
back to solastalgia and the other place-based illnesses where the human
cost of technology in the service of economic profit deeply affects the
body and soul. But it also brings us back to Jung's admonition regarding
the need to get close to evil as an unavoidable aspect of self-knowledge
and the generation of myth appropriate and sufficient to what we know
about the psyche, both individually and collectively.

Take the example of Massey Coal: this company's apparently
unrestrained acts of blowing up Appalachian mountains to strip-mine
coal can easily be condemned as economic titanism, in which the goal
of profit blinds itself to human costs. But is Massey Coal the only titan
involved here? Perhaps we need to turn the mirror upon our own titanic
complexes, as Lopez-Pedraza recommends. In this manner we can begin
to discern very uncomfortable facts about our own titanic, that is,
excessive desires for the many things made from coal. The list is very
long, and our collective addiction to its panoply of items blinds us to
the human costs that accompany their production. The dark, titanic
side of our consumption of coal and coal products is the destruction of
human lives occurring beyond our sight. This is not early Marx's notion
of the alienation of labor; this is our own alienated consumption. A
film like *The Last Mountain*, or Albrecht's work in Australian coal-
mining regions, brings those lives within our sight. When we
subsequently evade acknowledging what we now know, we are coming

into proximity with our capacity for evil. I read the passage from Jung's *Memories, Dreams, Reflections* to be saying that we need myth that keeps our feet to the fire or our awareness of this very human act of evasion.

This is an exceedingly uncomfortable corner into which Jung backs us. Here I do not want to know what I need to know—indeed, what I do know. Psychologists have long characterized this as cognitive dissonance. The fact that I share this evasion with others is no solace. I also do not want to acknowledge that lists other than the one for coal give me what I want for sustenance and comfort; the list of lists is too long. But knowing that I know what I do not want to acknowledge yields perhaps the most painful awareness. I mean simply this: by evading my own titanic psychological register, evading it perhaps titanically, I am polluting my own psychic home. This constitutes an inner, self-generated form of solastalgia, a home warring against itself, no longer providing the solace that comes from ignorance. Any notion of a quick solution to this condition is itself titanic. And hope for the working of the transcendental function, for some mediating third, for a symbol of transformation, may be misplaced. But Jung is undoubtedly right in stating that the issue at hand this time is the very *embodied* soul of humankind.

NOTES

1. Glenn Albrecht, Healthearth blog "Solastalgia," February 19, 2009. Accessed November 26, 2012, at www.healthearth.net.

2. Glenn Albrecht, Healthearth blog "Solastalgia," January 12, 2008. Accessed November 26, 2012, at www.healthearth.net.

3. Glenn Albrecht, Healthearth blog "Soundscapes," September 4, 2007. Accessed November 26, 2012, at www.healthearth.net.

4. Glenn Albrecht, "Environment Change, Distress, and Human Emotion Solastalgia," TEDxSydney, May 20, 2010. Accessed November 3, 2012, at http://tedxtalks.ted.com/video/TEDxSydney-Glenn-Albrecht-Envir;search%3AGlenn%20Albrecht. The typology is described in the course of the lecture.

5. *Ibid.*

6. S. P. Maesuibhne, "What Makes a New Mental Illness: The Case of Solastalgia and Hubris Syndrome," *Cosmos and History: The Journal of Natural and Social Philosophy* 5(2):217.

7. Glenn Albrecht, "Environment Change," TEDxSydney, May 20, 2010.

8. Robert Jay Lifton, *Witness to an Extreme Century* (New York: Free Press, 2011), p. 123.

9. The film's website, thelastmountainmovie.com, includes a trailer, purchase information, and information about activities in support of the film's mission.

10. Lifton, *Witness to an Extreme Century*, p. 108.

11. *Ibid.*, p. 112.

12. The film's preview, available on the director's cut DVD, *Walkabout* (Criterion, 1971), is a disgraceful reversal of the film's meaning and could be studied from that point of view.

13. Mark Achbar and Jennifer Abbott, directors, *The Corporation* (Big Picture Media Corporation and TV Ontario, 2003). The list occurs in the process of the film's diagnosis of the corporation as an individual. The film's website includes background materials, transcripts, study guides, a blog, and pointers toward action: www.thecorporation.com.

14. C. G. Jung, *Memories, Dreams, Reflections* (New York: Vintage, 1965), pp. 330–333.

15. Rafael Lopez-Pedraza, *Cultural Anxiety* (Einsiedeln: Daimon Verlag, 1990), especially chapters 1 and 2; and Lee Worth Bailey, *The Enchantment of Technology* (Urbana: University of Illinois Press, 2005), especially chapter 5, "Titanic: Utopian Triumphism." I have discussed Lopez-Pedraza at some length in an as-yet-unpublished essay, "The Titanic vis-à-vis the Archetypal in Jungian Cultural Criticism, Including Film Analysis," first presented at the Second International Conference of the International Association for Jungian Studies in 2009 at Cardiff University.

16. Lopez-Pedraza, *Cultural Anxiety*, p. 15.

17. Paul Diel quoted in Jean Chevalier and Alain Gheerbrant, *A Dictionary of Symbols* (Cambridge, MA: Blackwell, 1994), pp. 1009–10.

18. Bailey, *The Enchantment of Technology*, p. 104ff.

19. Lifton, *Witness to an Extreme Century*, p. 67.

20. Nicholas Gier, *Spiritual Titanism: Indian, Chinese, and Western Perspectives* (Albany: SUNY Press, 2000), pp. 12–17.

21. Isaiah Berlin, preface to H. G. Schenk, *The Mind of the European Romantics* (Garden City, NY: Anchor, 1969), p. xvii.

GLOBAL WARMING
INACTION, DENIAL, AND PSYCHE

LESLIE STEIN

*I see enormous stretches devastated, enormous stretches of the earth,
but thank God it's not the whole planet.*

—C. G. Jung

INTRODUCTION

The purpose of this paper is to explore the reasons, in terms of analytical psychology, for inaction and denial in relation to the looming catastrophe of global warming. Global warming is a unique and foreboding cause of potential destruction and disruption of modern civilization caused by rapid climate change, unique because it is a worldwide phenomenon distinguishable from transitory, localized events such as natural disasters, war, or even genocide. It is the possible destruction of humanity that is inexorably developing.

The United Nations Environment Programme warns that "(c)limate change is . . . considered to be the most significant problem related to changes in the atmosphere being faced by humankind" and concludes that "inaction will lead to changes that are irreversible."[1] The destruction of our way of life appears to be unstoppable without drastic and immediate intervention. It will lead to a catastrophic

Leslie Stein is a scholar in residence at the Center for Environmental Legal Studies, Pace University and an analyst in training at the C. G. Jung Institute of New York.

breakdown with "widespread social unrest, economic instability and loss of human life" as we approach a "planetary-scale critical transition."[2] Yet the catastrophe that will result from global warming does not, for various reasons, appear to engage us in a way that will mitigate that threat. There have been only ineffective responses in stemming the greenhouse gas emissions that lead to global warming.[3]

Inaction and denial with respect to global warming have been explained in several ways. It is said that a primary reason we are prone to inaction in the face of pending catastrophe is our inability to overcome feelings of helplessness and despair.[4] It is therefore less confrontational for an individual to perceive global warming as a political, economic, social, and scientific problem and not primarily a matter of personal responsibility.[5] This is coupled, the literature reports, with sociological considerations—such as a collective desire to maintain the social status quo, which requires ignoring the threat. There is also a strong bias against action and acceptance of the consequences of global warming in those who generally maintain negative ideologies about environmental issues, harbor disrespect for experts and politicians, and are acutely concerned with the perceived risks of change.[6] Another reason presented for inaction and denial is the historical development, brought about by Christianity, of the primacy of spirit and intellect over nature. This has the effect, it is argued, of making environmental problems, such as global warming, remote and abstract, leading to a devaluing of the bounties of the earth and the resultant diminution of the importance of the Great Mother archetype.[7]

In order to explain the process in the psyche that leads to inaction and delay from the unique standpoint of analytical psychology, it is first necessary to understand the threat of global warming.

THE THREAT OF GLOBAL WARMING

If a two degree Celsius (2°C) rise in global temperature occurs, many ecosystems will not adapt, leading to a steep rise in species extinction. There will be a severe decrease in the availability of water, an increase in drought in some areas, higher rates of flooding due to increased precipitation in other areas, and a worldwide decline in food production.

Carbon dioxide (CO_2) and other greenhouse gas concentrations in the atmosphere are increasing, causing a rise in average global temperatures. A rise of 2°C (or 3.6 degrees Fahrenheit) from preindustrial levels is associated with CO_2 concentrations in the atmosphere of 440 parts per million (ppm). At 3°C, or approximately 550 ppm, there will be catastrophic drought inland, extensive flooding in coastal regions, and a loss of all summer ice in the Antarctic.[8] A European Union analysis warned:

> Global warming of 2°C above pre-industrial levels cannot be considered safe. Considerable climate change impacts are already felt today and will have to be faced in the future—even below 2°C. Beyond this level, climate change impacts will increase substantially in scale and severity, including threats to unique ecosystems, risks of multi-metre long-term sea level rise, and both more frequent droughts and floods across the globe. If no action is taken, we may exceed 2°C already by the middle of this century. To avoid this, global emissions need to peak before 2015–2020 and to be at least halved by 2050 relative to 1990 levels.[9]

If all coal-fired power stations (a substantial source of greenhouse gas emissions) were closed down by 2030, the CO_2 concentration would still rise to 400 ppm.[10] In an interview following the American Geophysical Union meeting in December 2011, James Hansen, the director of the National Air and Space Administration (NASA) Goddard Institute for Space Studies in New York, and Eelco Rohling, from the University of Southampton, "agreed that if nations continue to emit CO_2 at current rates, the world could reach 560 ppm by 2100."[11] They suggested that the effect of such a rise in greenhouse gases could be a 25-meter sea level rise, destroying the infrastructure of all coastal cities, such as New York.

The current CO_2 concentration in the atmosphere at the time of writing in 2012 is 391.03 ppm.[12] In 1985, it was 350 ppm. According to the International Energy Agency, fossil fuel emissions increased 3.2 percent or 1 gigatonne (Gt) of CO_2 per year in 2012 alone.[13] To have even a 50 percent chance of limiting the increase in temperature to 2°C, the agency requires CO_2 emissions to peak at 32.6 Gt no later than 2017. This is, however, only 1.0 Gt above 2011 levels.

The continued increase in global warming is therefore profound, and the rate of concentration of greenhouse gases is exceeding the worst-case scenarios of the Intergovernmental Panel on Climate Change.[14] A report in 2012 indicated:

Models project substantial warming in temperature extremes by the end of the 21st century. It is *virtually certain* that increases in the frequency and magnitude of warm daily temperature extremes and decreases in cold extremes will occur in the 21st century at the global scale.[15]

Attempts at limiting greenhouse gas emissions have failed. The fifteenth session of the Conference of Parties (COP 15) to the United Nations Framework Convention on Climate Change (UNFCCC) resulted in the Copenhagen Accord of 2009, to which the United States is a party, which states that the Accord is made "with a view to reduce global emissions so as to hold the increase in global temperature below 2 degrees Celsius." This was to be accomplished by signatory nations pledging to stabilize greenhouse gasses at 450 ppm in the atmosphere, which would result in approximately a 40 to 60 percent chance of limiting global warming to 2°C above preindustrial levels. A Club of Rome report in 2012 indicates that it is too late and that a rise of 2°C by 2052 and 2.8°C by 2080 is now inevitable and irreversible.[16] The United Nations Environment Programme's report "Bridging the Emissions Gap" states that current pledges are at best 6 Gt short of keeping global average temperatures below 2°C.[17] Its report from the previous year stated that pledges were 5 Gt short, so the gap is increasing and the chance of limiting CO_2 concentrations to 450 ppm is decreasing. The International Energy Agency reported in its World Energy Outlook 2011 Factsheet that 80 percent of the cumulative CO_2 to be emitted worldwide between 2009 and 2035 to keep CO_2 concentrations below 450 ppm is already "locked in" with current infrastructure. It concluded that unless internationally coordinated action is taken by 2017, "all new infrastructure from then until 2035 would need to be zero-carbon, unless emitting infrastructure is retired before the end of its economic lifetime"; an impossible situation.[18]

The seventeenth Conference of Parties at Durban in 2011 recommended that there be a continuation of the Kyoto Protocol, to be adopted in 2015 and to come into effect in 2020.[19] The UNFCCC executive secretary stated that the new protocol would be a "universal participation in legally grounded mitigation targets, a departure from the past and Durban's major gift."[20] COP 17 also confirmed that the first review of the adequacy of the 2°C target should start in 2013 and should be concluded by 2015, when the COP shall take appropriate action based on the review. This puts off the problem to the future and offers no guarantees, but in the meantime, decisions are being made that have the effect of increasing greenhouse gases, such as the exploitation of Canada's tar sands reserves, about which one credible commentator stated:

> If we were to fully exploit this new oil source, and continue to burn our conventional oil, gas and coal supplies, concentrations of carbon dioxide in the atmosphere eventually would reach levels higher than in the Pliocene era, more than 2.5 million years ago, when sea level was at least 50 feet higher than it is now.[21]

The catastrophic effects go beyond species extinction, drought, and rising sea level. Each degree in temperature causes a 200–400 percent increase in the area burned by wildfire in parts of the western United States, a 5–15 percent reduction in the yields of crops as currently grown, and a 3–10 percent increase in the amount of rain falling during the heaviest precipitation events.[22] "Climates found at present on 10–48 percent of the planet are projected to disappear within a century, and climates that contemporary organisms have never experienced are likely to cover 12–39 percent of Earth."[23]

The results are already apparent. To name just a few examples, there has been a measurable increase in drought intensity, sea level rise is prompting relocation of the inhabitants of South Pacific Islands such as the Maldives, Marshall Islands, Tuvalu, and Kiribati, and extreme heat in North American cities has resulted in greater rates of heat-related deaths among the elderly and children.[24]

GLOBAL WARMING DENIAL AND INACTION

There is consistent outright denial of global warming that has appeared in the press and has confused public opinion.[25] The motivation for denial is often ideological, as the political parties have made the reality of global warming a political issue.[26] There is, as well, consistent outright denial by public opinion commentators of the phenomenon of global warming.[27] The deeper problem is the inaction of government in participating in international agreements, mitigating greenhouse gas emissions, or creating adequate strategies for adaptation to the effects of climate change.

Scientifically, the consequences of climate change cannot be denied but there is still debate as to the extent and rate of global warming. The World Resources Institute issued a paper at the end of 2011 to clarify the state of climate science. It starts with unequivocal historical data on temperature records from NASA that show the warmest decade since 1880 was 2000–2009 and that, as a matter of fact, the gap between record highs and low has been increasing rapidly since the 1980s.[28] However, in addition to facts, it also reports many scientific predictions, which are theoretical and are subject to interpretation. As an example, it is proposed that deep sea sediments that contain methane, a greenhouse gas more potent than CO_2, will become unstable because of warming and bubble to the surface, and therefore "if the Earth warms by 3°C, which is not beyond the scope of possibility during the next century, this feedback could add 17 percent to projected global average temperature increases."[29] It also states that "if current trends continue unabated, ice and snow loss will have significant ramifications for sea level rise and freshwater sources, with attendant, imminent impacts on both human and natural systems."[30]

The speculative or theoretical aspects of climate science have been used to discount the entirety of global warming projections. An editorial in the *Wall Street Journal* on January 27, 2012, signed by sixteen scientists from disparate fields, argued that there has been a smaller than predicted warming over the last twenty-two years which suggests that the models used by climate scientists have greatly exaggerated the effect of greenhouse gases. It added this view of why there is such concern:

> Alarmism over climate is of great benefit to many, providing government funding for academic research and a reason for government bureaucracies to grow. Alarmism also offers an excuse for governments to raise taxes, taxpayer-funded subsidies for businesses that understand how to work the political system, and a lure for big donations to charitable foundations promising to save the planet.

A reply on February 1, 2012, by thirty-nine climate scientists disputed these statements:

> Research shows that more than 97 percent of scientists actively publishing in the field agree that climate change is real and human

caused. It would be an act of recklessness for any political leader
to disregard the weight of evidence and ignore the enormous
risks that climate change clearly poses.[31]

This was followed by a further critique of those who deny the effects
of global warming by the American Physical Society, which represents
50,000 physicists. It indicated that the real significance of increasing
and extreme weather events is that they are harbingers of a changing
world subject to more frequent natural disasters. Extreme events were
labeled as teachable moments or "wake-up calls" to the realization that
an environmental crisis of global proportions is imminent: "much more
so than the subtle and sometimes ambiguous early warning signs of
global warming might lead us to believe."[32]

The effect of doubt is to create confusion in the political
constituencies of those who could be effective in mitigating the effects
of and strategizing methods for adaptation to global warming.
However, for there to be inaction and denial on such a scale in light of
indisputable scientific evidence, there must be a deeper cause.

IMPACTS OF GLOBAL WARMING IN THE PSYCHE

The phenomenon of global warming is unfathomable in the psyche,
which is the prime reason for inaction and denial. What is unfathomable
is the realization that nature is not reliable as the consistent, generative
principle that fosters life. For Jung, nature was the "nourishing soil of
the soul," the substratum of the collective unconscious, "God's world,"
which forms the bedrock of the alchemical and analytical psychology
opus.[33] The alteration in the character of nature from the beneficent
basis of life and the core of the *unus mundus*, the unified reality of all
things, to that which will destroy humankind is a betrayal of the sacred
and a casting out of man from God's world. This is contrary to the
fundamental orientation of the psyche, as it negates the basis of life.
The effect is to cause an unconscious primordial confusion in the psyche:
the chaos of the *massa confusa*.[34]

The confusion is further exacerbated because global warming is
not a clearly observable fact but a theoretical prediction proffered
by scientists and derived from complex data. Climate change is
observable through the interpretation of data, explained by
supposition and theoretical argument.[35]

An additional reason for inaction and denial is that the potential catastrophe is so unthinkable that even a partial consideration results in a psychogenic shock and a consequent disavowal of the idea. Freud expressed it clearly: "The ego rejects the unbearable idea together with its associated affect and behaves as if the idea had never occurred to the person at all."[36] It is, he suggested, the rejection of the unbearable idea that causes disavowal rather than the actual facts, meaning, in this context, that there is a tendency to ignore the consequences of global warming based on only a partial realization of its effects. The nature of disavowal triggered by only a partial realization of the consequences of the reality is explained by Jung as a consequence of the "repressive attitude of the conscious mind": the partial awareness of an unwelcome idea creates emotional responses, which come to the surface in thoughts or images, and then the ego momentarily identifies with these "only to revoke them in the same breath."[37]

The confusion exists in the psyche because of an unfathomable concept and an unbearable idea. This is the *cause* of denial and inaction that cannot be resolved by an understanding of global warming facts or a call to action; the confusion exists in the netherworld of the collective unconscious and leaks through into consciousness in annihilation myths such as the Norse myth of Ragnarök.

The annihilation myth of Ragnarök is presaged by climate events of continuous winter and has been said to be a component of an ecological codex revealed in the *Poetic Edda*.[38] There is in that myth a deep realization of the inevitability of a continuous cycle of climatic destruction and reformation symbolically illustrated by the survival of one human couple, the new sun and reborn earth, arising from the need for reinvigoration rituals to balance hostile forces.[39] The specific identification of global warming and inevitable climatic destruction in our time is, however, a recent concept, and its manifestation in the psyche is not yet patent, other than to foster inaction and denial.[40]

If the ego were to directly confront the confusion in the psyche, it would lead to the profound realization that God's purpose is completely unknowable and our speculations of the Creator's effulgence are only hubris. The mystery of life and nature in the case of global warming is not congruent with some higher purpose and would suggest that we have projected our own hopes and desires onto an uncaring soul.

Lack of hope or no possibility of eventual salvation is inconsistent with the Judeo-Christian outlook, which imbues the spirit and the Divine with this higher purpose; as Jung states: "we tend to identify our chthonic nature with evil and our spiritual nature with good."[41] The lofty spirit that we hope will be in relationship with God, if global warming effects are understood, therefore has a goal that we can never discover. In this confrontation between the aspiring spirit and the potential reality of a complete failure to achieve spiritual fulfilment, psyche has no alternative but to turn away from this conception because our Judeo-Christian ethos cannot conceive that we have perhaps fooled ourselves into believing that the path leads ever upward.

ANNIHILATION AND THE SELF

The Jungian orientation to the emergence of chaos in the psyche and to unconsciousness engendered by fear of annihilation or confusion is to cleave to the Self, the sense of wholeness, to find order. The Self is both an end goal and a process undertaken by the spirit in man (the Anthropos) attempting to realize its existence in the material world that yields the *Lapis* (the realization of the spirit within the stone).[42]

Annihilation and death are within the purview of the Self as elements of the shadow buried in the unconscious, felt in the *nigredo* stage of individuation as the dark night of the soul.[43] The *nigrum nigrius nigro* (the black that is blacker than black) is the experience of the raw, unconscious confrontation with emptiness, extinction, and nothingness, far removed from consciousness. Jung remarked that emptiness is "something *alien* to man: the chasm, the unplumbed depths, the *yin*."[44] The *nigredo*, however, does not begin to touch the catastrophe of global warming. It is a developmental stage in the symbolic process of alchemy that leads away from annihilation and death to the *albedo* or whitening, which is the dawning of consciousness. The alchemical opus is concerned with the evolution of the spirit, and therefore the unplumbed depths of annihilation and extinction, when recognized, are sublimated to the goal of the spirit and remain ephemeral as that which has been recognized but remains alien in the unconscious.

What global warming suggests—the negation of the Self by loss of life, the loss of soul, the inconceivable position of nothing, the rejection by nature and God—is contrary to all notions of individuation and appears, at best, in archetypal or symbolic form. This is because, in the quest for the spirit, these raw, unconscious forces are too frightening, making the entire unconscious something to be feared. Jung referred to "the totally erroneous supposition that the unconscious is a monster."[45] In the case of global warming, the unconscious becomes a monster. It is for this reason that the overwhelming nature of annihilation in any gradation is perceived in psychology as a pathological cause of anxiety but not something that must be confronted and understood.[46]

The notion of enantiodromia in analytical psychology is that the unconscious opposite will emerge over time; that which is submerged will always arise. In that sense, psyche has no choice; if it does not freeze in what Kierkegaard called "shut-upness," it finds a way to somehow confront that which lies in the unconscious, however deep and alien. Inaction and denial are embedded in chaos in the psyche and, by this argument, inevitably must be the subject of some reflection. Kierkegaard stressed that there is nowhere for psyche to go when the self is inclined to "run away from itself":

> The self becomes an abstract possibility which tires itself out with floundering in the possible, but does not budge from the spot, nor get to the spot, for precisely the necessary is the spot; to become oneself is precisely a movement at the spot.[47]

This means that the confusion will arise as it is within psyche and must be expressed. The manner in which it is expressed may be culturally determined and restricted or allowed by those gates of resistance that open and close when confronted by nothingness.

ANNIHILATION AND CULTURE

In the *Seven Sermons to the Dead* Jung carries on a dialogue with his guide Philemon, who starts the first sermon with the statement, "I begin with nothingness."[48] This nothingness is also the fullness that together is the Pleroma, the preexisting state beyond creation and which cannot be therefore named or understood. It is the *Ein Sof* of Kabbalah, the essence of God in Sufism (*dhat*), and the Sunya Brahman of classical Hinduism in a state prior to creation, and accordingly Jung states: "it is not profitable to think about the Pleroma, for to do that would mean one's dissolution."[49] The dissolution would arise because Jung states that we *are* the Pleroma and to "extend ourselves beyond the created world" will send us into an undifferentiated state, and we will cease to be created beings and fall into nothingness. Accordingly, the need to differentiate, to think, and to express one's individuality is essential because without it we are lost.

The essential observation of Jung is that the contemplation of the Pleroma is to be rejected ("bridle [one's] thoughts") and instead, it is critical to embrace distinctiveness to become a unique separated being, the precursor to the process of individuation.[50] This is a clear rejection of the contemplation of nothingness in oneself, as the primordial essence is inimical to individuation.

The God of creation is the manifestation of the Pleroma that Jung calls Abraxas, a living God of change that has no concern for man.[51] As man rejects the presence of the Godhead in himself (the *Imago Dei*), the dissociated God is one who "dissolves unity, who blasts everything human, who powerfully creates and mightily destroys."[52] Abraxas cannot be understood in the psyche because "you do not see it, because in your eyes the warring opposites of the power are cancelled out."[53] It is here that the confusion in the psyche that this causes is recognized. Jung asks: "Does this God not bring despairing confusion into the minds of men?" and Philemon answers that we (as the dead or unconscious) know only the "contradictoriness" of nature, but, "You know that this must be so, and at the same time you know that it did not have to be so and that at some other time it will not be so."[54]

In his analysis of the *Sermons*, Stephan Hoeller suggests that this represents a particularly Western concept:

> Individuation, especially defined in the First Sermon, is, then, a very specific and distinct idea of the Western tradition, adapted by Jung to psychological use . . . Unlike many (if not all) the spiritual systems of the East, especially of India, the Western tradition has never envisioned a permanent dissolution of human individuality in Divinity.[55]

It follows, as Jung makes clear, that fear of annihilation (phrased as death or ultimate dissolution) is endemic to the West:

> You will find in studying the culture of other civilizations that those people are far less afraid of death than we are. They take

things in a different way; they don't put so much store of life as
we do. To them, life and death are a matter of course; to us, it is
awful that there could be such as thing as death.[56]

This is perhaps why the Gorgon Medusa cannot be confronted
directly but only indirectly as a reflection in Perseus's shield.
Medusa is a symbol of death; her protruding, lolling tongue,
bulging eyes, and skin color are congruent with the decay of a
corpse.[57] Neumann explains:

> The petrifying gaze of Medusa belongs to the province of the
> Terrible Great Goddess, for to be rigid is to be dead. The effect
> of the terrible stands in opposition to the mobility of the life
> stream that flows in organic life; it is the psychic expression for
> petrification and sclerosis. The Gorgon is the counterpart of the
> life womb; she is the womb of death or the night sun.[58]

To experience the "womb of death" by reflection is both to reflect
on it and to distance it and, finally, if one is somehow able to confront
it, to remove its head to prevent its capacity to engage. The myth is
testament to the capacity to see a threat only by reflection and then,
even if one has courage, to render it harmless and no longer capable of
engagement. It has been explained that the ability to see, yet ignore
and thereby render the threat harmless, is the "hallmark of Western
subjectivity."[59] It is what Freud referred to as a state "in which one
both knows something and at the same time doesn't know . . . the
blindness of the seeing eye."[60]

Western subjectivity is based upon the proposition that any
thought is legitimate if it does not contradict itself, regardless of its
basis in reality.[61] This suggests an ability to observe any situation but
then to be able to think in a manner that is unrelated to the object,
allowing, for example, the topic of global warming to be discussed with
no relation to the experienced dread of the consequences of climate
change. Jung consistently placed this phenomenon, this splitting, at
the door of Christianity and its elevation of thought.[62] Possible
annihilation from global warming can thus be examined indirectly from
a distance by reflection and adjustments made to the thinking process
over time to accommodate the presence of the horror in the psyche.[63]
As there is great confusion in the unconscious about global warming,
the approach may be so indirect as to be meaningless.

The very indirect approach required into relationship with Medusa can be contrasted with the goddess Kali, worshiped in the stream of Hinduism that is Tantra. This contrast is significant in explaining the Western rejection of annihilation, and thus inaction and denial with respect to global warming as being culturally determined. This contrast is not evidenced by a different approach in the East to global warming; the orientalism of the East has now been absorbed into Western culture.[64] However, the myth of Kali stands as another perspective on confrontation with the unimaginable and brings the Western approach into focus.

The nature of Hinduism is to place all qualities of man and the divine in the visible forms of deities.[65] Kali symbolizes all that is benevolent *and* all that is destructive in the same imago. Kali has no parallel in Greek mythology and has been ignored in Western thought as being far too alien. The fierce, frightening nature of Kali—black, dishevelled hair, a necklace of severed heads, corpses of children for earrings, severed arms for a girdle, and standing on the inert body of Shiva—has not endeared her to psychology.[66] Kali offers a view of hell, present and future, that is so terrifying that she has often been reduced to a ceremonial role or watered down for modern India.[67] It has been pointed out that no figure such as Kali exists in Christianity, and it has been argued that she is therefore akin to Satan.[68]

Figure 1: Kali.

Her appearance un-equivocally conveys death, destructiveness, and terror, and her blackness is said to express that "she dissolves all in darkness, that is vacuity of existence, which is the Light of Being itself."[69] She is not the fertile, protective mother goddess but, with her lolling tongue, fangs, and emaciated body, that which takes away life. She is naked and therefore without illusions. The severed head in her left hand is symbolic of the annihilation of evil created by the ego and the sword is the discriminatory instrument to cut the thread of bondage.[70] She embodies the forbidden aspects of life: the terror of annihilation, the true negation of life that is evil, the stark reality of decay and death. She appears unstoppable, capable of a ruthless destruction, fuelled by the primordial Śhakti power, the essence of the divine feminine.

Destructiveness is, however, only one aspect of Kali. Her two right hands offer respectively a gift to dispel fear (the conch shell) and the trident of Shiva which represents spiritual courage. The arms around her waist in a girdle are the sign that she can free one from the bonds of karma. There are fifty skulls around her neck, the number of letters in the original Sanskrit alphabet, which combine to form "Om" or the sound of creation. It is explained that she "combines the terror of destruction with the reassurance of motherly love . . . She deals out death and terror while she offers fearlessness and boons."[71]

She is also said to be the "Mistress of Time," as her name is the feminine of *Kala* or "time." As such, she is also the goddess of all worldly change. The change is not just destructive but also *instructive* of the eventual loss and dissolution of all things: the destructiveness and the beneficence are completely interdependent. Sri Ramakrishna, a well-known adherent of Kali, states: "The two ideals are harmonized in her."[72] For the individual worshiper, it is required that there be acceptance of all her aspects. It is explained in this manner:

> Kali's boon is one when man confronts or accepts her and the realities she dramatically conveys to him. The image of Kali, in a variety of ways, teaches man that pain, sorrow, decay, death, and destruction are not to be overcome or conquered by denying them or explaining them away.[73]

The benevolence of the teaching arises from accepting annihilation in the psyche, rather than fighting to overcome it or denying its existence. Kali appears, at first glance, similar to the dual aspect of Mercurius, which suggests the emergence of a "third thing" that resolves the opposites.[74] However, Kali offers no reconciliation. There is, in fact, no counterbalance to the confusion and annihilation related to global warming in the psyche; no holding of the tension between the opposites of destruction and nondestruction; no *coincidentia oppositorum*.

Kali's reminder of the dark, avenging side of life, and the power of rage—posed against the contemporary backdrop of a plundered and wounded earth—is a vision of spiritually emerging power far removed from the benevolent mercy and accepting patience of Laksmi or Mary.[75]

CONCLUSION

The Jungian analyst Ronald Curran suggests that "like Mercury, Kali must be managed carefully in order to take from her murderous bloodthirst the transformative energy it contains. In this sense she is the curative bite we take of the hair of the dog that bit us."[76] It is reported that his understanding of the destructiveness of Kali gave Jung the conviction that evil was not negative but positive.[77] Kali is recognized as positive in the sense that she is instructive of our ultimate fate, the *momento mori*. She theoretically has the effect of forcing an examination of the catastrophic consequences of global warming.

The Zofingia Lectures, which Jung presented in his early years at medical school, contain a key to an orientation for global warming in psyche. He states that "the process of perfecting external relations has torn man way from his bond with nature, but only from the conscious bond, not from the unconscious."[78] The link with nature remains as part of the structure of psyche, and although it is submerged and clouded by confusion in the case of global warming, the psyche is oriented to the connection. The Self is not extinguished and still seeks its development, which explicitly requires perceiving the spirit in matter.

However, it is not the purpose of this paper to do otherwise than seek an explanation for the reasons behind denial and inaction in respect of global warming. No solution is offered. Even a full understanding of the effect of global warming will not bring the confusion and disavowal to consciousness. An intellectual understanding of a phenomenon such as global warming produces what Jung called, in a different context, a "treacherous sense of liberation and superiority," a sense that it can be worked out and a solution found, much like a crossword puzzle.[79]

The various effects of global warming in the psyche, as Jung put it in a discussion of the retention of ideas in the unconscious, "lose clarity of definition; the relations between them are less consequential and more vaguely analogous, less rational and therefore more 'incomprehensible.'"[80] If there is to be full acknowledgment of the devastating effects of climate change, the confusion, annihilation, and destruction must somehow be felt and integrated deeply by what Jung often referred to as the "integration into the psyche as a whole," where it is brought to the conscious mind so that one is confronted with what it really means and its inherent "moral demands."[81]

NOTES

1. United Nations Environment Programme, "GEO-5: Global Environment Outlook Assessment Report," June 2012, Part 1, pp. 36–37. Accessed November 12, 2012, at http://www.unep.org/geo/geo5.asp.

2. Anthony D. Barnosky, et al., "Approaching a State Shift in Earth's Biosphere," *Nature* 486 (June 7, 2012):52–58.

3. Haydn Washington and John Cook set out the forms of denial of global warming: see Hayden Williams and John Cook, *Climate Change Denial: Heads in the Sand* (New York: Earthscan, 2011).

4. Karl M. Norgaard, for example, promotes the thesis that because it is not possible to completely overcome feelings of despair and helplessness, silence or denial continue to be effective defenses; see Karl M. Norgaard, *Living in Denial: Climate Change, Emotions and Everyday Life* (Cambridge, MA: MIT Press, 2011).

5. See Susan M. Koger and Deborah Du Nann Winter, *The Psychology of Environmental Problems: Psychology for Sustainability*, 3rd edition (New York: Psychology Press, 2011).

6. Irena Feygina, John T. Jost, and Rachel E. Goldsmith, "System Justification, the Denial of Global Warming, and the Possibility of 'System-Sanctioned Change,'" *Personality and Social Psychology Bulletin* 36(3): 326–338; Robert Gifford, "The Dragons of Inaction: Psychological Barriers That Limit Climate Change Mitigation and Adaptation," *American Psychologist*, 66(4): 290–302.

7. This the starting point for any examination of individuals' refusal to participate in environmental harm. See, for example, Bruce. V. Foltz,

Inhabiting the Earth: Heidegger, Environmental Ethics, and the Metaphysics of Nature (New York: Humanity Books, 1995); Elizabeth Ryland, "Gaia Rising: A Jungian Look at Environmental Consciousness and Sustainable Organizations," *Organization Environment* 13(4):381–402; and Tom Cheetham, *Green Man, Earth Angel: The Prophetic Tradition and the Battle for the Soul of the World* (Albany, NY: SUNY Press, 2005).

8. Nicholas Stern, *The Economics of Climate Change: The Stern Review* (London: Cambridge University Press, 2007).

9. "The 2°C Target: Background on Impacts, Emission Pathways, Mitigation Options, and Costs," Information Reference Document prepared by EU Climate Change Expert Group "EG Science," final version 9.1, July 9, 2008, p. 51.

10. James Hansen, et al., "Target Atmospheric CO_2: Where Should Humanity Aim?" *Open Atmospheric Science Journal* 2:217–231.

11. Mark Fischetti, "2-Degree Global Warming Limit Is Called a 'Prescription for Disaster,'" Observations blog, *Scientific American*, December 6, 2011. Accessed November 12, 2012, at http://blogs.scientificamerican.com/observations/2011/12/06/two-degree-global-warming-limit-is-called-a-prescription-for-disaster/.

12. "Scripps CO_2 Data—Mauna Loa Observatory," CO_2Now. Accessed November 12, 2012, at http://co2now.org/Current-CO2/CO2-Now/.

13. "Global Carbon-Dioxide Emissions Increase by 1.0 Gt in 2011 to Record High," International Energy Agency. Accessed May 24, 2012 at http://www.iea.org/newsroomandevents/news/2012/may/name,27216,en.html. Based on a comparison with the IEA report "World Energy Outlook 2011," November 9, 2011. One gigatonne is 1,000,000,000 metric tonnes of carbon dioxide.

14. Established by the United Nations Environmental Programme and the World Meteorological Organization in 1988, endorsed by the UN General Assembly Resolution 43/53 of December 6, 1988.

15. C. B. Field, et al., *Managing the Risks of Extreme Events and Disasters to Advance Climate Change Adaptation: A Special Report of the Intergovernmental Panel on Climate Change* (Cambridge, UK: Cambridge University Press, 2012), p. 13; emphasis added.

16. Jorgen Randers, *2052: A Global Forecast for the Next Forty Years* (White River Junction, VT: Chelsea Green Publishing, 2012). One

paper, which has been heavily criticized in terms of the methodology used, suggests that there is to be a lower medium of 2.3 degrees; see Andreas Schmittner, et al., "Climate Sensitivity Estimated from Temperature Reconstructions of the Last Glacial Maximum," Science 334:1385–1388; for the criticism, see James Hansen, M. Sato, P. Kharecha, and K. von Schuckmann, "Earth's Energy Imbalance and Implications," *Atmospheric Chemistry and Physics* 11:13421–13449.

17. United Nations Environment Programme, "Bridging the Emissions Gap." Accessed November 12, 2012, at http://www.unep.org/publications/ebooks/bridgingemissionsgap/.

18. "World Energy Outlook 2011 Factsheet," International Energy Agency. Accessed November 12, 2012, at http://www.worldenergyoutlook.org/media/weowebsite/2011/factsheets.pdf. This is further verified in other research; see Steven J. Davis, Ken Caldeira, and H. Damon Matthews, "Future CO_2 Emissions and Climate Change from Existing Energy Infrastructure," *Science* 329:1330–1333.

19. The Accord endorses the continuation of the Kyoto Protocol, the treaty adopted December, 11, 1997, by the UNFCCC.

20. Christiana Figueres, Barbara Ward Lecture, International Institute for Environment and Development, London, March 9, 2012. Accessed November 12, 2012, at http://www.iied.org/tag/barbara-ward-lecture.

21. James Hansen, "Game Over for the Climate," *New York Times,* May 9, 2012. Accessed November 12, 2012, at http://www.nytimes.com/2012/05/10/opinion/game-over-for-the-climate.html.

22. National Research Council, *Climate Stabilization Targets: Emissions, Concentrations, and Impacts over Decades to Millennia* (Washington, DC: National Academic Press, 2011).

23. Barnosky, "Approaching a State Shift in Earth's Biosphere," p. 54.

24. See Craig D. Allen, et al., "A Global Overview of Drought and Heat-Induced Tree Mortality Reveals Emerging Climate Change Risks for Forests," *Forest Ecology and Management* 259:650–684. The full extent of the problem of rising sea level is discussed in Michael B. Gerrard and Gregory E. Wannier, eds., *Threatened Island Nations: Legal Implications of Rising Seas and a Changing Climate* (Cambridge, UK: Cambridge University Press, forthcoming). On heat-related deaths, see Peter Altman, "Killer Summer Heat: Projected Death Tolls from Rising

Temperatures in America Due to Climate Change," Natural Resources Defense Council Issue Brief, May 2012.

25. The role of the press and its influence is discussed in Maxwell T. Boykoff and Jules M. Boykoff, "Balance as Bias: Global Warming and the U.S. Prestige Press," *Global Environmental Change* 14:125–136; and Maxwell T. Boykoff and Jules M. Boykoff, "Climate Change and Journalistic Norms: A Case-Study of U.S. Mass-Media Coverage," *Geoforum* 38(6):1190–1204.

26. Riley E. Dunlap and Aaron M. McCright, "A Widening Gap: Republican and Democratic Views on Climate Change," *Environment* 50:26–35.

27. Described in detail in James Hoggan with Richard Littlemore, *Climate Cover-up: The Crusade to Deny Global Warming* (Vancouver: Greystone Books, 2009).

28. Aaron Strong, Kelly Levin, and Dennis Tirpak, *Climate Science: Major New Discoveries 2009–2010* (Washington, DC: World Resources Institute, 2011); "2009: Second Warmest Year on Record; End of Warmest Decade," NASA Research News, January 21, 2010. Accessed November 12, 2012, at http://www.giss.nasa .gov/research/news/20100121/.

29. Strong, Levin, and Tirpak, *Climate Science*, p. 7.

30. *Ibid.* These conclusions are reiterated in a comprehensive report on the state of climate science: Ian Allison, et al., *The Copenhagen Diagnosis, 2009: Updating the World on the Latest Climate Science* (Sydney: The University of New South Wales Climate Change Research Centre, 2009).

31. The research referred to is a meta-analysis of climate change research found in William R. L. Anderegg, James W. Prall, Jacob Harold, and Stephen H. Schneider, "Expert Credibility in Climate Change," *Proceedings of the National Academy of Sciences of the USA* 107:12107–12109.

32. John M. Wallace, "Weather- and Climate-Related Extreme Events: Teachable Moments," *Eos: Transactions, American Geophysical Union* 93(11):120.

33. C. G. Jung, "Soul and Death," in *The Collected Works of C. G. Jung*, vol. 8, *The Structure and Dynamics of the Psyche* (Princeton, NJ: Princeton University Press, 1960), § 800; C. G. Jung, *Letters, Vol. 2: 1951–1961*, edited by Gerhard Adler (Princeton, NJ: Princeton

University Press, 1953), p. 540; C. G. Jung, *Memories, Dreams, Reflections*, edited by Aneila Jaffé (New York: Vintage Books, 1989), pp. 67–68.

34. Matthew Feinberg and Robb Willer make a similar analysis concluding that global warming threatens deeply held beliefs that the world is just, orderly, and stable; see Matthew Feinberg and Robb Willer, "Apocalypse Soon? Dire Messages Reduce Belief in Global Warming by Contradicting Just-World Beliefs," *Psychological Science* 22(1):34–38.

35. The quality of communication of scientists influences the understanding of global warming; see Nick Pidgeon and Baruch Fischhoff, "The Role of Social and Decision Sciences in Communicating Uncertain Climate Risks," *Nature Climate Change* 1:35–41.

36. Sigmund Freud, *The Neuro-Psychoses of Defence* (1894), in *SE*, vol. 3 (London: Hogarth Press, 1961).

37. C. G. Jung, "The Relations between the Ego and the Unconscious," in *The Collected Works of C. G. Jung*, vol. 7, *Two Essays on Analytical Psychology* (Princeton, NJ: Princeton University Press, 1953), § 323.

38. The notion of the Ragnarök being presaged by a continuous winter is analyzed as having a possible scientific basis in Bo Graslund and N. Prince, "Twilight of the Gods? The 'Dust Veil Event' of AD 536 in Critical Perspective," *Antiquity* 86(332):428–443; see pp. 437–438.

39. John S. Martin, *Ragnarok: An Investigation into Old Norse Concepts of the Fate of the Gods* (Netherlands: Van Gorcum Assen, 1972).

40. Its evolution in current form is perhaps traceable to 2001; see Spencer R. Weart, *The Discovery of Global Warming* (Cambridge, MA: Harvard University Press, 2003).

41. C. G. Jung, "A Talk with Students at the Institute," May 1958, in *Spring* (1970):177–181.

42. Leslie Stein, *Becoming Whole: Jung's Equation for Realizing God* (New York: Helios Press, 2012).

43. See Marie-Louise von Franz, ed., *Aurora Consurgens: A Document Attributed to Thomas Aquinas on the Problem of Opposites in Alchemy* (Toronto: Inner City Books, 2000), chap. 6.

44. C. G. Jung, "Psychological Aspects of the Mother Archetype," in *The Collected Works of C. G. Jung*, vol. 9i, *The Archetype and the*

Collective Unconscious (Princeton, NJ: Princeton University Press, 1959), § 183; emphasis added.

45. C. G. Jung, "The Practical Use of Dream Analysis," in *The Collected Works of C. G. Jung*, vol. 16, *The Practice of Psychotherapy* (Princeton, NJ: Princeton University Press, 1954), § 329.

46. The background for this idea is discussed in Marvin Hurvich, "Traumatic Moment, Basic Dangers, and Annihilation Anxiety," *Psychoanalytic Psychology* 6(3):309–323; and Donald Winnicott, "The Fear of Breakdown," *International Review of Psycho-analysis* 1:103–107. It is analyzed more generally in Marvin Hurvich, "The Place of Annihilation Anxieties in Psychoanalytic Theory," *Journal of the American Psychoanalytic Association* 51(2):579–616.

47. Søren Kierkegaard, *The Sickness Unto Death* (Radford, VA: Wilder Publications, 2008), p. 29.

48. C. G. Jung, *The Red Book: Liber Novus*, edited by Sonu Shamdasani (New York: W. W. Norton & Company, 2009), p. 346, col. B.

49. *Ibid.*, p. 347, col. A.

50. *Ibid.*, p. 348, col. A.

51. *Ibid.*, p. 349, col. A.

52. *Ibid.*, p. 349, col. B.

53. *Ibid.*, p. 350, col. B.

54. *Ibid.*

55. Stephan A. Hoeller, *The Gnostic Jung and the Seven Sermons to the Dead* (Wheaton, IL: The Theosophical Publishing House, 1982), p. 70.

56. C. G. Jung, *Nietzsche's* Zarathustra: *Notes of the Seminar Given in 1934–1939*, edited by James L. Jarrett (Princeton, NJ: Princeton University Press, 1988), vol. 1, p. 252.

57. Stephen R. Wilk, *Medusa: Solving the Mystery of the Gorgon* (Oxford, UK: Oxford University Press, 2000), pp. 186–191.

58. Erich Neumann, *The Great Mother: An Analysis of an Archetype*, 2nd edition, edited by Ralph Manheim (Princeton, NJ: Princeton University Press, 1963), p. 166.

59. Samuel Weber, *The Legend of Freud*, 2nd edition (Stanford, CA: Stanford University Press, 1999), Introduction.

60. S. Freud, *Studies on Hysteria*, in *The Standard Edition of the Complete Psychological Works of Sigmund Freud*, vol. 2 (London: Hogarth, 1893), p. 117. This is discussed fully in Ronald Britton, "The Blindness of the Seeing Eye: Inverse Symmetry as a Defense against Reality," *Psychoanalytic Inquiry* 14(3):365–378.

61. See Murray Mills, *Insight and Inference: Descartes's Founding Principle and Modern Philosophy* (Toronto: University of Toronto Press, 1999), chap. 8.

62. C. G. Jung, "A Psychological Approach to the Dogma of the Trinity," in *The Collected Works of C. G. Jung*, vol. 11, *Psychology and Religion* (Princeton, NJ: Princeton University Press, 1958), § 261.

63. This process is described in Shelley E. Taylor, "Adjustment to Threatening Events: A Theory of Cognitive Adaption," *American Psychologist* 38(11):1161–1173.

64. See Gregory A. Barton, "Abolishing the East: The Dated Nature of Orientalism in the Definition and Ethical Analysis of the Hindu Faith," *Comparative Studies of South Asia, Africa and the Middle East* 29(2):281–290.

65. This leads to anthropomorphism and the living presence of deities. An interesting study in this regard is Justin L. Barrett, "Cognitive Constraints on Hindu Concepts of the Divine," *Journal for the Scientific Study of Religion* 37(4):608–619.

66. Her limited reception is discussed in Jeffrey J. Kripal, "Why the Tantrika Is a Hero: Kali in the Psychoanalytical Tradition," in *Encountering Kali: In the Margins, at the Center, in the West*, edited by Rachel F. McDermott and Jeffrey J. Kripal (Berkeley, CA: University of California Press, 2003), chap. 9.

67. See H. B. Urban, "'India's Darkest Heart': Kali in the Colonial Imagination," in *Encountering Kali: In the Margins, at the Center, in the West*, edited by Rachel F. McDermott and Jeffrey J. Kripal (Berkeley, CA: University of California Press, 2003), chap. 8.

68. R. T. Curran, "Kali, Individuation, and the Primordial Unconscious," *Psychological Perspectives* 48(2):172–189.

69. John Woodroffe, Śakti and Śakta (Madras: Ganesh & Company, 1927; reprinted: Dover, 2010), p. 26.

70. Ajit Mookerjee, *Kali: The Feminine Force* (New York: Destiny Books, 1988), chap. 4.

71. Elizabeth U. Harding, *Kali: The Black Goddess of Dakshineswar* (Berwick, ME: Nicholas-Hays, 1993), pp. 52–53.

72. *The Gospel of Sri Ramakrishna*, translated by Swami Nikhilananda (Madras: Sri Ramakrishna Math, 1974), p. 371.

73. David. R. Kinsley, *The Sword and the Flute* (Santa Barbara: University of California Press, 1975), p. 144.

74. C. G. Jung, "The Spirit Mercurius," in *The Collected Works of C. G. Jung*, vol. 13, *Alchemical Studies* (Princeton, NJ: Princeton University Press, 1967), § 267.

75. Linda. E. Olds, "The Neglected Feminine: Promises and Perils," *Soundings: An Interdisciplinary Journal* 69(3):226–240.

76. Curran, "Kali, Individuation, and the Primordial Unconscious," p. 183.

77. Fowler McCormick, quoted in C. G. Jung, *The Psychology of Kundalini Yoga: Notes on a Seminar Given in 1952*, edited by Sonu Shamdasani (Princeton, NJ: Princeton University Press, 1996), p. xxxviii.

78. C. G. Jung, *The Zofingia Lectures*, supplementary vol. A, *The Collected Works of C. G. Jung* (Princeton, NJ: Princeton University Press, 1983), § 170.

79. C. G. Jung, "The Psychology of the Transference," in *The Collected Works of C. G. Jung*, vol. 16, *The Practice of Psychotherapy* (Princeton, NJ: Princeton University Press, 1964), § 493.

80. C. G. Jung, *Psychology and Alchemy*, vol. 12, *The Collected Works of C. G. Jung* (Princeton, NJ: Princeton University Press, 1953), § 63.

81. C. G. Jung, "The Transcendent Function," in *The Collected Works of C. G. Jung*, vol. 8, *The Structure and Dynamics of the Psyche* (Princeton, NJ: Princeton University Press, 1960), § 131, *et. seq.*

The 2011 Earthquake in Japan
Psychotherapeutic Interventions and Change of Worldview

TOSHIO KAWAI

The Great East Japan Earthquake on March 11, 2011, was a tremendous disaster. It was the most powerful earthquake ever to be recorded in Japanese history with a magnitude of 9.0. The huge tsunami triggered by the earthquake, with a wave height of 30 meters, caused especially heavy damage. It destroyed many cities and villages near the coast and took many lives. About 16,000 people were killed; 3,000 are still missing. Because the damage was mainly a result of the tsunami, there was a clear contrast between areas that were severely hit by the earthquake and those that were not, which led to many stories about life and death. Some people narrowly escaped with their lives, while others unfortunately died or lost their family members. Moreover, the disaster became more complicated because the shock and the tsunami destroyed several nuclear power plants in Fukushima, which resulted in the secondary disaster of radiation leakages from the plants. There is still ongoing danger of nuclear contamination. These

Toshio Kawai is professor of clinical psychology at Kokoro Reseach Center, Kyoto University. He also works as a Jungian analyst. He has written on postmodern consciousness in connection with psychotherapy and the works of Haruki Murakami, autistic spectrum disorder, Jung's Red Book, and Jungian psychology in Japan.

triple damages of earthquake, tsunami, and nuclear leakage make intervention after the disaster especially difficult.

Right after the earthquake not only rescue parties and relief supplies, but also psychological relief teams were sent to stricken areas. Various natural disasters in the past, for example, the earthquake in Kobe in 1995, the typhoon in Toyooka on the Japanese sea coast in 2004, the Sichuan earthquake in China in 2008, and others, have taught us that the victims suffered not only from material damage, but also mentally. So when the earthquake hit on March 11, 2011, various kinds of psychological relief teams were organized and sent to the stricken areas. The Association of Jungian Analysts, Japan (AJAJ) and the Japanese Association for Sandplay Therapy (JAJP) organized a joint working committee for the psychological relief work; as chair of this committee, I reported on its activity on the International Association for Analytical Psychology (IAAP) website and in other papers.

In the face of earthquake disaster both material support and psychotherapeutic intervention are necessary for individual victims. Here I would like to address a third dimension: psychology of the earthquake from a global point of view. Although Japanese people are rather used to natural disasters, the 2011 earthquake brought about such unprecedented damage that it fundamentally shocked their existing worldview. In face of unexpected damages caused by the tsunami and the ongoing danger from the nuclear power plants, people no longer trust technology and the words of politicians and scientists. Unsatisfactory interventions and explanations after the disaster evoked more suspicion. In this sense, not only those in the stricken areas but the whole of the Japanese people were deeply touched by the disaster.

Jung believed that peoples' worldview and global psychology can be studied and changed through individual psychotherapy. In his concept of the collective unconscious the collective dimension can be found in the individual psyche. If this is the case, our psychological relief work with the victims of the earthquake can shed light on the changes in the worldview.

SMALL STORIES

Although our psychological relief work is fruitful and meaningful, we have to come to the conclusion that individual intervention and psychotherapy have less to do with the change in worldview. As I reported elsewhere our activity is focused on the care of care-taking persons, like psychotherapists and nursery teachers, in the stricken areas. The reason for this kind of intervention is that we cannot remain permanently on site, so it is better to work with people who are able to endure the difficulty for a certain period of time and wait for support. These care-taking persons have to hold the heavy stories told to them. It is important that these difficult stories are shared in a protective atmosphere offered by the psychological relief work team. Care of soul means care of stories.

As we made regular visits to the areas hit by tsunami, we could observe a general flow of psychological time after the earthquake. Right after the disaster everyone seemed to be overwhelmed and in great confusion. It was an extreme emergency situation. People were having to cope with the critical situation in every moment; they had to be evacuated, find food and clothes, rebuild their destroyed houses, and so on. There was no time for reflection. Generally a strong feeling of connectedness among the victims was noticed.

After about three months, the populace entered a phase of remembering and reflection. According to school counselors, children frequently reported nightmares concerning the earthquake and tsunami in June and July. From some people we had already met with, we heard about their life and death experiences for the first time. Such nightmares and critical stories should not be understood as the onset of trauma, but rather as a sign that the people have obtained a certain psychological distance from the disaster. The pictures drawn by an elementary school class support this hypothesis. Almost all the pictures drawn just after the earthquake have a distorted structure, while those drawn three months later were totally normalized and showed a clear recovery. A normal psyche seems to recover from crisis after several months if there is a supportive enough environment and if the crisis does not continue. So the reports of nightmares and the terrible experience of the tsunami three months after the earthquake do not mean that the psychic condition is getting worse, but rather that it is getting better.

After this period, and in some cases earlier, people start to talk about their personal problems in psychotherapy, but not necessarily about the earthquake. Children at school show various psychological symptoms, but as reported by the school counselors and nursery teachers, they complain about their relationships with their parents and schoolmates. We supervised several cases using sandplay therapy in a pediatric section of a hospital in Ishinomaki, a city that was severely hit by the tsunami. In every case the child expressed a psychological development that was pertinent for his or her age in the sandplay. For example, a ten-year-old boy had the task of establishing self-consciousness, which was expressed in his sandplay sessions. Traumatic experiences of the earthquake and tsunami were not a theme in the sandplay of the children. Only in the case of the mother of a girl did the sandplay show a literal reproduction of the tsunami; the mother was fixed on the traumatic experience, and her psychological condition did not get better.

We concluded from our psychological relief work that it is not the big story of the earthquake and tsunami, but small and individual stories that are important for the mental recovery of the victims. We can even suggest that a fixation on the big story of the earthquake disaster blocks psychological development, as the case of the mother hinted at. Psychological development and recovery from the shock of the earthquake are brought about by finding small stories. The big traumatic story of the earthquake and tsunami is replaced by small individual stories which are easier to cope with. Although each series of sandplay sessions was interesting, there was almost no indication of what the earthquake disaster meant for Japan and the modern world or how the collective psyche was reacting against the lost worldview.

PSYCHOTHERAPY AND PSYCHOLOGY

Our psychological relief work for victims of the 2011 earthquake suggests that psychotherapy does not have to do directly with the solution of a collective problem. The success of psychotherapy rather consists in the shift from the big story of trauma to small personal stories. Jung wrote in a letter, "If the individual is not really changed, nothing is changed."[1] Jung believed that a change of worldview would be brought about in the unconscious of individual persons. Jung wrote that the individual "is the one important factor and . . . the salvation of the world consists in the salvation of the individual soul."[2] As Wolfgang Giegerich pointed out, the concept of the collective unconscious might be problematic.[3] Jung assumed that the lost mythological world was still alive in the collective unconscious, which could produce new symbols. But as our psychological relief work suggested, psychotherapy has to do with the care of the individuals, but not with the salvation of the world.

Giegerich pointed out that the psychotherapy is insignificant for the *Menschheitsproblematik* (mankind's problems) and wrote, "The opus magnum is somewhere else: in those works that articulate and change the logic of our being-in-the-world."[4] Such works are created by great artists and thinkers. In this case, the big story tends to be symbolized and rendered in metaphors, in a work of art, a novel, or philosophy, instead of being replaced by small stories. We have to deal with such works if we would like to discuss our worldview, our being-in-the-world. In this sense it is probably important to distinguish psychology from psychotherapy. While psychotherapy has to do with care of small stories and individual persons, psychology is concerned with mankind's problems by interpreting works of artists and thinkers.

OLD BIG STORIES: LIFE AND DEATH

Since the 2011 earthquake numerous books and special issues of journals have been published. They not only report on the aftermath of the earthquake disaster and criticize the preparation before and the measures devised after the disaster. Some try to suggest a new worldview and being-in-the-world. In this sense they are attempts to cope with the big story not only on concrete and political levels, but also on metaphorical and conceptual levels.

It seems to me that it is still premature to propose a new big story concerning the Great East Japan Earthquake, so I would like to look back and consider two stories based on previous earthquakes. We may get some hints from them. One is from *The Legends of Tono,* a collection of tales from the Tono region in Tohoku, recorded and written by Kunio Yanagita.[5] Yanagita is the founder of Japanese folklore studies, and this collection has become a Japanese folklore and literature classic. This is a very interesting and peculiar work which has led to many studies and still deserves future study from new vantage points. As the exploration of folklore was not yet established in Japan at that time, the collection contains all kinds of stories from myths and fairy tales to gossip. I would like to mention one story which is directly related to a big earthquake. The coast of Sanriku has been hit several times by

terrible tsunamis caused by earthquakes. Historically, the one in 869
seemed to be the biggest. But in 1896 there was a famous Sanrikuoki
earthquake, which caused a tsunami and killed more than 20,000
people, almost as many as the 2011 earthquake. The story I quote, no.
99, is based on this tragedy.⁶ This story may be an answer to the life
and death question.

> Legend 99. Kiyoshi Kitagawa, an assistant headman in Tsuchi-
> buchi village, lived in Hiishi. His family had been roving priests
> for generations. His grandfather, named Seifuku-in, was a scholar
> who had written many books and done a lot for the village.
> Kiyoshi's younger brother Fukuji married into a family in
> Tanohama on the coast. Fukuji lost his wife and one of his
> children in the tidal wave [tsunami] that struck the area last year.
> For about a year, he was with the two children who survived in
> a shelter set up on the site of the original house.
>
> On a moonlit night in early summer, he got up to go to the toilet.
> It was off at some distance where the waves broke on the path by
> the beach. On this night, the fog hovered low, and he saw two
> people, a man and a woman, approaching him through the fog.
> The woman was definitely his wife who had died. Without
> thinking, he trailed after them to a cavern on the promontory in
> the direction of Funakoshi village. When he called out his wife's
> name, she looked back and smiled. The man he saw was from
> the same village, and he too had died in the tidal wave disaster.
> It had been rumored that this man and Fukuji's wife had been
> deeply in love before Fukuji had been picked to marry her.
>
> She said, "I am now married to this man." Fukuji replied, "But
> don't you love your children?" The color of her face changed
> slightly and she cried. Fukuji didn't realize that he was talking
> with the dead. While he was looking down at his feet feeling
> sad and miserable, the man and the woman moved on quickly
> and disappeared around the mountain on the way to Oura.
> He tried to run after them and then suddenly realized they
> were the dead. He stood on the road thinking until daybreak
> and went home in the morning. It is said that he was sick for a
> long time after this.

We mentioned that the story about life and death was important
in the case of a tsunami. Even near the coast, while some areas were
seriously hit, some areas were saved. In the same area some people could

barely escape, some were drowned and killed. Even within a family, such a drama occurred. How can the dead and living who were separated meet again? Or how can the living say farewell to the dead? In Japan there is a ritual to welcome dead ancestors during the Obon time in the summer. It is around the middle of August. In the case of the city of Kyoto, the dead come back to the city between August 7 and August 10, and they stick around and leave this world again on August 16. The famous sending fire of Five Mountains in Kyoto is a ceremony to send the dead souls back to the other world. In other places the dead are sent back to the other world by floating dedicatory lanterns on the river. Many dedicatory lanterns on the Kitakami River near Ishinomki in the year of the earthquake (2011) had a special meaning because they were not only symbolic ancestors but real recent dead by the latest tsunami. It was not a summer tourist festival at all, but a real ritual with sorrow and tears.

In the text of *The Legends of Tono* story no. 99 takes place in the summer of the year following the Sanriku earthquake, but in other texts based on the same colloquial tradition, it takes place in the summer of the same year as the earthquake. Considering the intensity of the story this must be the first Obon for the dead to return home, which is very important. I have heard many dreams of patients who did not believe in the return of the dead in Obon, but were surprised to dream of the dead who returned to this world exactly during this period. Fukuji, who had lost his wife, met her again; this story is a verification of the old story and belief.

But this story is not idyllic and sentimental. It does not end with a happy return of the dead. Fukuji's wife lives now with her former lover. This story should not be understood as a kind of gossip but as a truly psychological story. Fukuji lost his wife first physically in the tsunami and now loses her again psychologically because she seems to be living with her former lover. Meeting again leads to another separation. But this second loss is necessary to establish a new relationship between life and death and to recover from the disaster.

In Greek mythology Orpheus goes to the underworld to look for his dead wife, Eurydice. He is allowed to bring her back to this world with the promise of not seeing her on his way. But he looks back at her and loses her eternally. Orpheus's action should not be understood as a failure but as an accomplishment of love, sending Eurydice to her proper place since her name suggests that she is queen of the underworld.[7] In analogy to the myth of Orpheus our story from *The Legends of Tono* suggests that the dead wife is now psychologically lost and that she belongs to her own world. The film *Orphée* by French poet Jean Cocteau makes the double character of Eurydice clearer. In this film Orpheus loves *la princess de la mort*, "princess of death," and her driver Heurtebise loves Orpheus's wife Eurydice. Because these four figures make marriage quaternio (*Heiratsquaternio*), there are cross-cousin marriages or relationships to anima and animus between Orpheus and the princess of death and Eurydice and Heurtebise. But because the princess of death and Heurtebise remain in the other world at the end, Orpheus can come back to this world with his wife Eurydice. In comparison with Cocteau's film, we can conclude that the fourth element, a real woman in this world, is still lacking in our story from the Tono legends, which is probably the reason for Fukuji's sickness.

Because this story is based on the Japanese tradition of Obon ritual and is similar to the Orpheus's myth, it can be regarded as a collective answer to the tragedy of tsunami and the question of life and death. But it is at the same time Fukuji's personal story. In this sense this is an encounter of big story with a small personal story.

HARUKI MURAKAMI: GRATITUDE AND INVOLVEMENT

I would like to introduce another story, written by Haruki Murakami. Murakami is probably the most famous contemporary novelist in Japan. His recent novel *1Q84* was newly translated into English and published in October 2011. My understanding of his novel is that it shows the state of soul in Japan as having skipped over the task of establishing modern consciousness so that it now stands between the pre-modern world and postmodern consciousness.[8]

The original title of *After the Quake* was "All God's Children Can Dance," and it contains six short stories that take place between the Kobe earthquake in January 1995 and the poison gas terrorism carried out by a religious cult in the Tokyo subway in March 1995.[9] One is a natural disaster and the other a manmade disaster. The year 1995 was a turning point for Japan and also for Murakami's works, marking the end of Japan's economic flourishing and various kinds of Japanese systems, such as lifelong employment. Murakami's book marked a change from the detachment found in his earlier works to more involvement with society. I would like to focus on one of the six short stories, "Super-frog Saves Tokyo," which has a direct reference to the earthquake. The following is my summary of the story.

> Katagiri, a banker, was surprised by a huge frog who was waiting for him in his house. Frog explained that there would be an earthquake in Tokyo caused by a huge worm at 8:30 a.m. on February 18, which according to Frog's prophecy was in three days. Frog wanted to prevent it, but needed help. Frog subsequently proved the accuracy of his prophetic ability to Katagiri by predicting the return of a pending loan. Frog and Katagiri decided to go down to the epicenter, which was located exactly beneath the bank by which Katagiri was employed. But the day before the earthquake, just when they needed to go underground below the bank to fight the worm, Katagiri was shot and brought to a hospital. He woke up in the bed of the hospital and noticed that it was already February 18 and that the earthquake had not happened. A nurse explained to him that, contrary to his memory, he was found lying on the street without a gunshot wound. Frog came up to the hospital afterward and explained how he, Frog, had fought the worm. Katagiri apparently had been helping Frog in his dream. Frog started to fade out as he was telling the story about the fight with the worm. Boils burst out of the body of Frog and "wriggling, maggotlike worms of all shapes and sizes came crawling out." Hundreds of worms came and crawled up Katagiri's leg. He screamed and a nurse came. He told her, "He [Frog] saved Tokyo from being destroyed by an earthquake all by himself." The end of this story suggests that Katagiri was also about to die: "Then he closed his eyes and sank into a restful, dreamless sleep."

In contrast to the story in *The Legends of Tono*, which depicts what happened after the earthquake, this story shows how the earthquake was prevented. It is interesting that Katagiri has "no wife, no kids, both parents dead, brother and sister he had put through college married off. So what if they killed him?" The lack of relationship makes it possible for him to encounter Frog. In this sense he does not live in the old worldview with its story of meeting the dead ancestors. While in *The Legends of Tono* the motivation is a personal one of meeting the dead wife, the matter here is the collective task of saving Tokyo from the earthquake. So the dimension is totally different.

Frog fought the worm, while Katagiri wanted to help the frog and did help him in the dream. We can draw two conclusions. The first has to do with connection to the source of the power. The epicenter was located in the underground of the bank in which Katagiri worked. Is Katagiri a special person, a selected hero, or a godlike prophet? No, rather this suggests that every postmodern person who is not part of a community or a family nor in a personal relationship has his epicenter in his depth. To put it differently, the lack of horizontal relationships makes the vertical encounter possible and necessary. It is important to come into contact with this depth in the form of fighting. I don't think the point is to overcome the danger and to evade the disaster heroically. As Frog was transformed after the fight and died in the hospital, he was sacrificed by coming into contact with the power of the worm and was even embodied and transformed into worms. In the case of natural disaster there are very often aspects both of fear and of obtaining power from it. For example, on the coasts hit by the tsunami in 2011 there are hundreds of Shinto shrines. This is because people were both afraid of and at the same time thankful for the power of water, the rich power of the ocean which brings fish and other fruitful products. People were afraid of nature but, at the same time, grateful for its richness.

These two attitudes are somehow equivalent to the feelings of *tremendum* and *fascinosum* which Rudolf Otto described as feeling toward the "holy"; in face of the holy we have feelings of awfulness and fascination.[10] These two feelings have been noted historically in other rituals. After many natural disasters and epidemics around the ninth century in Japan, a festival was created in Heian time to drive away bad spirits: Gion Matsuri, the most famous festival in Kyoto. According to historians, it was important for people at that time not only to drive away but also to get the power of bad spirits; in the highlight of the festival people felt the power and presence of bad spirits. So there is a moment of both fear and fascination, presence and disappearance. In this connection I would like to mention that in several sandplay sessions after the earthquake a lot of animals were put in the sand tray. In one case, many animals were heading in the direction where the patient and therapist were standing. In another case a lot of animals were gathering around a sleeping rabbit (fig. 1). This can be regarded as the power of nature

Figure 1. Animals gathering (offered by Akiko Sasaki).

in a rather positive sense after people have experienced the extremely negative power of nature in the form of earthquakes and tsunamis.

After referring to the power of tsunami, I have to make a short remark concerning nuclear power plants. If we analyze the attitude toward nuclear power plants in Japan from this point of view, I have to say that it is totally out of this worldview. Nuclear power does not belong to environmental order and comes from outside of nature. It is no wonder the Japanese have not built any shrines to give thanks to nuclear power plants and want to discard them now without any gratitude for such powers. There has not been a grounded story around the nuclear disaster, but people now know that many of the stories about the safety and usefulness of nuclear power plants were false, manipulative, and served only the interests of the Tokyo Electric Company, the government scientists, and the mass media, all of whom colluded and spent billions of dollars developing their version of the story surrounding safe, clean nuclear power.

The second conclusion we can draw from Murakami's story is this: after the 2011 earthquake many writers, including scientists, highlighted the Japanese attitude of *mujō* the calm and passive acceptance of fate, thinking that nothing remains the same, that there is nothing in the end. While the Western worldview is aimed at attaining a better and higher point, the worldview of *mujō* is based on "ground zero," on nothingness. So even if people lose everything after the earthquake, they can accept the situation as a basic state. This attitude may have prevented them from chaotic rioting and it may have given them support to endure the difficult situation after the earthquake in the stricken areas.

But in Murakami's story, no passive acceptance of fate is recognized. Rather, the power is regarded as evil and the protagonist tries to fight against the evil. This is because this work evolved out of both a natural disaster, earthquake, and a manmade disaster, poison gas terrorism. The message is that we have to be active, we have to fight against the evil powers. We should not remain in a passive acceptance of fate. Because the earthquake of March 11, 2011 resulted in a combination of natural and manmade disaster, Murakami's story anticipated somehow a new attitude which may be necessary for the situation today. I would not say there is already a solution or a hint of a solution in this short work. But at least we may say that the highly praised attitude of *mujō* among the Japanese after the 2011 earthquake is not totally valid anymore. This is because we no longer have to deal only with natural power, which can be accepted with fear and gratitude in the exiting worldview. Besides the natural power, human and evil power played an important role in the disaster with extremely negative results. So the passive acceptance of power is not enough. We have to be active and fight against negative power. This means also that nature has lost its omnipotence. The 2011 earthquake surprised us with the uncontrollable power of nature on one side, but it made it clear to us that nature had lost its omnipotent power. This loss must be difficult for the old being-in-the-world.

LOSS OF NATURE AND OLD STORY: CONCLUSION

Though psychotherapy consists of the emancipation from the big story and the creation of small stories, the dimension of the big story is also important. While I have worked with people in Tohoku, I have keenly felt the loss of the old story, the old worldview, in the background. This loss overshadows the personal psychological problems. So there is a need for a new story.

But at the same time it is absolutely necessary to bring to light how the Tokyo Electric Company, the government, scientists, and the mass media colluded to create their version of the story and manipulated people. We have to learn from the negative consequences of this story.

There are several good ideas for a new story. For example the work of Japanese anthropologist Shinichi Nakazawa is worth mentioning concerning our relationship to the energy.[11] He analyzes the unmediated, immediate character of nuclear power; what happens inside the sun brought directly into a nuclear plant. This does not belong to the environmental order and hence the Japanese worldview. But instead of asserting a return to the old worldview and technology, he proposes direct but mediated use of sun energy, which is a dialectical negation of nuclear power. He points out the importance of interface in his further papers.

But it is premature to speak about a new story concretely. It is now important to accept and carry the loss as loss. It is a complicated situation in which human technology was defeated by the overwhelming power of nature on one hand, while on the other hand the omnipotence of nature was lost. This is so to speak a double loss because we have lost our trust in technology against the power of nature and our naive belief in the omnipotence of nature. I would like to respect this double loss so that the emptiness may become a place for the birth of a new being-in-the-world.

NOTES

1. C. G. Jung, *Letters, Vol. 2: 1951–1961* (Princeton, NJ: Princeton University Press 1973), p. 462.

2. C. G. Jung, "The Undiscovered Self," in *The Collected Works of C. G. Jung,* vol. 10, *Civilization in Transition* (Princeton, NJ: Princeton University Press, 1964), § 536.

3. W. Giegerich, "The End of Meaning and the Birth of Man," *Journal of Jungian Theory and Practice* 6(1):39.

4. *Ibid.*, p. 40.

5. Kunio Yanagita, *The Legends of Tono*, translated by R. Morse (1910; reprinted Lanham, MD: Lexington Books, 2008).

6. I would like to thank Professor Sukeyuki Miura whose paper in a seminar reminded me of this story and related materials.

7. T. Kawai, "Die Initiation ins Dichterische bei Heidegger und Jung: Der Ort der Psychotherapie," *Daseinsanalyse* 6:194–209.

8. T. Kawai, "Postmodern Consciousness in the Novels of Haruki Murakami," in *The Cultural Complex*, edited by T. Singer (London: Routledge, 2004), pp. 90–101.

9. Haruki Murakami, *After the Quake* (New York: Knopf, 2002).

10. R. Otto, *Das Heilige: Über das Irrationale in der Idee des Göttlichen und sein Verhälthis zum Rationalen* (Breslau: Trewendt und Granier, 1920).

11. S. Nakazawa, *Nihon no Daitenkan* [*Big Change of Japan*] (Tokyo: Shueisha, 2011).

THE GARDEN OF THE HEART AND SOUL
PSYCHOLOGICAL RELIEF WORK IN EARTHQUAKE ZONES AND ORPHANAGES IN CHINA

HEYONG SHEN AND GAO LAN

The Garden of the Heart and Soul project was first started at the orphanage in Guangzhou, China in 2007. Eva Pattis, a Jungian analyst from Milan, came to Guangzhou on May 1, 2008, and worked for ten days with the volunteers, making evaluations and supervising. Since then, we have set up forty-three workstations at orphanages in mainland China, including Lhasa (the capital of Tibet), Urumqi (the capital of Xinjiang Province), in Ningxia at an orphanage for Muslims, and in Beijing, Shanghai, and Guangzhou.

In the magnitude 8.0 earthquake in Sichuan, China, on May 12, 2008, about 69,000 people died, another 18,000 went missing, more than 374,000 people were injured, and 4.8 million survivors became homeless. The victims lost their family members and their livelihoods.

Heyong Shen is the president of the Chinese Federation of Analytical Psychology and Sandplay Therapy and a Jungian analyst. He is a member of Sandplay Therapists of America, the International Society for Sandplay Therapy (ISST), and the International Association for Analytical Psychology (IAAP) and professor at South China Normal University, City University of Macao, and Fudan University in China.

Gao Lan is professor of psychology at South China Normal University, a sandplay therapist, a member of ISST and an IAAP analyst in training.

This research project was supported by the City University of Macao (FHSS-2012-03).

A team from the Chinese Federation of Analytical Psychology and Sandplay Therapy went to Sichuan to provide psychological relief work the first week after the earthquake. We set up workstations in an area for the project that we called "the Garden of the Heart and Soul" and continued our work there for three years.

Figure 1. Heyong Shen with new students who came from Shui-mo, in Wenchuan, to the Garden of the Heart and Soul.

In December 2011, we returned to Sichuan for ten days with two friends, Lu Yuegang and Peng Xiaohua, who are well-known writers. Lu Yuegang, from his professional perspective as a writer, observed the deep emotional connection between the students and our volunteers at the Garden of the Heart and Soul. In three years, the children grow up fast and change a lot, but the intimacy, the feeling of family and of togetherness, which is so touching and moving, remains. This relationship is a basic element in the healing that occurs, especially in psychological relief work after earthquakes.

We had established a three-year plan at the very beginning of our work in May 2008, in the first week of the earthquake. Our primary effort was to build an effective relationship and a free and protected space that could offer the necessary safety and containing. "Hand in hand and heart to heart" is a vivid description of our work at the Garden of the Heart and Soul.

On this trip we visited the Garden of the Heart and Soul at two schools: Beichuan and Shuimo in Wenchuan. Beichuan Qiang Autonomous County is the only self-governing county for the Qiang people, a very special minority in China whose history goes back to Dayu (2200 BC) and Shenong Yandi (4300 BC). During the Han Dynasty (206 BC to 220 AD), there were about twelve million Qiang people in China, one fifth of the Chinese population. Before the 2008 earthquake, there were only about 280,000 Qiang people, and one-third of the people in Beichuan died. The school in Beichuan, where we have been working, suffered terrible damage; over half of the 3,000 students died in the buildings that collapsed in the earthquake.

We set up a five-level therapeutic plan of action, according to the situation—a small group working with a large population of victims:

1. Individual and family focused interventions;
2. Group work with 20–30 people;

Figure 2. Early meeting in a tent, Beichuan, May 18, 2008.

3. Large group activities for 60–100 people;

4. Film viewing, engaging greater numbers of people; and

5. Community and environmental work using music, broadcasting, printed flyers, pictures, and replanting the landscape.

Based on analytical psychology and the Chinese culture's psychology of the heart, we embraced the way of *ci-bei* (loving grief, compassion) as a guide in our work. *Ci-bei* is a combination of two characters: *ci*, which means love and compassion, and *bei*, which means grief, suffering, and pain. In the character *bei*,

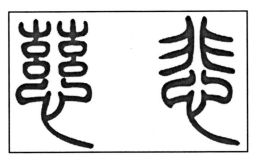

Figure 3. The Chinese characters for *ci* and *bei*.

the upper part of the symbol has the meaning of "split," "flying away," and "lost," while the lower part is the symbol for the heart. Thus we have the symbolic meaning of *bei*: when your heart is splitting and lost, you will have grief, suffering and pain. This is very close to the modern psychological interpretation of trauma.

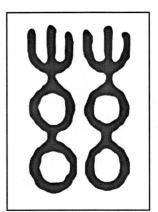

Figure 4. The Chinese character for *zi*.

How then to deal with such splitting, loss, and trauma? We can get the thread from the character *ci*. The character *ci* is also made up of two parts, the heart below and *zi* above. The symbol *zi* (figure 4) conveys the meaning of growing, associating, and connecting. So, from *ci*, we get the symbolic meaning of "associating with the heart" and "growing of the heart." Association, relatedness, and relationship are also important for contemporary psychotherapy.

According to Chinese philosophy, in particular the Doctrine of the Mean, when we have two opposite factors together, like characters of *ci-bei* (love and grief), then we have a third level of meaning that goes beyond the original two. For example, in the Chinese notion of *wei-ji* (crisis and opportunity) we find the idea of retaining the opposites and using the heart. This is also an important principle of Jungian analysis, which C. G. Jung called the transcendental function. The Chinese name for psychology, is "heart-ology" (figure 5). To rediscover the meaning of the heart and the soul is the main effort and the mission of a psychology of the heart.[1]

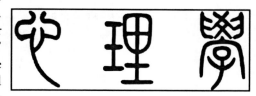

Figure 5. Chinese characters for psychology.

We based our work on analytical psychology and Chinese culture, especially the psychology of the heart. Sandplay therapy, combined with the Chinese five element principles, was the main method we used for the psychological relief initially. The practical and therapeutic process can be divided into three primary steps.

Figure 6. Setting up for sandplay, with a sign reading "The Garden of the Heart and Soul," at the school in Beichuan, May 26, 2008.

First, we worked to build an effective relationship, from heart to heart, using the first principle of the psychology of the heart, *gan-ying* (the thirty-first hexagram of *I Ching*, which can be translated as "touching the heart and responding from the heart"), to set up a contained, free, and protected space to reestablish and increase victims' sense of reality and safety. Qiang music and ritual were used, together with some breathing and body work to produce embodied resonance.

Second, based on the established relationship, we worked to enhance the therapeutic container by "attending and accompanying," active listening with the heart. (The Chinese character for "listening" combines the characters for "ear," "gestation," "ten eyes," or "straight," and "one heart." Such listening with the heart, as I call it, is referred to as "active listening" in the system of psychology of the heart.) We chose sandplay, music, painting, embodied dream work, and archetypal psychodrama for working with the clients individually and in groups.

Figure 7. Heyong Shen and one of his sandplay groups in the Garden of the Heart and Soul at the school in Beichuan, May 2008.

Finally, we offered sustained psychological support, using the psychology of the heart, employing the principles of "loving grief"(the Chinese character *ci-bei*, conveying the method and the way to work with trauma and healing) and *gan-ying* (wholehearted influence), and the healing and transformative function of the cultural archetypes (*dayu* for naming and initiating; *shennong* for taming and nurturing; and *fuxi* for timing and transforming).[2]

For the first six months, we could see in the sand trays the process and images as the victims expressed their trauma, their feelings of chaos and suffering, helplessness and wounding. In the next period, after several months, through the sandplay we can see that they were touched by the heart; images of angels emerged along with figures of the heart, and the healing process took hold in the Garden of the Heart and Soul.

Figure 8. Children working in the sand tray in the Garden of the Heart and Soul at the school in Beichuan, August 2008.

Figure 9. The students brought this heart-shaped stone to the Garden of the Heart and Soul. It was used very often in the students' sandplay process.

The image and symbol of the heart is very important in the Chinese culture. When we constructed the system of the psychology of the heart, we wrote about three levels of meaning: physiological, psychological, and metaphysical. The meaning of the heart from a physiological sense is this: the heart is the root and nature of life; the heart is the changing of mind and spirit. From a psychological sense, the heart is the totality of all psychological phenomena and processes. But besides the mind and body, the heart conveys a metaphysical sense: in Chinese the heart is used to express the heavenly mind or heavenly heart, and the heart of Dao. The Chinese characters for thought and thinking (figure 10),

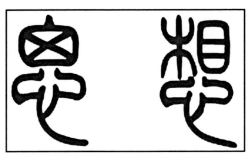

Figure 10. Chinese characters for thought and thinking.

emotion and feeling (figure 11), and will and ambition (figure 12)—the three most important factors in psychology—are all combinations that include the image of heart at their core.

Figure 11. Chinese characters for emotion and feeling.

As psychotherapists, we are all very familiar with therapy, but not so familiar with healing. We prefer to use the Chinese character for "healing" for our Jungian practice and psychological relief work because it has embodied the image of the heart, and the heart-related healing process (figure 13). It is a combination of the images for boat and the making of a boat (the upper part of the character) and

Figure 12. Chinese characters for will and ambition.

the heart (below) and it conveys a beautiful image of "boat of the heart."

For making a boat, especially in ancient times, the earliest image of a canoe, for instance, you need to make an empty space in the wood or tree trunk. This is the Chinese character *yu*, to make a boat or canoe by hollowing the log; it forms the upper part of "healing" (figure 14). But the accompanying image of "empty" has profound philosophical and psychological meaning; it conveys the meaning of empty and containing, and nothing and everything (figure 15). Empty, in the Chinese cultural context,

Figure 13. The Chinese character for healing.

is not only a term, but a very important philosophy. It is empty but also "containing"; we call existence in the empty *miao-you*: a wonderful having or containment. There is a Chinese proverb: "Having containment is great." That is the way and power of healing.

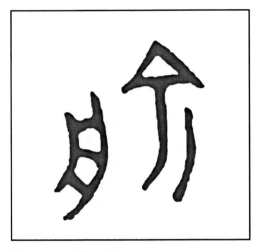

Figure 14. The Chinese character *yu*.

Figure 15. The Chinese character for "empty."

Figure 16. Early on in our work at the Garden of the Heart and Soul, for group sandplay, we used the ground with natural green grass as a sand tray.

On April 14, 2010, there was a big earthquake in Yushu, China. More than 90 percent of the local buildings collapsed; and several thousand people died, and more than 12,000 were injured. Yushu had been an old land for the Qiang people, and is now in Tibet, located on the Qing-Zhang plateau, with an average altitude of 4,500 meters. It is here that the headwaters for the three main rivers in China—the Yellow River, the Yang-zhi River, and Lanchang River—are found. Our team from the Chinese Federation of Analytical Psychology and Sandplay Therapy went to Yushu and set up three workstations there. We have continued our work for the last two years.

The model of the Garden of the Heart and Soul and the system of the psychology of the heart have been wholeheartedly accepted and are used widely in China today. Originally, our work was primarily for the psychological development of orphans and for natural disaster relief work, but it has now extended to centers for waifs and strays (runaways), stay-at-home children, children whose parents are incarcerated, and

Figure 17. The meaning of the Garden of the Heart and Soul and our work, embodied in the expressive sandplay process.

the inmates of juvenile detention centers. We plan to set up one hundred Gardens of the Heart and Soul in mainland China in the next two years. Working with the heart is our version of Jungian analysis and sandplay therapy practice in China, especially for the Garden of the Heart and Soul.

NOTES

1. Heyong Shen, *Psychology of the Heart*, Eranos Years Book, 1998/2008.

2. Heyong Shen, *San Chuan Xing Si: Record of Events of the Garden of the Heart and Soul in the 2008 Wenchuan Earthquake* (Guangdong Science and Technology Press, 2009–2010), pp. 151–152.

Figure 18. Eva Pattis (pictured here with Heyong Shen) and Luigi Zoja came to the earthquake zone in August 2008 and participated our psychological relief work in the Garden of the Heart and Soul. We used expressive sandplay therapy mainly and helped a lot of students.

EXPRESSIVE SANDWORK
A JUNGIAN APPROACH IN DISASTER AREAS

EVA PATTIS ZOJA

Translated by Mark Kyburz with John Peck

How easy it is to love a child,
how hard to love what a child turns into!
——J. M. Coetzee, *Age of Iron*

In a large hall, twelve children are immersed in quiet concentration, each one sitting or standing at a sand tray, busy creating their own inner worlds. On a large table in the middle of the room are countless miniature figures and objects, arranged by category: people, animals, houses, cars, trees, stones, bottle corks, shells, and marbles. Between the table, cluttered full of toys, and the individual sand trays, arranged along the walls, there is a hustle

Eva Pattis Zoja is a clinical psychologist and Jungian psychoanalyst and a member of Österreichische Gesellschaft für Analytische Psychologie, the Association of Graduate Analytical Psychologists, Centro Italiano Psicologia Analitica, and the New York Association for Analytical Psychology. She has a diploma in sandplay from the International Society for Sandplay Therapy and teaches at the C. G. Jung Institute, Zürich, the C. G. Jung Foundation, New York, and ÖGAP, Vienna. She is the author of *Abortion: Loss and Renewal in the Search for Identity* and *Sandplay Therapy in Vulnerable Communities* and editor of *Sandplay Therapy: The Treatment of Psychopathologies*. She is currently working in Colombia, Argentina, and Romania on a project in expressive sandwork, helping neglected children in areas where psychotherapy is not available (www.sandwork.org).

and bustle. The children move back and forth between the table, which they are all allowed to use, and their sand-filled rectangles, hundreds of times, carrying a small animal, two building blocks, three marbles, a handful of toy cars. No child disturbs any other. Each seems preoccupied with his or her own thoughts. Beside each sand tray sits an adult: sometimes their presence is so discreet that it passes unnoticed; sometimes an unexpected blushing reveals that he or she is exposed to strong emotions.

"It was one of the most moving moments of my life," one psychotherapist observes after his first experience of expressive sandwork. "It was like being in a delivery room, with us adults witnesses of their births and rebirths. What the children created in their sand trays mirrored their everyday psychic efforts. Normally, we don't get to see these."

Expressive sandwork is based on the sandplay therapy founded by Dora Kalff in the 1950s and '60s, but it is distinct from the latter in two important ways: first, expressive sandwork is conducted in a group; second, the adults assisting the children are voluntary helpers, who need not necessarily be qualified psychotherapists. Expressive sandwork was developed by Jungian analysts in the 1990s in several very different geographical and cultural contexts: China, South Africa, and Colombia, bringing psychological assistance to places where it is lacking. It could be described either as a minimalist, transcultural, and predominantly nonverbal form of psychotherapy that springs from analytical psychology or, alternatively, as an expression of the theoretical and practical foundations of social (and communal) life in Jungian terms. If a method is to be used in different cultural, social, ethnic, and linguistic contexts, its practical application must be flexible and its theoretical foundation needs to be solid. Adapting Margaret Lowenfeld's world technique, which she devised in London during the 1930s, expressive sandwork was devised as a tool that could prove beneficial for children forced to live in extremely problematic social environments, such as ghettos or slum areas in South Africa and South America or in vulnerable communities such as orphanages in Asia and Eastern Europe.[1]

THE BEGINNINGS OF EXPRESSIVE SANDWORK IN CHINA

In the late 1990s, two years after the first Chinese Jungian analyst, Heyong Shen, had completed his training at the Jung Institute in Zürich, he established a program in analytical psychology at the Normal University in Guan Zhao, where he held a lectureship. This was a considerable achievement, given that until that time behaviorist approaches were the only psychotherapeutic models to be taught at Chinese universities. Together with his wife, Gao Lan, a professor at the same university, he also began to introduce sandplay at an orphanage in Guang Zhao. There each child was accompanied by a facilitator over a period of five to six months. The facilitators were final-year psychology students.

Generally speaking, sandplay therapy made it easier to introduce C. G. Jung's work to China. Many Jungian premises already have correspondences in traditional Chinese culture. It is anything but strange for a culture whose writing system consists of ideograms (that is, pictorial symbols rather than alphabetical letters), which every child begins to learn from the age of four, to attach equal importance to mental images and conceptual thinking. Observing how swiftly and precisely Asians are capable of analyzing a sandplay image suggests that they are able to read the various figurative, chromatic, spatial, and geometical representations as though the sandplay image was a form of writing. A trace drawn in the sand recalls the traditional calligraphy classes taught in Buddhist monasteries, where daily practice involved writing the characters with a bamboo stick in a small sand tray. Thus, showing Chinese students and patients a sand tray for the first time and telling them that it can be used as a therapeutic instrument raises hardly any eyebrows. Quite the contrary, there often appears to be a clear sense of relief.

The notion of the psyche creating images as a means of self-expression, the idea of symbolic processes being initiated whenever psychic development is impeded, and the idea that dreams could have a prospective function: all these notions correspond profoundly and naturally with Oriental tradition. We could even say that analytical psychology speaks to our Chinese colleagues in a language that is both pre-Cartesian and post-Maoist (post-Maoist in the sense that the

individual matters, not the masses). In some, analytical psychology
awakens a need to take up a millenium-old tradition that we find in
the descriptions of the *I Ching*: for instance, that two so-called opposites
are not necessarily mutually exclusive but are complementary, like the
two sides of a coin. Through sandplay as a form of expression within
analysis, Jungian theory is cast in a concrete and tangible form. The
miniature toys convey the impression that we can touch symbols with
our hands. This aspect of sandplay corresponds to the idea, said to be
typical of Chinese culture, that everything that occurs in daily life also
has meaning, for instance, the color red means wealth, good fortune,
and abundance, while the number four stands for death. This does not
necessarily mean that signs and symbols are confounded, but rather
that symbols are experienced in a highly concrete manner.

Although sandplay therapy as developed by Dora Kalff fell on
fruitful soil in China, Heyong Shen and Gao Lan had to surmount
one obstacle: the individual setting of psychotherapy. Neither Margaret
Lowenfeld nor Dora Kalff, nor Carl Gustav Jung himself, had advocated
group therapy, whereas the number of children (in kindergartens,
schools, and orphanages) with behavior disorders who could benefit
from sandplay was enormous. It was obvious that the small number
of qualified therapists was inadequate to achieve even the bare
minimum, and thus the idea of sandwork groups gained ground,
despite the initial skepticism of Western therapists. Although Gao
Lan felt the need to adjust the method to her cultural surroundings,
she had no intention of contravening the instructions of her Western
teachers. She found a solution typical of Chinese culture, which prefers
to avoid outright confrontation: she organized group sandwork sessions
with lay assistants (students) and called these "sandplay without
therapy."[2] In doing so, she resolved her personal quandary elegantly
by remaining faithful to Western methods and their conditions while
respecting her own traditional cultural background, in which the
individual is subordinate to the community.

The method enjoyed great success in kindergartens and
protectories. The problematic behavior of the children attending
sandplay groups changed within a few months, just as their
psychosomatic symptoms improved noticeably. The adults
accompanying these sessions were teachers, educators, and pedagogy
or psychology students who had undergone brief training. In the

following years, sandwork groups were introduced in other orphanages and kindergartens in southern China. But the real breakthrough occurred in 2008, in the wake of the devastating earthquake in the province of Sichuan. In the two years after the earthquake, approximately 1,500 children, supervised by adults, were afforded the opportunity to go deep into themselves to shape and thus change their pain and hopes. In 2010, when an earthquake shook Yushu (Tibet), Jungian colleagues were among the first to arrive on the scene: they set up tents equipped with miniature figures and sand trays.

Subsequently, the Jungian analysts involved in these events, in cooperation with colleagues from South Africa and Colombia, developed clearer guidelines for establishing the setting in which expressive sandwork could be conducted, and a short training program for facilitators, who were neither qualified psychotherapists nor psychologists but volunteers from a wide range of occupations, was defined. These developments brought both new advantages and new risks. The training program emphasized that facilitators should withhold any kind of comment and that they should neither describe nor interpret what the children created: empathetic supervision meant becoming involved only with all one's feelings and thoughts. In other words, such facilitation amounts to what Winnicott has described as holding. At the same time, it was clear that individuals lacking psychotherapeutic experience would encounter countertransference reactions. However, experience has shown time and again that the group as a whole spontaneously develops a holding function of its own accord, and that acting out is rare among facilitators; if it does occur, it is swiftly neutralized by the other participants and can be discussed and worked through in the team meetings.

THE PRACTICE OF EXPRESSIVE SANDWORK

In a sandwork group setting, twelve sand trays are set up either in a large room or outdoors so that they are within easy reach of a large or several small tables on which rest miniature toys. If no tables are available, the play materials can also be placed on the floor. It is important that the material be ordered by categories and remain neatly arranged, so that the children are not rummaging through containers. When the children enter the room for the first session, the adult facilitators will already be sitting near each of the sand trays. It is left to chance which child sits next to which adult, whether male or female, older or younger. This process happens very quickly and many children do not notice the adults at first but instead are fascinated by the play materials. After their initial astonishment, they are reminded that there is a sand tray for each of them, and they quite spontaneously sit down on the nearest free chair. Once established, this pairing of child and adult at a specific sand tray remains unchanged for the duration of the project, which lasts four to six months. For the most part, a deep relationship develops between the adult facilitator and the child, even if—or rather precisely because—little is said.

During the twelve to sixteen weekly or fortnightly sessions, the children, who may come from a very difficult situation, are given the opportunity to engage in an experience that activates their own resources. Sessions are aimed at helping the children emerge psychically stronger from the experience, so that they can better perceive the developmental possibilities and offerings available in their surroundings—no matter how many or how few there may be. Sandwork offers a child who typically shares a very confined space— physical and psychic—with many family members and neighbors several previously unknown assets. First of all, the child has his or her own clearly defined place (the sand tray), including enough play material so that they need not fear missing out or going short; second, the child has a clearly defined amount of time, which no one will shorten; and, last but not least, an adult fully devoted to observing and taking seriously the child's outer and inner impulses, feelings, and thoughts is always present. This adult neither wants anything from the child (in terms of performance, relationship, or any other kind of communication), nor does the adult give the child anything (material things, advice, or instructions). The adult is simply on hand, available to enter into a relationship with the child on the *specific* level required by the child, in a verbal or nonverbal fashion. Usually, the children's body language expresses how close or far away they wish the supervisory adult to be: communication involves gazing or the avoidance thereof, the joint experience of being in each other's presence without harboring specific expectations, and the willingness to be touched by the other's life—in whatever shape or form this may express itself.

Offering children this free and sheltered space almost instantly activates their hitherto latent psychic potential. Scenes related to traumatic memories are given shape, conflicts are staged, and usually *at the same time* a possibility for the future processing of such events is hinted at. From the first session, a symbolization proceess is initiated, one that continues to evolve independent of the facilitator's capacity for grasping events on a cognitive level. Trusting his or her own fantasies, hidden wishes, and intuitions, the child creates a new world, first in the sand tray and thereafter also beyond—to the extent permitted by their surroundings—by discovering and expressing gifts and talents previously unknown to the child. Irrespective of a child's age and pathology, sandwork promotes one constant factor: each child begins to construct with instinctual and unmistakable certainty precisely what he or she needs at that particular moment.

In the first sessions, what the children create is usually not particularly coherent. Often, they simply place objects haphazardly in the sand, and while these cars, houses, animals, and so forth are carefully chosen, they are mostly unrelated. One could imagine that for some children this random collection of miniatures represents their own coincidental coming into the world, an event lacking any conceivable history and goal. Then the children might look around for the adult, to assure themselves that someone is there who sees what they are doing and can bear witness to their own existence. We can compare this moment to the one when an infant opens its eyes and— in the best case—meets its mother's affectionate gaze. At its heart, sandwork is about making up for the emotional failures of parental figures in the first few months of a child's life: once this most profound level activates itself, the adult will feel a strong emotion and be touched to the core. This reaction is certainly related to the child discovering something vital within, which his or her environment has so far denied. An instinct (or an archetype) breaks through all resistance (fear, aggression, apathy), making us realize that not only is something essential happening but also that the lost thread of physical and psychic development can be picked up again at this point. Put differently, even more than awakening vivid, symbolic representation, sandwork aims to reestablish the primary relational function.

Needless to say, the degree of attachment exhibited by the child toward the facilitator is respected. If the child wishes to turn the sand tray away from the facilitator, that is just as acceptable as any other position during the process. For instance, some children choose to sit beside their facilitator to create something next to or perhaps even from the adult's perspective. Careful attention to the children's need for closeness or distance affords them both a sense of security and the freedom to engage in the creative process in the sand tray. Thus, unconscious images begin to arise and become visible in the image created in the sand, in the relationship, and in the child's gestures. Incomprehensible and confusing experiences are sketched and gradually enriched by being given a context. Narrative fragments emerge, and unrelated elements come into contact and acquire direction, even a goal. Instances of resonance occur time and again between child and facilitator, expressed in a rhythm of gazes that resembles what Daniel Stern has described for the first few weeks of an infant's life. In the facilitator's gaze, the child discovers a first affirmation, which is subsequently repeated many times and gradually becomes anchored in the psychophysical entity, whereby a stable emotional basis is formed. The child begins to exist autonomously and will be able to draw on this feeling even if his or her integrity is under threat. This experience forms the basis for self-confidence and joy.

SANDWORK IN COLOMBIA

In 2008, I launched a pilot project in Bogotá together with five Jungian psychotherapists from Colombia. Space for the project was made available by the Escuela de la Paz, which is run by the Catholic lay organization Comunitá di Sant'Egidio near the Simón Bolívar park. The children involved in the project came from Soacha, an impoverished working-class city on the southern periphery of Bogotá. Initially, it seemed absurd to us that children would have to travel two hours by car (transportation was organized by the Comunitá) from a kind of everyday inferno to see us—a group of well-fed, well-dressed, and well-educated professionals—who were waiting to offer them something that might prove beneficial to their lives. In retrospect what we had to offer turned out to be useful if for no other reason than that nothing else came to them from the outside, from strange grown-ups, and foreigners at that. What the children discovered in doing sandwork were their own psychic energies. In that connection, it is worth reiterating the fundamental aim of this therapy: to provide a sheltered, free space and the presence of an empathetic adult. These basic conditions made available by sandwork allow the self-regulation of the psyche to become active, a dynamic to which Jung drew attention.

In 2011, we launched a second project in Bogotá. Darío Echeverri, who was serving at the Voto Nacional church in the Los Mártires district, provided us with a large room.[3] The church lies adjacent to an extremely impoverished area, which the locals refer to as "the Bronx." It consists of a collection of makeshift accommodations stretching out along several southbound streets, where drugs, weapons, and prostitution are the order of the day. Most of the families living here are refugees from other regions of the country, mostly farmers caught in the crossfire between guerilla fighers and paramilitary units who have been forced to leave their villages; the paramilitary are responsible for blackmailing and punishing the local population with mass executions. The children in this situation, from previously healthy families, inevitably witness horrific acts of violence and are now caught up in a crime-ridden and severely impoverished environment. Their parents have suffered traumatic experiences; the men have not the slightest chance of finding work. The unavoidable consequences are loss of identity and dignity, with consequent depression and escape into drugs and alcohol. This in turn leads to child neglect, maltreatment, and sexual abuse. The women find work a bit more easily, for instance, as housekeepers or street vendors selling used items or foodstuffs. Most of the time children are on their own, the younger ones entrusted to the care of older siblings and exposed to the violent transgressions of neighbors.

I have repeatedly interviewed social workers in Colombia about the predicament of families forced to flee their villages due to armed conflict and now living on the edge of a metropolis amid destitution and crime. My questions particularly concern what distinguishes those families that had fallen into drug and alcohol abuse from those able to protect their children and establish a livelihood—albeit a highly precarious one. Families that manage to save themselves from utter hopelessness and delinquency typically have maintained contact with their home village, whether through relatives or mere neighbors. Apparently the ties, which often seem loose, perhaps consisting of no more than a few telephone calls a year since every form of contact could be politically dangerous, contribute to remembering one's identity and membership in a healthy social unit.

Initially, the welfare assistants who decided which children would take part in the project shook their heads when they were introduced to expressive sandwork and inspected the play materials. They pointed out that these children had experienced the most brutal violence or had grown up in the Bronx, which amounts to the same thing. They thought it was highly unlikely that the children would play with these things, and they predicted that the children would take what they could use as a weapon. They said we must remove the metal parts, the shells, and the sharp wooden objects. Experience proved, however, that it was never necessary to remove anything: scissors, screws, nails, and sharp wooden sticks remained part of the stock of play materials. The children were so immersed in creating their own worlds that no conflicts between them ensued.

However, conflicts became evident in the sandplay, and this was difficult for the facilitators to endure. While the volunteers from middle- or upper-class backgrounds had better psychological training, nothing had prepared them to face a reality that they knew about only in the abstract. In weekly sessions (on Sunday mornings) in which facilitators shared their doubts, fears, and successes with the other volunteers, some likened the experience of accompanying a child through the sandplay process to an initiation. Of the twelve persons involved in the first round of this project, nine were prepared to continue in a new cycle lasting five months. A volunteer from Bogotá put it this way:

> The sand tray (the small "psychosocial box," as Marthika, the welfare assistant, calls it) clearly has a good influence on the children; this is also confirmed by the parents and their teacher. Based thereupon, one can afford to share one's doubts, starting with the use of Jungian analysis, which forms the basis of sandwork, and those concerning any kind of intervention in the social environment, which couldn't be more remote and more alien to those intervening. One can do nothing but cast aside one's personal motives and experiences and try to measure up to the "other"and the "outside."And yet, which outside is closer to us and affects us more deeply than whatever

we may be thinking—closer than that challenge behind which appears what is literally at stake, namely, the face of a child? Thus, I can become involved and bit by bit allow all kinds of questions to arise, always aware that my involvement will achieve no more and no less than a grain of sand.

Often the supervisors compare the relationship with the child that develops from one session to the next to an adoption:

> When I realized that a child would be assigned to me, I remembered the arrival of our adopted nephew. Most probably, he had already been born, had a face, a smile, had certain unfilled needs, and perhaps he was laughing in response to a place that we couldn't even imagine—and we were meant for him. But unlike an adoption, I would be accompanying a child only for a very limited amount of time, no more than sixteen sessions, mostly without speaking, and afterward I was supposed to forget about it again; in other words, this was like having temporary custody. I would accompany the child with my presence for a certain time and then abandon it, so that it could continue on its path—hopefully fortified. Precisely, I was a kind of transparent midwife-boat, which was supposed to break the power of the waves without marring or darkening the child's ambience, by temporarily providing a kind of skin: I gave the child the opportunity to "be in the water" in a different way, so that it could learn to regulate the pressure itself and to make better use of the currents that would drive it in the right direction.

One important moment in the training is the meeting between the new volunteers and those who have been with the project previously. This occasion provides new volunteers, who are about to have their first session with the children, with the opportunity to discuss their questions and doubts with experienced facilitators who are already seasoned in this role, which requires patience and great emotional involvement. What should I do if the child doesn't start playing? someone asks. The reply came after a few minutes silence:

> Well, every situation is unique. Speaking from my own experience, all I can say is that once you are sitting next to "yours," you will know exactly what to do and what not to do, what to say and what not to say: you will quite simply know.

Another question raised was, What it will be like when we and the children part company after five months? Won't be it difficult not to have contact afterward? After all, I'll be wanting to know how things have gone for the child.

> These thoughts also crossed my mind in the course of the sessions. Then, after the last one, I experienced a feeling that I hadn't expected or even imagined. I felt that the encounter with the child had taken place. That we had understood each other and experienced each other's pain and joy. Images had come into existence and a story was "told." All this took place, we experienced all of it. I'm not under the impression now that we have separated and lost one another and that we need to see each other again: the child and I continue to exist in this world. Something has survived and cannot disappear.

I would like to offer two examples of what survives, in an attempt to describe what expressive sandwork means for the children.

A six-year-old child, whose family had suffered violence and displacement as internal refugees, had repeatedly depicted scenes in which the lives of young animals and human beings were under threat and were forced to flee. In each session, the child buried a baby Jesus figure deep in the sand, for this seemed to be the only way it could survive. In the eighth session, the child was able to formulate a wish for the first time. On this occasion, she also selected a baby Jesus, but— in contrast to the previous scenes—the figure was not buried. Quite on the contrary, this time the figure was placed on a kind of throne, surrounded by a circle of precious stones and guarded by several animals. Next to the enthroned baby Jesus she placed the figure of a child and said that this child was praying to the baby Jesus. What was it praying? "It is praying to Jesus that nothing bad will happen" (*"Está pidiendo a Jesus que no pase nada"*). This girl had never experienced the world as a safe place. And yet being able to formulate a wish of her own, indeed being at all capable of imagining for once that nothing bad would happen, constitutes the subtle trait that we call resilience.

In the case of a seven-year-old girl, sandwork not only helped the child come to terms with a great burden, but also had a positive effect on the families in the neighborhood, in that it helped them discover a new kind of solidarity. Already in the first session, the facilitator noticed that the child was under great psychological strain. She was piling up an enormous number of objects in her sand tray, especially kitchenware and food, mixed with insects, snakes, soldiers, and small children. She filled some of the pans with sand and pretended to cook. Suddenly, she flung everything down, rummaged angrily among the objects, threw everything around, and also destroyed some of the objects. At the end of the session, she insisted on covering everything with a piece of cloth. Amid this chaos, the facilitator was impressed especially by one scene in which a reptile with a gaping mouth approaches a baby lying in a pram. This and various other clues that emerged in subsequent sessions suggested sexual abuse. Since the facilitators were not qualified psychotherapists and, seen institutionally, were not authorized to point out such a possibility without filing a complaint to the police, the matter was deferred for the time being. The sandwork was to continue for a couple of months, and several discussions with the parents were envisaged within the project. As long as the child continued to come to sessions, it was decided that no further steps would be taken other than keeping one's eyes open during the parent-facilitator meetings to establish whether or not suspicions seemed to be justified. The child's depictions became less chaotic every time; it seemed especially important to the child to distinguish clearly between good and evil. After the tenth session, these areas were clearly defined; the girl erected a high barrier in the sand and moved across to the facilitator's side—where the good area was located—as if to share this with the supervising adult and to be as far separated from the evil area as possible. In this session, the facilitator sensed the child's strong sense of intimacy and search for trust.

On the day after this session, the child asked to speak to her teacher and told her that she had something important to say. The teacher agreed and the child gave an account of being sexually abused by one of the neighbors. The teacher immediately took the medical, psychological, and legal measures warranted in such cases. The school doctor, school psychologist, and police contacted the child's parents. The accused, the father of a fourteen-year-old girl also involved in the project, left the neighborhood within a few hours. The parents of the other children were alarmed but reacted without panicking and tried to talk to their daughters in the days following this development. Four of the other girls reported similar incidents involving the same man. A fear that had seized the children of an entire apartment block had now been banished.

Under less optimal conditions, when a joint enemy is identified in an environment riddled with poverty and crime, such a disclosure can easily spark a campaign of hatred and entail even worse violence. In this case, however, the sandwork project had fostered a sense of solidarity among the affected families, especially among the women, and kept them together. The problem could be entirely resolved by socially binding means available within the community. Since the children were protected, the mothers were able to face reality in a quiet and rational manner. This was expressed especially in the solidarity shown toward the offender's daughter and wife, who had been terrified of possible revenge. On the other hand, it was an unspoken law of the Bronx that men would not wait for police to track down an offender; one particularly well-respected man, an industrious worker and the father of one of the molested children, said that he would kill the offender.

For the girl whose sandplay therapy had initiated everything, what appears to have happened was that the sessions and her growing confidence in her facilitator had affirmed her self-confidence and gave her the strength and conviction that she would be heard. Notably, she had not turned to her sandplay facilitator, nor had she requested an intervention where it would not have been possible in any direct shape or form. She left the role of her sandplay facilitator intact, instead seeking help where the most adequate response could be found, namely, at her school, a social institution. She did so in an incredibly efficient manner, probably because a corresponding structure had begun to emerge within her. While teachers and the school had existed for her prior to her experience of sandwork, only that particular kind of work strengthened her inner life and self-esteem sufficiently for her to turn to outer resources that she already knew, to make adequate use of them.

FUTURE PERSPECTIVES

In the past few years, certain private and public institutions have taken an interest in expressive sandwork. In Colombia, cooperation has begun with an organization that is actually skeptical toward psychological interventions: the Batuta Foundation, which provides free music lessons to 40,000 children and youths across the country.[4] Batuta receives four-fifths of its funding from the state. It is dedicated to supporting youths who have left armed paramilitary units and, with the help of music, assisting them in finding alternatives to crime and drug trafficking. Expressive sandwork unites two aspects that cultural or relief organizations often fail to provide jointly: the promotion of creativity and expert guidance for working through traumatic experiences.

Further cooperation has been initiated with the International Organization for Migration (IOM), which also works with the manifold consequences of conflict zones in Colombia. In psychological and sociological terms, the country faces a difficult task. Today the survivors of the massacres committed in recent decades, with entire regions having been razed to the ground, amount to millions of internal refugees, mostly farmers who have lost their livelihood. Now that some of these areas have been regained by the state, the displaced would—at least on paper—have the opportunity to return to their native villages. Reality, however, is different. For various sociological, political, economic, and psychological reasons, many do not want to return. Among other reasons, there is the insurmountability of traumatic events: "This is no longer the same soil," the survivors of massacres say, "this is a graveyard."

An intervention must, if at all possible, bring together deep psychological and cultural aspects. Certain rituals are needed, but every anthropologist knows that these cannot simply be invented; they can only gradually evolve in each culture. In this connection, expressive sandwork—which offers children the opportunity to establish for themselves a neutral ground on which they can create a world of their own using miniature figures—could prove to be an auxiliary tool capable of setting in motion a broader healing process. A group of Jungian analysts is currently discussing whether and how a return of displaced populations to their native territories could be fostered. Working with dreams and other expressions of the unconscious could be helpful in this respect.

In 2012 expressive sandwork was introduced in the Macrina child care center and in a elementary school in Bucharest. Teachers, school counselors, and psychologists have been trained as facilitators.

In March 2013, the first expressive sandwork project will be organized in Buenos Aires in conjunction with the Vocación Humana Foundation (http://www.vocacionhumana.org/_31/), a cultural organization with a Jungian orientation, which has been working together with the Eranos Foundation in Ascona since 2011.

NOTES

1. Bringing psychoanalysis to places where it is needed most and offering it free of charge is by no means a new idea. Rather, this has been one of its aims, ever since its Freudian beginnings. The free clinics opened in Vienna and Berlin from 1920 to 1933—where patients who could not afford analytic treatment were treated by a team of psychotherapists, who are today considered the pioneers of psychoanalysis—by now have faded almost entirely from memory. But at the time, the psychoanalysts offering such treatment dedicated one fifth of either their time or their income to the clinic. See E. A. Danto, *Freud's Free Clinics: Psychoanalysis and Social Justice, 1918–1938* (New York: Columbia University Press, 2005).

2. Gao Lan, "Supervision of Sandplay Therapy in Preschool Education in China," in *Supervision of Sandplay Therapy*, edited by H. S. Friedman and R. R. Mitchell (London: Routledge, 2007).

3. Father Darío Echeverri is secretary of the National Commission of Reconciliation. He is recognized by the Colombian government, by FARC (Forze Armate Rivoluzionarie di Colombia), and by ENL (Esercito Nazionale di Liberazione) as a mediator in the process of reaching a humanitarian agreement.

4. The Batuta Foundation is inspired by Antonio Abreu's Venezuelan El Sistema, which is now called Fundación Musical Simón Bolívar: http://www.fundacionbatuta.org.

HEARING THE BUGLE'S CALL
HURRICANE KATRINA, THE BP OIL SPILL,
AND THE EFFECTS OF TRAUMA

RANDY FERTEL

From Chicago to New Orleans
From the muscle to the bone
From the shotgun shack to the Superdome
We yelled "help" but the cavalry stayed home
There ain't no-one hearing the bugle blown
We take care of our own
We take care of our own
Wherever this flag's flown
We take care of our own
          —Bruce Springsteen, "We Take Care of Our Own"

A native of New Orleans, Randy Fertel, Ph.D., has taught the literature of war at Harvard, Tulane, the University of New Orleans, and the New School for Social Research. He heads the Ruth U. Fertel Foundation, which is devoted to Louisiana education and (which) brought Alice Waters's Edible Schoolyard project to post-Katrina New Orleans. He also heads the Fertel Foundation, which sponsors the Ron Ridenhour Prizes for Courageous Truth Telling. A contributor to NPR, *Huffington Post,* the *Smithsonian,* the *Kenyon Review,* and *Creative Nonfiction,* he wrote *The Gorilla Man and the Empress of Steak: A New Orleans Family Memoir* (University Press of Mississippi) and *A Taste for Chaos: The Hidden Order in the Art of Improvisation* (forthcoming from Spring Journal Books).

The experiences of Hurricane Katrina and the BP oil spill both invite the questions that Bruce Springsteen poses on his album *Wrecking Ball*: Do we in America take care of our own? What does it mean for a society when the bugle is blown but not heard, when the cavalry stays home? What are the effects on citizens and on civic society?

Wrecking ball indeed.

I have taught the literature of the war for many decades, and I view trauma through that lens. For Harvard trauma psychiatrist Judith Herman the effects of trauma are fundamental: "Traumatic events call into question basic human relationships. They breach the attachments of family, friendship, love, and community."[1]

While we associate these effects with extreme violence, natural or human, some trauma is the result of subtler forms of abuse by figures of authority that disturb the tacit social contract between leaders and those they lead. In fact, when the abuse of power accompanies violent trauma, it increases the likelihood of post-traumatic stress disorder (PTSD). As Veterans Administration psychiatrist Jonathan Shay writes, in his superb *Achilles in Vietnam: Combat Trauma and the Undoing of Character,* "moral injury is an essential part of any combat trauma that leads to lifelong psychological injury. Veterans can usually recover from horror, fear, and grief once they return to civilian life, so long as 'what's right' has not also been violated."[2] Again Herman: "Every instance of severe traumatic psychological injury is a standing challenge to the rightness of the social order."[3]

Trauma is always an experience of powerlessness. Facing a traumatic situation, a person can sometimes minimize long-term effects by taking action. In the 1976 Chowchilla school bus kidnapping in California, twenty-six children were buried alive in a moving van; one child took the lead in digging them out. "[A]cknowledged by all the other children to be the 'hero' of Chowchilla," writes psychiatrist Lenore Terr, who examined the survivors some months after the abduction and longitudinally for years thereafter, this "hero" child "showed no personality problems after the kidnapping."[4]

Empowerment can prevent or minimize trauma; so too, recovery from trauma depends first upon the survivor's re-empowerment. Herman writes: "The core experiences of psychological trauma are disempowerment and disconnection from others. Recovery, therefore, is based upon the empowerment of the survivor and the creation of new connections."[5] Thus, suffering the violence of a natural disaster, survivors' trauma can also be minimized by the proper deployment of societal care, which minimizes disconnection and helps to re-empower. The natural world may be out of joint but fulfilling the social contract ensures that the survivors' experience of powerlessness does not spin completely out of control with lifelong effects.

If re-empowerment is the first step toward recovery, next comes the effort to reconstruct the trauma narrative in order fully to understand the trauma experience, what happened, and what it means. In the aftermath of Katrina, in almost every social encounter, survivors manifested a compulsion to tell their Katrina story. But such compulsive storytelling is not always the path to recovery. As one sees in war narratives, there are "stuck" trauma narratives and there are "recovered" trauma narratives. Trauma psychologists offer a mnemonic for a more rigorous and effective process. BASK stands for behavior (what happened), affect (what it felt like to experience it), senses (what happened in all its sensuous aspects), and knowledge (understanding what it means that this could have happened).[6] Trauma, always an intrusion of the unexpected, has the effect of breaking the life story we each and all deploy to make sense of our lives: pulling the rug out from under us, trauma makes nonsense of that sense that served us until then. Recovery can be understood as knitting the lifeline or life narrative back together, telling our story in such a way that the trauma experience is now explained as part of the life narrative. To a rape victim, it makes no sense that a near relative could do her such harm; and yet it *was* always possible. A recovery narrative not only recounts what happened but the human truths behind what happened, for example, that those who love us, or should love us, sometimes do us grave harm.

Although it disrupts the mnemonic, the last rubric should not be knowledge but rather wisdom: truly understanding how, for example, a nation that believes itself morally exceptional could wage immoral wars for cynical reasons, how such a nation could allow one of its finest cities to drown, how that nation could put an entire ecology and way of life in jeopardy for the sake of corporate greed. How, in short, the cavalry could stay home.

ഌ   ൪

One sure way to provoke a fistfight in New Orleans these days is to speak of Hurricane Katrina as "a natural disaster." On the Mississippi coast, in Biloxi, Gulfport, and Pass Christian, where the full brunt of a Category 5 storm was felt—*that* was a natural disaster, with peak winds above 170 mph and a storm surge of about 30 feet. What we suffered in New Orleans was a Category 2 storm and "the failure of the federal levees"—a locution that will help you avoid that fistfight. New Orleans suffered the result of years of neglect from the powers that be and a government that, at every level—local, state, federal—did not show up. President Bush *literally* stayed home for days—his vacation home in Crawford, Texas. President Johnson, by contrast, after his visit to the city immediately following Category 2 Hurricane Betsy in 1965, instructed the Army Corps of Engineers to construct levees that would protect New Orleans. Yet, years of sub-code work and indifference ensured that the federal levees would fail—in more than fifty locations. Call the experience of Hurricane Katrina an example of trauma by neglect, before and after. Neglect trauma renders the survivor hopeless (*the cavalry will never come*) and instills a double bind: *Is the cavalry at fault or am I?* Katrina and its aftermath were, as Jed Horne puts it in one of the best books about the storm, a breach of faith.[7]

The blowout of the British Petroleum Macondo well fifty miles off the coast of Louisiana was of course and without question an entirely man-made disaster, a tissue of corporate and governmental fecklessness, dishonesty, and greed. The only thing natural about the event was the petroleum crude and natural gas that gushed unabated for three months. Not nature's hand but man's alone can be seen in the factors— deregulation; a federal regulatory body, Marine Management Service, that was wildly understaffed and whose personnel had recently been caught doing drugs with and accepting sexual favors and gifts from the oil companies they regulated; and above all the corporate imperative to maximize profits at all costs—that led to eleven deaths and perhaps ultimately to the end of a way of life in Plaquemines and much of the Gulf Coast.

℀   ℁

I grew up fishing in the Mississippi River delta below New Orleans in Plaquemines Parish. The delta is a thing of great if subtle beauty. The expanse of marsh with its slow-moving bayous—distributaries from the Mississippi River—extends as far as the eye can see. The only visual relief came from fishing camps on stilts along the bayous' banks. If we returned at night from our camp at the mouth of Grand Bayou, New Orleans, eighty or ninety miles to the north, was at most a faint glow. I never saw a creamier Milky Way. As the outboard motor roared in your ears, you'd look down at the boat's wake unfurling behind and see just as many stars in the water: plankton and other sea life lit up by the agitation of your passing. You could reach out and let stars rush through your outstretched fingers. You'd feel both how vast was the universe and how close the vastness.

A tomboy, Mom had grown up in Happy Jack, Louisiana, hard by the levee and twenty miles from Venice where Highway 23 turns liquid at Head of Passes—nothing but water beyond. More than once on these excursions, it was just Mom at the tiller, taking us out beyond the relative safety of the more sheltered bayous and bays. We knew we were safe in her hands.

We fished on a fourteen-and-a-half-foot lap-sided speedboat with a single 35 hp Evinrude. We would wake before dawn and trailer it across the Mississippi River on the ferry—this is before the bridge was built—then through the Belle Chasse ("good hunting") tunnel under the Intracoastal Waterway, which sweated and leaked so much that we held our breath till we saw daylight coming at the other end, then past the Gulf chemical refinery, where we closed the windows and again held our breath, this time against the acrid chemical stench. After Belle Chasse, there were few landmarks to keep our young eyes occupied during the long drive down to the river's mouth. We'd pass the huge house of Judge Leander Perez back off the highway with its incongruous moose head hung on the porch. President of the parish for decades and an infamous racist, Perez had stolen a princedom's wealth in mineral rights from the citizens of Plaquemines. Then Myrtle Grove and West Pointe à la Hache, where pirate Jean Lafitte used to supply slaves for Magnolia plantation, where Mark Twain once stayed. By now we were fully awake because Happy Jack was just a few miles on. Ten miles beyond the home of Mom's brother, Uncle Sig, we would launch in Empire at Battistella's Marina. Out Grand Bayou, the few remaining scraggly cypress trees, vestiges of once grand freshwater cypress swamps, soon gave way to expanses of marsh with nothing more substantial than low wax myrtle bushes. We'd cross Bay Adams, then Bastian Bay, where you'd smell the menhaden or pogy boats, whose purse seine nets hauled in that stinky fish by the millions. Beyond the bays, the rest was marsh grass. Orange-toothed nutrias and masked raccoons fed along the muddy bank, the only break from the monotony, while Mom expertly monitored the impossibly subtle landmarks (watermarks rather) that were her guides. *Turn right at the second cane pole marking the Christovich oyster bed. Bear left at the second sign for underwater pipelines—"Do Not Drag Anchor."* We'd fish the lower reaches of Grand Bayou where Mom once caught a thirty-six-inch bull redfish, fighting it on her light tackle for forty-five minutes, or the Rocks, an outlet to the Gulf that had been reinforced with granite boulders that, like Judge Perez's moose, came from somewhere far, far away—nothing here but alluvial muck. If you stopped to cast from the bank rather than the boat, and if you ventured at all back into the marsh, you could find your foot suddenly deep in the smelly muck of the *flottant* or *pré tremblante*—"trembling prairie" that floated with the tides, unattached to the bottom. Bedrock lay two hundred feet below the muck. Despite the boat's diminutive size and no backup power, on calmer days we'd venture miles into the Gulf of Mexico to fish near the oil rigs where red snapper and other reef fish congregated.

ᛞ   ᚳ

Mom's independence and self-sufficiency seemed an outgrowth of the landscape. A creolized corruption of the Native American *piakimin,* Plaquemines was named for the persimmons that once grew wild on the river's banks. In 1727, less than a decade after New Orleans was settled, Sister Marie Madeleine Hachard, an Ursuline nun traveling to the Crescent City to found the oldest all-girls school in America, described these and other fruits of this cornucopian land:

> Wild ducks are very cheap. Teal, water-hen, geese and other fowl and game are also very common but we do not buy it as we do not wish to indulge in delicacies. Really, it is a charming country

> all winter and in summer the fish are plentiful and good. There
> are oysters and carps of prodigious size and delicious flavor . . . It
> is full of orange trees . . . [Reverend Father de Beaubois] gave us
> about three hundred sour ones which we preserved.[8]

My maternal ancestors arrived in the New World at about the same
time as Sister Marie. Carpenter Simon Hingle (sometimes Engel or
Yngle in the genealogical record), probably settled first in Mobile, then
traveled to La Côte des Allemands, on the river a dozen miles below
Baton Rouge. The name means German bank (literally "coast") of the
Mississippi. John Law brought Alsatian immigrants from the
Rhineland-Palatinate in 1721 to settle there as part of the Mississippi
Company monopoly he was granted by the French government. Law
promised a mountain of gold and paradise and delivered a
hardscrabble existence to the hundreds of Alsatians who fell for the
lure. Law's Mississippi bubble soon burst. Some of his Alsatians or
their descendants migrated one hundred miles south, where the
land with its surrounding waters, in terms of fecundity, wasn't so
far from *le paradis* Law promised. By 1789 Jacques-Santiago Hingle
was established in Plaquemines.[9] The rich environment that Sister
Marie described called him and his descendants to farm rice, indigo,
and oranges. But in their hearts, they were all hunters and fishermen.
In their parish they enjoyed the fruits of 15 percent of the wetlands
in America in an area that would one day provide 20 percent of the
nation's seafood. (Southern Louisiana has 40 percent of America's
wetlands.) Their land was the culmination of a million-square-mile
funnel and a layover on the great Central Flyway for the annual
migration of songbirds and waterfowl (altogether 353 species). From
Canada's boreal forest and parklands across the Great Plains down to
the Gulf Coast, this route is home to a large percentage of North
America's ducks and geese. According to Rowan Jacobsen, "one fifth of
all the ducks in America overwinter in the Louisiana wetlands."[10]

If the land was paradisal, the weather . . . well, as their laconic
descendants might today say, *not so much*. The heat and moisture
brought vector-borne diseases—malaria, yellow fever—that were
unrelenting before efforts to control mosquitoes came in the mid-
twentieth century. My great-great-grandfather Jules Hingle died of
lockjaw, his daughter Angeline, my great-grandmother, of anthrax. Life

was hard in the delta. But it *was* the land of plenty. In the Depression, according to my mother, "we never knew we were poor. There was always plenty of food for the taking."

The weather was extraordinary and not just for the verdant winters. The hurricane of 1856 washed away Isle Dernière, a barrier island and rich man's retreat in the Gulf of Mexico thirty miles due west from Happy Jack. It took 320 men, women, and children with it. The hurricane of 1893 killed 2,500 in Louisiana, 300 in Plaquemines alone. My great-uncle Nick Jacomine recalled the hurricane of September 1915 in his shakily handwritten memoir, "The Story of My Life: Things I Can Remember":

> The Mississippi River ran over its bank and drowned all our cattle which we had driven on the levee for protection. The water was so rough that the cattle were swept so far that some of them were never found. Up to five feet of water . . . every thing was destroyed, rice ready to be threshed and all foods and small animals. The government sent a relief boat with food and all twice a week and that's what kept us going till the water receded.

The cavalry had shown up.

A few hours after the Jacomines took to the levee, high winds tore New Orleans apart. Uptown in Audubon Park winds flattened Horticultural Hall, built for the 1884 Cotton Exposition. Streetcars in New Orleans stopped operating. Downtown, Jackson Square was in shambles. The clock on the St. Louis Cathedral stopped at 5:50 p.m. Nearby, on the Pontalba Buildings, ironwork and chimneys were ripped away. Next to the cathedral, the Presbytere's cupola was demolished and the Cabildo, its sister building where the French transferred ownership of Louisiana to the Americans in 1803, lost most of its roof slates. The dome and the upper floors of the vacant St. Louis Hotel—once a thriving slave market—received heavy damage. The steeple of the First Presbyterian Church on Lafayette Square across Canal in the American Sector was hurled through the church roof and two adjoining rooming houses. Just blocks away on South Rampart Street, my paternal grandparents, the Fertels, born in Krakow, huddled in their pawnshop unscathed, little knowing this climatic event linked them by a future grandson's marriage to some Alsatian farmers who huddled on the levee downriver.

More than eight inches of rain were recorded in the next twenty-one hours. (Katrina would drop eight to ten inches.) But the levees held and the twelve-foot screw pumps, invented by New Orleans engineer Albert Baldwin Wood and installed just that year, delivered as promised, removing more than nine billion gallons of water from the city streets. The city was saved. The cavalry heard the bugle call—in advance—and did not stay home.

Ninety years later, those same pumps worked during the rains of Hurricane Katrina until the levees were breached, until the city power cut off and the pumps' dedicated generators flooded. That breach catastrophically affected tens of thousands who were left stranded or died in their homes, in the Superdome, and in the convention center and, it is no exaggeration to say, hundreds of thousands who faced exile and the task of rebuilding, problems that continue even seven years later. After Hurricane Betsy in 1965, not only did President Johnson make a commitment to better levees but he also mobilized the federal bureaucracy to provide relief. Forty years later, under Mayor Ray Nagin, Governor Kathleen Blanco, Brownie's FEMA, and the Bush administration, the cavalry stayed home. There is no need here to rehearse their oft-told bungles and failures.

Since the time of Lyndon B. Johnson's Great Society, and in large part because of its many bureaucratic failures in other areas, the social contract in America has changed.[11] There is less belief in the social safety net and far more in privatization of government functions. Not only did the cavalry not show up, they've been disbanded.[12] FEMA director Michael "You're doing a great job" Brown was slow to respond because he was incompetent and unprofessional, but also because he, like his boss, wanted to mobilize not the bureaucracy but the disaster-industrial complex: Halliburton, Bechtel, Blackwater, and the like.[13] Sad to say, he *was* doing a great job at the task he was at least implicitly given. When the cavalry finally did show—the Army and the National Guard—they carried assault rifles and rode Humvees and helicopters, and rather than providing water, food, and shelter, they treated Katrina survivors as if they were criminals or the enemy. The social fabric was rent along with the social safety net.

⁞    

Despite all these breakdowns in the social contract, New Orleans has experienced an extraordinary rebirth since Katrina largely because of grassroots efforts. As *Nation* urban reporter Roberta Gratz points out, "the barn-raising instinct in America is alive and well. Though Michael Brown turned away offers of private and international support in order to make sure private contractors got the jobs, thousands of individuals, local and national, came to the rescue" (personal interview, July 23, 2012). Faith-based and other charitable and educational organizations from across America descended upon New Orleans in the immediate aftermath to help in the rescue and for years afterward, and to this day, to help gut and rebuild homes. Twenty- and thirtysomethings, sensing an opportunity both to do well and to do good, flocked to the city, making it the top entrepreneurial city in America according to *Forbes*. Actor Brad Pitt and his Make It Right Foundation built more than seventy homes in the Lower Ninth Ward. In Gentilly (where I was raised), Leonard Riggio of Barnes & Noble and his Project Home Again built the one hundred homes he promised and one for *lagniappe,* our local word for something extra, the thirteenth donut in a baker's dozen, which suggests how thoroughly he embraced the local culture. The cavalry came; they just didn't wear uniforms.

Even more important psychologically were local efforts. "The network that helped New Orleanians return and rebuild was only available at the grassroots level," reports Gratz, whose book on the city's rebirth is forthcoming. "There was no ombudsman except grassroots organizations." Start-up neighborhood associations throughout the city fought the "green dot plan" that, coming from the powers that be and driven by developers, would have sacrificed neighborhoods deemed too far below sea level to be rebuilt. Slogging through a recovery bureaucracy, whose rules were plagued by a "fog-of-war" vagueness and catch-22s, was almost impossible without the help of neighborhood organizations that counseled how to wrestle with the incompetent, many-layered bureaucracy. One must not forget the many New Orleanians who continue in exile because of poverty and inadequate government programs to ensure their return; but, nonetheless, in the estimation of many, New Orleans has been reborn, smaller perhaps but perhaps better, and while much is left to be rebuilt, ahead of expectation.[14]

That New Orleans's rebirth was all bottom-up contributed to the self-re-empowerment of the citizenry and helped many work through their trauma.[15] Working together, community action groups re-created, as Judith Herman describes, "the psychological faculties that were damaged or deformed by the traumatic experience," faculties including "the basic capacities for trust, autonomy, initiative, competence, identity, and intimacy."[16]

Which is about when the Macondo well blew and oil and gas began to gush. Many experienced the catastrophe as a repetition of that powerlessness felt after Katrina. This first and quite profound effect on the city's populace—the return to helplessness—has been hard to shake. New Orleans had just elected Mitch Landrieu with some 67 percent of the vote and wide support across racial and demographic lines. Landrieu had been beaten in 2006 by the incumbent's racially divisive campaign, "Our Mayor," by which Nagin meant the mayor of the black majority. In 2010 Landrieu's theme was "one voice, one fight, one city." But in his inaugural address on May 3, only two weeks after the Macondo disaster, and though a superb public speaker, Landrieu's theme—"Today is a new day; today is a new time"—fell upon wishful but unbelieving ears. At the moment of the cavalry's arrival, a *diabolus ex machina* had stolen Mayor Landrieu's thunder. As the oil gushed and came ashore, as toxic dispersants were deployed not to cure the harm done but to hide it from view and thus causing more harm, as corporations and government agencies and leaders covered their asses, the question in many New Orleanians' lowered eyes seemed to be, "What's the point?"

Repetition compulsion, the psychological phenomenon in which a person repeats a traumatic event or its circumstances over and over again, is a common effect of PTSD. For Freud such behavior contradicted the pleasure principle; he explained it by means of his death drive theory, often referred to as *thanatos*. Later trauma psychologists explain it rather as an effort to achieve a belated mastery. Surprised the first time by the extraordinary traumatic event, the trauma survivor unconsciously creates echoic situations where she or he can achieve a better outcome. Seeming to have succeeded, suddenly New Orleans found itself back in the same soup, a repetition not of its own making and certainly offering little prospect of mastery. And so, once again, New Orleans was faced with government and corporate fecklessness and incompetence and a recovery bureaucracy seemingly determined to prevent recovery. A deflated and passive mood settled over New Orleans.

But there were important differences between the two events. The BP oil spill repeated the experience of government and corporate fecklessness, incompetence, and greed in overwhelming amplitude. But where after Katrina, one's personal and the city's future was uncertain, at least the problems were concrete and obvious: eighty percent of the city had been destroyed along with much of its infrastructure, levee system, and government. How fully to rebuild was unclear, but at least the task was clear: to rebuild. With the BP oil spill the ambiguities were compounded. Who knew what the effects of the oil and the Corexit, criminally used to disperse it, would be and for how long?[17] Who knew what the effect on the fisheries, at the height of their spawning season when the well blew, would be?[18] Who knew if there was any future livelihood to be made in waters that had nurtured families, including my own, for almost three hundred years? With Katrina, rebuilding began perhaps with picking up a hammer. After the BP oil spill, how does an individual have any impact on 206 million barrels of oil and 1.8 million gallons of toxic dispersant? Oystermen, who lost one spawning season, put out tons of cultch—the limestone or oyster shells used to create habitat for the oyster spat or embryos; but in the years that followed they had no say over whether the oysters that had not been killed would spawn or if their spat would set. Few did. And if the fish came back, would they be contaminated? If so, was there a remedy? The state bird, the brown pelican, covered in oil became the media darling and icon. But what of the millions of migratory birds that would be diving into fouled waters for food or, for the first time in history, let alone during their lifetime, would not find the food they need to get them through the winter or on their way across six hundred miles of the Gulf?

§ ☙ ❧

Another similarity between the two events is difficult to draw a bead on and a challenge to talk about. Blaming the victim is commonplace in trauma experience and one does not wish to fall into it. Survivors commonly blame themselves: "I shouldn't have been caught out." This is cause for sympathy and therapeutic treatment. More reprehensible is the phenomenon wherein witnesses after the fact blame the survivor: "They asked for it."[19] After Katrina, New Orleans was blamed for a multitude of sins, from living "below sea level" to the racism that put poor blacks at risk. Both claims are far from the whole truth. New Orleans was settled on high ground and pushed into the newly drained low ground of the back swamp as it grew into a port serving the nation; and the low ground sank further because of subsidence, an effect of the levees' preventing annual inundation. Like much of America, New Orleans is guilty of racism, but the breaches in the federal levees also flooded largely white middle-class Lakeview and upper-crust Old Metairie.

I do not want to participate in such hatefulness, but if as James Hillman writes, "fear, like love, can become a call into consciousness," then we must answer the call that the fears of Katrina and the BP oil spill have generated.[20] My point is this: it is a hard truth, but though the failure of the levees lies mainly at the feet of the Army Corps of Engineers and the federal executive and legislative branches that underfunded the levee program for decades, it is also true that, as Harley Winer, a retired Army Corps engineer, told me, "it was not an engineering failure but a political failure—the system was not designed; it was negotiated." No apologist for the Corps, Winer reports that many of the levees failed because local governments—levee boards, police juries, etc.—often had their own agendas in negotiating levee planning. Lots of decisions—where the levees were placed; rights of way; the quality of the borrow (clay) used to build them (often determined by whose land was chosen to take it from, at great profit to the chosen)—were based on immediate self-interest, not long-range community safety. Winer exaggerates: the Army Corps of Engineers pulled the trigger with shoddy engineering and workmanship. But, famous for our corruption, we in southern Louisiana helped load the gun. The degrees of culpability are incomparable; nonetheless we need to own our small share.

A similar point can be made with regard to the BP oil spill. Just as Louisiana senator Mary Landrieu was quick to object to Obama's moratorium on drilling in the Gulf, southern Louisiana from the very beginning made a bargain with the oil industry: jobs in exchange for license to decimate the environment.[21] Of the eleven men who died, five were from Louisiana, the rest from Texas and Mississippi—so all were from the Gulf Coast. Oilmen and fishermen, often from the same family, live and work side by side. Though we know for a certainty now that up to 50 percent of the wetlands' erosion is due to oil industry canals, "there was a time in Louisiana, not very long ago," writes Tulane environmental law professor Oliver Houck, "when the U.S. Fish and Wildlife service was contending that oil and gas canals benefited the environment," and, he notes, "at least part of this support came from Louisiana fish and wildlife agencies, for whom more canals meant more boating access."[22] Rowan Jacobsen explains further, "The four-thousand-plus rigs in the Gulf . . . are the world's largest artificial reef system" and, because they attract fish, a favorite destination for game fishermen.[23] All of which is to say that environmentalists are the exception rather than the rule in the Louisiana wetlands.

The BP oil spill compounded our self-victimization. Our discomfort with the diabolical bargain is reflected in the language used to describe, often self-describe, those who, now unable to fish, got rich hiring themselves and their boats out in the cleanup: *spillionaires*. This is not to point a finger, to blame the victim, but to call attention to the unease, the disjunction and cognitive dissonance, felt by those who know that they had a role in their victimization, "victim-perpetrators" as some recovering Vietnam veterans called themselves.[24] All the human truths that led to the trauma must form part of a healing trauma narrative. The larger fault lies beyond us; but we own a small piece of the catastrophe that befell us. That is a part of our story.

ຽ   ໕

Trauma breaks a survivor's life narrative, "undermin[ing]," Judith Herman tells us, "the belief systems that give meaning to human experience."[25] But both Katrina and the BP oil spill broke something much larger. Katrina disrupted our sense that the American infrastructure was secure, that there was a basic safety net in place, that our leaders and the nation itself cared about us. Bad enough. Far worse, Katrina gave us a glimpse of a break in the way Nature has performed since the dawn of history: caused by industrialization and fossil fuel consumption, climate change is certain to bring ever more violent climatic events—storms, tsunamis, changes at the poles, the rising of the oceans—and with them the specter that we may be unable to adapt.

Because it was about fossil fuels and the desperation that led to ultra-deep drilling, the BP oil spill partook of those themes and reinforced them: the spill gave us a glimpse of an uncertain future with less oil, and more storms and water. But the spill had a mindboggling aspect: the disaster was so catastrophic that it gave us a glimpse of the end of an ecology, the Gulf's and even perhaps the ecology of the world's oceans. To put his or her life narrative back together the trauma survivor must, through BASK, make sense of the past leading up to and causing the trauma. Knitting your life together you may see the world differently, but the world has not fundamentally changed: the potential for the trauma had been hidden from your view but was always there. In this instance, *the world has changed.* How can you put together a life narrative if the trauma doesn't just mark a radical break in *your* time line, but in Time itself?[26] As Sonya Robinson, a friend from Mobile whose family has lived on the Gulf Coast for eight generations, told me, "We are used to the rhythm of destruction and repair, but now this . . ."

The narrator of Jesmyn Ward's *Salvage the Bones*, Esch, whose name perhaps in part looks toward "eschatology," the end of times, sums up her experience of Katrina on the Mississippi Gulf Coast, "suddenly there is a great split between now and then, and I wonder where the world where that happened has gone, because we are not in it."[27] In *Tar Ball Chronicles*, David Gessner argues: "We are witnessing no less than a radical cutting off from our past. An eradication of a way of life that has worked pretty well for human beings for a millennium or two. Right before our eyes the line is being cut."[28] And not just for the fisherman, shrimpers, and oystermen of Plaquemines Parish, for, as Gessner adds,

> Maybe at this moment in time we all belong to Plaquemines Parish. I can't help but feel that this at least edges close to the truth. That is, I can't help but feel that while most of us may not have any official allegiance to Plaquemines, we are all still a part of this fucked-up place in this fucked-up time.
>
> What I am seeing down here is the future. For most of us it may still just be something you glimpse on TV, but this is where we are all heading. Here you can witness the sacrificing of our places, our homes, in a desperate attempt to gulp up what is left. . . .

And here you can feel all that like no place else. This is where it is
happening, where you can experience the shuddering of the death
pangs. Welcome to the future. While the rest of the country may
not know it yet, down here they're already living inside of it.[29]

∾ ∿

Trauma survivors' vision of life and of the world are often darkened
to the point of despair that Gessner articulates. But the experience of
trauma often galvanizes trauma survivors to make what repairs can be
made in the torn fabric. Doing so heals. Another link between Katrina
and the BP oil spill is that while the immediate repairs differed—better
levees versus better oversight of drilling—for most, the long-range repair
was the same: to save and rebuild the wetlands. In both cases—Katrina
and BP—the people of southern Louisiana have felt victimized by the
loss of the wetlands at the hands of both the Army Corps of Engineers
and the petroleum industry. Paradoxically the levees built since 1927
to improve navigation on the Mississippi have made life possible in
Plaquemines Parish but also ensured that the wetlands surrounding
us would eventually melt away into the Gulf. Without the annual fresh
water inundation and the silt it left behind, the land was subjected to
erosion, allowing the salt-water intrusion that killed off plant life and
caused more erosion. The marshlands were further jeopardized by more
than ten thousand miles of canals dug by sulfur, natural gas, and oil
production companies seeking more direct routes to their working fields
and to pump out the mineral wealth. By bringing tidal and wave action
deep into the wetlands, these canals led to more erosion, more than a
third of the loss the wetlands have suffered.[30]

The future of the fisheries hinges on the wetlands, which as
Christopher Hallowell points out, "serves as breeding ground, nursery,
food source, and buffer."[31] "Buffer" refers to the truth that the longevity
of New Orleans also hinges on the wetlands' restoration. Every two
and a half miles of wetlands the storm surge must travel, according to
some scientists, reduces it by a foot.[32]

Victimized but not necessarily playing the victim. Not only is New
Orleans the key river port servicing the entire Mississippi River
drainage, but the wetlands themselves are of great value even without
the minerals beneath their muck. Drawing on *Gaining Ground*, an
analysis by the nonprofit Earth Economics, Rowan Jacobsen argues

that the wetlands are "worth up to twelve thousand dollars per acre in annual benefits. The entire delta provides twelve billion to forty-seven billion dollars in annual benefits, depending on how you value certain services . . . Over a century, that makes the delta worth more than a trillion dollars . . . This trillion dollar asset will be lost if we continue to practice business as usual."[33]

ꟸ ꟸ

At Studio in the Woods, an artist colony south of New Orleans and just north of Plaquemines Parish, Joe and Lucianne Carmichael were faced with the question of what to do about the devastation Katrina had wreaked upon the bottomland hardwood forest that made their artist retreat so unique and special. Situated in organic peat soils created by eons of the Mississippi's annual inundation, much of its canopy of oak, elm, hickory, maple, hackberry, cypress, and sweet gum had been ripped down by Katrina's winds. David Baker, their environmental curator, a research botanist from Tulane University, told them, much to their surprise, *to do nothing*, that the destruction of the canopy was part of the life cycle of bottomland hardwood forests in a hurricane zone; allowing sunlight to filter onto the forest floor would allow new growth. At a presentation on the natural reforestation program, Baker recounted that the first saplings that popped up were persimmons, the namesake of Plaquemines Parish.

I have seen no such signs of rebirth after the BP oil spill. Congress has passed the Restore Act which promises to deliver 80 percent of BP's penalties to the Gulf states to aid in restoration. But, given the history of the federal government's delivery on promises, few are counting on those monies showing up.

ꟸ ꟸ

Establishing safety and re-empowering the trauma survivor to understand his or her trauma is not sufficient; the trauma narrative must be *told* and must be *heard*. If trauma rends the social fabric, telling your story to those who really listen re-knits it, creating a new, perhaps smaller, but wiser social world. A longing for good listeners and the renewal of American society is where Bruce Springsteen wistfully takes us in his song:

Where the eyes, the eyes with the will to see
Where the hearts, that run over with mercy
Where's the love that has not forsaken me
Where's the work that set my hands, my soul free
Where's the spirit that'll reign, reign over me
Where's the promise, from sea to shining sea
Where's the promise, from sea to shining sea
Wherever this flag is flown
Wherever this flag is flown
Wherever this flag is flown[34]

While the government did not show up, the nation's artists did, and they helped to tell the story, drawing upon and mirroring the survivors' stories and in effect providing listenership and extending audience. In film and television, Spike Lee's *When the Levees Broke: A Requiem in Four Acts* and David Simon and Eric Overmyer's HBO series *Treme*; Harry Shearer's film about the culpability of the Corps, *The Big Uneasy;* Sundance award-winners *Trouble the Water* and *Beasts of the Southern Wild*—these all helped persuade New Orleans that its story was heard and understood. So too, works of fiction, memoir, reportage, and historical narrative have helped us re-knit our civic life story, better understanding what happened, how it could have happened, and what it means that it happened: Jesmyn Ward's National Book Award–winning *Salvage the Bones: A Novel;* Dan Baum's *Nine Lives: Death and Life in New Orleans;* Dave Eggers's *Zeitoun;* and New Orleanian Jed Horne's *Breach of Faith;* Ivor van Heerden and Mike Bryan's, *The Storm: What Went Wrong and Why during Hurricane Katrina—The Inside Story from One Louisiana Scientist;* Ken Wells's *The Good Pirates of the Forgotten Bayous: Fighting to Save a Way of Life in the Wake of Hurricane Katrina;* and Lawrence Powell's *The Accidental City: Improvising New Orleans.*[35] Jazz trumpeter Terence Blanchard's Grammy Award–winning *A Tale of God's Will (A Requiem for Katrina)*, composed for Lee's *When the Levees Broke*, expressed our grief and invited our mourning.[36] Clarinetist Dr. Michael White's breakthrough album *Blue Crescent*, a response to Katrina composed during a residency at A Studio in the Woods, rather than focusing directly on the storm, returned us to the traditions of improvisation and emotional release that are the heart of what Powell argues makes New Orleans "a state of mind, built on the edge of disaster."[37]

Springsteen himself moved many of us to tears at the 2006 Jazz Fest when he opened his set with the spiritual "O Mary Don't You Weep for Me," which in his version includes the lyric:

> Brothers and sisters don't you cry
> There'll be good times by and by
> Pharaoh's army got drownded
> O Mary don't weep

It didn't quite apply unless you identified Pharaoh's army not with New Orleans but rather with the cavalry that showed up (National Guard and Halliburton) or didn't (various levels of government), but that subtle calculus was unnecessary: we melted. This year, with the lingering tragedy of the BP oil spill now on our minds, it was the second song of Springsteen's set, "We Take Care of Our Own," that liquefied us when it asked the questions we were all asking.

There have been excellent pieces of reportage that are the beginnings of a BP oil spill trauma narrative, some—Jacobsen's and Gessner's—mentioned in these pages. But the future is too uncertain for the final healing narrative to emerge. The three stages of recovery—reestablishing safety; coming fully to understand the trauma; and finding an audience who will really listen—are still in the making. Recovery—both environmental and psychological—hangs in the balance. That we have hung fire so long on that uncertainty and have much longer to suffer it surely will be part of any trauma narrative to emerge from the Macondo blowout and the oil spill that may have erased a way of life.

℘   ℅

And then in late August 2012 there was Hurricane Isaac, which, on second thought, decided not to stay its hand and dealt us more than a glancing blow. Their PTSD reactivated, New Orleanians learned that beefed-up levees notwithstanding, under the new climate change dispensation even a Category 1 storm can do us serious harm. Slow moving, Isaac (8 mph compared to Katrina's 13; forty-eight hours of tropical storm force winds compared to Katrina's eight hours) dumped a lot of rain on New Orleans (20.66 inches compared to Katrina's 8 to 14)[38] and brought a stronger storm surge than anticipated (9 to 11 feet at Shell Beach in St. Bernard Parish).[39] Had the biblical promise to Noah been rescinded? The levees held but many Katrina survivors were re-traumatized by Isaac, more than a Category 1 storm ought to have done.

Repetition compulsion is the neurotic version of a healthy task in the process of recovery: to reexperience the traumata but now without a loss of power and autonomy. And so, while Isaac re-traumatized some, the storm's long-term effect was more positive. Isaac gave New Orleanians an opportunity to revisit the trauma of Katrina and to experience the sense of empowerment and mastery that preparedness and civic coordination affords: better levees, better evacuation planning, better government involvement at all levels.

Yet a third fact is also true of Isaac: the extensive flooding in Plaquemines reinforced the abiding lessons of Katrina and the BP oil spill, that in the final analysis, the key to New Orleans's future is the revival of the coastal wetlands.

NOTES

1. Judith Herman, *Trauma and Recovery: The Aftermath of Violence from Domestic Abuse to Political Terror* (New York: Basic Books, 1992), p. 51. Psychologist Terrence Real differentiates between active trauma—usually boundary violations of some kind—and passive trauma—a form of emotional or physical neglect. Real notes, "Rather than a violent presence, passive trauma may be defined as a violent lack—the absence of nurture and responsibilities normally expected of a caregiver, the absence of connection" (*I Don't Want to Talk about It: Overcoming the Secret Legacy of Male Depression* [New York: Scribner, 1997], p. 107).

2. Jonathan Shay, *Achilles in Vietnam: Combat Trauma and the Undoing of Character* (New York: Atheneum, 1994), p. 20. Moral injury is caused, according to Shay, "by 1) a betrayal of 'what's right' 2) by a legitimate authority 3) in a high-stakes situation. Rather than a clean wound, it is like a contaminated wound that has the potential to kill the patient and harm others around him/her" (personal interview, August 2, 2012). Shay explains "what's right": "No single English word takes in the whole sweep of a culture's definition of right and wrong; we use terms such as moral order, convention, normative expectations,

ethics, and commonly understood social values. The ancient Greek word that Homer used, *thémis*, encompasses all these meanings. A word of this scope is needed for the betrayals experienced by Vietnam combat veterans. In this book I shall use the phrase 'what's right' as an equivalent of *thémis*" (*Achilles in Vietnam*, p. 5).

3. Quoted in Shay, *Achilles in Vietnam*, p. 3.

4. Lenore Terr, *Too Scared to Cry: Psychic Trauma in Childhood* (New York: Basic Books, 1990), p. 61. This prophylactic helps explain the mystery that sent Freud in the wrong direction in his effort to understand trauma. Faced with the fact that traumata may or may not lead to long-range trauma affect, Freud speculated that not just the experience but the fantasy and meaning associated with the experience could be traumatizing. For Freud, his patient Little Hans, for example, was not threatened by his father with castration; that's just how Little Hans interpreted his father's admonishments. Whether or not the survivor fell into a state of helplessness better explains different reactions to traumata.

5. Herman, *Trauma and Recovery*, p. 133.

6. BASK was developed by Dr. Bennet Braun. See "The BASK Model of Dissociation," *Dissociation* 1(1988):4–23.

7. Jed Horne, *Breach of Faith: Hurricane Katrina and the Near Death of a Great American City* (New York: Random House, 2006).

8. *Letters of Marie Madeleine Hachard,* translated by Myldred Masson Costa (1727; rpt. New Orleans, LA: Laborde Printing Company, 1974).

9. William R. Stringfield, *Le Pays des Fleurs Oranges.* Self-published genealogy, 2001. Retrieved from http://www.rootsweb.ancestry.com/~laplaque/order.htm.

10. Rowan Jacobsen, *Shadows on the Gulf: A Journey through Our Last Great Wetland* (New York: Bloomsbury, 2011), p. 29.

11. See Nicholas Lemann, *The Promised Land: The Great Black Migration and How It Changed America* (New York: Knopf, 1991).

12. See Naomi Klein, *The Shock Doctrine: The Rise of Disaster Capitalism* (New York: Metropolitan Books, 2007), where she argues that privatization has largely been put in place by exploiting crisis and trauma.

13. At a press conference following the 2007 Ridenhour Prizes at the National Press Club, Ridenhour Courage prize winner President

Jimmy Carter was asked by *Times-Picayune* reporter John Pope how he would have "done things differently" after Katrina. His response surprised many. FEMA was the creation of his administration, Carter explained, the effort of four years and a response to the fact that the duties assigned to FEMA had been split among thirty-three government agencies. FEMA was founded with "three mandatory characteristics": 1) that FEMA's director would report directly to the president; 2) that it would be well funded; and 3) that it would be "headed by the most outstanding experts on disaster relief that we could find in America." "So," he summed up, "I think everything that was done in the New Orleans and Mississippi and Alabama area after Katrina was a disaster as far as FEMA was concerned because it did not have a competent person in charge, it was not adequately financed—its finances had been reduced dramatically—and it was under the still-struggling Homeland Security agency searching for its own role and its own identity. Other than that," he smiled, "it was ok."

14. In 2007, I teamed up with James Hillman to explore New Orleans's rebirth in a film project we called *Sea Level: Reviving the Soul of Cities*. Hillman had long been a commentator on cities and a believer in cities as an articulation of the psyche. The project was curtailed at the onset of his final illness, but not before the theme of self-empowerment emerged. Though the film did not see the light of day, this theme has become the dominant narrative about New Orleans's rebirth, and I believe we were early in settling on it as the important narrative.

15. Rebecca Solnit's chapter on New Orleans in *A Paradise Built in Hell: The Extraordinary Communities That Arise in Disaster* (New York: Penguin, 2009), pp. 231–303, offers a good account of this multifaceted grassroots community effort.

16. Herman, *Trauma and Recovery*, p. 133.

17. The Environmental Protection Agency disallowed the use of Corexit 9527 as unacceptably toxic. BP switched to Corexit 9500, apparently without the EPA's weighing in. Corexit in either form does not get rid of the oil but only disperses it, which led to multiple underwater oil plumes thousands of miles long. As a result less oil made itself visible on beaches, but the oil plumes held the oil in suspension in the water column, preventing the natural action of bacteria that

would have consumed the oil and ensuring an even greater impact on the fisheries and the food chain than the oil alone would have had.

18. For example the bluefin tuna, a magnificent megafauna already much endangered by our craving for sushi, spawns in the vicinity of the Macondo well in late April. The National Oceanic and Atmospheric Administration (NOAA) estimates that 20 percent of the 2010 spawn were lost. Bluefin spawn take eight to ten years to reach sexual maturity (see Pew Environmental Group's factsheet: http://www.pewtrusts.org/ uploadedFiles/wwwpewtrustsorg/Fact_Sheets/Protecting_ocean_life/ PEG_BluefinOilSpill_14may2010.pdf?n=4455). As Michael Conathan writes for the Center for American Progress, "Shrimp harvests are down, and many with no eyes are turning up in nets. Fisherman are landing red snapper and more than twenty other species covered in lesions" ("RESTORE Act Would Boost Gulf Coast Fisheries," retrieved from http://www.americanprogress.org/issues/2012/06/ fof_061512.html).

19. See William Ryan, *Blaming the Victim* (New York: Vintage, 1971). Theodore Adorno argued that blaming the victim was "one of the most sinister features of the Fascist character," in "Wagner, Nietzsche and Hitler," *Kenyon Review* 9(1947):158.

20. James Hillman, *Pan and the Nightmare*, rev. ed. (Putnam, CT: Spring Books, 2007), p. 37.

21. According to Oliver Houck, "Today we tell Congress that we 'sacrificed' ourselves for the national good . . . Never has there been such a willing, complicit sacrifice. We made a bundle of money, wasted most of it, and blackballed anyone who questioned what it was doing to the Louisiana coast. About seventy years ago, Louisiana made a deal with the oil industry. The industry would get what it wanted; the state would get a piece of the take" ("Can We Save New Orleans?" *Tulane Environmental Law Journal* 20[Spring 2006]:20). The most thorough analysis of how to save New Orleans, this piece is available online at: http://www.google.com/search?client =safari&rls =en&q=Can+We+Save+New+Orleans%3F"+in+Tulane+ Environmental +Law+Journal+20&ie=UTF-8&oe=UTF-8.

22. Houck, "Can We Save New Orleans?" p. 55 and 55n.

23. Jacobsen, *Shadows on the Gulf,* p. 137.

24. Larry Rottmann, Jan Barry, and Basil T. Paquet, eds., *Winning Hearts and Minds: Poems by Vietnam Veterans* (New York: First Casualty Press, 1972).

25. Herman, *Trauma and Recovery,* p. 51.

26. Lenore Terr writes, in *Too Scared to Cry,* "Fitting a frightening event into 'time,' either personal time or world time, helps a person to cope with that event. Feeling rhythms, in addition, helps maintain a person's sense of balance. If all of these time awarenesses fail, however, to prevent a person from becoming traumatized, the person's time sense will undergo some damage. . . . time functions both as a protection against damage and as a marker of the damage" (p. 148).

27. Jesmyn Ward, *Salvage the Bones: A Novel* (New York: Bloomsbury, 2012), p. 251.

28. David Gessner, *The Tarball Chronicles: A Journey beyond the Oiled Pelican and into the Heart of the Gulf Oil Spill* (Minneapolis: Milkweed Editions, 2011), p. 148.

29. Gessner, *The Tarball Chronicles,* pp. 149–50.

30. Christopher Hallowell, *Holding Back the Sea: The Struggle for America's Natural Legacy on the Gulf Coast* (New York: HarperCollins, 2001), p. 17.

31. Hallowell, *Holding Back the Sea,* p. 197.

32. Oliver Houck writes, "The coastal marshes act just like a levee, only a flat one. They knock down storm surges, and over the eighty-some miles between New Orleans and the Gulf that amounts to the height of a tall man, six feet or more. That's a lot of free levee. All we had to do was nurture it and leave it alone. Instead of course, we starved the marshes from the main river and then started cutting them up with canals"("Can We Save New Orleans?" p. 35).

33. Jacobsen, *Shadows on the Gulf,* p. 171.

34. Bruce Springsteen, "We Take Care of Our Own," *Wrecking Ball* (Columbia, 2012).

35. Dan Baum, *Nine Lives: Death and Life in New Orleans* (New York: Spiegel and Grau, 2009); David Eggers, *Zeitoun* (New York: Vintage, 2010); Ivor van Heerden and Mike Bryan, *The Storm: What Went Wrong and Why during Hurricane Katrina—The Inside Story from One Louisiana Scientist* (New York: Penguin, 2007); Ken Wells, *The*

Good Pirates of the Forgotten Bayous: Fighting to Save a Way of Life in the Wake of Hurricane Katrina (New Haven, CT: Yale University Press, 2008); Lawrence Powell, *The Accidental City: Improvising New Orleans* (Cambridge, MA: Harvard, 2012).

36. Terence Blanchard, *A Tale of God's Will (A Requiem for Katrina)* (New York: Blue Note, 2007).

37. Powell, *The Accidental City,* p. 81.

38. For these statistics thanks go to Mark Schleifstein, staff writer of the *Times-Picayune,* email correspondence, Sept 18, 2012.

39. http://www.accuweather.com/en/weather-news/the-life-of-isaac/71857.

HURRICANE KATRINA
THE TEQUILA, THE KLEENEX, AND THE IVY

T here is something captivating about the power of a hurricane.
My first experience of this power was in 1957 as a six-year-old
sitting in my grandparents' house as Hurricane Audrey
devastated Cameron, a coastal community in southwest Louisiana
about sixty miles south of their home. I watched with awe through
a window as the trunks of the giant elms in the yard swayed in the
howling wind and branches high in the canopy whipped and
cracked as Audrey moved inland. As a resident of several towns
throughout southern Louisiana and of New Orleans since my late
twenties, I remember the threat of many hurricanes and the indirect
impact of others. There were those with winds that demanded taped
or boarded windows, snapped telephone poles, mangled power
lines, felled trees; others ushered mammoth tidal surges, unleashed
torrential rains, and flooded coastal communities. Others, many in fact,

Marilyn Marshall, M.A., LPC, is a Jungian analyst practicing and teaching in
New Orleans. She is a graduate of the Inter-Regional Society for Jungian Analysts
(IRSJA) and a faculty member of the New Orleans Jungian Seminar. She is the author
of published articles and has cowritten, with analysts Connie Romero and Charlotte
Mathes, the play *Vault of the Heart*, adapted from selected themes and dialogues in
Jung's Red Book. The play has been performed by analysts in New Orleans, Fall
2010, and in Boulder (IRSJA Conference), Spring 2011.

changed course or passed by with a stormy warning and headed west
or east along the Gulf of Mexico.

Missile from the Sea

Missile flying through the air
Brings destruction as I stare
Buildings crumble one by one
Dust, debris does block the sun
This invasion, I surmise,
Takes this world, now, by surprise
Chaos reigns through city streets
Raging fires compound the heat
Here and there a bomb explodes
Calling for survival mode
On and on the chaos reigns
People in a trance-like pain
End is near, there is no doubt
No rescue and no way out
Climb the ladder and I see
Woman's objectivity
Struggle there on ladder's steps
She and I, the one adept
On and on the chaos reigns
But for me there is no pain.

This was my journal entry on July 22, 2005, five weeks before
Hurricane Katrina. I was in analysis at the time and in training to
become a Jungian analyst. Part of the way I worked with my dreams
after putting them on a computer disc was to paint them or engage
with them in poetic form or dialogue. In this dream the night before
I watched a missile, launched from the depths of the sea, break the
moonlit surface, arc through the night sky, and destroy a city alongside
the water. At first, I was just a distant observer as the missile traveled
and the chaos in the city began. Then, I was in the city witnessing all
manner of response to such a catastrophic event and needing to respond,
as well, for it was the city in which I lived.

My strongest association to this dream related to war. Foremost
was the reality that, at that time, one of my sons, a member of the
National Guard, was in the war in Iraq: in the external world missiles
had been launched, bombs had exploded, and his life was threatened

daily with destruction. His death would have had the impact on me of the "missile from the sea." This association once again flooded me with the emotions of fear and anxiety I first experienced when my son told me his unit was going to Iraq. Tender memories had surfaced and assailed me with a longing for the past. In my mind he became a little boy again, wrapped in my arms, protected from harm, and years younger than the man of twenty-eight. Regression had pulled me down into a whirling vortex of emotion and back to a time when the sweetness of life as mother and child existed in its infancy of development. For all mothers the physical umbilical cord is cut at the birth of the child; the initial separation is mandated, and for the first time the child is forced to breathe separately. For many mothers the psychic cord remains and is only periodically cut away as *we* are forced to breathe separately and yet relate in a new way.

My identity had been formed around the role of mother. Until college, I was of necessity a second mother to ten brothers and sisters born within a twelve-year span. Then after college and marriage I wanted children and, in time, had three boys. Through the years, other parts of me had interfered with the mother and demanded their places in my life. These new expressions of myself had helped me breathe separately. Yet, this dream with its turbulent association was another invitation to respond consciously to the archetypal mother within and to recognize the power and complexity of the psychic relationship between mother and child. It had invited me to acknowledge at a deeper level the separate destinies of individuals. I had my own life with its path, its necessity, and my son, along with his brothers, had his. This seems a simple realization and one that began long before my sons were adults. But I think anyone who has identified with or depended upon a particular role or attitude in life, with its defenses in place, knows the difficulty of experiencing the internal chaos incumbent with the necessary destruction or loss of that one-dimensional way of being.

There was no denying or avoiding this destruction. I had been clumsily, gradually changing through my relationship with the unconscious, but there are those pivotal experiences or defining moments that usher in, even force, change, and my dream seemed to indicate one of those. It presented me with a sudden and immediate image: from the depths of the collective unconscious an aggressive, masculine archetypal force was destroying an established interior city,

the psychic home of an identity as well as the collective structures—
its standards, attitudes, and ideals—that formed and protected it.

In the dream, in the end, I left this city. Subsequent dreams
offered additional images to help me process this experience. Then
one month later, on August 21, 2005, I made this journal entry in
response to a dream:

The Wall, Cracked Open

There against the wall she cries
Telling me her sorrow
Noise that keeps the air in flow
Prevents me from hearing
She thinks I can help
She thinks I can at least listen
Her dam has broken
And tears spill out
As the rain pours through
Cracks in a brick wall that
Can no longer hold up
The young woman crying
And the dissolving wall
And the new cat that comes to investigate
My watch has stopped
And so has another
While two other clocks announce I'll be late
There is tension everywhere
The woman, the wall about to crumble,
The watch and clock
And then falling, falling
Her tears come forth with a force that breaks walls,
once again allowing the flow of life.

Through my analysis during the previous ten years, I had also
struggled in the anguishing tension produced by the awareness of many
unconscious complexes and the turmoil of their effects on my
relationship with myself and with others. The young woman of this
dream was symbolic of that process. She evoked a quality of the feminine
that had been born at a time when I began to express my own voice
rather than the echo of another's. Then she was lost. In the dream,
even though I could not hear her voice, the at-oneness of the image

and emotion, the tension, and the dissolving wall communicated her message. Grounded in the experiences of beauty and ugliness, of mistakes and imperfections, and of the descents and ascents of my life, this figure represented a new feminine consciousness.

The synchronicity of these dreams and internal processes and what occurred the following week with Hurricane Katrina was a powerful personal experience of what many in depth psychology describe as the *anima mundi* or world soul. That intimate relationship of inner and outer, of the individual and the collective, of above and below, and of the human and divine held me in awe.

Hurricane Katrina adjusted my memory with the words "before the storm" and "after the storm." I was no longer the little girl looking through a window at the captivating power of a hurricane's winds. I was a woman experiencing the cataclysmic destruction of its power. I lost my house. I lost all of its furnishings. I lost the clothes in closets and drawers that had not made it into a large suitcase. I lost precious artwork of psychic life I had created throughout my analysis and family photographs of the past that I had thought safe up on a closet shelf. And, with the exception of personal journals, my laptop, Jung's *Collected Works*, and a few other books I could fit into the trunk of my car, I lost my library.

BEFORE THE STORM

What do I remember: the experience of an energy that surfaces from within, permeating cells, moving bodies, creating words, catalyzing thoughts, communicating life and death; emotions of excitement and dread, awe and fear; and the storm, whose satellite images showed its monstrous counterclockwise spin encompassing much of the Gulf of Mexico, still hundreds of miles away but with a possible eye on the city I loved and on my home.

What do I remember: the neighbors helping one another in preparation, boarding up windows and storing away or anchoring down large objects in our yards that could become projectiles in the catastrophic winds of a category 5 hurricane. I remember the critical announcement for the voluntary evacuation and the organized process of geographical phases of movement for the coastal population of southeast Louisiana, including the New Orleans area;

the lines at gas stations and strangers at the pumps talking of routes and destinations; the many cell phone calls between loved ones about plans and emergency numbers, just in case; and then the hours of driving west on crowded interstates and highways to my mother's house in southwest Louisiana.

Mercifully, Katrina's ferocious winds had calmed from 175 mph to 125 mph, a category 3, by the time she hit on the morning of August 29, 2005. Gratefully, she made landfall to the east of New Orleans near the Louisiana/Mississippi border rather than the expected and feared path of a direct hit. Relief! Relief? These words *mercifully* and *gratefully* could suggest the belief or idea that, like Michelangelo's painting in the Sistine Chapel of God's finger pointing toward Adam, reaching out to give life, the god's finger reached out and pointed to a different target of destruction, sparing New Orleans. But what of the new target, of the others who would not be able to use these words?

What do I remember: the disbelief, the numbness, the inability to think—struck, hit, stopped, staring, unable to move from the television's images of devastation and despair. In New Orleans? This couldn't be—the category 5 had become a manageable 3, and Katrina had even missed the city! What I was seeing was not the direct impact of Hurricane Katrina's wind and rain but a flood described in the news as biblical and caused not by the "breach of" but by the "breaks in" the earthen walls, the levees built to protect New Orleans. I had evacuated but others hadn't or couldn't, and there they were, projected on this screen for the world to witness their plight—standing on rooftops, wading through chest-high water, clinging to rescue lines, clutching children, carrying elderly, floating dead; waiting on overpasses, waiting at the convention center, waiting at the Superdome, waiting in hospitals, waiting in makeshift triage at the airport; waiting for drinking water, for food, for medical supplies, for transportation out. Thousands waiting for help.

How could I not remember—the missile from the sea! The chaos, the trauma, and the trance-like pain. The woman's tears and the wall, cracked open! A city destroyed. Order destroyed. Safety destroyed. Protection destroyed. Control dissolved. Capacity dissolved. Mercy denied. Humanity exposed. The archetypal power of the god's pointed finger.

I had had a simple dream in the early hours of that morning of the storm:

> *My analyst (who also lived in New Orleans and had evacuated) stood before me, looked directly into my eyes, and, with his hands chest high, he began purposefully pounding his right fist into his left hand.*

This was an aggressive gesture depicting a side of him I had not known, a gesture a man could use to indicate he was inviting a fight or warning he would fight. He showed no emotion, just the action. Synchronisticly, my brother in Austin, Texas, called me that morning. Affected also by these images on major news channels, he responded with a practicality that had not occurred to me: "Get to Baton Rouge right now and find a place to live. Hundreds of thousands of people are going to be displaced and looking for somewhere close to New Orleans to live." The commanding intensity of his voice suggested the aggressiveness of my analyst's fist. Reality defied disbelief and action dislodged my numbness: my own aggression was launched.

After the question of a place to live was settled that day in Baton Rouge, I returned to my mother's house holding onto magical thinking: despite the report of the break at the 17th Street Canal levee, which was two miles north of my house, and despite the images of flood waters surrounding the Superdome, which was about five miles south, I thought that maybe the area around my house had not flooded; I could, gratefully, be spared. Internet access and its satellite images in the days that followed deflated that psychic defense.

I continued watching the news as more and more images and information assailed me. Chaos reigned in floodwaters, on the concrete islands of refuge, and in the city streets unaffected by flooding. I began to feel a rising anger at the slow response to people's vulnerability and need. The United States has the capacity to send humanitarian aid to countries that are devastated by tsunamis and earthquakes in a matter of hours, distributing water, food, and medical supplies where necessary from helicopters, ships, or planes. Its military proudly displays its capability to destroy with a weapon from the air a single building, among many surrounding it, hiding a terrorist in Iraq. But in a port city thriving alongside the legendary mighty Mississippi River, where cruise ships and tankers deftly snake through the river's curves and currents, and in the Superdome with its heliport on a high and dry upper parking lot, thousands of men, women, and children were left without water, food, medical supplies, or assistance for days!

It was all unbelievable—the impersonal, unavoidable power of Nature or of the god who points a finger and the incapacity of humanity to control it and, in this case, defend against it. Parts of the levee system built surrounding the city to protect it from just such a flood had failed and 80 percent of New Orleans, which had been established centuries ago in a bowl-shaped topography, remained underwater for weeks.

After the Storm

I was allowed to return in October because my office was in the uptown area of New Orleans which, along with the French Quarter, did not flood. Had I not had that address on my business card, I would have had to wait another six to eight weeks: the return to the city had been systematically organized for citizens living in certain zip codes with the most heavily flooded areas scheduled at the latest dates. I had tried to prepare myself for the shock of what I would find but that preparation failed.

I had decided to return to my Lakeview neighborhood via a main boulevard that crossed the short bridge over the 17th Street Canal, not far from where this levee gave way. This canal and the protective levee on either side serves as a boundary between the suburban city of Metairie and the city of New Orleans. If you can remember in *The Wizard of Oz* Dorothy's experience of moving suddenly from black-and-white Kansas to the vibrant color of the Land of Oz, imagine it in reverse. On the Metairie side of this bridge, where police waited to check for confirmation of my zip code, life was in Technicolor—streets bustling with cars, businesses open, neighborhoods populated, and landscapes thriving with flowering plants, carpets of green, and trees dripping with thick leaves offering shade in the 90 degree heat. Here, there were cats scurrying, dogs barking, and people everywhere going about their day, albeit with an unfamiliar solemnity. I imagined words like *mercifully* and *gratefully* peppered their compassionate distress for New Orleans and their understandable relief about the finger that had pointed to the other side of the canal.

On the New Orleans side, a mere thirty yards away from the checkpoint for entry, a desolate black-and-white landscape spanned every direction for miles. Made ghostly by a malodorous gray dusty residue left by the floodwaters and baked on by the sun, the surreal scene was heartbreaking. Sailboats and speedboats, two miles from their harbor at Lake Pontchartrain, lay battered on their sides or upside down along the boulevard. Magnolias stood exhausted, but tall regal palms and mammoth oaks had succumbed to the force of the flood, gouging roofs and blocking passages down neighborhood streets. Farther down the boulevard at the intersection of an even wider boulevard, tireless workers with trucks and cranes were piling debris on top of what was now a monument of destruction fifty yards wide and three stories high that extended a mile north toward the lake. Gray-crusted cars left parked in driveways and on what was deemed higher ground significantly outnumbered the few traveling the eerie streets. Every bush had been stripped bare of leaves, and their branches, as well as the dead grass, wore that lifeless gray. And house after haunting house, marked with the infamous red or black paint to designate inspection for dead bodies, sat anguished in a wasteland of devastation that even the birds had abandoned.

What do I remember: on the front door of my small cottage was the sign of the black *X* with numbers in each quadrant indicating the completed search, the date, the searcher (who had broken a window to enter), and number dead—0. I unlocked the swollen, saturated door, but I could not budge it, even with a friend's added body weight for force, so a crowbar and sledgehammer broke me in. That sordid smell polluting the open air was concentrated and assaulting in a boarded-up house with mud carpeting the buckled wood floors and mildew texturing the walls like repulsive, greenish-brown patterned wallpaper. The watermark, as distinct as a horizontal line of graffiti drawn throughout the house, indicated eight feet. Everything that wasn't in the attic had drowned; even the refrigerator had been turned on its side in a position that seemed impossible in the small kitchen.

The curious thing about this nightmarish image, like something in a dream that stands out strangely different from the expected, was a synchronistic three-ness. Resting upright on a wooden chair leaning against a corner of the dining room, ten feet from its place on a glass shelf, was a bottle of tequila, its golden liquid holding a message emblematic of alcohol's potential to medicate or numb pain. In the living room a box of Kleenex I had left on the upholstered ottoman, which must have floated like a buoy, looked as though someone could have placed it there that day; the tissue was white, fluffy, sticking out from its plastic box top ready to absorb a flood of tears. And in the kitchen, high atop a cabinet in its decorative clay planter was the ivy; weeks of enclosure in sauna-like moisture and heat had provided the perfect conditions, and its bright, rich green variegated leaves grew prolifically in graceful vines, promising life.

The tequila, the Kleenex, and the ivy. It sounded like the title of a fairy tale. Why tequila, I wondered? I rarely drank it. Why not wine or vodka, which would have been a more comprehensible image for me then? No, tequila did not make sense to me and I dismissed it; however, in time, I would come to recognize its image as symbolic of any form of retreat into a false spirit—a spirit of rising above all the loss and pain with rationalization, of being a kind of superhuman able to handle anything, and of flying into thoughts and ideas rather than staying on the ground of a vulnerable reality.

This tequila I did drink, especially its intoxication of ideas and thoughts. Despite having lost my library in the floodwaters I escaped into study, the rigorous intellectual component of training. This was the same spirited defense enacted via graduate school twelve years earlier that had protected me from the full experience of the destruction and pain I caused by leaving my twenty-two-year marriage, including the guilt of leaving my adolescent sons and the home I had helped establish.

The archetypal process of destruction constellates such past traumas, including those of childhood. The little six-year-old who watched the hurricane's winds through a glass window felt vulnerable and helpless in the storms she witnessed at home. The vows she had made for protection from the emotional turmoil and loss had become the cement for similar bricks of experience. The wall behind which she had been silently hiding also began to crumble in the floodwaters of Katrina.

Destruction cannot be experienced all at once or once and for all. Defenses serve a purpose and only with time, attention, and, perhaps with the god's influential finger, do those protections crack and give way. Gratefully, this defensive flight with a false spirit did not have the same strength. Gradually, through confrontations in the external and internal worlds, through the vessel of analysis and the added fires of the training process, the Kleenex was called to serve its purpose.

Although Hurricane Katrina was not a missile, it was a force of nature that destroyed a wall of defense and ushered in a period of renewal for New Orleans, just as a flood of tears had dissolved my particular wall of defense and ushered in a new consciousness. The collective forces of destruction had started gathering energy in the waters off the coast of Africa to create eventually the conditions for the flood that broke the levees surrounding New Orleans, just as the forces in my individual journey of destruction and transformation began years before in the unconscious waters of the archetypal mother and child. The god(s) had pointed a finger at this individual and at the collective. Something crucial was needed and could no longer be avoided. But with the destruction would also come transformation; the ivy would thrive.

This third image, the ivy, was symbolic of the new growth that would come from the tension between the defenses that protect and the emotional experience of the protected. Ivy is a plant associated with Dionysus, a god who has a place in the soul of New Orleans. For me, the ivy symbolized a spiritual growth and awareness of the value of the Dionysian, the loosening of the collective standards and expectations I had unconsciously adopted, of my ideals of perfection, of my one-sided identity as mother, and of the dominating value of the intellect. I also hoped that it represented growth and new life for this city that honors Dionysus. The yearly celebration of Mardi Gras, in particular, pays homage to this god. This is a celebration that ritualizes the disrobing of convention and the donning of masks of perversity, a celebration that provides a container for the expressions of the irreverent, the irrational, and the irascible and allows for the loosening and unbinding of rigid attitudes and defenses. It seemed to me that such a city which hosts and contains the Dionysian might, itself, need to experience the god's pointed finger—the destructive dissolution and dismemberment that accompanies a process of transformation.

SEVEN YEARS LATER

After the storm, I commuted from Baton Rouge to New Orleans twice weekly to see individuals for psychotherapy. With different mythic motifs and symbols of meaning, the many stories of suffering I heard gave witness to this archetypal underpinning of destruction and transformation. Although Katrina and the flood created the disaster for such constellations, this pattern lives in the natural processes of psyche and is a universal human experience. On the collective level, I watched as the city began to rebuild and renew itself with the help of those of its citizens who could return and the aid of people from all over the United States and other countries who joined in the effort. These processes continue to this day.

I moved back to New Orleans in January 2009 to my old neighborhood in the Lakeview area. Gratefully, my sons are on their paths with their families and work, and right now this brings a smile to my face; tears of joy glisten. It is good to be home.

When I was asked to write this article about Hurricane Katrina, I agreed to do it because I thought it might be an invitation from the psyche to process yet another layer of that experience. It was. The first invitation came at a yearly weekend get-together with friends with whom I had trained. One of the women made the most delicious margaritas for us, strong margaritas. Too many drinks, too much tequila for me. I was not only terribly intoxicated but sick to my stomach. My gratitude for the compassionate care of one friend in particular that night was matched the next morning by the shame I felt, despite everyone's empathy, for the dissolution into such a state. Why did this happen and to what purpose? The second invitation came two months later with three women with whom I meet to share our internal work. I talked with them about the experience of writing this article and remembering Katrina. When they asked me to read aloud "The Missile from the Sea," I broke down in tears on the word *destruction* in the second line. I was surprised by the strength of this emotion. This informed me that there must be more to experience than I was capable of before now.

When I processed these two difficult experiences in my journal, I remembered my interpretation of the tequila as a false spirit. With the margaritas in mind, I decided to look into that particular type of alcohol. I discovered that tequila is made from the agave plant, a fact that offered me a more specific meaning than I had discerned seven years ago. Although there are other amplifications for agave, one in particular had meaning for me. Agave (Agaue) was the name of one of four daughters of Cadmus and Harmonia of Greek myth. One of her sisters, Semele, was the mother of Dionysus. Agave, along with her two other sisters, were driven mad in punishment for not honoring the divinity of their nephew. During a Dionysian rite in the depths of the forest, gripped in the very madness they had rejected with domestic fervor and collective prejudice, Agave and her sisters tore to pieces Pentheus, Agave's son. Gratefully, the interior wall behind which Agave retreated had cracked open when I experienced the young woman's voice as my own with the word *destruction*. And life began to flow.

I know my own sons have been wounded and hurt by my unconsciousness and by the destruction of their image, and mine, of mother. I also realize that psychic sons, masculine qualities within, have been affected. I am grateful for depth psychology, for the experience and awareness of the difficult and painful processes of destruction and transformation, and especially for my two analysts. Had I not had the vessel created by their respect for and attention to the depths of the psyche and its archetypal dimension, I may have suffered the peril of Agave and Pentheus.

The tequila, the Kleenex, and the ivy. I am in awe of the mystery!

IN MY BACK YARD
LEGACIES OF THE AMERICAN WEST

STEPHEN FOSTER

> Unfortunately there can be no doubt that man is, on the
> whole, less good than he imagines himself or wants to be.
> Everyone carries a shadow, and the less it is embodied in the
> individual's conscious life, the blacker and denser it is. If an
> inferiority is conscious, one always has a chance to correct it.
> Furthermore, it is constantly in contact with other interests, so
> that it is continually subjected to modifications. But if it is
> repressed and isolated from consciousness, it never gets corrected.[1]

Over the past twenty-eight years I have calculated the human
health and ecological risks associated with chemical dumps,
spills, and hazardous waste sites in the United States, Europe,
South America, and southern Africa. These sites have become so
commonplace that we rarely give them much thought unless they are

Stephen Foster has a B.S. degree in chemistry from Sussex University, and Master's
degree and a Ph.D. in organic chemistry from Imperial College, London. He has post-
doctoral fellowships from the University of Wisconsin in biochemistry and toxicology,
and Harvard University in cancer research, and has worked as an environmental consultant
in hazardous waste for over 28 years. Foster also has a Master's degree in counseling
psychology from Regis University, and graduated as a Jungian analyst from the Inter-
Regional Society of Jungian Analysts in 2009. His book, *Risky Business: A Jungian View of
Environmental Disasters and the Nature Archetype*, expands on the archetypal aspects of
environmental psychology and shadow.

near our homes or appear on the evening news. In fact, many people are unaware that there are hundreds, if not thousands, of sites across the United States and that the developing world is now taking the lead in these environmental disasters. For part of this work I have been a Jungian analyst. I will not elaborate on the symbolism of dumping wastes into towns and homes across America, or on the unconscious process by which this occurs; I plan to focus here on the human experience of these events and the cleanup. However, one of the key aspects of Jung's work that applies when working with all of these sites is one's ability to hold the tension. There is always a tension between known and unknown, responsible party and affected party, regulator and regulated, health and sickness, vocal and silent, and action and inaction. The damage or pathology at a site is suspected, but its degree or extent is unknown. As with the human psyche, when one starts the process of discussing the malady, the remedy or cure cannot be fully predicted.

In this process, approaching each site is like undertaking analysis: one holds the tension and waits for the transcendent function. About this psychic function Jung states:

> From the activity of the unconscious there now emerges a new content, constellated by thesis and antithesis in equal measure and standing in a compensatory relation to both. It thus forms the middle ground on which the opposites can be united. If, for instance, we conceive the opposition to be sensuality versus spirituality, then the mediatory content born out of the unconscious provides a welcome means of expression for the spiritual thesis, because of its rich spiritual associations, and also for the sensual antithesis, because of its sensuous imagery. The ego, however, torn between thesis and antithesis, finds in the middle ground its own counterpart, its sole and unique means of expression, and it eagerly seizes on this in order to be delivered from its division.[2]

When the transcendent function emerges in this process there is often a solution, unknown to either pole at the outset, but ending in a reasonable outcome for most. And like the analytic process, the solution may not become apparent for many years. Being engaged with the daily material, talking about possibilities and activating the imagination is undoubtedly required.

Rather than attempting to describe a wide range of sites in several countries, I will focus here on three types of sites common in the United States, all located in the American West (Montana, Colorado, and Wyoming): metals in soil related to the mining industry (lead, arsenic, copper, and zinc), chlorinated solvents in groundwater (dry cleaning fluid and laboratory solvents from the analysis of road materials), and petroleum in soil and water. Each of the three sites has large numbers of individuals or wildlife affected. The wastes affect each community in which they are located on personal and collective levels. Each community responds out of both ecological and cultural complexes based on their relationship to the environment, and as a community with their collective history in relation to the wastes, the landscape, climate, lifestyle, and each other. Therefore, the work is not just with individuals, as one might find with analysis, but also with the community as though it were an entity with its own purposive mind, cultural characteristics, patterns of behavior, biases, and desires that will impact the outcome.

BACKGROUND

The U.S. Environmental Protection Agency (EPA), which manages many of America's most toxic sites, was founded in 1970. Ten years later Congress enacted the Comprehensive Environmental Response, Compensation, and Liability Act (CERCLA) in response to the high number of abandoned sites such as Love Canal, NY, and Times Beech, MO, and the mounting environmental contamination that resulted from industrial dumping. Under this 1980 law, any company, entity, or individual who dumped, handled, or contributed to a waste problem was liable for the cost of cleanup. The funds generated a "Superfund" to pay for these abandoned hazardous waste sites.

When William Ruckelshaus, the first and fifth EPA administrator (1970 to 1973, and 1983 to 1985), implemented the Superfund program in the 1980s, he stated that the risks from substances at a waste site should be calculated and that they should be clearly and effectively communicated to the public; thus a scientific foundation for the cleanup process was established. The Superfund process determines what substances are present, their effects, and ways to clean them up. Remediation (cleanup) always involves a great deal of science and engineering, and often the science is complicated and uncertain.

At the heart of the Superfund program is a process called risk assessment that determines how "clean" is clean enough. It involves physical and biological sciences, toxicology and mathematical modeling, and it determines how much engineering is required to make a site "safe" for reuse, if that is possible. I have prepared a hundred or more of these risk assessments over the past thirty years. More important here, I have been involved in the personal and collective experiences of those affected by toxic wastes. Residents have invited me into their homes and their lives, to sample their air, soil, water, and food. It was also my job to explain the results of the risk assessment process. Inevitably, psychic and emotional issues were mixed into our risk communications because health problems, cancer, and environmental trauma were ever present.

Risk communication brings together science and psychology because to communicate the complexity of risk requires an understanding of the triggers that can be activated in individuals and communities. Environmental triggers are another name for highly charged eco-complexes related to environmental images. In Jung's work with the word association experiment, he described complexes as autonomous, affect-laden images; eco-complexes are associated with the environment in relation to one's home, its physical and ecological setting, culture, family, economics, and survival. Eco-complexes encompass the fear of developing cancer, protecting one's children from neurological damage, or losing the financial and emotional investment in one's home. When one engages with those affected by toxic substances, the psychological components are often the same: disbelief that this is "happening to me and my family," anger at those responsible, shock that the effects can be so severe, anxiety about what will happen next, fear for one's family, livelihood, and lifestyle, and the trauma of it all. These occur initially on a personal level, and then, when the community realizes that it is threatened as a whole, a form of collective shame and trauma sets in. The community feels dirty and abandoned. The emotional components of exposure to hazardous waste are rarely addressed in any formally organized adequate way. Superfund is a concrete science and engineering program with mandated communications, but communities must necessarily deal with the emotional aspects of exposure, illness, and harm regardless of Superfund because of the community members' emotional reactions to the situation.

The toxic substances present at these sites are as varied as the chemicals mined, manufactured, or enriched by industry and government over the past century. If you live in the United States, the chances are high that there is a national or state Superfund site near you. For many it comes as a shock to find that they actually live on a site and that their drinking water or air has been polluted for years. Imagine your own feelings if you found out that the water you once assumed to be clean was contaminated. Movies such as *Erin Brockovich* tell the story of drinking water contaminated with chromium, bringing this scenario to the silver screen. But this wasn't just a Hollywood screenplay; it was real. Similar events, with various other chemicals, continues to happen across the country and adds to the number and magnitude of environmental disasters that the public does not hear about.

Likewise, the movie *Michael Clayton* highlights the effects of toxic chemicals on a farmer's family and a scientist when agricultural runoff poisons the family's well. Like any disaster, it is both an individual and collective tragedy. But unlike a short-lived hurricane or earthquake, environmental disasters can be years in the making and take lifetimes to heal. Toxic waste may affect each family or community differently. Some people are more predisposed to cancer or liver or kidney damage because of genetics, diet, lifestyle, and the degree of exposure. For sites where many people may be exposed, whole communities may have to relocate or rebuild as part of the cleanup process. Higher priority sites are evaluated and dealt with more quickly; however, investigation and cleanup continues on a great many sites.

BUTTE AND METALS IN MONTANA

Some of the mining sites in the United States are so old that generations lived there before they were ever deemed hazardous, and there are many sites where families were exposed to hazardous chemicals before there was a Superfund program. In the western states, particularly the mineral rich Rocky Mountain states, the 1872 Mining Law was designed to open the West's resources to the developing nation. Placer gold mining in Butte, Montana, by the Anaconda Mining

Company started in 1864, and by 1882 the area's rich copper vein was discovered.[3] Between then and 1964, an estimated 7.3 million tonnes (a tonne is 1,000 kilograms) of copper came from Butte's Berkeley Pit. To understand the nature of the environmental disaster associated with mining and the human and ecological tragedies that ensued, one needs to know that the ore that comes out of the ground is actually a mixture of metals and other chemicals. Copper ore is often rich in lead, zinc, silver, and arsenic. After the ore is mined, it is crushed and enriched by separating out and discarding rock and low-metal ore. This rock is called tailings and is often dumped close to the mine.

Tailings are fine sand-like grains that still contain metals in the form of sulfur salts which have a distinctive yellow or yellow-green color. If one drives around the West, tailings clearly mark the presence of old mines because over time the sulfur picks up oxygen from the air to form metal sulfides and sulfuric acid, which kill vegetation and leave the land denuded and barren. Historically, as mines grew, so did the tailing piles, and eventually they became the land on which mining towns were built. One can see this same pattern today in developing countries, where miners want or are forced to live near the mine. In 1997, I visited gold and copper mines in South Africa, including Soweto, where the gold mine tailing piles tower over the townships. The wind blew tailings into homes and yards. It is a consistent and underreported piece of information that the economically disadvantaged are disproportionally exposed to these types of toxic wastes.

Western miners are characteristically a resilient, independent people who work hard and play hard. Hunting and fishing are more a way of life than recreational sports. The challenge of mining under the harsh conditions of a Montana winter requires a fierce tenacity that draws individuals into these communities with a common cultural attitude, value system, and philosophy. So when the EPA started the process of investigating how mine tailings had impacted western towns, and the degree to which children had been harmed, there was skepticism and often anger toward this outside group. People found it unbelievable that the tailings were in fact significantly toxic and that the place they called home was a toxic waste site.

Lead, a neurotoxic metal now known to damage developing brains, lower intelligence, and alter brain function, is common in tailings and is exacerbated in mining communities by lead-based paint. Aging houses drop paint chips onto the soil, increasing lead levels to highly toxic, especially for children who play in the yards. While managing the investigation at one site, I remember having my team sample a house, inside and out, according to a very specific protocol to determine lead and arsenic levels in house dust, soil, gardens, and play areas. I talked to the mother while we sampled her child's sandbox, in which her young boy often played with his big yellow digger, trucks, and trailers. The sandbox was filled with the fine-grained bright yellow tailings that were mined by his father. We helped her swap the contaminated sand for clean sand, but the feeling that she might have contributed to harming her child was overwhelming to her. With tears in her eyes she shook as she carried her son into the house to wash him off. It was the late 1980s, and she had no idea of the danger. Public health as well as general education in this area was nearly nonexistent. Once parents became aware that their children were at risk, communities became outraged and wanted action. While the entire town was affected by the mine tailings, cleanup was expensive and took time. When the tenacious community focused on removing or covering up the wastes with clean soil (removing all of the old soil was impossible), they became an unstoppable force, and their resiliency and independent nature led to an eventual solution for their community.

Unknown to many now, the town of Butte has a unique place in the history of the West, western mining, and the struggle between mine unions and owners. In June 1917, the Butte Granite Mountain fire killed 168 miners, and Butte's miners went on strike to protest safety and working conditions. Occurring during World War I, the government saw their actions as treason, and the owner's private force, the FBI, and the U.S. Army forced the miners down into the mine at gunpoint. Some union miners were killed as a warning to others. The bonds forged between miners from the shared dangers and losses experienced in the mines were strengthened when outside forces entered the town. Because of the time spent underground in the mine and the anxiety of those waiting for the men to return, Butte neighborhoods had transcended ethnic and racial boundaries. The town became polarized between miners and mine owners during the strike. It is within this historic cultural backdrop, cultural complexes, and animosity toward outside groups that the EPA started the Superfund process years later.

Regular public meetings are part of the Superfund process; the city council is actively involved with the EPA, the health department, the potentially responsible parties (PRPs), and the public. Investigations require going into many homes and yards to collect data. In Butte, a health study was also conducted to measure lead levels in children's blood. These studies were invasive and anxiety provoking. I conducted a similar study in another town where we checked for arsenic and lead contamination in homes, yards, urine, and food. I felt the anxiety, fear, and anguish of the parents during this period. They feared the results would find these chemicals at levels that would damage organs, form cancers, or harm a child's brain. They wanted the results immediately, and when body chemical levels came in high, reactions were strong and immediate. Mothers went from home to home comparing results, speculating and talking about what to do next. This increased the sense of community, but also fueled the trauma.

The Superfund process has been criticized because it spends millions of dollars studying and characterizing conditions at waste sites before action is taken. Unlike other types of cleanup, after a fire or flood, for example, attempts to clean a site can spread contamination. Scientists and engineers do not always agree on the best type of cleanup, and the debate between experts at public meetings undermines the public's confidence in the process. Scientists are often held in high regard within these mining communities because of the complexities of extracting, enriching, and smelting ore. Conflict between experts leads to a general deflated feeling from the public: "If they can't agree, and they are the experts, what chance do we have?"

When mining ceased in Butte, the pumps that prevented mine flooding were turned off. As a result, the Berkeley Pit (one of the world's largest open pit mines) filled with 37 billion gallons of acidic, toxic, metal-laden water over 900 feet deep. There is something darkly beautiful about this water-filled pit that sits above the town. It will require water treatment in perpetuity and is a permanent reminder of the past.

Within a few miles of the mine, on a railroad spur, there is a smelter at Anaconda where enriched ore was chemically reduced to form metal ingots. Arsenic is a relatively low-melting metalloid, meaning it has some metal properties, and is present in copper, zinc, silver, and lead ore. Smelting separates the metal from its impurities and heat makes glass out of the sands in the rock. Impurities such as arsenic and lead are blown out of the liquid ore into a flue as fine particles. These toxic substances concentrate in flue dust or leave via a stack as smoke. Arsenic and lead levels in flue dust and soil near the Anaconda smelter were extremely high, and workers were exposed. Arsenic in this form causes lung cancer in addition to liver and skin cancer, and lung cancer is a common cancer in Silver Bow County (the county where Butte and Anaconda are situated). Cancer statistics for 1979 to 1999 showed higher levels of skin cancer in Silver Bow County compared with reference populations.[4] Respiratory disease mortality was in Silver Bow County relative to the rest of Montana was 28 percent higher in 1979–88, 16 percent higher in 1989–98, and 27 percent higher in 1999–2008. Montana cancer statistics also show there was a higher mortality in Silver Bow County compared to other counties in the state.[5] However, it is difficult to distinguish between respiratory disease and cancer caused by arsenic or by smoking cigarettes, skin cancers caused by arsenic or the sun, and liver cancers caused by arsenic or by drinking alcohol. Many miners smoke, drink, and are exposed to sunlight. The inability to point to a specific cause of disease adds trauma because each worker or resident feels, or knows, they have been exposed to lead and arsenic, and they believe it is one more insult they have to bear from the mine owners in the one-company town, but it cannot be proven.

In the end, yards and gardens at residential properties were covered with clean soil, general health improved, and child blood-lead levels dropped. The individual/community transcendent function was expressed in the form of improvements to amenities, a golf course, and grants to the university and community colleges. As with psychoanalysis, gathering energy through talking gave way to positive action to make improvements; individuals live with what they cannot change—a pit of contaminated water that will be there in perpetuity.

The Anaconda smelter was closed in 1980, and I did not have a chance to visit the smelter while it was active. However, in 1998 I visited the active copper smelter at the Chuquicamata copper mine in northern Chile. The smelter and mine are in the Atacama Desert, which receives 0.04 inches of rainfall per year on average. Acidic mine drainage is not an issue because of the arid climate. At a depth of 850 meters, this is the second deepest open pit mine in the world. It is 4.3 kilometers long and 3 kilometers wide; the trucks at the bottom look like small insects. The first thing that struck me when entering the high plateau near the smelter was the smell and taste of sulfur dioxide. It permeates the nose and mouth with a choking, acidic taste and reminds me of Tolkien's description of Mordor. The smelter is a large warehouse-like building that contains large metal cauldrons of liquid metal heated by furnaces that are controlled by one man in a small control room at the very crest of the building's ceiling. The control room is on a track and shuttles back and forth along the length of the furnaces. When the smelting process is over, the purified liquid copper is poured from the cauldrons into molds to make huge copper ingots. As the liquid hits the mold, a plume of hot gaseous fumes and dust—high in arsenic—clouds the air and engulfs the boxlike control room in toxic smoke. Operators are only allowed to work two days per week at this job because it is so dangerous and exposure is so high. Their body arsenic levels reflect their exposure. However, it is the highest paying job in the smelter, and everyone wants it. It has money and prestige. Workers here tend to have a particular type of skin disorder that is characteristic of arsenic toxicity. There are no available respiratory disease or lung cancer statistics for these workers. Being located in a barren high desert helps minimize the impacts on human health, and only workers and their families will know the true impacts of this exposure.

Tailings Downstream

The mine tailings and smelter emissions from Butte and Anaconda entered the Clark Fork River, were dispersed along 125 miles of the river system, and collected as six million cubic yards of contaminated sediment behind the Milltown Dam, near Missoula. Throughout the river system, the toxic metals killed fish and poisoned water wells, and acidity killed vegetation. Families consumed arsenic-contaminated water for years before the problem was discovered and bottled water was provided. Site-related public meetings at the local school were well attended, and emotions ran high. Residents vented their feelings, formed groups that empowered rather than isolated the individual, and were told about investigation and cleanup plans. The group process provided a container for community rage. When I participated in or ran these public meetings, I could feel the energy in the room. Beneath the surface, the group mind held anxiety, anger, and unresolved feeling that had not taken shape or form. Groups were distrustful of those presenting information. When information is complicated, residents wonder if experts are hiding something, and when it is simple, they suspect a cover up. As for many sites, the EPA funded a Technical Advisory Group, experts selected by residents to help explain technical aspects of the cleanup. Credibility and trust can be built through personal contact and relationship, but when children are affected or residents develop health problems, anger and frustration increase, resistance hardens, and there are no compromises. At this site a tension existed between the Milltown Dam owners, Montana Power, and the Clark Fork Coalition, which wanted the dam removed. The dam indirectly impacted the town because it collected the contaminated sediments, creating conditions that changed the chemistry of the groundwater and released arsenic into it. The town considered the dam an eyesore, and it interfered with the trout fishery on the Blackfoot and the Clark Fork Rivers. In this case, public meetings and a public process ensued over several years. Eventually the images from the movie *A River Runs Through It* became persistent references for the locals to rally around. Their heritage was about fishing and wildlife, and the dam did not fit with this image. In the end, the group mind settled on the removal of the Milltown Dam and its contaminated sediments as the much needed symbol of closure. In 2010 the dam was removed, and fish can now swim up the Blackfoot or Clark Fork Rivers without hindrance. The community participated in the selection of the remedy.

The Clark Fork River problem was created through poor management and disposal practices; this is the mechanism by which most hazardous sites are created. In the United States, worker exposure is now relatively well managed, and under the Resource Conservation and Recovery Act, industry is required to manage its wastes.

Solvents in Groundwater

Historically, good chemical management was not always the norm. It was common to find industrial facilities with leaking pipes, unlined pits, and tanks on bare ground. Throughout the United States, small industrial companies and commercial productions used the dry well concept to dispose of waste. This meant taking a 55-gallon drum with a series of holes in the bottom, burying it in the ground, and putting a lid on top. Workers then simply filled the buried drum with waste solvents, and it would be empty by the next day, ready for the process to be repeated. In addition, when chlorinated solvents or paint residues were stored in underground tanks that rusted through, solvents entered the groundwater. Where groundwater flowed under houses and apartment buildings, these solvents flowed with them, and toxic vapors could percolate up into residences. Residents may be exposed for years to these unseen, odorless vapors without their knowing it. Sites are still regularly discovered where vapor intrusion, the presence of an unseen vapor with no odor or taste, enters schools, homes, apartment buildings, and office buildings and exposes children, families, and workers. Unknown exposures, when discovered, lead to understandable fear and anxiety.

I started working at one such site in Denver in 1994, though the spill had occurred earlier when a tank used to store spent solvents from a material testing laboratory rusted through and contaminated the groundwater. A second adjacent site in a residential neighborhood, involving similar degreasing solvents used by a rifle scope manufacturer, resulted in the same problem. These are the country's landmark sites for vapor intrusion, which is currently a national contamination issue because of the number of people affected and because the situation highlights a flaw in the Superfund program, which until this point had focused primarily on drinking water. Both sites are still in the process of being cleaned up. Many apartment buildings and houses were affected, and hundreds of residents were exposed. The percolation of unseen chemicals into buildings, especially homes, through the floor is terrifying because it is insidious. When chemical vapors enter homes through basements, floorboards, and cracks, indoor air chemicals are measured. Technicians go into the home and set up sampling devices next to beds, cribs, and living room couches. The results tell the residents of their cancer risk.

In the open format portion of a public meeting for the site, on older woman said to me: "I feel so terrible. It's like I've been socked in the stomach. I don't know if breathing all of those chemicals over the years has made my health worse. My husband died last year, could these chemicals have killed him? I know I will get sick later. I just don't understand what they are saying, and what all the maps and numbers mean." These comments express the feelings of desperation and isolation felt by many living on these contaminated sites. They also express the unsolvable quality of never really knowing what might have killed those who die in this situation, illustrating a different sort of eco-complex that touches on uncertainty and a lack of safety within one's home. One of the key characteristics of this particular site was the tenor of the residential neighborhoods, represented by an older generation of people who had raised their families in these homes. Another section of the affected area was a close-knit immigrant Russian community. All the literature was translated to respond to the needs of this population; their cultural attitude toward authority was distinctly different from that of traditional western families, who tended to be more forceful in their questioning of authority.

Public meetings for these sites are important and cathartic events. They provide an opportunity for affected residents to express their anger, concern, and anxiety. It has been shown in other areas of psychological therapy, such as sexual trauma, that talking about one's experience in a public setting helps recovery.[6] It is the recognition that something has emerged from the unknown to confront the individual that must be retold. The repeated exposure to vapors every day caused these individuals to recall each ailment, each cough, and each cancer on their block. As the investigation process required continual house sampling for the unseen vapors in basements and bedrooms, individuals were confronted with the invisible intrusion at each entry into their home. The meetings provided a space for the residents to bring the test results and talk about them.

In these group settings, a person's typology will affect how they approach the problem. Sensation types will want to know all of the details, while feeling types will circle around the subject from all directions. Intuition can quickly turn dark. Home visits are often required to work one-on-one with those most affected, and repeat visits may also be required. As with the analysis of trauma, the story has to be told over and over: "Why me? What does it mean when I have this number? How many times do you have to come back?" This type of environmental trauma is sudden and shocking for the community, while sites like Butte and Milltown have a history of contamination that people have grown up with and physical manifestations of the problem that they can see every day. The difference in the traumatic quality consists of disbelief, paranoia, and distrust. In both instances, individuals and communities need time to integrate the full range of the problem, possible effects, and resolutions.

Imagined symbolically, the conscious rational mind and the unconscious imagination are in tension and the solution appears simple—"remove the chemicals from my home." However, the transcendent function may have another preferred outcome such as incorporating low volatile organic paints to reduce background exposure, implementing medical monitoring, or even forming tenant associations that encourage group education and responses. In Denver, the spill radically impacted the responsible party, and we could say that they, too, experienced the effects of the transcendent process. In this case, the Colorado Department of Transportation, the entity that owned and operated the laboratory where the release occurred, implemented internal reviews of chemical use within the department and by its contractors to ensure these types of exposures did not occur again. In addition, they conducted environmental management of new properties, and continued to implement education through an internal Web site.

PETROLEUM, ANOTHER LEGACY OF THE AMERICAN WEST

Leaks and spills at gas stations and petroleum refineries were and still are common. Gasoline floats on water, including groundwater, and vapors can migrate into the basements of homes over contaminated groundwater. The cancer-causing chemical benzene is present in gasoline at 2–4 percent, but benzene has a low odor threshold compared to other solvents, and the smell of gas means these sites are usually found relatively quickly.

In the late 1800s, oil was discovered in the Teapot Dome formation just outside of Casper, Wyoming. The Teapot Dome oil reserve was leased by Interior Secretary Albert Fall to private oil companies (including Marathon Oil, a subsidiary of Sinclair Oil) without competitive bidding, in exchange for approximately $5 million in kickbacks. Oil from the Teapot Dome was refined in Casper at a number of refineries, now known as the former BP/Amoco refinery, the former ChevronTexaco refinery, and the Sinclair refinery. I worked with the Wyoming Department of Environmental Quality (WDEQ), the state's EPA, to assist in developing risk-based cleanup goals for wastes at all of these refineries. The former BP/Amoco refinery finished operations in 1991, at which time the site was fenced, leaving behind 4,000 acres contaminated with almost one hundred years of spilled oil, sludge, and hundreds of miles of buried pipeline.

At the outset of the investigation process, tensions between the US EPA and Amoco were high because of an enforcement order issued by the EPA and an appeal filed by Amoco. Legal activity led to delays in cleanup, causing citizens in the community to file a lawsuit in federal court. A judge intervened, requiring cleanup to occur within a limited time. When BP acquired the property in a merger with Amoco, they entered into a consent decree with the citizens, the city, and the state that required a collaborative process in which the citizens, the city, the potentially responsible party, and the state identified reuse options and cleanup strategies (remedies). The collaborative process ensured that every meeting was a public meeting where the citizens were active participants.

The refinery had consisted of a processing area in the center of town, a tank farm with a view of the North Platte River, and Soda Lake, into which sludge from the refinery was pumped, forming a pond used by migratory birds and bird watchers alike. The wastes at this site were generally petroleum wastes consisting of gasoline chemicals, including benzene, lead, and oil sludge containing coal tar residues that also cause cancer and skin and liver problems. Breathing coal tar residues can also lead to lung cancer. Free-floating liquid oil and gasoline several feet deep settled on the water table and would bubble up into the adjacent river as iridescent chemical rings that floated downstream. The heavier oily residues adhere to the soil in the ground and did not move. These unseen residues can remain for hundreds of years unless repeatedly treated.

Once the cracking towers and tanks had been removed, the area became an open space where teenagers parked at night or broke through the fence to access the good river fishing. I myself have eaten fish from the river, generously shared by an old-timer. At one public meeting, many of the interested locals gathered to mark spots on a map projected onto the walls of the meeting room where they thought contamination lurked under their homes or civic buildings. It was here, in front of his neighbors, that one retired worker told of opening a spigot to let the oil flow into the river when cleaning out tanks. His admission was a powerful moment that allowed others to talk of the sludge, tank bottoms, and tar dumped in the river, which had been acceptable practices at the time. There was a sense of guilt and real shame shared by many of the workers and their families. "We didn't know any better," another man said. He now lived in fear of the gasoline under his house. He couldn't smell it, but he knew it was there, seeping up through his floor. With palpable emotion, he told the group that he thought it had killed his dog. Talking about these past practices gave way to a spontaneous truth and reconciliation process. Old-timers could speak of their crimes against nature, and the group could hold and witness the emergence of guilt, shame, and grief.

The public meetings also evoked anger and frustration at the refinery owners that could be expressed, heard, and contained by the group. The original refinery owners had retired to nice houses on the Texas coastline, and surrogate managers took the brunt of the aggression. But that did not matter; someone was doing something, and the town had a vision. A group came together, rented a basement office in a bank, and made plans to change the face of this part of town with an eighteen-hole golf course, a civic center, and a kayak run during the spring flood. As part of the remediation process, more than two thousand trees were planted to help break down and clean up the oil.

These are all transformational acts by the community to bring about the healing and beautification important to those who felt wounded by the experience. The company that created the problem invested in the town, and this felt right to the citizens. The revitalized town expressed hope for healing a scarred landscape and enjoying the river again. Is this an image of the transcendent function on the group scale? It certainly appears that way. This example highlights an ecological problem and demonstrates that the ecology has value and is a priority. In addition, it shows a town that was conscious of the need for revitalization and encouraged this through group responsibility so as not to lose the community's vitality. When one drives around Wyoming, it is not uncommon to see abandoned towns that no longer are vitalized by ranching or oil.

The cleanup of the refineries in Caspar is an example of how the group mind can commit to maintaining the life and history of a community, so that the Western lifestyle can continue. This, too, is a cultural complex rooted in environmental issues. Over the years, there were many public meetings for this project. At the larger meetings the group energy sometimes threatened to get out of hand, voices were raised, and the police officer who was always present paid more attention than usual. A group mind can coalesce and escalate quickly. At the smaller meetings, more people spoke of their feelings and relationship with the land. The trauma was readily apparent in the vacant glassy eyes, the looking away, the memories of finding dead wildlife trapped in the tar, the dead fish, and friends who died young of cancer. The one-on-one conversations are not unlike moments of analysis when intimate details are revealed and confessions are made and witnessed.

As part of the investigation of the river, we rafted downstream and watched the osprey fish for trout and blue herons stalk the reeds. The cleanup involved planting wetlands to replace those that had been lost, and the redwing blackbirds swayed and nodded with the tall grass in the breeze. It was as though the actual sign warning us not to eat too many fish had simply encouraged the fish to spawn and the wildlife to burgeon. The swallows used the sign as a perch from which to catch the spring aphids as they emerged from the shallows.

One of the unique aspects of this site, which is now a model or example used almost exclusively in WDEQ's Voluntary Remediation Program, is the collaborative process developed at Casper where all interested parties have a seat at the table. Residents who were part of the lawsuit were valued in the process. Experts answered questions about the complicated relationship between the oil at the refinery and the river. Throughout this process, which took several years, scientists were required to drop persona defenses and authentically relate to the public or risk being dismissed as not credible or disingenuous, compromising the collaborative process. A local breakfast restaurant near the former refinery was a place where all parties would meet with their own teams and technical consultants to plan for the day's activities. Breakfast meetings often became informal discussion groups or breakout meetings; parties would try out ideas and develop closer ties. In the end it was the authentic resolution of conflict through discussion and personal interactions that led to the selection of a remedy. This is not unlike two-person therapy, when the analyst becomes part of the process as a real human being who is touched and changed by the analysand's story.

Some of these relationships were poignant. Mr. C, a local resident who worked at the refinery, would attend carrying his oxygen tank. He always came with another elderly man who had worked with him. Mr. C was vocal at meetings and his heavy, labored statements and pauses to catch his breath always added emphasis to his opinions. Early in the process we talked during a break in a meeting. "You never forget your exposure," he said, and thinking back to my days in the laboratory I understood what he meant. When gas escapes to form a cloud that envelops you, you feel like you are drowning. Your lungs burn, your head spins, and you always wonder about long-term effects. He reminded me of my uncle who was gassed in the Great War. Over the course of the project Mr. C's lung cancer worsened, and it was only toward the end that I realized I had not seen him at meetings for a while. When his friend told me Mr. C would not see the beginning of the cleanup, we were both emotional about this news.

Through the collaborative process all voices were heard, and in 2002, the site cleanup procedures were selected and implemented, indicating that cleanup, restoration, and reconstruction was under way. This process demonstrates that when the public takes action, expresses its concerns, and has an imagination of what it would like to achieve, the affected group can bring about change.

From a psychological perspective, work at these sites shows that the exposed groups go through the same range of emotions as the individuals in the same situation, except that when the group settles on a particular direction, or image, it gains momentum and can prevail quite effectively in ways an individual cannot because of the collective power of the group. The tension created between the individuals/ communities and the responsible parties can ultimately lead to a creative solution where the public meeting process provides a forum or container for community exchange, discussion, and opportunities for the group to coalesce, both consciously and unconsciously. Within the group process at any of these sites, individuals can get their psychological needs met through grieving, talking about possibilities, and activating the imagination. Under these conditions, I have seen the transcendent function expressed within a group and in service of cleanup.

NOTES

1. C. G. Jung, "Psychology and Religion" (1938) in *The Collected Works of C. G. Jung,* vol. 11, *Psychology and Religion* (Princeton, NJ: Princeton University Press, 1958), § 131.

2. C. G. Jung, *The Collected Works of C. G. Jung,* vol. 6, *Psychological Types* (Princeton, NJ: Princeton University Press, 1971), § 825.

3. Placer gold mining is a technique that extracts gold from alluvium, or streambeds. It is one of the oldest mining techniques, used particularly by the ancient Romans, and one of the easiest because it does not require the crushing of hard rock (quartz) to retrieve gold deposits.

4. Agency for Toxic Substances and Disease Registry, Health Consultation for Silver Bow Creek/Butte Area, Silver Bow and Deer Lodge Counties, Montana, 2001, retrieved from http://www.atsdr.cdc.gov/hac/pha/pha.asp?docid=1232&pg=1#T1.

5. Cancer statistics from the Montana Department of Health; see http://www.dphhs.mt.gov/publichealth/cancer/documents/MortalityinSilverBowCountyandMontana.pdf.

6. Bill O'Hanlon and Bob Bertolino, *Even from a Broken Web: Brief, Respectful Solution-Oriented Therapy for Sexual Abuse and Trauma* (New York: John Wiley and Sons, 1998), p. 104.

CATASTROPHE
AND DREAMS

LUIGI ZOJA

Catastrophe is a "turning upside down" (Greek *katastrephein*, to overturn) of the world in which the individual finds himself. Catastrophic dreams reveal an extreme product of the unconscious, but also a continuity between the individual psyche and the surrounding world, and hence the collective psyche. In these cases an individual's dream can express the common suffering better than the complaints of the masses can. This implies another Jungian concept in addition to that of the collective psyche: at particular moments an individual's unconscious can produce "big dreams" whose images derive from the individual, but whose meaning belongs to the whole people.[1] How do you know if one of your dreams is big? The dreamer will know it instinctively: he is overcome by a feeling of collective participation.[2]

Luigi Zoja, Ph.D., is a former training analyst of the C. G. Jung Institute in Zürich, past president of the Centro Italiano di Psicologia Analitica, and former president of the International Association for Analytical Psychology (IAAP). He has taught at the School of Psychiatry, State University of Palermo, and at the University of Insubria and practiced in Zürich, New York, and Milan. He is the author of many papers and books, published in many languages, including *The Father* (2001), *Cultivating the Soul* (2005), *Ethics and Analysis* (2007), and *Violence in History, Culture and the Psyche* (2009).

This paper was first presented at the Fifth International Conference of Analytical Psychology and Chinese Culture, held June 6-10, 2012 at the University of Macau, Macau, China.

We usually feel that a dream is something intimate, even embarrassing, which we prefer to keep to ourselves, but in this case we feel uncomfortable if we don't share it with the community, to which it clearly belongs. When a man dreams of a collective catastrophe in which he is involved, he sinks into a Dantean hell, but at the same time he is elevated to a rare state of grace: he feels an instinctive, simple, indisputable sense of sharing.

In such cases, the overwhelming predominance of collective content over individual content makes a particular form of dream analysis possible: it makes sense to discuss such dreams even without possessing the associations and other amplifications that the dreamer can provide, indeed without even meeting him personally.[3]

Here we will examine two dreams of Primo Levi (1919–1987), a Jewish Italian writer who survived Auschwitz, and two of Michihiko Hachiya (1903–1980), the director of the Communications Hospital in Hiroshima, who survived the dropping of the first atomic bomb (*hibakusha*).[4] What follows is intended as a psychological discussion, not one of those comparisons between Auschwitz and Hiroshima which have already been the subject of much needless debate. Auschwitz was part of a deliberate and complex genocidal project; the bombing of Hiroshima was an intentional trial of a new weapon on a mass of civilians, so that historians and jurists reject the notion of genocide. Both, however, were examples of huge shared catastrophes. Levi created the concept of a grey area to discuss the ethical problems of Auschwitz: even there, good and evil were not as clearly distinct from one another as black and white, but overlapped. Dreams of catastrophe are a doorway into what is a moral problem before it is a clinical one. So this idea which embraces complexity applies all the more to Hiroshima: the American attack was monstrous, but from the general viewpoint of civilization victory by the United States was more desirable than that of the Axis.

Levi's chapter "Le nostre notti" ("Our Nights") in his book *Se questo è un uomo* (published in the U.S. as *Survival in Auschwitz*) describes dreams dreamed in a concentration camp, specifying that they recur in different ways: the same dreamer often had the same dream at different times; but the same dream might also be dreamed by a different person, at a different time or even at the same time.

Levi describes how he lies down on his bed. Each narrow pallet is shared by two prisoners; his neighbor is a stranger much bigger than him who falls asleep immediately, forcing him to sleep on the edge. After fruitless attempts to gain a few centimeters, Levi too falls asleep, exhausted; lacking physical space, he chooses psychic space, which seemingly even the worst of tyrants cannot take away from us.[5] His neighbor's snoring merges with the puffing of a locomotive which appears to him in a dream pulling the wagons unloaded by the prisoners during their daily work. Levi hears the whistle of a train, which is perhaps both real and dreamed, for trains travel by night as well as by day. It's a sound that forms a constant acoustic background to the obligations and sufferings of the camp. In the dream the train and the torments of Auschwitz cease to be images; they are transformed into a story which the dreamer tells to his sister and other loved ones.[6] He is at home; the surroundings and the fact of narrating to these people give him an almost physical enjoyment. But little by little the dream degenerates irremediably into a nightmare: no one listens to him, everyone is indifferent; they talk among themselves and his sister gets up and goes off without saying a word. At this Levi feels a "pure pain . . . like certain pains of early childhood," when you still lack any of the tools that might help you understand it and can defend yourself from it by attributing them to reality and life.[7] He rebels so strongly that he wakes up. At this point, although reality is the worst possible nightmare, he is still paradoxically tormented by his dream. He remembers that he has had this dream many times before. He remembers Alberto, his best friend in the concentration camp, telling him he had had the same dream, that in fact many, perhaps all, of the prisoners have it.

Everyone around him dreams. Their mouths emit noises, not because they want to express themselves, but because they dream that they are eating. The senses and needs of the tortured body continue to permeate the diaphragm between dream and reality. The little food they are given is diluted in watery soup. To attenuate their hunger they swallow as much of it as possible. So the night is filled with a constant trooping out to urinate. The sound of these walkers mingles with the dream, becoming a single, never-ending procession:

> It is us, grey and identical, as small as ants and as high as the
> stars, packed together, in infinite numbers right across the
> plain to the horizon; sometimes we are fused into a single
> substance, an anguished mixture in which we feel trapped
> and suffocated; sometimes we are walking around and around
> in circles, without a beginning or an end, with blinding
> dizziness and a tide of nausea.[8]

The impulses of the body are not the only things that oscillate
back and forth between dream and wakefulness. The whole of reality
acquires dreamlike characteristics; and dreams acquire very real
characteristics. The psychic force of modern man, accustomed to
keeping the two experiences clearly separate, can no longer prevent
them from coming together and being confused. The ego of the
dream is shaken and annihilated, just like the prisoner's ego in
reality. Their place is taken by a dreamlike fatalism. *Se questo è un
uomo* is one of the most well known and significant autobiographical
books of the twentieth century, not least because we feel in the
depersonalization of the author's dreams the universality of the
catastrophes that have devastated him. He delivers them to the
reader with the same solemnity with which, according to Jung, the
shaman shared his big dreams with the whole tribe.

The frequent oneiric repetition of a trauma is considered to be an
unconscious attempt to integrate a suffering that is too acute to be
accepted as part of one's psychic history. So we would expect the dreams
of the prisoners in the concentration camp to concern the greatest
traumas to which they are exposed: violence, the death of their
companions, their own daily exhaustion. Instead, their oneiric suffering
takes two disconcerting forms.

First, although by now Primo Levi is familiar with the dream of
his sister and his indifferent friends, he finds himself defenseless,
unprepared for its recurrence. The scenes always take him by surprise,
the suffering starts all over again. In a sense, the unbridgeable gap
between him and his loved ones, who behave as if they didn't know of
his existence, repeats in an interpersonal form the temporal gap in his
psyche. It is fragmented into compartments that lack continuity in
time: today's dreamer knows nothing of yesterday's dreamer, he has
learned nothing from having already had that dream. So the first form
of suffering is an irremediable splitting of experience itself.

The second is complete insignificance and alienation from a context of places and people in any family sense, which may be a translation into spatial terms of the split that the first form of suffering represented in time. Both in the first scene and in the following one, surprisingly, there is hardly any trace of the horrific physical sufferings that surround the dreamer. The prisoners are not far from the gas chambers and the crematory ovens, and the most trivial event might result in their torture and death; and yet the torment, which becomes unbearable and leads to awakening, is existential, almost an emblem of an ordinary day and an average inhabitant of an anonymous modern city, where *what is in danger is not physical life but psychic identity.* The real suffering is the lack of I-you relationships and of the integrity of the ego itself, which is reduced to the level of a ghost, an anonymous shade, a number. For on close analysis, this general absence of a human dimension is the collective terrain that has generated the individual sufferings in which they are immersed. The dreamer-prisoners swarm "like ants" and spread out "as far as the stars . . . as far as the horizon."[9] The anonymous mass floods the landscape, occupying every space in the scene. There is nothing else. The individual's solitude now corresponds to a world solitude. The world of the concentration camp is not a horrific medieval residue in modernity, but a laboratory that anticipates the anomie and alienation of postmodernity. The dream, so to speak, is not a self-analysis of a condition from which one disappears because death wins, but a prognosis of a return to normal life in which one disappears because anonymity wins: the disappearance of identity.

The dropping of the atomic bomb on Hiroshima is unparalleled as a catastrophe that history has concentrated at one point in time and space. Dr. Hachiya's diary, according to Canetti, embodies an incomparable humanity: in the depths of such a disaster we feel that others are the same as us.[10]

Dr. Hachiya's condition is formally very different from Levi's. Close to the hypocenter of the atomic explosion, hit by the radiation and by countless pieces of shrapnel which penetrate his flesh all over his body, the head of the Communications Hospital had his wounds briefly medicated.[11] But he resumed his work as director almost immediately. Unlike the prisoners in the concentration camp he was, on the face of it, free. But unlike the prisoners (who at least had a longer nocturnal rest in the winter: their work was in the open air and was impossible to do in the long northern nights because of the darkness), from this point on he had practically no rest.[12] His body was not a prisoner, but his time was. His work was never-ending: almost the whole city needed treatment, but most of the nurses and doctors had been killed. In addition, Hachiya frenetically wrote in a diary in his spare time. The population of Hiroshima had fallen into *koyodatsu*, a Japanese concept which indicates a state of extreme dejection and apathy.[13] In his mind, language itself needs to be reformulated. The words *recognize* and *identity* lose their function now that many people are so disfigured that they don't recognize themselves in the mirror; Hachiya realizes that he has lost any sense of the word *destruction* when he looks at his city: what can one talk about?[14] Although they share this state of mind, the functions of his ego seem intact: indeed he takes on what is the heaviest medical responsibility in all Japan.[15] We might suspect that he is prey to a maniacal reaction to events, but that is not the case: the details, and the memories of those who knew him, depict a man who always takes time to reflect and weighs every word carefully.

The doctor's diary contains two dreams, on the 24th and 31st of August.[16] During the early days images of untold sufferings were reported to him: one man burnt to a cinder was still sitting on his bicycle; many people ran along with skin hanging off their bodies like a scarecrow's rags; one man held his own eyeball in his hand: "Is it possible," the person who reported this to him asked, "that he could still see? That eye was staring at me."[17] Hachiya is bored by these anecdotes, but three days later that eye comes back to him in a dream. Significantly, the eye is at the center of many episodes of paranoid delirium; among the *hibakusha*, Lifton diagnoses a survivors' paranoia.[18] The survivors feel, so to speak, as if they are being observed and judged by a supernatural gaze. By what incomprehensible will has a whole mass of people been exterminated while they have been left alive? They feel as if they are being watched over by the invisible authority that decided this; they have been given their lives as a gift, but have not been given any explanation of why. They feel that they owe the dead a debt and are tormented by the possibility that someone may ask them to pay it.

In the dream of August 24 the doctor is in Tokyo, at the time of the great earthquake. Psychoanalysis teaches us that, faced with an impasse, the psyche returns to the archetype that provides familiar tools for processing it; so when a man meets a woman who disorients him, his unconscious will try to grasp the experience by dreaming of the woman who is the root of all his experiences: his mother. Here the person who has been afflicted by an evil that he feels is absolute dreams of a previously known prototype of the evil. For Hachiya this was the 1923 earthquake, of which he had certainly heard much talk in his youth. In the dream the streets are occupied by a mass of decaying corpses, turned toward him as if they were looking at him. An eye lies in the palm of one young woman's hand; suddenly it takes off and flies around in the sky, before coming back down to alight on him. The doctor looks at it, and it looks at him. The eye is an immense sphere which occupies the sky. He wakes up in terror.

Like Levi's anonymous mass of people, the immense eye concentrates a nameless suffering which comes to fill the entire horizon. It is menacing not because it threatens anyone but because there is nothing else, because it is meaningless and nameless. But this meaninglessness and this namelessness are the whole of the dreamer's psychic horizon. This condenses an existential condition into which the doctor, despite his outward efficiency, has started to slip mentally since the day of the explosion: time is liquefied, losing meaning; he feels an animalesque loneliness.[19]

On August 31, Hachiya dreams he is in Tokyo again: this continual movement toward the geographical and political center of Japan confirms that the dream is primarily an inner representation of the whole population's soul, rather than of the dreamer's personal soul. The American battleship *Missouri* is still anchored in the bay. The dreamer is part of an immense crowd that has come to watch the emperor go on board. (In fact, Japan's surrender was indeed signed on the *Missouri*, but by plenipotentiaries. By tradition the emperor, a divine figure, could not show himself in public or even speak on the radio, which everyone listened to at that time. On August 15, his subjects for the first time heard a radio broadcast of his voice: asking them to bear the unbearable, he announced the surrender. Hachiya perceptively noted that those crackling sentences had a far more devastating effect on people's minds than the bomb).[20]

The dream becomes increasingly vivid. The scene shifts back from Tokyo to Hiroshima, near the Communications Hospital and the fork in the river Ota, which is still remembered today as the hypocenter of the atomic explosion. The bodies of the dead or dying are heaped on the banks by the thousands. But the ship is preparing to leave. Then, as in Dante's hell, the bodies writhe and implore the ship not to take the emperor away; some jump into the water to stop it raising anchor. Again the dreamer wakes up in a cold sweat.

As in Levi's dream, despite the immediate presence of devastation, the unbearable trauma repeated in these two dreams is not that of the atomic explosion or the mass of dying people. In the first dream the anguish of the eye becomes everything. In the second the Japanese people become nothing: their voices are not heard, the loss of the emperor becomes the irremediable loss of the collective soul; an irrevocable separation between speaking mouths and unhearing ears. Only on the last day of his diary does Hachiya explain to an American official how his Buddhist faith has helped him: "I lost my house and all my possessions, I was wounded. But I and my wife are alive, while around us others died, and for this I am grateful."[21]

A stifling aspect of these dreams is the way in which they reflect everyday life as if in a mirror. Wakefulness seems to be the converse of the dream, and the dream the converse of wakefulness—identical but opposite, like an image seen in a mirror.[22] Levi feels relief when he escapes from a dream by waking up, and so does Hachiya. But just as this experience is possible, so is its converse. In discussing his own survival in the concentration camp, Victor Emil Frankl describes a prisoner having a nightmare.[23] His instinctive reaction is to wake him up. But he realizes that he would not be helping him: What is the point of taking him out of a nightmare to bring him back into the concentration camp? That a dream is, as Freud originally held, a mechanism whose function was to preserve sleep is considered by many to be a reductive interpretation; but it takes on a different perspective in a catastrophic situation from which anyone would like to escape, and seemingly at any price. Why "seemingly"? Because one doesn't escape by paying with one's life; it has often been noted that catastrophic conditions do not necessarily lead to an increase in the suicide rate.[24] The situation of extreme suffering in which one is immersed and the proximity of death do not seem to have a significant influence on voluntary decisions to die. Someone who lives in a catastrophe, despite his extreme depression, despite his being like a living dead man, will often say in retrospect that he felt a strong desire for life—release from the concentration camp or an end to the radiation. And when he was tempted by death, he often seems to have asked himself: Is death another dream, or another nightmare, which could be a mirror image of the tormented condition from which one wishes to escape at any price?

Dreams of catastrophe, then, almost seem to ignore the direct sufferings under which they were dreamed. Rather, they are a far broader emblem of the existential condition to which the dreamers have been reduced: as if their unconscious produced a self-representation of the inhuman anonymity in which the shattering experience that has enveloped them was planned and of the mental degeneration which risks making its perpetuation possible. Catastrophe, rather than causing a direct pathology limited to that catastrophe, reveals a general loss of meaning on the part of the individual. This process of revelation will be completed in the normal society to which he will return after the trauma, and, on more than one occasion, it will cause his death by delayed action.[25]

NOTES

1. C. G. Jung, "The Relations between the Ego and the Unconscious," in *The Collected Works of C. G. Jung*, vol. 7, *Two Essays on Analytical Psychology* (Princeton, NJ: Princeton University Press, 1953), § 250, note 2, and § 277.

2. *Ibid.*, § 277.

3. Although we refer to them as dreams, they might more accurately be described as nightmares. See my *Contro Ismene. Considerazioni sulla violenza [Violence in History, Culture and the Psyche]* (Torino: Bollati Boringhieri, 2009; English edition: New Orleans: Spring Journal Books, 2009), chap. 3; C. G. Jung, "The Spirit Mercurius," in *The Collected Works of C. G. Jung*, vol. 13, *Alchemical Studies* (Princeton, NJ: Princeton University Press, 1967), § 249.

4. Primo Levi, *Se questo è un uomo* (1947–1958), in *Opere I*, edited by Marco Belpoliti (Torino: Einaudi, 1997); in English: *If This Is a Man and The Truce*, translated by Stephen Woolf (Boston: Little, Brown,

1991). Michihiko Hachiya, *Hiroshima Diary: The Journal of a Japanese Physician, August 6–September 30, 1945* (1955) (Chapel Hill: University of North Carolina Press, 1995).

5. In fact Charlotte Beradt shows how situations of extreme politico-social restriction like that of Nazism have an effect on sleep, generating dreams emblematic of that collective anguish. See Charlotte Beradt, *Das Dritte Reich des Traums* (1966) (Frankfurt am Main: Suhrkamp, 1981), and her commentary, "Terror und Traum: Metodologische Anmerkungen zu Zeiterfahrungen im Dritten Reich," in *Vergangene Zukunft. Zur Semantik geschichtlicher Zeiten*, edited by Reinhardt Koselleck (Frankfurt am Main: Suhrkamp, 1979).

6. Anna Maria Levi, a very important figure "to whom Primo would remain closely attached all his life." Marco Belpoliti, Cronologia in *Opere I* (Torino: Einaudi, 1997), p. lxxiii.

7. Levi, *Se questo è un uomo*, p. 54.

8. *Ibid.*, p. 56.

9. *Ibid.*

10. Elias Canetti, "Dr. Hachiyas Tagebuch aus Hiroshima," in *Die gespaltene Zukunft: Aufsätze und Gespräche* (München: Carl Hanser Verlag, 1972), p. 58.

11. An American doctor who interviewed him when his diary was published in the United States ten years after the bombing noted that Hachiya bore marks of the explosion all over his body and that the mobility of one of his arms was impaired, but he still couldn't find the time to have an operation. William M. Hitzig, "Faith from the Inferno," *The Saturday Review*, August 6, 1955, p. 13.

12. Levi, *Se questo è un uomo*, "it's winter and the nights are long" (p. 51); "In winter the nights are long, and we are allowed a considerable amount of time for sleeping" (p. 52).

13. It may correspond to the mechanism that Lifton, using the language of American psychology, has called psychic numbing. Robert Jay Lifton, *Death in Life: Survivors of Hiroshima* (1968) (Chapel Hill: University of North Carolina Press, 1991), p. 506. If, however, we pursue the comparison with the prisoners of the concentration camp, it corresponds to the state of physical and psychic dejection that the prisoners described as becoming *Musselmen* (Muslims). Levi, *Se questo è un uomo*, p. 84 note; Viktor Emil Frankl, *Trotzdem ja zum Leben sagen:*

Ein Psychologe erlebt das Konzentrationslager (1977) (München: DTV, 1982), p. 40; Bruno Bettelheim, *Surviving and Other Essays* (1952) (New York: Vintage Books, 1980), p. 106.

14. Lifton, *Death in Life*, p. 26; Hachiya, *Hiroshima Diary*, p. 31.

15. Only on the first day after the explosion does he confess to having felt that he was beginning to feel "lonely with an animal loneliness, part of the darkness of night." Hachiya, *Hiroshima Diary*, p. 24.

16. That is, the eighteenth and twenty-fifth days after the explosion. Hachiya, *Hiroshima Diary*, pp. 114–115 and 145–146.

17. *Ibid.*, p. 101.

18. Lifton, *Death in Life*, pp. 512–516. See also my *Paranoia: La follia che fa la storia* (Turin: Bollati Boringhieri, 2011), chaps. 1 and 11.

19. The entry is dated August 6 (but he says he is not sure about the date and that it could have been the following day). Hachiya, *Hiroshima Diary*, pp. 8, 24.

20. *Ibid.*, pp. 81–82.

21. *Ibid.*, p. 229.

22. See Levi, *Se questo è un uomo*, p. 66.

23. Frankl, *Trotzdem ja zum Leben sagen*, pp. 52–53.

24. Although there has been some debate, there is general agreement on the question. Whereas Bettelheim (*Surviving and Other Essays*) oscillates, sometimes stating that suicide was not frequent in the concentration camps (p. 106), and sometimes stating that it was (p. 308), Levi is quite clear: people in the concentration camp didn't think of suicide. And the reason he gives is convincing. The prisoners were reduced to an almost animal form of existence, and animals can wait for death, but not actively choose it (interview by Alessandra Carpegna in *La Stampa*, May 24, 1983). Christian Goeschel, *Suicide in Nazi Germany* (London: Oxford University Press, 2009), notes a high suicide rate, but in small camps before the war (p. 78), and he repeatedly points out that statistics on the suicide rate were artificially exaggerated: they included extrajudicial executions (pp. 115, 126). See also Erwin Ringel, *Der Selbstmord: Abschluss einer krankhaften psychischen Entwicklung* (1953) (Eschborn bei Frankfurt am Main: Verlag Dietmar Klotz, 2008), p. 68; Herrman Langbein, *Menschen in Auschwitz [Hommes et femmes à Auschwitz]*

(1972) (French edition: Paris: Tallandir, 2011), pp. 128–133. Langbein cites at length testimonies of other authors, almost all agreeing with Levi's; he points out that Bettelheim knew the concentration camps, but not the extermination camps, and argues that Bettelheim is therefore a limited witness. Levi's arguments provide indirect confirmation of James Hillman's *Suicide and the Soul* (New York: Harper and Row, 1964): contemplating suicide may form part of a particularly complex process of identification, and as such is unlikely to occur when life is restricted to its most elementary features. From this point of view, the experience of Hiroshima is difficult to compare with that of the concentration camps, because the horror did not concern an interminable everyday existence but was concentrated in the dropping of the bomb, which led to the war ending within a few days. According to Lifton (The Survivor), however, as in the concentration camps, there was no significant rise in the suicide rate in Hiroshima (p. 507). Of course, this assessment leaves open a vast grey area of people who were so weakened that they died (because they couldn't keep going or because they had "chosen"' to stop living?): the *Musselmänner* in the camps and people affected by *koyodatsu* in Hiroshima.

25. Some authors well known for having written about the extermination camps and then living mentally with the aftereffects for a long time after their liberation, such as Primo Levi, Jean Amery, and Odette Abadi Rosenstock, committed suicide decades later.

CHILDREN'S DREAMS CAN SEE THROUGH

ROBERTO GAMBINI

DREAMS OF URBAN YOUTH

Many years ago, in 1997, I suggested to the board of directors of a school in São Paulo that an experiment be made. The main idea was to build a bridge between education and the unconscious by setting aside one hour every week dedicated to dream sharing in the classroom. The principals agreed, on the condition that this new activity be restricted to pre-elementary school, comprising some three hundred children age two to five or six. The experiment has revealed a dimension of the children's inner world that had never been taken into account by their teachers, as is the case with education in general in most schools around the world. This private school had been in operation for some thirty years, with a staff of highly trained teachers. I once asked them if they had any idea what kind of dreams those children might have, and the answer was that they had no idea at all. When they started collecting dreams and corresponding drawings, many of them were overwhelmed by the monsters, killings, dramatic scenes, and heroic acts that appeared every week as small groups gathered to tell their dreams. I have coached these teachers and followed their activities for years, observing all the beneficial effects this simple activity had, ranging from heightening the children's readiness

Roberto Gambini is a Jungian analyst in São Paulo, Brazil. His books include *Indian Mirror: The Making of the Brazilian Soul* and *Soul and Culture*.

to learn to widening the teachers' field of vision about the inner reality of their students. To date, more than twenty-five thousand dreams have been collected, which allows us to say that we now have an idea what are the main dream motifs of white, upper-middle-class children living in privileged conditions in the city of São Paulo. Their dreams correlate to the social class they belong to.

Nine years later, in 2006, I decided to try the experiment again, but at the other end of the social spectrum. Would the dreams of underprivileged children, living in a poor and dangerous environment, present the same motifs and images as my original sample? So, I went to Rio de Janeiro to talk to a schoolmaster in one of the largest favelas of the Marvelous City.

Favelas are, in some ways, like fortified citadels; the few entrances are kept under strict surveillance by the drug traffic security agents. My guide, a friend who had been training teachers in fundamental health care, and I had to be picked up at Rio's airport by a taxi driver who had free pass, being herself a resident of the "community" (the word *favela* has become politically incorrect, even offensive to those who dwell there). The school head accepted my proposal, and I trained, on that first day, a group of some twenty teachers. It was necessary to be quick and practical. They were asked first to try to relax their students in any way they saw fit, for example, by having them lie on the floor listening to music. The dreams had to be recorded verbatim, accompanied by a drawing on the other side of the page. That was all. They got the main idea: dreams were to be told and not interpreted. We just wanted to know what these children dream of.

A few weeks later a huge package came in the mail containing around four hundred dreams. I studied them and tried to organize the material, as I had done years ago with the larger sample from the affluent children. What a surprise! One hundred dreams, more or less, had to do with violence, and another quarter of the sample were dreams depicting environmental degradation. So from the beginning, I had to wonder why is it that in the Jungian tradition there is so little theoretical attention given to the relationship between the unconscious and social structure.

As I examined the dreams and attempted a working classification of them, I began by trying to empathize with the feeling atmosphere, before adopting the analytical attitude. Of the dreams with the motif of violence, two especially stood out. So on my second visit to the school in Rio, I asked the principal to tell me who those kids were; in the case of these two dreams, I felt I needed some biographical data, which was not the general rule. I was referred to a woman who knew all the students, and her reaction was very interesting. When I asked her who these two children were, she was very surprised and replied: "But Dr. Gambini, do you have a crystal ball?" And then: "Among all others, you picked up the only two children whose fathers are rival drug traffic chiefs. One has an adolescent daughter, and the other a nine-year-old son. How could you possibly know?" I simply said: "I knew nothing about them. It was because of their dreams."

In a brief survey of the subsample of dreams in which violence is the central motif, we hear short and radical stories, accompanied by corresponding images. "I dreamed that my uncle was shot and I was with him." "While I was dying, I raised from my bed and cried loud 'Dad, Mom,' but no one answered." In his drawing, the dreamer shows several people being shot, and one can see a thin line representing the course of a bullet before it reached his body and killed him. This dream works with two moments of extremely accelerated time, which nonetheless allow him a minimal fraction of a second to cry out for help, and no help came. So this must represent an inner state to which most of the children living in the community have adapted, namely, living with the feeling—or fear, or high probability—that death could come any moment, any time, a common occurrence of daily life. Imagine a child trying to concentrate while listening to the teacher trying to teach them some math exercise with this image in the mind's background. It could be observed that most teachers complain that the pupils get distracted, looking out the window and paying no attention to what the teacher is saying, with an understanding that some disciplinary measure should be taken. I wonder if the teachers also look out the window while they teach. They might, and the reason would be the same.

Another example of a dream is minimal and expresses the awful awareness that there will be a total lack of protection in the event of imminent danger of being shot: "Help, help, help." That is the whole dream, just this repeated word. Another dream: "I dreamed that I was dead." In his drawing, the boy is lying on the floor, surrounded by a group of passive adults looking at him.

It should be kept in mind, while we try to empathize with the inner experience of children assaulted by these frightening images during sleep, that they are only six to nine years old. In the following material we have a piece of important information about the origin of such frequent and gratuitous shooting that appears in so many dreams. A boy reported: "In my dream I was returning home from my *capoeira* class [*capoeira* is an Afro-Brazilian type of fighting]. The police was after me, but I was innocent." The first traumatic event, whether in dreams or in actual situations, is that an innocent child can, for no reason, be shot to death. The other factor, which must be highly confusing if the goal is a clear understanding of the rules of the world, is the illogical bias that contaminates a child's progressive attempt to make some sense of what is right and what is wrong, a bias created by the criminal and ambiguous attitude of the police force, officially presented to the youngsters as a law-enforcing power, a promoter of justice, law, and order. In fact, the students we met feared the police and their black van painted with the emblem of a skull even more than they feared drug dealers.

The next dreams elaborate the situation still further, posing the problem of a dangerous, but lucrative, working relationship with drug dealers: "I had this dream twice. I accepted a bag given to me by a stranger and the guys came after me. They shot at me several times and I died." This is a bag of cocaine, and it has appeared in several dreams. It was this dream that caught my attention when I first began examining the material. The boy's father is the second most powerful drug lord. For other boys, the dream conflict is different: they are shot if they refuse to take the bag. This is a crucial moment in which one must be able to say yes or no, but neither answer gives the youngster any sense of security, since death may result in either case. We would prefer that these boys say no. But can they, psychologically speaking? Don't their dreams tell us that, unprotected and left alone, they are facing an impossible dilemma?

Even the presence of a concerned mother in the dream, or in real life, giving good advice to her son, is of no avail. One boy reported: "I dreamed that a man wanted to hand me a small bag. My mother told me not to accept it, but I did. Then the police arrested me and shot me dead." Sometimes it is the police, sometimes it is the drug dealers who shoot. And the mother (fathers never appear in this role) has no influence at all. The aspect of psychic energy devoted to self-preservation at any cost occupies such an enormous part of these young boys' and girls' inner worlds that other archetypes of the soul have no chance to make an appearance.

In the other dream that initially caught my attention, the dreamer, an adolescent girl, is the daughter of the chief drug dealer in this community. In her words: "In my dream my parents were having a fight and my mother jumped through the window." I made a comparison between this dream and another collected at the upper-class private school in São Paulo, in which a boy dreamed that his mother threw a spider out of the window. Both dreams are drawn taking place in an apartment building, with an amazing structural similarity. The boy's mother is represented as being positive to his development, as she helps him to get rid of his nocturnal fears, symbolized by the spider, a weaver of uncontrollable fantasies. As for the girl, she has not nocturnal, but daylight fears about her mother's physical integrity, and therefore lacks any sense of protection from her mother, who in her dream commits suicide.

Alongside the motif of violence, the theme of ecological angst, to my great surprise, appeared in equal proportion, that is, one fourth of the whole sample. And in this context a synchronicity has to be recognized. The dreams dealing with the motif of ecological disaster, which were delivered to us in São Paulo in December 2006, precede by two months the publication in Brazilian newspapers, on February 3, 2007, of the official report on the conclusions reached by an international forum working on the subject of global climatic changes. This joint work of 2,500 scientists deals with topics such as increase of temperature, greater incidence of hurricanes, polar ice melting, and the increasing rise of ocean levels, clearly linking these dangerous changes to human activity, especially deforestation and gas emissions from burning fossil fuel. It seems to me that, coinciding in time, the dreams of children living under aggressive conditions produced the same diagnosis. So, in order to further our hypothesis about a deep connection between dreams and social structure, we could here consider the possibility that children who are suffering psychologically, as a result of devastating conditions in their physical and psychological environment, are deeply connected to the sufferings of the earth. It seems that one function of the unconscious, that of signaling imminent danger, runs through the channel of common wounds.

What I came upon in my research was a ghostly series of frightening images. "I dreamed of a queer beast in the water." It is not a fish, but a composite figure displaying bird traits combined with four legs, walking on the sea surface. Such a water animal might be expected the dreams of indigenous children, who live in a more natural environment (as we will examine further in the next section), but in that of a child from one of Rio's poorest suburbs? In this case, both the meaning and the context are of another nature; such an animal is mythological and can only be the announcement that a new mythology of incoming catastrophe is on the make. In this context, this beast is an alien or a bizarre Darwinian mutation. I submit that there are alien, unheard of psychological intrusions taking place in the inner world of some of our young ones.

"I dreamed that my house turned into a sea." In this boy's drawing there is a blue whale, a yellow shark, some rays, and many small fish. Why would one's house turn into a sea? A house, a home, needs an earthy basis, with roof, walls, doors, and windows, warmth, protection, father, and mother. When the house changes into a limitless expanse of water, inhabited by predators like the shark, the whole cultural creation of "home" disappears. If nature is our home, what is changing it into something that consciousness cannot figure out?

A dream by a ten-year-old girl: "I was journeying with my family and then everything disappeared and turned into a desert." If in the previous dream the unconscious is attuned to global warming, the rising sea level, and the acidification of the oceans, here it registers the threat of desertification, the gradual disappearance of fertile soil for agriculture and food supply. For this girl, the image is one of abandonment, loss of vital bonds, and the shocking situation of having to go on living in a devastated land, in a true wasteland. Does this dream originate in a particular problem of this girl, or is she unconsciously expressing a threat on a much larger scale?

We have this report by a boy: "I dreamed that the sun had disappeared, and I went searching for it because it was already 10 a.m. After some time I found it again." This child is perhaps dreaming of a startling and unexplained alteration of the rotation of the earth around the sun or a thickening of the atmosphere keeping the sun from view. Ten a.m. refers to a previous condition of normality, because the perception of time depends on the absolutely ordinary fact that the sun rises predictably and regularly. If the sun is not where it is expected to be at the appointed time, what is happening with Time? What is happening to the very principles and laws that rule the cosmos? What can one do, or feel, or think, at the mere suggestion that natural events are running astray? The experience of awe conveyed by this poor child's dream echoes a similar experience our ancestors must have had even before language was invented to express their horror whenever the sun disappeared during a daytime eclipse.

Dreams of the Kamaiurá

Now we will travel to another world and visit an indigenous tribe called the Kamaiurá. Although they came into contact with Western culture more than a hundred years ago, their culture today is practically intact. They live in the central area of Brazil, close to the Xingu River, an affluent of the Amazon, in the state of Mato Grosso. German anthropologist Karl von den Stein was the first to visit them in 1884, but it was not until 1946, when governmental policy launched a westward march, that the first official settlement was established in the area, followed by the opening of roads. In 1961, the Xingu National Park was created, an immense territory measuring 27,000 square kilometers, in which 5,500 people belonging to fourteen different tribes could preserve their traditional way of life, relatively protected from invasion by loggers or farmers in the vicinity looking to expand their huge farms. Together, the tribes form a sort of native confederation, practicing intertribal marriages, as well as exchange of artifacts and ritual gatherings and festivals. They speak different languages or dialects and have their own mythological systems. Every tribe has a shaman, generally an older man, who has the task of transmitting to the younger generations their mythological heritage, which, together with possession of a territory, is some guarantee that their identity is not destroyed.

Carmen Junqueira, one of the leading Brazilian anthropologists, began studying the Kamaiurá in the early 1960s, and it is to our friendship that I owe the privilege of having received permission from the shaman Takuman to research their children's dreams. Takuman, now eighty years old, is relatively well informed about the outside world and is able to keep alive the traditional Kamaiurá life. He only dresses up for certain occasions, most of the time living nude, which only indigenous are able to do with dignity. I visited his village twice, in 2006 and 2008, and explained my project with children's dreams to him. He had an understanding of my work as a therapist, being himself a specialist in the field of dreams.

Takuman instructed the children, about fifteen of them, to gather every morning in a hut used as a school, where they learn to read and write in their own language, for the purpose of telling me their dreams with the help of a translator. I handed out sheets of paper and colored pencils for drawing, as I had done in previous fieldwork. Takuman was interested to hear what the children were dreaming so at the end of my stay I gave him my general impression of their highly positive psychological situation. He always laughed when I reported each day the dreams I had heard, but he never said what he had seen in them and never asked me for my interpretation. But his help was crucial in the case of two dreams that I was not able to understand using our symbolic codes, since they referred to Kamaiurá myths. After he told me about the myths I could understand the purpose of those two dreams, as we will shortly see.[1]

A typical behavior, which can be observed in any tribe, is that mothers carry their babies for most of the day, when they go out to gather food and during their other daily chores. The mother carries her baby close to her naked body, with the help of a cotton band worn diagonally across the chest, in a position makes it possible for the baby to reach the breast at will, leaving it free to suckle intermittently at will, without any restriction from the mother. One could say the baby owns the breast and has its mother entirely for itself for at least a year or two. If the mother has another child, the older one can give its place to the newborn without further difficulties simply because it has had enough of what was needed to acquire emotional self-confidence. Small children are calm and peaceful, and in the same way the role of the mother can be played by any woman if necessary at a given moment, the older children take care of the small ones. What one sees in the village is a group of self-sufficient children helping each other and enjoying each other's company to amuse themselves. Only if a child has a serious problem will it cry out for mother's help. The mothers are not overly anxious about protecting their young from learning through experience. Being aware of this dynamic from earlier fieldwork with another indigenous tribe, the Zoro, I was curious to learn what the Kamaiurá children might dream of.

I made two visits, collecting fifty-five dreams altogether. As was to be expected, the dream motifs here differ completely from previous collections and portray images of growing up quickly and performing adult tasks, learning, being courageous, facing danger without protection from adults, and being heroic. All the dreams are staged in the village and its surroundings, at the lake and in the woods. All the dreams have a lysis, there are no threatening figures, and, most important, parents play no active role in these dreams.

A six-year-old boy tells his dream: "I went to a hut in the bush and found a pig. I threw an arrow, killed it, cut it open with a knife, roasted it, and everybody ate it." Of course, at this age, the boy is not capable of doing all these things, but in waking life he will soon be participating is such an activity. Boys and girls mature early as a matter of survival; at thirteen, they can already have children. Coming of age is not a psychological event, but the general rule according to cultural provisions. So the boy dreams today of himself tomorrow, and there is no arrogance in that.

Similarly, a small girl dreams: "I went to the clearing in the bush to uproot some manioc, I put it all in a basin on top of my head, then I fell into a hole and broke my leg." Maybe because she is still too small, she falls at the end of her task. But she faces the accident alone, without crying for mother's help; her dream ends with her broken leg as something that simply happens to one. A boy, five at the most, reported: "I went fishing, caught some fish, took it home, grilled it and gave to my mother and brother, and they ate it." The image of feeding the adults is of special relevance, both in the dream and in real life, for it marks the beginning of independence and cooperation. Someone who is able to feed others is a valuable member of the tribe and a provider of life's continuity.

The children dream of daily life in their village, of things and beings that belong there, which indicates adaptation and integration to present life as it is. Accompanied by a carefully executed drawing depicting the village in detail, a girl dreamed that she was dancing there in the open center. One might disregard this as a banal dream, but in its simplicity it shows how psychologically healthy it is to love the place one belongs to and to be able to express this feeling publicly. This girl is a true flower of her culture; she is happy to be Kamaiurá, to be as she is. What inner state is more likely to promote growth than this? Similar dreams: "I sat under a tree to eat a tangerine." "I had a parrot perched on my arm. I fed him, put him on a tree branch, and went to the lake shore to play there."

Three final dreams contain another kind of material. The first is told by a six-year-old boy, who volunteered to start this experiment of sharing dreams in my first meeting with the group. Perhaps he was excited, knowing that he had something interesting to tell: "I stepped into a canoe and went out to fish in the lake, and then the water animal appeared. It came after me. I rowed fast to the shore, stepped out, and ran to my house." He drew three different moments in the dream: standing in the center of the village, then walking to the lake shore, and then meeting two water animals. With the help of the interpreter, I asked him what this water animal was, and he said, "It is a water pig." At the time, I thought, well, here we are in a mythical ground, and I don't know what this is. How will I understand this dream? The first action, going out to fish, is comprehensible in the light of previous dreams in which boys or girls anticipate their imminent maturity. But this dream has a different atmosphere, with the appearance of a mythic element.

I went to Takuman for assistance. He listened to the dream and immediately said: "This is very dangerous. The boy cannot go so far into the lake. What he did is wrong. If the boy had told me this dream, I would not let him go there, it is too dangerous." "Why so?" I asked. "Because near the shore one can swim, play, or fish, but if you go to that faraway place, there is where the spirits that inhabit some animals live. Here in our big lake there are three underwater villages, one is of wild pigs, the other of jaguars, and the third of armadillos." When I asked him to tell me this story of villages, he went on: "They exist, under the water there are villages with houses, hammocks, fire, and in each one live some of those animals I told you." I wanted to hear more about whether Takuman considered them to be real animals or not, and he said: "They appear as animals except for the shaman. To me, what I see is a spirit, a *mamaé*. To the others, they are an illusion that

is real. This spirit is very nasty because it does not want anybody to
get too close; he kills you if you do that. You have to respect the laws
of nature, isn't that so?"

In the boy's dream, what has he really done? He transgressed a
mythical taboo. Anthropologists teach us that myths in all preliterate
societies are transmitted orally, from time immemorial, from generation
to generation. This function is performed by the older people of the
tribe, the shaman being the one who knows all the details and the
proper narrative, as he heard it from the previous shaman who taught
him everything he knows. In the cosmology of the Kamaiurá there are
three times: 1) mythic time, in which the creation of the world and of
man takes place; 2) the time of the elders, in which events prior to
contact with white men's culture occurred; and 3) present time, from
the moment of contact onward. In their myth of origin, the civilizing
god Mavutsinin, who is still alive and lives an enchanted place called
Morená where three rivers join their waters to form the Xingu
(Takuman tells me that whenever he goes to this place he can see
Mavutsinin), took five tree trunks, made four little holes in each,
and then inserted twigs in the place of arms and legs. These trunks
he turned into the Kamaiurá, to whom he gave bows and arrows,
and he taught them all they know: from planting to weaving cotton
for hammocks, from clay gathering to making pots, from hunting to
cooking, from knowing herbs to curing. The myth is long and detailed,
having "chapters" explaining the conflicting relationship between the
siblings sun and moon, the origin of day and night, of fire, what
happens after death, where the souls go to, and the role of good and
bad spirits. So the mythology about the *mamaé* and the underwater
villages are part of this much broader narrative.

It must have been in the time of the elders that an interesting
mythic variation took form, explaining that the Kamaiurá and the
whites were created together and in the same way. Mavutsinin wanted
them to live as twins. In another version, he scarified the skin of a
Kamaiurá and with his blood created a white man, with the intention
of them living together in a very large village by the enchanted waters
of the Morená. Mavutsinin created two types of weapons and presented
them for both to choose: the black bow and a fire weapon (gun). His
intention was that the Kamaiurá should choose the second, but the
reverse happened. Mavutsinin got very angry and told the Kamaiurá

to choose the rifle, but they were enthralled by the arrow, so the white man ended up with the stronger weapon. Perhaps anticipating the danger of future domination, and his plan of a mixed village having failed, he sent white men away to a remote place and ordered the Kamaiurá to stay in the area where they had been created. To the Kamaiurá he gave fish and manioc, and to the whites he gave rice, grease, bricks, knives, axes, and a long list of goods. So this myth explains to the Kamaiurá that whites have superior technology by will of the creator god, a fact to be accepted as coming from a higher order of determination, but the important element is the forsaken divine project of a life in harmony between different people, which the Kamaiurá still accept as a possibility (demonstrated, for instance, in the way they welcome white researchers and people who are really their friends). But they are quite aware, since the time of the elders, that whites can destroy them.

But why would the Kamaiurá disregard the possibility of future confrontation, becoming enchanted by the black bow, knowing full well that the other weapon would be so clearly effective for hunting? It must have been, it seems to me as I try to penetrate the spirit of the myth, that Kamaiurá were created to be Kamaiurá and to remain so forever. Their choice of the black bow meant that they were created with the capacity to choose on the basis of their own nature, of their own way of understanding life and the world. So this mythical disobedience, like that of Adam and Eve, is the very basis of a certainty that they have had a clear identity since the moment they were created—that what makes them what they are is precisely the way they understand the world and how life should be lived from their own perspective, that is to say, supported by their mythology. The preservation of living myths in consciousness and in the unconscious is therefore the sine qua non for Kamaiurá to remain Kamaiurá, even if they drink Coca-Cola or absorb elements from Western culture. They even have guns today, and they use them alongside bows and arrows.

This is the imaginal and actual context of the boy's dream about the water animal. Myths have been transmitted orally from a very remote past and are alive in the unconscious, and because they are alive they respond, through a dream, to a situation of transgression and its dangers (the water animals chasing the boy). If the unconscious has a compensatory dialogue with consciousness, this dream might indicate that for the Kamaiurá children of the present there may be a growing number of lacunae in the conscious integration of mythical narratives, which depend upon a feeling of resonance with the shaman's stories. A lack of resonance is certainly a result of the way acculturation is taking place since the introduction of diesel generators and television sets.

I observed that young kids, when watching TV, could not follow the stories told in American films or the very popular Brazilian soap operas, but they are fascinated by commercials for tennis shoes, bicycles, cell phones, watches, sunglasses, hair creams, and Bermudas shorts, and girls get excited about cosmetics, hairdos, fashion, and the behavior of urban girls. The fact that Kamaiurá are curious about and desirous of our society's goods and gadgets is no novelty. It was first recorded in a letter written in 1500 by the first Portuguese explorers who expected to receive gold and silver in exchange for their cheap gifts of mirrors and beads. Whenever there was contact, it always began with an offering of gifts such as mirrors, metal cooking pans, combs, knives, and axes, along with rice, grease, sugar, and clothes. These objects, once accepted, soon became part of the Kamaiurá way of life. But these are things. What the young are being offered now is the subtle mythological narrative that a pair of tennis shoes, or sunglasses, or lipstick, makes one happy.

In the course of unpacking all the implications of this dream, as well as the one that follows, I formulated the hypothesis that the mythical stories told by the shaman are losing their magnetic power to entice fantasy and imagination in the face of the overwhelming efficacy of advertising narratives that have become a strong stirring force in the imaginal world, cleaving the space for growing lacunae in mythical scripts. It was not the rifle after all, that has proven to be the great menace, but an attack on the roots of Kamaiurá mythical imagination.

I think Takuman understood this new situation immediately when I asked him to interpret the boy's dream. The worried and sad expression on his face was a sign of this newly acquired awareness, knowing, as he did, that the young were becoming less interested in the stories he had to tell. He knows well how to deal with evil spirits, but what should be his attitude toward this surreptitious poisonous snake sneaking into the young Kamaiurá minds? How can he counterattack it? He is getting old. His successor will not be his son, who is quite fluent in Portuguese and clearly becoming a political man, interested primarily in making money through the tribe's contact with our civilization. Instead he chose his daughter, Nekumalu, who still bares her breasts and speaks no word of our language. Women shamans are a rarity but have existed in the past. Does he intuit that a feminine approach to contemporary challenges to the tribe's identity might be more effective than the male shamanic tradition?

The next dream was also told by a six- or seven-year-old boy and is also an indicator of a deep problem taking place at the unconscious level: "In my dream I awoke at night and went outside of my house to take a pee. Then I looked up at the sky and saw the eclipse of the moon." Here again, it was obviously wrong to interpret this dream with Middle-Eastern, Greek, Nordic, Hindu, Japanese, African, alchemical, or any other symbolism one might want to project onto this indigenous boy's eclipsed moon, so I again turned to Takuman for help. One thing I knew about Kamaiurá customs is that if you had physical needs at night, researchers included, you stayed close to the hut's outside wall and avoided going too far in the dark because a bad spirit might be stalking you. Looking at the sky also seemed quite innocent. I had to find out if there was a mythical lacuna here too, and what was the specific implication of this night sighting of an eclipse.

Takuman was as concerned about this dream as he had been about the other and immediately stated: "It is very dangerous to look at the moon during an eclipse. The moon is not very high up, it is quite close to us.[Sun and moon, as twins, are the offspring of one of Mavutsinin's daughters, and there is a whole epic about them, involving the jaguar and several metamorphoses.] The eclipse is because the moon is menstruating and the dripping blood can fall on anyone down here, looking stupidly at her without the necessary protection. This boy could not do that." So here we have another mythological transgression.

Takuman's immediate reaction was to express his conviction that he had to insist that children should be interested and pay more attention when listening to his storytelling. As I did in the favela in Rio, advancing the hypothesis that poor or underprivileged children are unconsciously linked to the earth's sufferings, here we may conjecture that children's dreams may be an indicator of deep dangers threatening cultural survival. Myths cannot be broken, nor ignored. They are the uniting force, the only one that can enable these ancestral populations to resist the assault of white civilization's greed for their land or the unforeseen consequences of new roads, huge agricultural projects, or the construction of power plants in their vicinity. Only supported by myth will they be able to continue to choose the black bow.

Another dream, told by a boy nine to ten years old, also depicts a mythic element, but in this case the dreamer is aware of the meaning of the oneiric scene: "In my dream I saw some kind of animal behind my house. Then I fainted. It was not a real animal, but a spirit, the soul of a deceased person." Here there is no transgression and no innocence. Quite the contrary, it is the living myth in the unconscious that explains to the boy what he experienced in the dream. Takuman found this dream somewhat reassuring.

The last dream in our research leads us to other thoughts and concerns. Meri is a sweet girl approaching puberty. In her words: "I was chewing a sugar cane stick under the parabolic antenna. The antenna fell over me. A snake appeared and bit my foot." Some years ago, this antenna was installed behind Takuman's house as a gift after he gave his permission to a powerful TV station to film the ritual for the dead (*kuarup*), during which neighboring tribes come to the Kamaiurá village for an impressive funeral festival. This antenna was truly a Trojan horse hiding the enemy in its belly, and the image of a snake bite on one's foot is archetypal, be it Greek or indigenous Brazilian. In the dream, the girl is innocently enjoying something sweet (though bad for her teeth; sugar is also a white present), unaware of any predictable danger. There were other snake dreams in this series, but in this one we have the two symbols, one for a danger that all children know about (the snake), and another for a less obvious danger, seductive technology (the antenna, which makes TV transmissions possible). The girl is ignorant of the fact that technology in her village can be a poisonous snake, but as we have seen, it introduces a cleavage in the young generation's imaginal world. Her dream further elaborates the threat to her sense of identity and tribal belonging. What it says here is that our society hides a danger for her, which weakens her standpoint, her very contact with her reality.

DREAMS OF THE PATAXÓ

Our last sample comes from the Atlantic coast, in the southern part of Bahia, where the Pataxó have lived since the sixteenth century— that is to say, they were already there when the land was "discovered" by Portuguese explorers. My contact with them, as in the previous cases, was made possible by a friendship, in this case with Iani Petrovitch, a very devoted woman who decided to found a nongovernmental organization called the Institute of Young Tribes. Her aim is to work with young descendants of the Pataxó so that they would not forget where they come from and who they are. As many readers certainly know, the conquest of the Americas is a bloody and cruel story marked by genocide, cultural destruction, decimation of indigenous populations, and theft of the lands they lived on from time immemorial. In the old town of Porto Seguro, where I met with a group of Pataxó youngsters, there are today four scattered Pataxó settlements; originally they owned a continuous territory that was, step by step, overtaken by land seekers. If this institute had not been started more than a decade ago to revive the idea that there is a history, a culture, and a valuable dignity to regain and preserve, these survivors would be inevitably marching toward assimilation into the lowest social strata of the larger society. The Pataxó neighborhoods do not look indigenous, not like the magnificent villages that can be visited in the Xingu National Park; they look like any poor neighborhood in any Latin American town.

The young folk who have been coming to this organization's meetings for years learn how to sing in the Pataxó language or dance in their traditional way taught by the elders or take part in workshops to keep alive the old skills of bead weaving, body painting, and clay modeling. They could live in any coastal town and pass for urban citizens, rather than Pataxó, since they look very trendy and up to date, are fluent in Portuguese, and attend school; many of them have jobs in offices, shops, tourist attractions, or in positions that require knowledge of computer technology. So for them what is happening, through intelligent and empathic effort, is the rehabilitation of a lost identity that might become again their first and predominant one. But on some occasions I had the impression that they had two personas and could choose which one would fit a given situation, or that they learned how to impersonate a Pataxó. Maybe the process of retrieving lost roots is really more intricate than one is led to believe.

On my third visit to Porto Seguro, in 2010, I proposed that a mixed group spend a whole morning with me under an old mango tree in one of the reserves. I say mixed because white people working with them also participated, as did some Afro-Brazilian descendants who have become their allies in many acts for civil rights. So this sample is more indicative of the whole Brazilian society, with the impressive mixture that characterizes our people and our culture. After hearing fifteen dreams, I noticed that something like a mosaic appeared, a common symbolic field, as there was some interconnection between dream motives, for example, the image or symbol of something new emerging out of decayed matter in the dreams of a Pataxó youth and a white educator. This phenomenon has been observed in dream-sharing groups in several countries.

I will briefly mention a few dreams to give the reader a general idea and then concentrate on a very important one told by a young Pataxó man. The woman who leads the organization had a dream in which her present conflict was exposed through an image of an upside-down bride standing on her hands. Privately, she told me that she cannot go on working in the present institutional framework, always trying to get some help from governmental agents, wasting energy with endless technical reports and feeling constrained to limit the scope of her projects. An old Pataxó woman dreamed that her daughter, who in reality has joined a Pentecostal church, abandoned her and would not listen anymore to what she had to say. Talking to the group, she said her daughter thought it was a mistake to insist in this folly of an indigenous identity, that for her this was finished, proposing that her mother also join the church. In the dream, she says to the daughter that she wants to stay where she belongs.

One of the educators, who works specifically on the subject of cultural preservation, dreamed that he had to go into the sea but was terribly afraid and anguished. He said this motif was recurrent, and when asked by the group what he was so afraid of, he said he was afraid of spirituality. Talking to him privately, he told me he knew the importance of indigenous religion but feared that some so-called shamanistic healing practices were too uncanny for him, and yet he had to theorize about it and defend it in his workshops with Pataxó youngsters. That was his anguish.

Out of the fifteen dreams, one really stands out. It points directly to the core symbolism and the real psychological difficulty of regaining a lost cultural identity as an inner, centering experience and not just as a second persona. The dreamer, a young man in his early twenties, is bilingual and very articulate. In his dream he and two companions had to go to the airport. Some white men offered them a ride in their car, but he refused, saying he and his companions would rather walk. As they followed the road, they had to climb a steep muddy slope. Transparent water was running down. He saw a hole filled with water in the ground and knelt down to look into it. At the bottom there lay an old Pataxó clay pot. While he was using a stick to bring out the pot, the white men appeared again, shouting at him that he should leave that business aside, as they had to hurry to the airport.

Here we can see clearly that the possibility of contacting the old indigenous soul is constellated in the unconscious. But a conflicting counter-tendency is also activated. It might be a resistance on the part of the "white" component of the Pataxó psyche, that is, their adapted side, which is surely instrumental for survival, acceptance, adaptation, respect, assimilation, job opportunities, and so on. Going to the airport and flying away to somewhere else is in total contrast with kneeling down and finding something submersed in a hole in the ground. In this connection, we might also consider that only a minority of the larger society understands and supports the courageous quest of a group of Pataxó youngsters to be accepted and respected for what they are, first of all by themselves. The larger part of society in fact would prefer that the indigenous disappear as such and that their land be liberated for sale or direct use by the rest of the population. It would be a naive mistake to imagine that Brazilian collective consciousness has a correct historical and ethical perspective through which to understand the indigenous dilemma. Many sectors of society simply ignore it, while others fight against indigenous rights. So this dream might be pointing to two adverse forces, one in the inner world of the Pataxó themselves, another emanating from outside reality.

I asked the dreamer if there were clay pots in his house. The answer was no, neither his mother nor his grandmother cooked in such traditional vessels. But could they make one, if they wished? No, they had never learned how to do it. He then said that he had seen such an old clay pot once, when a relative was digging a hole in their yard to set a wooden pole. The pot was broken, and they glued the pieces together. Then the grandfather said: "If this pot was here, it is because there were Indians living here in the past."

In our group under the mango tree, we then talked about archaeology, and I suggested to the educator that they could look at books in which many of these pots can be seen, coming from all parts of our country, all dated and identified. The dreamer then said he would like to study archaeology; perhaps they could start a workshop. If they found an old native woman who still remembered how the Pataxó made their pots, they could then learn again. Here the dream speaks clearly, there being no need to introject any external content; it says that the core of a lost identity is still alive and lies in the depths of the indigenous psyche (the hole filled with water). The main task to be pursued is to bring back to consciousness what once was there and is already within reach, not so far from the surface. But one has to kneel down to the buried ancestral soul, valuing it for what it is. This old clay pot is a perfect symbol for all that was lost and has to be regained. It is their grail. It is the alchemical vessel for the rebirth of Pataxó culture, which in this case, unlike the Kamaiurá, has to integrate creatively all the already acquired contents of white culture and not simply throw it away.

As in many other countries that were colonized, something very precious historically has been considered of no value at all: the ancestral soul that supports our collective psychology. I adopted the expression "patrimony of sensibility" to name a process of soul making that started probably thirty thousand years ago, as some rock paintings indicate. The original inhabitants of the Americas developed an awareness of having inner images, and this is visible in engravings and drawings on stone. The creation of myths, religion, rituals, beauty, culture, society is ancient. This is one polarity, and it is clearly threatened if understood as implying backwardness and irrationality.

Psychotherapists, educators, social scientists, thinkers, and artists who have a commitment to humane values therefore act as defenders of this patrimony of sensibility, as listeners to the voices of all that is denied, as witnesses to dreams that are bridges between what was and what can become. The preservation of cultural diversity is in opposition to a tendency toward general homogeneity. As in the alchemical procedures, no element must be left out for the production of a new synthesis.

There are a considerable number of young Pataxó, firmly rooted in their cultural identities, who are seeking higher education. They will soon write another version of Brazilian history, from the point of view of the defeated. They are not mere survivors, but the ferment of a critical mass of people able to act, take positions, interfere, debate. They are making films about indigenous life, collecting information, gathering myths, and at the same time finding a way to live in our society without losing their original outlook to what life is all about. They now understand deep and complex conflicts through a new paradigm and will bring about change, innovation, and creation, synthesizing in their souls and in their minds both the old and the new.

NOTE

1. In the way most indigenous children are raised and how they live, provided their culture is preserved, there is an element of wisdom in the relationship between mother and infant that unfortunately has never garnered serious attention from psychologists or educators. Only anthropologists have described it. My conviction remains that throughout five centuries of contact between Europeans and the native peoples of the Americas there has always been a devaluation of any wisdom the ancestral indigenous soul might have. It is inconceivable that in a country such as Brazil there is not one single psychology department studying how indigenous peoples educate and relate to their children.

Acknowledgments

I want to express my gratitude to the following friends, who made this research possible: Eda Canepa and Jeanete De Vivo, heads of an elementary school in São Paulo; Joyce Capelli, director of the Brazilian office of International Medicine, who introduced me to a school in Jacarezinho, Rio de Janeiro; Carmen Junqueira, who introduced me to the Kamaiurá tribe; Iani Petrovitch, director of the Instituto Tribos Jovens, who invited me to work with the Pataxó; Eva Pattis, who suggested this research for possible publication in *Spring*.

SONS OF NARCISSUS

EVANGELOS TSEMPELIS

I grew up in Greece feeling, for as long as I can remember, a sense of pain. A sense of loss impinged on my being and defined my existence for many, many years. There was always the sense that somehow I clung desperately to a world that was slipping by as new changes made themselves present in so many facets of life. I remember the old neighborhood where I lived as a kid. How we played on the street. The dirt road where we rode our bicycles next to the big asphalt road. The open-air cinema where we saw movies on hot summer nights while savoring cheese pies bought at the nearby bakery. And even though our lives were admittedly already modern lives, it was possible still to see open fields from the window of our apartment in Athens. I could even sometimes see a shepherd as he took his sheep to feed on the grass.

Yet, I think that already then I somehow knew that the image of the fields and the lonely shepherd, the open-air cinema, our bicycles on the dirt road, and our forgetful play were all symbols of a bygone era. In many ways, that was the paradox of my childhood and perhaps the childhood of my generation in Greece: our present was already the past.

Similarly, today our future appears as an empty promise, an expired ticket, worthless like a downgraded junk bond. I close my eyes and I

Evangelos Tsempelis is an analyst in training at ISAPZURICH.

am transported to that time in the mid-seventies when the world, our world in Greece, was smaller, not so much because we were kids but because the world altogether was smaller, less complicated. Greece was a country at the far end of the Balkan Peninsula, fixed in the curious balance of cold war reality. It had recently recovered from a seven-year military junta that would leave its marks and redefine a whole society for the next thirty-five years. This is how long it took for all those hopes and aspirations for democracy, European-style affluence, and modernization, shared by a people, to run their full course and reach the point where we are today.

My country is bankrupt. I will not lie—there is a sense of relief that comes with this painful predicament. This death has been hanging over our heads, a Damoclean sword, for a very long time. A sense of decay, of stagnation, pressed down on our bodies and souls since we were kids. The poets spoke about it long before, even though we did not know it then. In retrospect, I can see how we lived the agony of an impending disaster. We grew up half conscious of a certain falseness that made itself evident in so many countless ways that each one of us can now describe it in our uniquely personal respective experiences. There is a wonderful scene in one of Theo Angelopoulos's magnificent films, *Ulysses' Gaze*, where the main character is traveling to the north of Greece by taxi in order to reach the border of that unknown "other" country, which Albania was for us all the way up to the 1990s when the border was finally opened and an official peace treaty ended a forty-five-year armistice in place since the end of World War II. At one point, as a blizzard sets in, the taxi driver stops his car on the top of a hill. He looks at the mountain peaks in the distant horizon and confides that he has heard that Greece is dying: "It is said that after more than two thousand years of history it is finally dying, not able to endure any longer the weight of such a long decay: old marbles and ruins lying everywhere as reminders of past forgotten glory." He then wishes that "this death might be quick as the waiting is unbearable." So it is perhaps understandable how there is a certain relief that comes with the news that finally this long-anticipated death is now somehow, at last, an acknowledged reality.

My country has gone under. So many people—political analysts, economists, journalists, experts, officials, and specialists foreign and local—have explained and described the numbers behind the financial collapse. The International Monetary Fund and the European Union have imposed an austerity policy of shock therapy comprised of radical reforms of the public sector aiming to streamline the economy, cut the enormous deficits, and hopefully put the country back on track. But can you tell the story of a country in numbers? Does a life—yours, mine, anyone's—fit within an algorithm? And what does this enormous debt really symbolize? I know we have to repay it, I know that repaying will be damn hard, almost impossible. But what is that act of repaying really? What does it stand for and what does it mean? What expert can offer a reasonable answer to these awkwardly pressing questions? As I scribble these thoughts, as I think of pain, collective and personal, and as I ponder the collapse of entire horizons, thinking what this might mean to our lives, I have no intention of even trying to be smart or to offer answers or posit theories, economic, political, psychological, or what have you. The only decent thing, it appears, is to describe the pain. To trace the loss. To mourn.

I think of the island where we spent our summers. I remember how in its remoteness—it took ten very slow hours by ferry to get there from the port of Piraeus—it represented a perfectly beautiful and perfectly complete world. I remember arriving there, how in the early hours of the morning as the summer sun was rising in the Aegean sky, we would see in the far distance the subtle contours of the island's body. It was an almost mystical experience to be out on the deck of the ship, face hit by the seasonal northeastern wind, the *meltemi*, and to see the island slowly materialize in our vision. Love. How long should one pause before it? And how to even begin to describe it? As the island comes closer, I can see the lighthouse at the left side of the natural bay defining the port. And as we enter the harbor I see the whitewashed church right next to the newly built pier over a streak of sandy beach. Gaze farther up and you will see the most beautiful Cycladic village clinging to the rocks of a steep hill. It was built up there, who knows when, to protect the villagers from the pirates who roamed the seas in the old days, all the way back to the time of Homer, whose tomb people claim still lies here on the other side of the island. We got to the village from the port on donkeys and mules.

As a kid, I heard so many stories from my parents about the old days when the island was even more remote, and I never realized that those times, when I was told these stories, would become my old times to cherish. I was too busy then trying to hold on to that fleeting image of a still older world. I remember how appalling and injurious it seemed when our house was connected to the island's main electrical supply and the old petrol lamps and the candles, whose flickering light shaped the background of our summer nights, were extinguished and replaced forever with the familiar banal electric light. Or when the road was built over the beach so that the increasing number of tourists from all over the world, looking for sex, drugs, and rock 'n' roll, could reach the far end of the bay by bus. So, just like the protesters in Paris in 1968, in my own way, I too remember *"sous les pavés, la plage"* ("under the paving stones, the beach"). The acts of sacrilege to this paradise would be countless. These acts were joined by a million others on the body of Greece in each and every corner as the country was on its way to a hasty full-blown modernization, which turned islands of childhood into lucrative and now defunct real estate projects. Each of us has a story of desecration to recount. My wife and our friends can tell you what happened, respectively, to their little paradises. And if you've lived this pain, you can immediately recognize it in other people's lives and in the stories they have to tell. This pain defines a whole mood, a whole world—our world, the one that is now bankrupt and subject to treatment by people who call themselves experts, modernizers, or technocrats and who define another world, an almost impossible one for all of us left lingering in the pain to partake in: the real world of numbers, reforms, and balance sheets.

I have heard a story. The European Commission has established a certain quota on fishing in the Mediterranean, and so they have come up with a policy whereby they pay a lucrative sum to fishermen to stop being fishermen. The story goes that in order for a fisherman to receive this life-changing sum of money, a certain autopsy has to take place. A committee of functionaries goes to the island to witness the destruction of the fishing boat. The boat is actually cut in two before the eyes of the committee. Now you see these boats are more than boats. Made of wood, they are called καΐκι (kaikee), and they have been sailing these now overfished seas for as long as anyone can remember, all the way back to the time of the pirates and perhaps long before. To destroy these boats is to commit some act for which no name has yet been coined because the pain of that act has still not reached the collective psyche of our language. But I am pretty sure that there will be a name for it in the future. I hope. Just as I hope that people will one day find some word to redeem our lost dignity for having called the murder of civilians in surgically precise modern war interventions "collateral damage." But that is another story.

It would be a momentous occasion to attend one of these autopsies, an opportunity to see two different worlds come into contact and face each other. On the one hand, the world of functionaries, holders of a technocratic knowledge, executioners of EU policies; on the other, an island fisherman, representative of an old world, a world of tradition and custom with links to a premodern way of life. Today it is still possible to find fleeting vestiges of this demurring world in Greece. You can go south to a remote island and meet such a fisherman. Or you can go north to some remote mountain and meet an old solitary priest. I remember meeting such a man some years ago. He was in his seventies, or he may have been younger, but his face had been deeply etched and curved by the relentless elements of his world: the sun and the salt of the Aegean Sea. He had the only *καΐκι* on the island. In times of trouble, when someone was in urgent need of medical attention or when the seas were too rough for the ferry to approach this remote island, people always turned to this man. I remember sitting in a taverna on a windy summer day and listening to a song that had been inspired by his epic acts of seamanship as I stared at the far horizon and the menacing roughness of the Aegean archipelago. One barely needs to amplify this with references to Homer or to mythology to understand the meaning and the sacredness of that vessel, the boat which carried men and women, sick and pregnant, old and young, from a small island to a bigger and safer land in times of trouble. To destroy such boat is not merely an act of cruelty, or even an act of brutality. The closest description that comes to mind is "ontological destruction." There is something essential, something in the deepest and most profound sense of being, that is wounded and offended. Something so abysmally primordial and basic is invoked here that I am inclined to make a lengthy deviation, by means of history and philosophy, in order to begin to trace the gravity of what is implied here.

I would want to talk of philosophers and their tireless plight, a heritage running back more than 2,500 years, to capture the meaning of the world in terms of basic essence or elements. I would want to make references to metaphysics and its long history in order to reacquire and retrace the meaning of the word *being,* in Greek ον, hence the English word *ontology.* I would want to pause long on a certain modern philosopher who spent a lifetime trying to answer, *What Is Called Thinking?* I would want to retell the story of how he wanted to turn thinking back to itself and ask what makes it possible. I would want to recount how, reading rigorously the long heritage of Western thought, he reminded us that our very heritage had forgotten, for more than twenty centuries, to inquire into the meaning of one simple word that conditions everything else: *is.* I would want to speak of how he points out that in the very memory of language something of enormous proportions is preserved even though otherwise long forgotten. I would tell how he looks at the etymology of the Greek word for truth, αλήθεια, stemming from α (anti) and λήθη (forgetfulness), to point out how in that ancient language the word for truth implies some action of wrestling with oblivion. I would try to show how, from that vantage point, truth is not some visible, all-present, and objective fact but a certain relationship with the abysmal realm of forgetfulness from which all springs forth and all retracts in the endless circle of veiling and unveiling we call life or history, in a chain of brief moments, events, forming an eternity and which are none other than the collisions between self and Being. And then I would want to show how this man's philosophy points to a very similar direction as the work of another abyss-of-a-man who started off to become a scientist but had to let himself drop all the way to the bottom of existence in order to find some truth capable of holding him and who subsequently spent a lifetime building a bridge back, from the dreams and images that came to him at the time of his breakdown, to the world of science and rational thinking that (wo)men tended so forgetfully to inhabit in his (and our) time. I would tell how this man's suspension over the void and the bridge he never stopped building have allowed so many other people after him to hang onto an image—of a horse, a snake, or a fish—as the last resort to come back from the most dark and desperate times of *their* existence. And after this long pilgrimage, perhaps I might feel myself justified to deploy, with all its powerful and newly rediscovered meaning, the term *ontological destruction,* feeling that it may now capture something of what is here at stake.

But it would be tedious and convoluted to follow such a path in the purview of this essay. Rather, by means of circumambulation, I will allow myself to be pulled back to "collateral damage." A term coined to make a crime, the "accidental" killing of civilians, appear to be a technical issue, involving some form of abstract mathematics rather than what it is: the harsh reality of the death of human beings caused by modern warfare. To begin to understand the violence of what this term does to the reality of human beings—men, women and children—you would have to put yourself in a place where these modern means of war are engaged in order to witness in your own eyes what the disembodied language of virtual war attempts to place in forgetful obscurity. Or you would have to read a firsthand account of a massacre by someone who spent a life covering such stories of violence and death. You would then have to endure a new act of violence committed by means of words carefully chosen by such a woman or man, who dedicated his or her life to this task, to vividly account for murder. This self-inflicting homeopathic cure, consisting of exposing oneself to the violence of language, would be necessary to restore dignity to words alluding to acts of unfathomable violence, which if left to their own devices would otherwise simply echo that violence in injuriously perpetuating euphemistic oblivion. Where does unfelt, forgotten pain go? And what kind of mysterious debt does it accrue on human existence?

Consider men and women, but primarily men, sitting in big conference rooms in sovereign towers of opulence and power speaking a language of technical terms to "reflect" and "analyze" a certain reality, to devise a policy, or a cure. They use words, big words, which always refer to a certain capability to effect outcome, in action or in inaction alike, in great volume and scope, almost always without properly accounting for the very simple, the very small—that forgotten word of the philosopher that still (mysteriously) keeps the world (meaningfully) together: ὄν, being, être, Sein. An austerity program; a "shock therapy"; a "life-saving intervention" to streamline another people's deficit; to balance a budget; to revise a treaty or to end some man-made calamity in some godforsaken corner of the world. These are examples of modern versions of hubris, emblematic reflections of a technological civilization having made possible the use of power in such grand scales and in such wide-ranging forms (intellectual, technical, and material) that it is capable of defining and shaping reality, in magnitude and speed, like never before, albeit in striking forgetfulness.

I have an image. It consists of a woman being taken away—
evacuated in an armored tank—from her house, where her husband
and his elderly father are left behind to defend the livelihood of the
family, which consists of produce, sheep, and the simple goods that
make a peasant home. The woman and perhaps her children are being
evacuated by an international force of peacekeepers to protect them
from the vengeance of an ethnically polarized crowd approaching with
murderous intent once again to commit violence, once again to
condemn to oblivion not just one family, this family, but a whole world
of families just like this one. The woman, as she is being whisked away,
has a frantic look in her eyes. It is the look of silent terror, pure human
terror, and pain, endless pain. The men are left behind to face destiny.
To struggle, to fight, to try to salvage something of what "is" from
unfolding, imminent oblivion.

I have another image. The general secretary of a world-renowned
international security organization comes to visit all the women who
have been evacuated after the ethnic violence has unleashed its fury on
their homes and after their husbands and fathers-in-law have lost the
battle against that faceless force served so blindly by angry men. This
man comes seemingly to console and to listen. He approaches the square
of a city, becomingly named after an adjacent field that marks the site
of a battle heroically lost almost seven hundred years ago and which
still weighs in as a point of reference for a beginning in the collective
memory of an entire people. He is followed by an awe-inspiring escort
of guards in elegant two-piece suits carrying machine guns in suitcases
and wearing earphones made of transparent plastic. Their attire is meant
to exude an air of sovereign and conspicuous presence. The metal
suitcases enclosing the machine guns present the most intimidating
form of power, the one that affords the privilege of subtlety and
decorum. The general secretary approaches the exasperated crowd of
women in black. One, relatively young, for no apparent reason steps
up and comes to tell him her story face-to-face. She is shattered. She is
furious. She is possessed by the primordial truth of her victimhood. A
crowd of people circle around; journalists keep close to capture the
moment; body guards are vigilant lest something goes wrong and the
situation gets out of hand. Here it is again, the moment when two
worlds come together to stare at each other. The world of the ivory
tower, of sovereign stately power, of aloof clarity and intervention, and

the other world, the small world of anonymous men and women struggling to stay afloat in the high seas of their time. Grand narratives stumbling on everyday people's stories, changing their lives forever, beyond recovery, beyond relief.

The secretary listens to the shattered woman. He attempts to utter some words to fill the gap that separates them. His words are commonplace, consisting of such hopeless platitudes, so out of sync, so below par in human terms that they simply insult. There are situations where the only decent thing, it seems, is to be frugal with words, to be utterly laconic. In these situations one ought to go for small, as small as one can get; all the way to the very microscopy of the minute caring for the endangered species of the what-is-as-it-is-on-its-way-to-no-longer-being-any-more. To hold. To respect. To wait and allow the otherness of the void which envelops, surrounds, and conditions language and life to be properly felt. Above all, there are situations where one ought to avoid putting up pitiful abstractions, or big consoling gestures, or all-encompassing notions, all of which are direct insults to the vastness of an already perpetrated injury. The secretary now reaches out with a consoling gesture to the woman. He attempts to caress her at the back of her neck in an act of affection. He thinks he is caressing. He is not. He thinks he is consoling. He is not. He is hurting. He does not even know. He is battering. He does not realize. Even this simple human act is impossible under these odd, so very odd circumstances.

I think of numbers, again: €260 billion. That is the latest estimated cost of the damage caused in Japan by the largest earthquake in its recorded history, plus a giant tsunami that drowned entire cities in the north of the country, plus a nuclear accident almost reaching the scale of Chernobyl. The enormity of this human and environmental catastrophe, which includes tens of thousands of casualties, in actual monetary figures is still smaller than the debt of Greece. Against the background of this disaster, against the background of the enormity of some other people's suffering, what is the meaning of the €300 billion worth of Greek debt? Is it possible to talk of €300 billion worth of oblivion? Of €300 billion worth of borrowed affluence and false entitlements? Of €300 billion worth of pompous, self-absorbed, forgetful existence? How could so much damage—equivalent, in the cold language of numbers, to the apocalyptic proportions of what has happened in Japan—have occurred undetected? How can that equivalence in numbers be broken down into actual human acts, acts committed and acts suffered over time? And what kind of existence is required or implied in order to be able to both suffer and perpetrate such awesome damage so self-forgetfully? And finally, the relentless question: how is the voice spoken here—in defense of lost paradises, in memory of acts of sacrilege, and in alliance with victimhood—also liable for this self-indulgent forgetfulness? How is the voice spoken here echoing this self-indulgent pompous existence? How is its victimhood a function of some form of clinging to false entitlements?

I have a dream:

> *I am on a boat approaching a shore. Alongside, a series of other similar boats are moored. I jump into the sea. I dive deep. At the sandy bottom I see a big red fish. It looks old. It has corals on its scales. I stare at it and then watch myself ascend to the surface.*

Who is ascending? Who is watching the ascent? Is it the same entity that looks at the fish and the same one that ascends to the surface? What might be that internal imaginary split between self-entities and levels of depth? And how to approach this odd, so very odd, question without having to echo borrowed words and notions? Moreover, how is one to distinguish between a personal entity and a collective one? How could the very idea of personhood even be postulated without first laboring to uncover what conditions its existence and what separates it from a collective? Similarly, how to trace the (hi)story of the collective conditioning of this entity without falling prey to prescribed notions always available in the reading of the past? How to talk of the history of Greece without once again accounting for ontological destruction? Where to stand so as to begin to speak of the many old ways of being and seeing which had to be condemned to oblivion along a continuum of time until a modern national reality was forged and inculcated in individual consciousness? Forgetfulness upon forgetfulness: the story of the unfolding of historical consciousness. How difficult it is to distinguish between what is an authentically personal affect from what is part of a collective conditioning when even the very categories of this impossible distinction are not sitting on safe ground, as one stands reflected against the other in echo. Yet, strikingly, what drives this line of thinking other than the yearning for some "deeper," "authentic" grounding?

Another dream:

> *My father and I are digging a grave. It is the grave of Greece. We are looking for its buried corpse. My father is digging on the upper half of the grave and finds nothing. I dig on the bottom half, from waist down. I dig and feel that perhaps if I dig deeper, I will find her.*

Father and son digging a grave, looking for the corpse of Greece. Looking for a buried yet still absent corpse. And what would it mean to find that corpse? Would it signal the same kind of relief that was mentioned at the beginning of this essay, when the notion of an imminent and long-anticipated death was described? The presence of a dead body has always been, in myth and reality alike, a prerequisite for the rites of mourning to take place and the pain over death to be finally expressed and come to terms with in consciousness. Would finding a corpse then mark the end of some long-lived inner death, bringing a period of nostalgic yearning finally to a close? And how is this search one that involves a father and a son, the former belonging to the baby boom generation, fraught with opportunity, and the latter to the lost generation that fell through the cracks of a transition from one world to another, from one state of consciousness to some other? Our fathers. Their generation. Their world. Ours. In the middle the absent corpse of a woman. Our country. Their absent and estranged wife (wives). Our missing mother(s). From absence to loss the unfolding of unaddressed pain. Fathers and sons. Two different levels of reality within the same patriarchal order. Upper body and lower body. Two different levels within the same missing corpse. Our dead country missing in our bodies. Digging.

Riding.

> *It is high summer in Greece. I am riding a motorcycle in the Peloponnese. An enormous sense of joy overtakes my being as I cruise leisurely across the beautiful landscape. I find a small remote beach. The sun is burning hot. On this mile-long stretch of sand I only see another couple with a dog playing and splashing in the water. I take my clothes off and dip in. A sense of pleasure envelops my entire*

existence. I lay still and let the water carry my weight. I hear the
sound of the sea as my ears are covered by the water, and my body
drifts away. Heavenly. Later in the evening I ride back to the ancient
theater of Epidaurus to attend a showing of Orestes. *After the play,*
I spend the night in a tent at a nearby camp site by the seaside of
ancient Epidaurus. The next day, I continue to wander with no
sense of destination. I am now climbing the winding road of a
hill. I see signs to a temple of Apollo Epikourios (Apollo the Helper).
I follow with a sense of urgency. It's late afternoon. I am at the top
of what feels like a very remote cliff. There is nobody around. I
marvel at the view of surrounding mountains and the sea at the
end of the distant horizon. I park my motorcycle and ascend the
steps leading to the temple. I see a young man sitting alone in front
of a kiosk making obnoxious sounds with his cell phone. We chat.
I ask him about the temple. He is clueless even though his job is to
guard it. I buy a ticket and climb the steps leading to a giant tent.
I enter. I am dazzled by what confronts me so unexpectedly. A
stunningly imposing ancient temple. It is reminiscent of the
Parthenon. I am standing breathless in awe.

What is that temple? What is that sense of awe? What is that
serendipitous encounter? Who is Orestes, avenger and murderer of his
mother and son of a murdered father? Who is Apollo? How is he a
helper? What is that tent? What does it mean to put a temple in a
tent, to bracket it in an act of "preserving" it? I think of bracketing,
putting within parentheses, as a gesture that a whole heritage of
philosophy has used as a way to dig to the bottom of things, in search
of the ultimate ground for truth. How I would like to trace and retell
the story of that act of bracketing/digging. To tell how it started with
a man, who still defines our era, all the way back to the seventeenth
century. A man who bracketed the entire world, doubting its validity
in search of the one certain thing for which proof could be given and
on which the whole world could be subsequently built up on newly
found certainty. Bracketing the entire world. Imagine doubting the
validity of mountains and seas and other people and awe-inspiring
temples all the way to the one certain thing: the (f)act of thinking.
And I would like to recount how that bracketing and the new certainty
that it produced led eventually to a whole world of certainty. A world

of objects. A world of measurable space. Eventually, an objective malleable world that we are still trying to inhabit today.

I would want to speak of how that certainty was purchased at the cost of a certain exile or alienation from the world. Man would now be the perpetual observer, looking at a world of objects, reflecting and mastering them by means of reason but at the cost of being aloof and immune to the world's awe inspiring mystery, deaf to the enigma of its being. (Trapped within parentheses.) Certainty was purchased at the cost of standing suspiciously before the world asking for proofs of its existence while entertaining the thought that it actually might not exist. I would like to talk of how that gulf between what man could now know in certainty and how that knowledge applied to the world outside himself was an impossible one to cover. And of course there would once again be a story about forgetfulness within this account. It would be a story of how so many men who followed this great thinker conveniently forgot to ask the dormant questions waiting to be addressed in this new form of thought and instead busied themselves measuring and mastering a newly emergent world of objects, erecting a promising world of science based on positive (objectively measurable) proof.

I would also want to talk of another great thinker whose only known pastime was to play billiards when he was not in his study thinking. I would like to recount the story of his bracketing, how he tried to bridge that unbridgeable gap between what we know and what is. How he achieved the most groundbreaking synthesis in proposing that the world exists and that we know it according to our pre-given apparatus of knowing. In this way, doubt could be dispelled for a while, and the busy men could continue their measuring and mastering unperturbed. God could also momentarily find respite as God was placed safely in a realm beyond what can be known, in the world of the "thing in itself, " which always lies beyond our capacity to know. And the story would go on to how this remarkable accomplishment was once again achieved at the cost of positing a whole realm of things which could not be known in themselves, banishing man from any access to the actual truth of the world: $\alpha\lambda\dot{\eta}\theta\varepsilon\iota\alpha$. Do you remember that old word for truth belonging to an older world that we spoke of at the beginning?

I would speak of another wise old man who lived a life trying, with all the meaning that can be mustered, to express this: to be a serious philosopher. With the clouds of the Second World War approaching ominously, banished from the university because of his persuasions and literally locked outside its library by the very man who had been his own very favorite student, this wise old man took it upon his shoulders to carry the burden of a last attempt to reground philosophy and salvage the sciences from what he saw as a profound and threatening crisis to European civilization. Positivist science, the science of reason based on objective facts, had overshadowed the old philosophical claim to universal truth. From that point of view, everything not able to answer the test of objective truth as a fact was dispelled to the realm of relativism, insignificance, meaninglessness, or of some form of self-enclosed psychologism. The wise old man, through his own careful bracketing, took upon himself the heroic task of rehabilitating the alienated and exiled subject. He tried to show that at the root of everything lies the subject. And he tried to reach that deep subjective ground by once again bracketing the entire world, by dismissing all things taken for granted in the natural attitude through which we look at the world. There at the desperate hours of a life coming at an end, at the very end of an era, at the brink of a world war, he found his ultimate ground in a certain entity, which always discreetly announces its presence in the form of subtle intention(alitie)s. However much and however long I bracket the world I can never go beyond that presence which always sets me on the way to something. A purely "objective red fish with corals on its scales" simply does not exist independent from the intention(alitie)s to look at it or to move away from it. All of the wise men before, according to his argument, had not bracketed enough. In their reductions there was always something left unaccounted for: the subtle subjective intention at the background.

Even that other wise man, who liked playing billiards, in his gigantic synthetic philosophy had implicitly discounted this subjective presence. He never asked how something obvious is in fact obvious. How else then by reference to this subtle intentional presence? The subject. In wanting to ground knowledge onto pure reason, in separating the world into a phenomenal world and a world beyond our capacity of knowing, the world of the "thing in itself," in assuming the same suspicious attitude to inner experience, to what can be known intuitively about the actual world, the billiard man was (aloofly) assuming the very same dichotomy that he was trying to bridge. A temple is a temple only within a horizon of possible perceptions, a multiplicity of objects relating to it internally. A temple is a temple within an external horizon of things, mountains and rivers and people all connected. And the world is a perceptual world. So the argument went. And at that liminal hour for philosophy, at that liminal hour for Western civilization and for this wise and serious man, whose time was running out, that last book was left unfinished.

"Bracketing" a temple within a tent, to preserve it from erosion. A perfectly rational explanation, a perfectly rational act. Yet, there is something odd, so very odd, in the sight of this rational act. By means of undertaking this preventive action against erosion, the temple is turned momentarily into an object that needs to be preserved: a monument. A bracketed temple is no longer a temple. Rather, it becomes something else within a new horizon of inner and outer perceived objects. It is a monument. A token of time passed. A timeless token of a finite temple. The bracketed temple is no longer a temple. It is no longer a sanctuary. This temple was a sanctuary. It was erected sometime in the fifth century B.C. as the Messinians and the Arcadians were trying to protect themselves from the ever-expanding Spartans. In building this temple the Arcadians were invoking the protection of Apollo, sun god, god of light. With his help they could perhaps defend themselves against the menacing forces they were pit against by the darkness of nonbeing. At one point in time, a Christian time, the temple was entirely forgotten. Many centuries later, in the late eighteenth century, the century of newly fervent and enlightened interest in classical Greece, a Frenchman discovered it "accidentally." He correctly identified it in terms of its history and by doing so instantly bequeathed it to the horizon of archaeological monuments that was slowly emerging at the time: a horizon of multiple archaeological objects relating to each other perceptually. Why was this temple forgotten? Why was it rediscovered? What was that act of rediscovery? And how may the awe that I experienced in "rediscovering" this temple, which is no longer a temple, be entered into a relation to the serendipitous experience of that Frenchman more than two hundred years ago?

The temple was forgotten, was rendered redundant or obsolete, as a temple in a Christian era and was rediscovered as a monument in a premodern time of enlightened interest in the past. For two hundred years it has been standing as a monument to that past. These two hundred years of erosion also mark (roughly) the "lifetime" of our modern Greek state (of mind). Imagine measuring that in terms of erosion. These monuments covering the body of Greece are not simply tokens to times past. They are, as objects, mostly tokens to a time present. They carry, each one of them, the long story of forgetfulness between the time that they were forgotten and the time they were remembered, rediscovered. They were forgotten as objects of reverence to a deity, as parts of a wholesome world in relation to truth and beauty, as sanctuaries at times of menace. They were remembered as monuments. Each one of these objects, as a monument, carries a very long history of unaccounted and unmourned *ontological destruction*. As such, these objects, which are not objects, silently impinge the weight of their lost dignity on our being. Their dead, missing corpses call for burial rites. And every person who is born in that land and who grows to speak that language which is still called Greek and which still uses the same word for truth, $\alpha\lambda\acute{\eta}\theta\varepsilon\iota\alpha$, always in relation to (forgetfulness), carries, whether he or she knows it or not, part of the indecency of this belated and long overdue burial.

This temple to Apollo was already not a temple when it was discovered by that Frenchman. It has been a monument for the past two hundred years, since that day, long before it was covered by a tent to protect it from erosion. As a bracketed temple, the-temple-which-is-no-longer-a-temple might no longer even be a monument. It is some new entity not entirely intelligible in the horizon of familiar and perceptible objects. Neither is it clear what the sense of awe that its rediscovery inspires today "is." It is not religious piety, as it no longer is a temple. It is not scientific archaeological numinosity, as it has been already discovered as an object two hundred long years ago. And in any case, in the realm of objective discovery, the moment of eureka is reserved only to the one who invents or discovers first: in this case, the Frenchman. Nobody feels elated in rediscovering penicillin. So what is it? Some new possibility may be announcing itself, which is not fully grasped here. Could it be that the sense of awe is related not so much to what is present, the temple-which-is-no-longer-a-temple, as to what in bracketed form is now rendered absent? Covered, the monument is no longer a monument. It is no longer a token of the past; it no longer acts as a summons to commemorate remembrance now. It had already been all of that for the past two hundred eroding years. The covered monument is a bracketed monument: a non-monument. It is no longer identical to itself. It is absent. An empty shell released.

And yet, it is such a remarkable experience to enter that tent. Unknowingly one is confronted not by a temple-which-is-no-longer-a-temple but by some event. Something momentous and instantaneous hits; an encounter with some unknown other is revealed. There it is, sitting. I can hear outside in the distance the locusts singing the eternal song of the (Greek) summer. I think of horizons lost. Horizons collapsing. We are going down. We are going to our death. I am. But there is something in that absence that magnificently announces itself now, which gives me courage. I can feel in my heart something growing. Who knows what will announce itself in some new emerging horizon?

MELANCHOLIA AND CATASTROPHIC CHANGE
AN ESSAY ON THE FILM *MELANCHOLIA* (2011)

P rominently in writer/director Lars von Trier's mind, when he developed his latest film, *Melancholia* (2011), was his own mental state. Struggling with depression, he searched for inspiration for a new project to follow the dark, pornographically violent, nearly unwatchable *Antichrist* (2009). Hearing about how depressives react in the face of disaster became a seed. "My analyst told me that melancholiacs will usually be more level-headed than ordinary people in a disastrous situation, partly because they can say: 'What did I tell you?' But also because they have nothing to lose."[1]

Von Trier saw a TV documentary in which he learned that Saturn is the planet for melancholia; he read about cosmic collisions on the Internet; he listened to music; and he went to museums. He said, "I think Justine is very much me. She is based a lot on my person and my experiences with doomsday prophecies and depression. Whereas Claire is meant to be a normal person."[2]

Pamela J. Power, Ph.D., is a clinical psychologist and Jungian analyst practicing in Santa Monica, CA. She is an analyst member and on the faculty of the C. G. Jung Institute of Los Angeles, where she also served as training director and clinic director. She has published numerous articles, film essays, and book reviews for *Psychological Perspectives* and articles for *Journal of Jungian Theory and Practice*. Her most recent article is "Violence and the Religious Instinct," *Psychological Perspectives* 54(4), 2011.

The film begins with an eight-minute opening sequence of extreme slow-motion images that take one through the story from beginning to the final swallowing up of Earth by a massive planet. The viewer now knows what will eventually occur. Von Trier wants to get the ending out of the way—no distracting suspense. After the opening sequence, the film is divided into two parts. Part one is the reception for Justine's wedding at the elegant estate of her older sister, Claire, and Claire's husband, John. Part two takes place in the aftermath of the wedding reception. Justine has fallen into a severe depressive episode and has come to stay at the estate where Claire is nursing her. At this time a rogue planet called Melancholia is approaching and threatens to collide with Earth. Justine is the first to notice an unusually bright star, and later she notices when it disappears. At the end of *Melancholia*, Justine helps her young nephew Leo gather sticks to make a "magic cave" that will "protect" them. She brings her distraught sister, Claire, with Leo into the structure. The three sit together, holding hands, waiting for the end.

Justine is a depressive personality for whom the ordinary demands of life are too great. She does not know how to participate in life in a meaningful way. She has episodes where she flouts collective expectations. She acts out impulses and creates emotional turbulence with everyone; or she falls into a deep depression, unable to bathe or eat. Food tastes like ashes, and all she wants to do is sleep. However, Justine is gifted; she "knows" things that others don't, and she senses beyond ordinary reality. But she is unable to use what she knows to benefit herself or to live a creative life, and she always expects the worst to happen. As the disaster approaches, Justine's depression improves. She becomes calm while Claire becomes increasingly anxious.

Claire is caring, loving, more normal and adapted. But there is a thin quality to her personality, intimations of a life not fully lived. Claire cares deeply for her sister, but can make no sense of her. She is disturbed by Justine's erratic behavior. Claire needs life and people to be nice and untroublesome. Eventually, through the sister connection, Claire, too, begins to sense that something is off with the mysterious planet moving closer to Earth. She tries to allow herself to be reassured by her husband but secretly checks out rumors on the Internet that claim Melancholia is in a dance of death with Earth. Claire becomes increasingly anxious because she, in contrast to Justine, has everything to lose: her life, her marriage, and her young son, Leo.

John is the abnormally normal husband of Claire—wealthy, pompous, competent, sure of himself and his values. An amateur astronomer, he tells everyone that the new planet is no threat. He believes the scientists who assure the public that Melancholia will give Earth an unprecedented, dazzling display as it passes close by. When he realizes he is wrong, he tells his son: "There is nothing to do, there is no place to hide." In the face of this shattering fact, he takes an overdose of sleeping pills and dies in the barn among the horses.

Another major player in this film is the lush, hyperbolic, over-the-top music of the prelude to Wagner's opera *Tristan und Isolde*. The images in the opening scene, which move the viewer through the story of *Melancholia*, are drenched in emotionally evocative, chromatically ambiguous tonalities. After the beginning, the music slips in here and there in the form of judicious intimations and suggestions. It comes fully forward only in a few specific places and, of course, throughout the ending.

Experienced at the level of a literal story, it is difficult not to be moved by the emotional ending. Previously, Justine had been unable to participate meaningfully in any ritual, including her own wedding. Forced into an extreme situation, she is able to create a rite of passage, a meaningful final ritual. All of this is foreshadowed in images from the initial sequence. We, the viewers, know what is to come. Still, it is emotionally wrenching when we finally see it happen.

JUSTINE

After the opening sequence, Justine and her new husband arrive very late to their wedding reception in a stretch limo that moves slowly up a narrow dirt road to the estate. Toasts to the bride and groom are interrupted by Justine's estranged parents' highly charged, vitriolic animosity. Her mother denounces the very idea of marriage while her father sits with several dates, floozies all named "Betty," stuffing spoons into his lapel pocket. The parents steal the moment from the wedding couple, and as they do, Justine disappears into a dissociative state.

As a depressive personality, Justine longs to end it all, to get it all over with. This ridiculous life of disingenuous relationships, values she cannot believe in, promises that feel vacuous seems disgusting to her. She wants to believe her new husband, Michael, can bring her happiness, but this hope falls flat over and over during the wedding reception. Justine attempts to approach and engage her parents. Her mother is walled off in a castle of bitterness and resentment while her father is lost in a haze of self-indulgence and hedonistic womanizing.

We can justifiably infer that Justine's parental relationships left her unprepared to engage with life in a fulfilling and meaningful way. Life and people, once a source of hope, have left her disconnected and filled with despair and disappointment. Not knowing how to repair these gaps in herself, she settled into a pattern of life that left her isolated from herself and others.

Justine tries unsuccessfully to talk with her mother, and she begs her father to stay overnight so they can talk the next day. She needs something, she longs for something, but she does not know what or how to get it. In this vacuum, the planet Melancholia appears on the scene. What Justine longs for is, in Christopher Bollas's terminology, a "transformational object."[3] In face of not being able to think or feel what she really longs for, and convinced that what she longs for does not exist, she longs for the end. The planet becomes for her a transformational object and, at the same time, synonymous with the end of everything.

The search for the transformational object is the earliest search, according to Bollas, to repair the connection to life that was lost at an early stage of development.

> To seek the transformational object is to recollect an early object experience, to remember not cognitively but existentially— through intense affective experience—a relationship which was identified with cumulative transformational experiences of the self. Its intensity as an object relation is not due to the fact that this is an object of desire, but to the object being identified with such powerful metamorphoses of being.[4]

Justine follows "the call" of Melancholia and moves into a psychosomatic fusion with the mysterious planet. During one scene she goes into the woods and lies naked in the planet's light. This is one of the moments when Wagner's music comes forward. The music is an intimation of another world.

> On the occasion of the aesthetic moment . . . an individual feels a deep subjective rapport with an object and experiences an uncanny fusion with the object, an event that re-evokes an ego state that prevailed during early psychic life . . . This anticipation of being transformed by an object inspires the subject with a reverential attitude towards it, so that even though the transformation of the self will not take place on the scale it reached during early life, the adult subject tends to nominate such objects as sacred.[5]

After her communion with Melancholia, Justine is cured. She regains her appetite and her sanity. Meanwhile, everyone around her begins to disintegrate into panic and anxiety. Justine idealizes destructive change; destruction becomes a healing symbol for her. Once she recognizes what is going to happen, she worships the deadly planet and becomes its devotee. She understands that the world is evil and that it deserves to be destroyed. To add distress to despair, she states, in her knowing way, that there is no other life anywhere in the universe. It is all over. Depressive thinking, par excellence! But it is also melancholic thinking; and the giveaway is the moralistic stance Justine takes toward the world—and ultimately, toward herself.

In *Mourning and Melancholia* Freud lays out the psychology of melancholy. He writes that both normal mourning and melancholy begin with the loss of an object. The loss can be literal, as in death, but can include "all those situations of being slighted, neglected or disappointed."[6] In the condition of melancholy, the process of grieving and mourning goes awry. The libidinal cathexis of the lost object is not withdrawn and placed onto another object, as is the case with normal mourning. In melancholy, this libido is withdrawn into the ego and serves "to establish an identification of the ego with the abandoned object. Thus the shadow of the object fell upon the ego, and the latter could henceforth be judged by a special agency [the superego], as though it were an object, the forsaken object."[7] An intrapsychic sadomasochistic activity takes place in which the superego berates, debases, and abuses the ego "making it suffer and deriving sadistic satisfaction from its suffering."[8]

One can readily observe how Justine has become melancholic due to the loss (through neglect) of her parents. And one can see how this led her to search for the transformational object. The intrapsychic sadomasochistic activity is not apparent or observable in the character of Justine; it must be inferred by her psychopathology. In her mind, it isn't herself that Justine wants to destroy, but the world. We must look to an earlier state of mind to discern the meaning of this. The child's omnipotent mind can destroy the world and make it disappear by magical thinking. The child pulls the blanket over her head and the world disappears (and the child cannot be seen). The world is herself, her ego; it is evil, and, when it is gone, Justine states: "No one will miss it." She means, "No one will miss *me* when I am gone because I am so bad." But it also carries a more narcissistically destructive message: "I will destroy the world because it has been such a disappointment to me."

Justine is sure there is life nowhere else in the universe. And because she alone guessed exactly how many beans there were in the jar at the wedding reception, one tends to believe what she says! "I know things; I've always known things," she tells Claire. There is no life like hers anywhere in the universe, she is unique and will destroy herself, everything and everyone in one grand gesture.

Viewing the ending of the film from the perspective of the inner world of the melancholic personality, it is horrifying. In this version of the story, Justine is *not* a helpful sister and aunt; she has brought disaster down on everyone. We see the playing out of narcissistic destruction to the point of suicide, not an unreasonable conclusion given the depth of depression and despair she felt. And how many times has she been there? How many times has Claire nursed her back from the brink of death? Maybe this time it really *is* the end. Did the end of the world happen literally, or was it all in her head?

PSYCHE

In 2040 a large asteroid will orbit close enough to the earth to be pulled by the earth's gravitational field. NASA scientists claim the odds are remote that 2011 AG5 will make direct impact, but those odds could change with future readings. Asteroids are really planetoids, space rocks that orbit the sun. There are millions of them, mostly small ones that would burn up in the earth's atmosphere. AG5 orbits the sun between Venus and Mars and is 460 feet wide. NASA's Near Earth Object Observations Program searches for and monitors threats to the earth from those asteroids large enough to do damage should they collide with the earth.

Apparently, sky anxiety is so pervasive that a NASA scientist, David Morrison, has coined the term *cosmophobia* to describe this new emotional and psychological disorder. Cosmophobia is the fear of the cosmos, particularly "the terror that the world will end by means of some astronomical occurrence."[9]

Jung was intensely preoccupied with UFOs in the late 1940s and 1950s when sightings were numerous. He gathered factual data and dream material that eventually became his book, *Flying Saucers: A Modern Myth of Things Seen in the Skies* (1958). Jung considered UFOs to be either a mass hallucination or a factual occurrence. In his psychological exegesis of the UFO phenomena, Jung commented on the flying saucer as a symbol of wholeness constellated in the collective unconscious to compensate for the disintegrative and dissociative effect on the psyche caused by the cold war and the threat of a full-out nuclear war.

Wilfred Bion described catastrophic change as any change that threatens to subvert a given psychic order or structure, for better or for worse. Bion wrote: "It is catastrophic in the sense that it is accompanied by feelings of disaster in the participants [and that] it is sudden and violent in an almost physical way."[10] Resistance is always part of the change, but when resistance is predominant, the change becomes a catastrophe. Bion noted: "Mental evolution is catastrophic and timeless."[11] A feared inner truth deposes an established truth. Any significant movement in mental evolution challenges all our resistances and defenses.

Disasters close to home are monitored with alarm: climate change, rising sea levels, shrinking food supplies, increasing population, severe droughts, global financial instability, collapse of governments, collapse of the middle class, basic education moving out of reach, water supplies threatened, and more. One does not need to be entertained by a doomsday disaster movie; these days we seem to be living in one.

In *Archetype of the Apocalypse,* Edward Edinger described apocalyptic images as the "the coming of the Self into conscious realization."[12] He believed the wheels of the apocalypse have long been set in motion.

"It is a momentous event—literally world-shattering. This is what the content of the Apocalypse archetype presents: the shattering of the world as it has been, followed by its reconstitution."[13] Edinger argued:

> The apocalyptic events depicted in the Book of Revelation are at hand. Jung's *Answer to Job*, if we can assimilate it, provides us with the meaning of these events. Certainly, Jung thought his understanding of these matters was worth his best efforts to communicate: "rather than allow laxity to let things drift toward the impending world catastrophe."[14]

Edinger's perspective is a continuation and extension of Jung's "myth of meaning." The process of individuation replaces the loss of containment in traditional religion or ideologies. Jung's psychology recognizes that the individual has a soul, that the ego is not the center of the personality, and that there is a regulating archetype within called the Self. In Jungian psychology there is a gradual change of the ego through repeated encounters with the shadow, anima/animus, and the Self. Contents of the unconscious reveal themselves to be inner contradictions to the ego's attitude and will. The ego learns it is not master in its own house. There are repeated, noisy collisions between the ego and the Self. "[God] is the name by which I designate all things which cross my willful path violently and recklessly."[15] This process leads to a gradual relativization of the ego and the establishment of a relationship between ego and Self. Jung believed in the cosmic and redemptive role of the human psyche. When we change ourselves, we change the world: "The world hangs on a thin thread, and that thread is the psyche of man."[16]

MEANING

Wolfgang Giegerich writes:

> something new is trying to enter the consciousness of "modern man" in order to radically transform it . . . Sinister and uncanny though it may be, meaninglessness is like a guest who knocks at our door asking for shelter. Perhaps we even need disillusionment through spiritual emptiness and meaninglessness as something necessary . . . Perhaps the experience of meaninglessness is an initiation into the disillusioning and liberating knowledge that

we are not ourselves divine children nor do we have to be, but mortal men: "children of death" born of the death of the child. And perhaps the loss of the center means a crumbling of the ontological totalitarianism of Christianity. Perhaps it could open up a distant vision of a psychology without ego and self, without wholeness and centroversion, without person and development, without meaning and salvation—a psychology devoid of all this theological ballast.[17]

For Giegerich, meaninglessness is meant to be something liberating, something that opens a door. It is not about learning to live without meaning, but rather to experience how bondage to meaning can limit psychological evolution. Because we have taken Jung (and others) so seriously, we've overdone our "modern man in search of a soul," and we have outguessed and outrun "God's secret intentions."[18]

Meaninglessness is unbearable. It intrudes as an uninvited guest. The reaction is an attempt to plaster meaning onto events as a way of managing, tolerating, or controlling them. Jung questioned whether humans could survive without meaning. Jung's psychology was meant to address the alarm and anxiety of the modern individual and to replace lost meanings of religion and myth with a "myth of meaning." As part of this new myth, the human psyche has a cosmic role. The process of individuation assists in the evolution of the God-image. Jung writes in *Memories, Dreams, Reflections*: "That is the meaning of divine service, of the service which man can render to God, that light may emerge from the darkness, that the Creator may become conscious of His creation, and man conscious of himself."[19]

But if, as Giegerich suggests, meaninglessness may be a liberating guest, then the whole enterprise of meaning making is brought into question; it isn't thrown out altogether, but the potency of meaning is modified, lessened, attenuated. The rogue planet Melancholia, as the "uninvited guest" is an agent of catastrophic change, and an image of the terror of change that we cannot understand and cannot influence. A menacingly huge planet swallows up a diminutive earth. All biological development, all human evolution and culture, is destroyed. We feel small, helpless, and terrified.

At the beginning of the film, Justine lives in a state of longing. She does not fit into life. She cannot find meaning in life's rituals or ordinary human relationships. She knows that she cannot participate in such things because, for her, they are vacuous and empty. According to Giegerich,

> The longing for meaning is deluded about itself . . . Meaning, where it indeed exists, is first of all an implicit fact of existence, it's a priori. It can never be the answer to a question; it is, conversely, an unquestioned and unquestionable certainty that predates any possible questioning. It is the groundedness of existence, a sense of embeddedness in life, of containment in the world—perhaps we could even say of in-ness as the logic of existence as such. Meaning exists if the meaning of life is as self-evident as the in-ness in water is for fish.

> The search for meaning is in truth, but secretly, the longing for a state of in-ness.[20]

Justine longs for what is not available. This is the dilemma for modern consciousness: We cannot go back, but how to go forward, and to what? Giegerich argues:

> The kind of in-ness that is longed for, if it were indeed realized, would be intolerable for the modern subject. It would collide with our inalienable insistence on emancipated individuality and rationality. It would necessarily be felt as imprisonment, as a nightmare, of which the 20th century experience in totalitarian states and with fundamentalist sects has given us a taste.[21]

Understanding and feeling this dilemma induces a painful state of mind, feelings of loss and disorientation. One searches for a verisimilitude of "in-ness" (meaning) in a relationship, a psychology, or a theology. Instead, there is a collision between a previously held cluster of assumptions and a new, as yet unknown reality.

Foreshadowing by an unusually bright star in the constellation Scorpio catches Justine's attention. Later, after she cannot get her horse Abraham to cross over the bridge, she looks up and sees that Melancholia has emerged into full view. She is compelled to understand what is happening and moves into the unknown. She walks into the woods at night, takes her off her clothes, and lies near the water in the light of the planet. Justine now knows how to live with catastrophic change. Living with it would mean facing with full consciousness *what is*. No dissociation, no covering it over or making it nicer than it is. Justine declares sharply, "You want to meet on the patio, sing a song, have a glass of wine? Why don't we meet on the toilet, Claire?" Justine tries to shake her sister out of her need for everything to be nice and wrapped up.

The soundtrack—Wagner's prelude to *Tristan und Isolde*—reflects the idea of catastrophic change. Wagner's prelude has been described by many musicologists as marking the start of the disintegration of Western tonal music. The so-called Tristan chord right at the beginning resolves in an unconventional manner for the times. Throughout the entire opera, the music never comes to a resolution until the very end when the lovers are dead. Instead, any momentary resolution in the music is merely a step to further chromatic dissonances. It is a musical representation of endless longing, yearning, desire, and delusional hopefulness.

We have Justine inside us as well as John, Claire, Leo, the parents, and the horses. John prefers to die rather than live through any significant change in his well-established life. He cannot tolerate a challenge or affront to his superior, know-it-all narcissism. Claire is overwrought with anxiety: "But where would Leo grow up?" She worries about the discontinuity caused by a huge shift. She clings to what is known. When John discovers the truth, he says, "There is nothing to do, there is no place to hide." The horses panic and behave frantically in response to the impending doom.

Tolerating living in a state of not knowing, without accepting an easy fix, is the doorway to a future psychology. *Melancholia* can be seen as a vision of catastrophe in which the idea of a saving myth or redemptive religion is lost, and the role of the individual psyche that Jung and Edinger put forward undergoes a shift. What we, as individuals, can do is limited. While not turning a blind eye, and continuing to recognize the importance of doing whatever we can to help with the pressing issues of our time, there are hints that the effect of these efforts may be far less than we would hope.

How might Giegerich's "distant vision of a psychology without ego and self, without wholeness" appear? The end of the world as the end of ego gives a clue. It is not the loss of the ego, but the loss of the ego in the position of the child, and it is the loss of the other since the child always has an other, something outside itself. The ego as the child has longings, fantasies, delusions, magical thinking, projections, and a belief in the totally other. The end of the world, as the end of ego, is not just a relativization of ego, but the end of the ego as the centerpiece of psychology.

From Giegerich's perspective, it is a psychological act that Justine, as Soul, pulls the planet Melancholia from behind the sun and surrenders to it. She recognizes the other in Melancholia as belonging to herself, as her own interiority. The end of the world is the end of the other. The collision and swallowing up of Earth is the other finally coming home to itself. The dance of death that Melancholia does with Earth is the dance of negation, and it is the end of longing because there is no other to long for anymore.

In addition to terror of the future, and in part because of it, there exists collective melancholy. Blaming ourselves, in a melancholic way, results from an inflation that insists we should have and could have done better. We could and should have been better custodians of our planet, just as we could and should have been better parents to our children.

It is possible that we have lived to the end of what was once a useful system of moral life and is now an oppressive moralistic system that prevents life from opening, moving, and evolving. Our moralistic system is so much the water in which we live that we hardly realize it is there; we live it as assumption. Every significant movement beyond our current way of thinking/feeling challenges our protective moralistic conditioning.

All our hopeful psychologies have a scent of moralism in one form or another. There is a correct way, a right way as opposed to the wrong way. There are writers who stimulate a sense of responsibility to the point of guilt toward what "we" have done and are doing to planet Earth. While these are facts not to be disputed, it appears to evoke an unhelpful response. One gets drawn into a melancholic state of feeling bad, an emotional state that is a defense against further evolving, creative thinking, appropriate (not sentimental) feeling, and effective actions. All blaming and moralistic thinking can be viewed as a defense against the Kleinian depressive position, or against the "accomplished" stage of shadow integration.[22]

A quiet scene of the two moons late in the film foreshadows this authentic feeling state. One is Earth's moon, the other is Melancholia shown in the nighttime sky as the moon's twin. The realization that Melancholia is in a direct collision course with Earth ushers in a period of quiet sadness. Justine is serious and calm. She eats, she is real, and she coaxes Claire into acceptance. The use of silence underscores the change, the shift; the two moons suggest a non-ego-centered event and is an image of the change in the cosmic syntax.

Greg Mogenson writes: "The negation of the negation is more depressive and sad. Cringing at the thought of its former righteousness and naïveté, it [consciousness] starts to collapse from within and go under. Its shame, however, is a higher shame, the beginning of its sublation."[23]

End

Lars von Trier has powerfully expressed the current collective panic and anxiety about the end of the world. He searched for answers to the dilemmas of our time. By creating *Melancholia* he intuited a *telos* that is revealed in the film. The realization of this is far into the future, if at all: there are no more redemptive myths or messianic deus ex machina. Instead, there exists a reality that we must face and manage with our limited human abilities. With the end of the other, there are no more victims and perpetrators, no more innocence and evil. There is no more tension or reconciliation of the opposites. No more "the one after the other [followed by] the side-by-side."[24] Instead, contradictions and the opposites are squarely (logically) within each other and, perhaps most important, are *recognized and accepted as such*.

Melancholia is a ravishingly beautiful film with gorgeous images, breathtaking cinematography, and evocative music. Perhaps Lars von Trier did not have a visionary perspective such as I have outlined in this overview, but he said that he hoped viewers would take a deeper look: "You can skate across the polished surface in this film. The style is polished, but underneath the smooth surface, there's content. And to get to that, you need to look beyond the polish."[25]

NOTES

1. Nils Thorsen, "Interview: Longing for the End of All," accessed September 7, 2012, http://www.melancholiathemovie.com/#_ interview.
2. *Ibid.*
3. Christopher Bollas, *The Shadow of the Object* (New York: Columbia University Press, 1987), p. 17.

4. *Ibid.*

5. *Ibid.,* pp. 16–17.

6. Sigmund Freud, *Mourning and Melancholia,* vol. 14, *Standard Edition of the Complete Psychological Works of Sigmund Freud* (London: Vintage, 2001), p. 251.

7. *Ibid.,* p. 248.

8. *Ibid.,* p. 251.

9. Ralfee Finn, "Tame Your Cosmophobia," *East Bay Express,* October 21–27, 2009, http://www.eastbayexpress.com/ebx/tame-your-cosmophobia/Content?oid=1371603.

10. Wilfred Bion, "Transformations," *Seven Servants* (New York: Jason Aronson, 1977), p. 8.

11. Wilfred Bion, "Attention and Interpretation," *Seven Servants* (New York: Jason Aronson, 1977), p. 108.

12. Edward Edinger, *Archetype of the Apocalypse* (Chicago: Open Court, 1999), p. 5.

13. *Ibid.*

14. *Ibid.,* p. 182.

15. C. G. Jung, *Letters, Volume 2: 1951–1961* (Princeton, NJ: Princeton University Press, 1971), p. 525.

16. William McGuire and R. F. C. Hull, eds., *C. G. Jung Speaking: Interviews and Encounters* (Princeton, NJ: Princeton University Press, 1977), p. 303.

17. Wolfgang Giegerich, *Soul-Violence* (New Orleans: Spring Journal Books, 2008), pp. 72–73.

18. From an unpublished letter by C. G. Jung quoted in Gerhard Adler, "Jung's Personality and Work," *Psychological Perspectives* (Spring 1975), p. 12:

> Can man stand a further increase of consciousness? . . . Is it really worthwhile that man should progress morally and intellectually? . . . But I confess that I submitted to the divine power of this apparently insurmountable problem and I consciously and intentionally made my life miserable, because I wanted God to be alive and free from the suffering man has put upon him by loving his own reason more than God's secret intentions.

19. C. G. Jung, *Memories, Dreams, Reflections* (New York: Pantheon Books, 1961), p. 338.

20. Wolfgang Giegerich, "The End of Meaning and the Birth of Man," *Journal of Jungian Theory and Practice* 6(1): 2–3.

21. *Ibid.,* pp. 3–4.

22. The concept of the depressive position was originally formulated by Melanie Klein in "A Contribution to the Psychogenesis of Manic-Depressive States" (1935). Klein observed that it follows an earlier stage in development dominated by the process of splitting wherein the good object is seen as separate from the bad object. The realization that the bad object and the good are the same is accompanied by the "depressing" realization that hatred and aggression is directed toward the same object one loves. Klein and those after her wrote that the depressive position is never fully achieved, that it is worked on throughout one's life. Depressive position counters the natural tendency to split, to see matters in terms of mutually exclusive opposites.

Regarding shadow integration, Wolfgang Giegerich writes:

> The apprenticeship of consciousness is concluded. It has been a constant climb from complete innocence to full psychological awareness. . . . Now our logic can accept and affirm the inherent contradiction of our being, namely our *being* consciousness. . . . All the forms of killing of the previous stages—the theological, moralistic, enlightened, pietistic killings—have been overcome, not only empirically, but logically: because the form of otherness has been overcome. "First Shadow, Then Anima, or the Advent of the Guest," in *Soul-Violence* (New Orleans: Spring Journal Books, 2008), p. 108.

23. Greg Mogenson, "Different Moments in Dialectical Movement," in *Dialectics and Analytical Psychology: The El Capitan Seminar* (New Orleans: Spring Journal Books, 2005), pp. 94–95.

24. C. G. Jung, *Mysterium Coniunctionis*, vol. 14, *The Collected Works of C. G. Jung*, translated by R. F. C. Hull (London: Routledge and Kegan Paul, 1966), § 206.

25. Thorsen, "Interview."

Trauma, Mourning, and Renewal
Agnieszka Piotrowska's *Out of the Ruins*

HELENA BASSIL-MOROZOW

I n February 1989, Agnieszka Piotrowska, then a BBC trainee on a new contract with the BBC Elstree Studios, set off for a ten-day pre-filming visit to Armenia in order to research the possibility of a documentary about the earthquake that had taken place December 7, 1988. Months later, she returned to Armenia with a film crew for eight weeks to make her first documentary film, *Out of the Ruins* (1989). The original research trip became the pivotal event of her life and career. It profoundly affected the young director both personally and professionally as well as repositioned her ethical views and beliefs.

This article traces the rebuilding of hope and meaning, in the lives of the film's participants and in the filmmaker herself, after the catastrophic earthquake. The fact that the director lacked both professional and life experience during the making of this documentary makes the communal quest for hope, meaning, and spiritual rebirth all the more heroic and special. The filmmaker joined the victims of

Helena Bassil-Morozow is a cultural philosopher and film scholar, researching the dynamic between individual personality and sociocultural systems in industrialized and postindustrial societies. She is an honorary research fellow of the Research Institute for Media Art and Design, University of Bedfordshire. Her books include *Tim Burton: The Monster and the Crowd* and *The Trickster in Contemporary Film*.

the earthquake in their trip through physical and spiritual hell—which, luckily for everyone involved, ended in symbolic renewal.

For Piotrowska, *Out of the Ruins* was a tough initiation into the directing profession. Since then, she has made more than a dozen documentaries and TV series and won countless awards. However, the significance of that first film made twenty years ago is still important both for the director and the nation she observed and filmed, a nation whose psychological fragments she was painfully trying to piece together in her first work. In fact, the film was rebroadcast in Armenia in 2011. It is as topical now as it was in 1989 because it discusses the ways in which we—human beings— deal with mass trauma and personal grief. Apart from the horror of loss, it shows the power of empathy and the ability of the human psyche to regenerate itself, to find a way out of an existential crisis, and to lift itself "out of the ruins."

TRAUMA

On December 7, 1988, the Spitak region of Armenia (part of the former Soviet Union at the time) was jolted by a magnitude 7.1 earthquake which was followed by a magnitude 5.8 aftershock. The tremors devastated an area 80 kilometers in diameter, including the cities of Spitak, Leninakan, and Kirovakan. At least twenty-five thousand people were killed, fifteen thousand were injured, and many more lost their homes. A number of factors contributed to the high death toll, including freezing winter temperatures and poorly constructed housing. Many victims died because poorly designed multistory apartment blocks were shaken to the ground in a matter of seconds. The floors collapsed, crushing anyone who did not escape.

Piotrowska's film opens with a panorama of Leninakan shot from a helicopter. The aim of this long—and rather shaky—establishing shot is to show us the scope of the disaster. Its details are revealed in the subsequent sequences: suddenly the generalized human grief, which looks so neutral and airbrushed in the news, faces us in all its raw emotionality and corporeality. We are shown blood, dead bodies, funerals, mourning and grief, therapeutic sessions, and childbirth. Participants do not hide anything from the camera and express their thoughts and emotions openly. The hardest thing for the audience to deal with, however, is the existential despair and loss of faith from which the families who lost their loved ones in the earthquake suffer. It is this Job-like pain, caused by the demiurge's brutality, that is difficult to grasp and accept. Yet, at the same time, with so much real grief and mourning, there is a glimmer of hope for rebirth and renewal in the film.

A major adverse event with a large number of deaths is certainly a very difficult subject for a young female documentary director to tackle. It took Piotrowska and her crew two months to complete the principal photography. The time spent on location was traumatic—and particularly so because the director was emotionally unprepared to deal with a mass outpouring of human grief. She reminisces:

> I have no idea how I managed to raise the money to make *Out of the Ruins*. This really would be tough now. It was not a commercial movie—and I have no idea how I got through the two months on location in Armenia with zero experience or training of dealing with profound grief. I spent the first month completely on my own, and the second leading a BBC crew for the first time on such a big project. I remember crying all the time, looking at all the sadness and physical destruction; seeing women giving birth in the middle of the rubble. I was just writing notes for my film—as I was really a cyborg there, and not a young woman out of her depth. I learnt then that crying can be a good thing—for me it has since been a good defence, a way of getting rid of negative feelings, and carrying on.
>
> It was very important to me at the time to make this film—I really, really wanted to see what the pain really meant "behind the scenes." So often films about natural disasters are but "weather pornography"—no real in-depth narratives. I think over the years this got worse, not better. From that point of view, I still think this is a really good film.[1]

We are used to thinking of feature films as artificial, and documentaries as "depicting real life." However, documentary narratives are not entirely real—they have to be reconstructed and manipulated into storylike sequences to create meaning for the audience. One can only show a segment of the vast narrative that is life, and this segment has to be carefully chosen and polished. Similarly, Piotrowska constructs a story that lends itself well to Jungian analysis—the characters' struggle for meaning after the catastrophe, their struggle for the explanation of God's cruelty and injustice, transforms into a heroic journey that ends with the birth of a child. The new meaning can be said to be born "out of the ruins."

For her film, Piotrowska chooses an extended family living in a shanty town amidst the wreckage. Two cousins live opposite each other—Asthik and Gina. Asthik lost both her children, a boy and a girl, while Gina was lucky and her two children survived. Now Asthik is pregnant again, and she and her husband are impatiently waiting for the baby to arrive.

Living conditions are cramped, which means that many people have to sleep on the floor in tiny rooms; for instance, Gina's family lives in a garage. Piotrowska follows both families as they go about their daily lives—looking after relatives' graves at the cemetery, attending religious services, cleaning up the rubble, making bread, playing with the children, working, sleeping, attending therapy sessions. All the while, the director's main attention is on Asthik's growing belly as the unborn child symbolizes hope for the mourning family. The film ends with the birth of a baby girl in an overcrowded hospital with minimal sanitary conditions. The baby is healthy, and Asthik and her husband are finally happy after months of pain and despair.

The director constructs the narrative of *Out of the Ruins* as a series of juxtapositions that gradually grow and expand into a linear narrative concentrating on the struggle for meaning and order in the cruel and unpredictable world. These juxtapositions represent the struggle between darkness and light, death and life, despair and hope, chaos and order, nature and mankind.

For instance, because their children survived, Gina and her husband are interviewed against ordinary backgrounds: streets, room interiors. Natural light is used. By contrast, Asthik's mourning and inner emptiness are conveyed by dark backgrounds and low-key lighting.

The victims' "inner darkness" conveyed by cinematic means is linked in the film to their loss of faith—the result of the trauma. In her interviews, Asthik keeps expressing her disappointment in the imperfect world and in the Christian Orthodox religion which failed to protect her children: "This compels me to say there is no God . . . Before the earthquake I used to dress in colourful clothes. I used to dress up and go out a lot. Black is the colour of my dress now."[2] Her existentialist stance is echoed by her husband: "Our nation has lived for its faith and by its faith. Now God ceased to exist for us. We always lived a hard life for the sake of that God. But that God is no more. I used to look at my children and say: 'I'll lay down my life for God so that you may live in peace.' But God has betrayed us. He has forsaken us . . . All that you had may vanish without trace, leaving you in ruins." Asthik keeps looking at Gina's daughter because she reminds her of her own lost child.

Gina's postcatastrophe view of God is deist rather than existentialist. Deism presupposes that God created the universe and left it to exist and operate by itself. Consequently, he is in no way responsible for any natural disasters or man-made nightmares (such as genocides) that happen in the world. Gina has transferred all the blame for the earthquake onto Mother Nature: "I still have my faith. This was not God—but nature was at fault here. God could not have been so cruel."

MOURNING

The survivors' transition from the vision of God as a force that organizes the world according to rational laws and governs it justly to deist explanations of the disaster or even blatant existentialism is understandable. A tragedy on this scale has many facets—physical, psychological, ontological. It severely distorts the spiritual matrix of the survivors' lives. For the survivors, it is not just their houses that turn to rubble—the entire universe, with its rational laws, scientific rules, and Kantian categorical imperative comes crashing down. The human mind wants its surroundings to be predictable and logical. Jung writes in "Archaic Man" (1931):

> We distinctly resent the idea of invisible and arbitrary forces, for it is not so long ago that we made our escape from that frightening world of dreams and superstitions, and constructed for ourselves a picture of the cosmos worthy of our rational consciousness— that latest and greatest achievement of man. We are now surrounded by a world that is obedient to rational laws. It is true that we do not know the causes of everything, but in time they will be discovered, and these discoveries will accord with our reasoned expectations. There are, to be sure, also chance occurrences, but they are merely accidental, and we do not doubt that they have a causality of their own. Chance happenings are

repellent to the mind that loves order. They disturb the regular, predictable course of events in the most absurd and irritating way. We resent them as we resent the invisible, arbitrary forces, for they remind us too much of Satanic imps or of the caprice of a *deus ex machina.* They are the worst enemies of our careful calculations and a continual threat to all our undertakings. Being admittedly contrary to reason, they deserve all our abuse, and yet we should not fail to give them their due.[3]

Theodicy of any kind is no consolation for those who lost their relatives in a natural disaster. The earthquake survivors' anger at God is a very ancient form of spiritual and psychological injury that Jungian thought has touched upon many times. The biblical Job's search for an explanation of his sufferings makes for a powerful story because it presents the individual as being inexplicably, desperately, irreversibly out of control over his life and fate. The individual in this biblical tale is lonely and abused. Moreover, his friends and family side with the abuser that is the all-powerful God. Therefore, the deity is a cruel and cunning trickster and not at all the rational ruler of the world. Stanley Diamond argues in his analysis of the Book of Job:

> Job . . . despairs of his friends, along with, in the passion of his suffering, his family. God is torturing him for unknown reasons, he replies. His friends, he continues, desert him when they insist that he is undergoing a just punishment, and he warns them of retribution.
>
> But they prove relentless and Job finally responds that the wicked often go unpunished in this world, giving many examples of this state of affairs. In so doing, he not only unwittingly questions his own implicit conviction of the connection between piety and the worldly reward, but his more recently stated belief that God punished the wicked only. He also asserts what the Book has ostensibly set out to question: Why do the just suffer and the wicked flourish? And so the dialogue comes to a close, Job seeking sympathy and defending his behaviour, his friends accusing him of impudence, perfidy, hypocrisy, and self-righteousness.[4]

Existential crisis not only affected the film's participants—it also profoundly affected its young director. Piotrowska, who met Asthik in a hospital in Yerevan and became friends with her, was profoundly moved by the woman's plight and her loss of basic trust in the world.

She says: "The entire experience was just transformational. I had to deal with grief, sadness, and loss on a grand scale. At the same time, I knew that I had to complete this film. It felt like I had no choice, really: either I complete it—or I will never make a film again."

Jung, with his profound interest in Gnosticism, had a lot to say about God's dark side—not just in his famous book *Answer to Job* (1952), but elsewhere in his writings. He famously (and consistently) criticized the Christian doctrine for separating the "benevolent God" from its adversary, the Devil. For Jung the Gnostic, God's darkness cannot be separated from his goodness. Jung writes:

> The world is not a garden of God the Father, it is also a place of horror. Not only in heaven no father and earth no mother and men are not brothers, but they represent as many hostile destructive forces to which we are the more surely delivered over the more confidently and thoughtlessly we entrust ourselves to the so-called fatherly hand of God.[5]

Psychologically and ontologically, natural disasters are numinous—shocking, unconscious, primordial, way outside of human control. They defy meaning-making processes characteristic of the human mind. In fact, they eliminate and erase meaning. The very scale and impact of natural disasters make meaning as a concept obsolete. They leave human beings at a loss, at developmental crossroads. These terrifyingly gnostic moments retain their powerful numinosity many years after the catastrophe. Gnostic theodicy hands the problem of evil over to the numinous—where it disappears and dissolves—for the numinous is vast and unknowable. It does not do meaning, explanations, or apologies. Human beings can only try to argue their case before God—like Job or like Jacob in Jung's analysis of the biblical story of Jacob wrestling with the angel:

> Without wishing it, we human beings are placed in situations in which the great "principles" entangle us in something, and God leaves it to us to find a way out. Sometimes a clear path is opened with his help, but when it really comes to the point one has the feeling of having been abandoned by every good spirit. In critical situations the hero always mislays his weapon, and at such moments, as before death, we are confronted with the nakedness of this fact. And one does not know how one got there. A thousand twists of fate all of a sudden land you in such a

situation. This is symbolically represented by Jacob's fight with
the angel at the ford. Here a man can do nothing but stand
his ground. It is a situation that challenges him to react as a
whole man. It may turn out that he can no longer keep to the
letter of the moral law. That is where his most personal ethics
begin: in grim confrontation with the Absolute, in striking
out on a path condemned by current morality and the
guardians of the law. And yet one may feel that he has never
been truer to his innermost nature and vocation, and hence
nearer to the Absolute, because he alone and the Omniscient
have seen the actual situation as it were from inside, whereas
the judges and condemners see it only from the outside.[6]

The encounter with the unfathomable and numinous nature of
God is rephrased by Piotrowska (who is a Lacanian) as "the encounter
with 'the (Big) Other.'" In Lacanian language, the Big Other
designates "a radical alterity, an other-ness which transcends the
illusory otherness of the imaginary because it cannot be assimilated
through identification." The Other is thus beyond conscious
control; it is another place, a place outside consciousness.[7] The
Other is rationally and emotionally unfathomable. In the situation
where the director is dealing with a mass catastrophe, creating a linear
and meaningful narrative out of the ruins becomes an almost
superhuman task. Piotrowska asserts:

> Documentary filmmakers create visual narratives out of the
> experience they have had with the Other. Once made, the
> narrative of a film lives on and the memory of the experience
> lives on too—but the two, of course, are different. My
> assertion is that, for the audiences, the filmmakers and the
> contributors alike, it is important that the record of their
> experience together has elements of "the production of
> meaning," rather than being just made as entertainment.
> Modern television practices and objectives make it near
> impossible for the production of meaning to take place.

Interestingly enough, Piotrowska's solution to the characters'
existentialist nightmare and loss of meaning is to go back to the basics
of life—to rebuild it from scratch, from simple, uncomplicated everyday
tasks; to concentrate on the bricks of everyday existence. In the state of
psychological twilight, meaning is found not in religion or philosophy

but in everyday, ritualized tasks such as the making of bread or in special events such as the birth of a child. Theodicy is shoved aside and replaced with uncomplicated reality.

RENEWAL

Even filming a world in ruins, an absurd world in which nature's cruelty is both horrendously superfluous and terrifyingly inexplicable, the director needs a narrative structure. When the big meaning is lost, when the human mind is struggling with the eternal problem of evil, cinematic narrative becomes dependent on smaller building blocks. Piotrowska structures the narrative around Asthik's pregnancy and childbirth. Narratives are structures, and, man-made or naturally emerging, they ameliorate the absurdity of the world. The narrative structure of *Out of the Ruins* mirrors and replicates the participants' rediscovered hope and meaning that had been destroyed by the earthquake.

Piotrowska goes back to the basics of life; she leaves the realm of the abstract and the philosophical and enters the world of raw existence, day-to-day survival, and powerful emotions. While the child is the core of the narrative—and the treasure of Asthik's female hero quest— the rest of the story is filled with blood, tears, funerals, nightmares, and communal cleaning of the debris. Many of the scenes in *Out of the Ruins* are chillingly naturalistic, brutally candid, or outright unwatchable. The new meaning—rather like the child—is born out of these naturalistic, bloody truths rooted in the hardship of everyday existence and survival.

For instance, one of the scenes in the film depicts an animal sacrifice. A goat is dragged mercilessly to the place of the sacrifice and its head is cut off. The entire community, including small children, is present at the ritual. Piotrowska does not spare the audience from the most brutal elements of the ritual: we are shown the slow ritual murder, the pool of blood, the carcass-cutting process. The brutal ritual reminds the community of the death of their loved ones; some people are crying. Another scene shows a funeral with loud female wailers and mourners whose grief is terrifyingly exposed, which makes for very uncomfortable watching.

One of the most uncomfortable scenes depicts Asthik playing with Gina's little girl, stroking her hair and telling her that she reminds her of her own dead child. In another part of the film an elderly woman is walking along a line of cheap coffins and opening the lids—apparently looking for a dead relative. Her demeanor is so shockingly businesslike that the viewer becomes appalled by the dehumanized way in which the dead bodies are handled—particularly because of the stark juxtaposition between the lifelessness of the bodies and the powerful and painful grief displayed so openly by the film's participants.

Some domestic scenes are almost peaceful—like the one in which the surviving women of the family are making bread together in a garage. Creative activities spread into the realm of mourning and loss—while the women are baking bread and collectively looking after the children, the men are carving gravestones and cleaning the rubble.

A significant portion of the film is devoted to the psychotherapeutic treatment received by the affected children after the disaster. Psychotherapy and psychology were seen in the Soviet Union in a negative light and were considered to be pseudosciences. In 1989—when Piotrowska was making the documentary—the official attitude toward therapy was gradually changing. The director of the children's therapy center featured in the film explains that the Armenian government underestimates the seriousness of the psychological trauma received by the children. Left without treatment, their mental health may deteriorate.

We are shown the minimal mental health services available to the young victims: group art and drama therapy. We get to see children's painting sessions and a recording of a drama therapy class. Both make for disturbing viewing. Children use black and red in the majority of their pictures while the main subjects, predictably, are ruined buildings, dead bodies, graveyards, and ambulances. Many children suffer from insomnia and nightmares—and during the drama therapy session they are asked to act out the worst of their dreams. A little boy tells fellow patients and the therapist that his recurring nightmare is the one in which the earth opens up and all of his family falls into the gash. The group then relives the nightmare together with the dreamer.

Finally, there is the scene of childbirth—grotesque in its crudity, fragility, and exposedness. The heavily pregnant Asthik is taken to an overcrowded maternity hospital where several women are forced to share the same prenatal ward. Women also have to share one birthing unit. There is a shortage of staff, hospital beds, and instruments. Water to be used in procedures is boiled in large metal tubs by middle-aged nurses on gas hobs. Amid all this chaos and lack of privacy, amid all the moaning and crying women, Asthik gives birth to a baby girl. The birth and the washing of the child are filmed in detail. This moment is as liminal as it is carnivalesque in its indelicate yet truthful corporeality.

New meaning is born out of the ruins in these nightmarish, ritualistic—yet realistic—moments. It is born out of the shifting layers of life; it gradually emerges during transitional, liminal periods. In an absurd world civilization starts to question itself and its own right to exist—but the physical, the basic, the everyday remains intact. The director makes a film about the world on the edge, the world as it is rebuilding itself from the basic bricks of life. In fact, Gohar—the child born in the film—said twenty years later that watching herself being born out of the ruins was a revelation, an amazing feeling. It was certainly an important scene, in all its emotional and corporeal naturalism.

Piotrowska's decision to show the terrible reality—the physical and psychological fragility of mankind—can even be said to be Bakhtinian. During the liminal shifts, when the thin veneer of civilization wanes, when theodicy fails in its task of explaining the origins and purpose of evil, the physical becomes the source of life, and the source of all theological and philosophical explanations. The search for meaning after the catastrophe leads back to the body: death and birth, communal bread making and meat sharing (the latter involving the hapless goat). *Out of the Ruins* is terrifyingly grotesque in the sense that it is full of images that we civilized Western human beings would rather not see.

For the civilized mind, the human body is private, hidden, sacred. By contrast, in Piotrowska's film, it is sprawled out for everyone to see; it is unprotected. From the dehumanization of dead bodies to the maternity ward conditions, the fragility of human life lies terrifyingly exposed. Nature is powerful; it destroys the human spirit. It destroys faith, hope, civilization. All that is left is the flesh.

Yet, this prevalence of the physical in the film, disturbing as it is, is also a positive sign. Hope—like the new baby girl—is born out of this simple, raw life that survived under the ruins of civilization. It is this new life that marks the end of mourning and the beginning of the period of social and personal rebirth.

In *Out of the Ruins,* life and death coexist in claustrophobic proximity. Renewal after the catastrophe comes out of this controversial coexistence which our civilized mind—relying on science and rationality for answers—is reluctant to acknowledge. The result is the gnostic unity of the corporeal and the spiritual via suffering and subsequent renewal. The director renders the idea of the body as the source of life with her powerful—and disturbing—shots of people carving tombstones for their dead loved ones, of children overcoming their fears and nightmares in collective drama, of babies bathed in Soviet metallic tubs. The film's principal juxtaposition—that of life and death—gradually disappears and turns into a Rabelaisian-Bakhtinian unity.

According to Russian cultural critic Mikhail Bakhtin, the idea of the human body as something private emerges in European culture after the Renaissance. By contrast, the medieval and Renaissance vision of the world did not separate the physical from the spiritual. It also did not draw the distinction between death and life. The images that seem to us grotesquely realistic and excessive were normal in medieval folk culture. This attitude toward life and death is also present in some rebellious Renaissance literature—particularly in François Rabelais's epic trilogy *Gargantua and Pantagruel,* and also in Shakespeare's texts. Bakhtin writes in *Rabelais and His World* (1981):

> The grotesque image reflects a phenomenon in transformation, an as yet unfinished metamorphosis, of death and birth, growth and becoming. The relation to time is one determining trait of the grotesque image. The other indispensable trait is ambivalence. For in this image we find both poles of transformation, the old and the new, the dying and the procreating, the beginning and the end of the metamorphosis.[8]

Interestingly enough, even though Piotrowska's camerawork and choice of narrative moments called for a degree of intrusion into the personal lives of the participants, looking out for emotionally and physically intimate moments, the director herself does not see her actions as being particularly intrusive. Moreover, she remained friends with the female protagonist, Asthik, and the two kept in touch after the filming had ended. Piotrowska explains:

Asthik and her family moved to Moscow and I moved too. Apparently, they had tried to find me for ten years. Eventually, through the Internet, Asthik got in touch again and we did meet in Moscow in 2006. I sensed they thought it was a disappointing meeting: we traveled in very different directions in the seventeen years that intervened, and the Agnieszka they met in 2006 was too different from their internal image of the Agnieszka who had made a beautiful film of their loss and their survival. . . .

Did they feel colonized all these years ago? Actually I do think they might have done—but they thought it was well worth it: it was good to have their story retold with pretty music by Michael Nyman and the beautiful crane shots. It validated the nightmare they went through. It helped. It really did.

And so I thought in a way they sought me out in lieu of God, or some kind omnipotent agency which could change their lives again—even if just on the screen. And that was not something I could offer—and they were sad about that.

The director as a god that transforms the world and is in charge of life and death is an interesting idea. According to Bakhtin, the death-life opposition is a psychological by-product of the modern mind. It is deeply existentialist and it simply did not exist in medieval folk culture:

Such an opposition is completely contrary to the system of grotesque imagery, in which death is not a negation of life seen as the great body of all the people but part of life as a whole—its indispensable component, the condition of its constant renewal and regeneration. Death is here always related to birth; the grave is related to the earth's life-giving womb. Birth-death, death-birth, such are the components of life itself as in the famous words of the Spirit of the Earth in Goethe's *Faust*. Death is included in life, and together with birth determines its eternal movement. Even the struggle of life and death in the individual body is conceived by grotesque imagery as the struggle of the old life stubbornly resisting the new life out to be born, as the crisis of change.[9]

By contrast, the contemporary image of the body, which began to emerge in European literature and culture from the seventeenth century onward, separates the physical from the spiritual. The body becomes secondary and the life of the spirit takes precedence in human existence:

> [B]odies and objects begin to acquire a private, individual nature, they are rendered petty and homely and become immovable parts of private life, the goal of egotistic lust and possession. This is no longer the positive, regenerating and renewing lower stratum, but a blunt and deathly obstacle to ideal aspirations. In the private sphere of isolated individuals the images of the bodily lower stratum preserve the element of negation while losing almost entirely their positive regenerating force. Their link with life and with the cosmos is broken, they are narrowed down to naturalistic erotic images.[10]

Thus, from our point of view as contemporary Western individuals, realism is always grotesque and indecent because it has no respect for individual human beings, reducing them to flesh and bones. It has no respect for our uniqueness, for the human mind. It does not take into account the fact that we are all different. Nature itself is grotesque, and it prompts in us something akin to an existentialist revolt. And yet, the grotesque, the realistic, and the naturalistic are closely linked to life. They are life itself. The birth of Asthik's baby at the end of *Out of the Ruins* marks the end of the cycle of death and birth, which can be said to be truly Bakhtinian. Something good is born out of something terrible.

And here we have come back to Jung's Gnosticism: in the words of Marie-Louise von Franz, Jung's psychology does not ask *why* something happened (that is, what caused it), but what did it happen for?[11] Similarly, in Piotrowska's film, where theodicy fails, where science is powerless and technology insufficient, where rational explanations stopped working—the body becomes the source of renewal. Meaning is born out of absurdity, out of the meaningless. And it is the body that gives birth to the spirit and keeps it alive.

NOTES

1. This and all subsequent interview passages with Agnieszka Piotrowska are from a private interview given in July 2012.

2. All interview quotes used in this article are taken from Piotrowska's documentary.

3. C. G. Jung, "Archaic Man," in *The Collected Works of C. G. Jung*, vol. 10, *Civilization in Transition*, trans. R. F. C. Hull (London: Routledge and Kegan Paul, 1966), § 113.

4. Stanley Diamond in the introduction to Paul Radin, *The Trickster: A Study in American Indian Mythology* (New York: Schocken Books, 1972), pp. xv-xvi.

5. Jung, "Archaic Man," § 224.

6. C. G. Jung, "Good and Evil in Analytical Psychology," in *The Collected Works of C. G. Jung*, vol. 10, *Civilization in Transition*, trans. R. F. C. Hull (London: Routledge and Kegan Paul, 1966), § 869.

7. Dylan Evans, *An Introductory Dictionary of Lacanian Psychoanalysis* (London: Routledge, 1996), p. 133.

8. Mikhail Bakhtin, *Rabelais and His World* (Bloomington: Indiana University Press, 1984), p. 24.

9. *Ibid.*, p. 50.

10. *Ibid.*, p. 23.

11. Marie-Louise von Franz, "The Process of Individuation," in *Man and His Symbols*, ed. C. G. Jung (London: Picador, 1964), p. 384.

Archetypes Assemble
How Superhero Teams Save the World from the Apocalypse and Lead the Way to Individuation—Marvel's *The Avengers*

James Alan Anslow

Marvel's The Avengers (*Avengers Assemble* in the UK). 2012. Directed by Joss Whedon. Written by Joss Whedon (screenplay and story) and Zak Penn (story). Based on the comic book by Stan Lee and Jack Kirby.

Introduction

The Avengers is a recent example of the apocalyptic superhero genre which has been prevalent in Hollywood since the start of the twenty-first century. The popularity of such movies, and TV series, is due to the crisis of the individual in a complex and fractured postmodern society. This crisis is played out in disasters—man-made, natural, supernatural, or extraterrestrial—that cannot be countered by the lone heroism of a single protagonist. Instead a collective, a team,

James Alan Anslow is a media psychology researcher working on his Ph.D. at the Centre for Psychoanalytic Studies, University of Essex, and formerly a journalism lecturer at City University London. Before becoming an academic, he worked for thirty years on Britain's biggest-selling newspapers, *The Sun* and the controversially discontinued *News of the World*. He was chief production editor of *News of the World* in the 1990s and ran its editorial output the night Princess Diana died.

of heroes gathers together to save humankind. The superhero teams created by Marvel comics in the 1960s and re-presented in blockbuster films, notably since the year 2000, have typified this movement: in 2006 an idiosyncratic band of talented young mutants saved the world in *X-Men: The Last Stand* and in 2007 a tightly knit quaternity fended off the planet-eating Galactus and his glistening interstellar herald in *Fantastic Four: Rise of the Silver Surfer.*

Now the third of Marvel's "big three" collectives has hit the screen like a thunderbolt from a mythic realm beyond the Internet. *The Avengers*, directed by Joss Whedon and released in 2012, is a fast-paced, comic book journey of individuation fueled by powerful archetypal projections vividly enhanced through computer-generated imagery (CGI). Based on a set of superheroic characters invented (sometimes reinvented) by Marvel Publishing in the 1960s, the billion-dollar movie is the culmination of an interwoven plot explored to varying degrees in five earlier films: *The Incredible Hulk* (2008), *Iron Man* (2008), *Iron Man 2* (2010), *Captain America: The First Avenger* (2011), and *Thor* (2011). It is not necessary to see these prequels to understand the film plot, nor does a viewer need to be aware of their nuanced fifty-year-old roots in the silver age of comic books, generally considered to stretch from the late 1950s to the mid 1970s. If, however, as I did, you saw the other five movies and if, as my twelve-year-old self was, you were steeped in the Marvel magic conjured up by Stan Lee and his comic book artists, led by Jack Kirby, then your enjoyment of this film will have been amplified many times over. It has taken half a century for cinematography to acquire tools nimble and subtle enough to capture and emulate the graphic imagination of Kirby, Steve Ditko, and other leading Marvel artists of their time. *Avengers Assemble* and its prequels sit comfortably among hitherto unconnected films from the Marvel pantheon including those about Spider-Man, the X-Men, and the Fantastic Four.

The Plot: Facing the Threat of the Other

The film is set in the present or immediate future in a place that is recognizably our planet. One of the hallmarks of Marvel superheroes is that they operate in actual cities referred to by name, not the fantastical ones of DC Comics' Superman and Batman: New York not Metropolis nor Gotham City. The juxtaposition of the mundane and supra-mundane—superheroes battling amid known landmarks—is thrilling; it provides a conscious landscape with a bridge to the unconscious in which archetypal tensions can unfold; it portrays a *coniunctio* of body and soul. The movie opens with the Asgardian trickster Loki (Tom Hiddleston) making a Faustian deal with a shadowy, supremely powerful extraterrestrial called the Other (Alexis Denisof), whose name blatantly announces its psychological meaning and requires little interpretation. Loki promises to retrieve a mysterious and numinous power source called the Tesseract and in return the Other will provide him with an army of Chitauri, monsters with which he can conquer the earth. The planet is secretly protected by an organization called S.H.I.E.L.D. led by Nick Fury (Samuel L. Jackson), one-eyed like his all-father Asgardian equivalent Odin. In response to Loki's threat Fury invokes the Avengers Initiative and begins to gather together a tempestuous collection of superheroes, some of whom have been previously introduced in the prequels mentioned above.

The most powerful is Loki's adoptive brother Thor, the hammer-wielding Norse god of thunder (Chris Hemsworth). In the original Marvel comics, starting with *Journey into Mystery* #83 (August 1962), Thor had a human identity in the form of a crippled doctor—a wounded healer—but in the films he is simply the rather Shakespearean warrior god, entertainingly played by handsome Hemsworth, formerly an Australian soap opera star in TV's *Home and Away*, who was brilliantly directed by Kenneth Branagh in his eponymous film debut as the displaced golden-locked immortal.

In *The Avengers*, Thor is yoked with three heroes, each of whom is undergoing tumultuous differentiation and reintegration of their psyches. Tony Stark (Robert Downey Jr.) is the hyperinflated genius playboy industrialist and show-off philanthropist who struggles with an almost all-consuming ego, an alcohol problem, and a heart kept beating by a complex artificial power source; his persona is Iron Man, a twenty-first-century superpowered suit of armor that is both the personification of Western weaponry and an altruistic protector of the weak, in "stark" contrast to Tony's selfish hedonism, seemingly recently modified by his love for Pepper Potts (Gwyneth Paltrow). Steve Rogers (Chris Evans) was a feeble, sickly wannabe warrior transformed into muscular supersoldier Captain America by a scientific experiment during World War II; he is frozen in ice and reborn in this century to help redeem the world once more. He has a near-magical mandala-like shield which, like S.H.I.E.L.D., protects all of humanity from the disruptive shadow lurking in the collective unconscious. Bruce Banner (Mark Ruffalo) is one of the world's leading scientists; he is ostensibly recruited by Fury for his intellect, his logos, but inevitably his powerful shadow, the Hulk, overwhelms him through anger and adds his brute strength to the emerging Avengers team. "Hulk smash" is this green monster's war cry, and Banner's Jekyll-and-Hyde psychological angst matches the inner, less overt conflicts of Stark and Rogers, the latter displaced in a new age as well as a new body. As viewers we are, of course, attracted by the power of Banner's shadow rather than his cerebral ego. We secretly commend Stark's observation: "Dr. Banner, your work is unparalleled. And I'm a huge fan of the way you lose control and turn into an enormous green rage monster."

The two remaining members of the collective psyche that is the Avengers are Clint Barton aka Hawkeye (Jeremy Renner) and Natasha Romanoff aka the Black Widow (Scarlett Johansson). As trained agents without superpowers they differ from their more maverick teammates; they are a syzygy with an ambiguous interpersonal history and their personal psyches are more opaque than those of Stark, Rogers, and Banner. These two characters are spirit-like, inhuman—even though, on the face of it, they are the most human of the team. They are projections of the team's collective psyche rather than psychological entities in their own right. Romanoff's nom de guerre defines her presence as the feminine force of creation and destruction; black widow spiders notoriously eat their males after mating. Mookerjee has drawn attention to the sex, death, and rebirth images of the Indian deity Kali and her representation of the Black Goddess known in Finland as Kalma (Kali Ma).[1] Romanoff is the only strong female presence in the film and, given its martial content, her projection as the darker side of the Great Mother feels appropriate. As the main anima projection in the storyline (Pepper Potts is subsidiary) she is often underestimated by foes and allies alike. Hillman discusses the perceived inferiority of anima projections thus:

> For anima presents herself in fantasies, rather than meanings. It
> is implied that the anima as function is superior to the anima
> personified. Further support for anima integration as "breaking

up the personifications" can be drawn from other passages where Jung talks of the "dissolution of the anima" and of "depersonalizing" and "subjugating the anima."[2]

Jung says:

> When projected the anima has a feminine form with definite characteristics. This empirical finding does not mean that the archetype is constituted like that in itself. The male female syzygy is only one among the possible pairs of opposites albeit the most important one.[3]

Her archer partner is almost sprite-like; indeed Stark jokingly calls him Legolas in a reference to the bow-carrying elf in Tolkien's *The Lord of the Rings*. The bow is often associated with the spirit of the Green Man, who is described so comprehensively by Anderson and Hicks.[4] The green man of Sherwood, Robin Hood, is a legendary archer, and even Shakespeare's trickster Puck departs "faster than an arrow from an archer's bow."[5] The archer's bow and arrow provide a concretely manifest connection between the internal and the external world; it is a key trickster function threading together conscious and the unconscious.

The blood sacrifice of Agent Phil Coulson (Clark Gregg), whose admiration of Captain America is unmistakably Patroclusian, spurs the Avengers to integrate their efforts and confront Loki and his unearthly army. New York City itself proves to be the portal for the Chitauri fleet waiting in space to subjugate the world, and Loki's scepter provides the mythic key to the world's defense. The extended CGI-enhanced apocalyptic battle that almost lays waste to the city will be familiar to those who remember such destruction meted out almost every month to the Big Apple in the aforementioned Marvel comics and also to the newer generations of computer gamers. (At the time of writing there is no game product on the market based on the film. However, there have been discussions, and gamers expect one to appear before long. The computer game market dwarfs Hollywood's sales, and this commercial truth impacts the plots and graphics of superhero films.)[6] The result of the battle is a predictable victory for the Avengers and S.H.I.E.L.D., while Loki and the Other, as psychological facts of life always with us, survive. The film's conclusion makes it clear that the way is left open for a sequel—or perhaps several.

THE FRAGMENTED INDIVIDUAL

Apocalyptic films and TV series, as entertaining as they are, signify profound uneasiness in the psyche of the postmodern man or woman. We are not truly liberated individuals; we are still of the mass—in the West now cultural rather than ideological—and dominated by the collective unconscious described by Jung, who writes:

> The "common man," who is predominantly a mass man, acts on the principle of realizing nothing, nor does he need to, because for him the only thing that commits mistakes is that vast anonymity conventionally known as the "State" or "Society." But once a man knows that he is, or should be, responsible, he feels responsible also for his psychic constitution, the more so the more clearly he sees what he would have to be in order to become healthier, more stable, and more efficient. Once he is on the way to assimilating the unconscious he can be certain that he will escape no difficulty that is an integral part of his nature.[7]

It is this assimilating of the unconscious that emerges time and again in *The Avengers* and provides its relentless psychological tension. In this fiction the world is undergoing the most important moment of its existence: its potential subjugation by an alien ruler. Yet the real story in the movie is the psychological one of the six-in-one entity that is the Avengers. Jung explains:

> The great events of world history are, at bottom, profoundly unimportant. In the last analysis, the essential thing is the life of the individual. This alone makes history, here alone do the transformations first take place, and the whole future, the whole history of the world, ultimately spring as a gigantic summation from these hidden sources in individuals. In our most private and most subjective lives, we are not only the passive witnesses of our age, and its sufferers, but also its makers.[8]

The core psychological themes of *The Avengers* are predicated on this fragmentation; if the team is viewed as a single psyche, then it is often dysfunctional, its limbs working in mutual conflict. Brokenness is a key theme of the film; the group scatters away from each other, propelled by internal tensions and aspirations. This brokenness is reinforced, sometimes triggered, by confrontations with their individual shadows, those of each other, and of the team's collective unconscious. Loki, the shadow trickster, has opened up the portal to the Other, the unconscious, and the team, the collective psyche, is fighting to close it, fighting to avoid being sucked into the unconscious. They only conquer or tame the unconscious when they face their own anger, embodied in the Hulk, and make their own heroic efforts, typified by Iron Man's epic concluding battle. Jung describes this struggle with the unconscious thus:

> Instead of being at the mercy of wild beasts, earthquakes, landslides, and inundations, modern man is battered by the elemental forces of his own psyche. This is the World Power that vastly exceeds all other powers on earth. The Age of Enlightenment, which stripped nature and human institutions of gods, overlooked the God of Terror who dwells in the human soul.[9]

Christopher Hauke invoked Jung's concept of the collective unconscious in helping us understand the postmodern man and woman following the "death knell of the "bourgeois ego or monad or subject." He writes: "Jung's development of the concept of a collective unconscious, and ultimately Jung's collective 'subject' which he called the self, helps us with understanding the postmodern subject in a contemporary way less dependent on modern formulations."[10]

Hauke said that what Jung called "internationalism" and "mass man" are in fact global capitalism and "the culture of mass consumerism and communications of the cultural theorists." He adds: "The fragmentation and 'schitzophrenia' of the postmodern subject can be viewed as arising out of the fragmentation of human qualities beyond any choice or control of the individual."[11]

It is this fragmented, dispersed, disconnected, seemingly powerless postmodern condition that sees the Avengers on the point of losing their collective cohesion and being scattered to oblivion by the invaders. It is their reassembling as a psychic, functioning collective whole that saves the day. In fact the word *assemble* in the film's UK and Irish title is a key to its message. It is historically the group's call to arms, although the words are never uttered in this film.

Assembling the Fragments

Avengers #1 (the comic book) was published by Marvel in September 1963, and I bought it shortly afterward, tired of the formulaic superhero plots and characters of the dominant publisher in the genre then, DC Comics, which were utterly lacking the energy and attraction I would later understand as numinosity. On the edition's cover, the back of a shadowy Loki faced the team as it was then comprised (it was slightly different from the movie lineup, although it included the Hulk, Iron Man, and Thor). A lurid tagline splashed in red on the page asked: "Can the combined power of the Avengers defeat the sinister spells of Loki, god of evil?" I was hooked. I had been reading the tales of the Norse gods since I *could* read, and I knew Loki was the god of fire and mischief rather than evil, but such quibbling did not matter; the selling point of the tagline was "the combined power." Assembling that power, represented as the team's manifold archetypal projections, in order to confront and reintegrate with the unconscious shadow of Loki and the well-named Other, is the task with which all human beings are faced from birth: the journey identified by Jung, however inexactly, as individuation. We all instinctually admire individual heroes. (Recently Andrew Samuels asked, after playing the evocative theme tune from *The Good, the Bad and the Ugly* by Ennio Morricone, "Where have all the individuals gone?")[12] But, equally instinctually, we sense that it is a *combination* of traits, strengths, and insights that serve us best as individuals and societies; with skillful and illuminated spiritual mentoring and/or therapeutic guidance, we can also differentiate these psychic elements and reintegrate them with "the other." Jung explains:

> I use the term "individuation" to denote the process by which a person becomes a psychological "in-dividual," that is, a separate, individual unity or "whole." It is generally assumed that consciousness is the whole of the psychological individual. But knowledge of the phenomena that can only be explained on the hypothesis of unconscious psychic processes makes it doubtful whether the ego and its contents are in fact identical with the "whole."[13]

But *The Avengers* is not primarily about the individual, it is rather about the differentiated and reintegrated contents of the individual, represented by this incohesive team. Jung himself might have failed on his quest for individuation in his "dark night of the soul" just as the psychic collective that is the Avengers could fail.[14] As Banner himself observes: "We're not a team, we're a time bomb." But, like Jung himself, in the end they do not fail.

Human beings respond to the team whether it is a hunting party, a football squad, a rock band, or a group of superheroes. A soccer team may have their star player, their David Beckham, but time after time the fate of ego inflation awaits the individual who thinks he or she is bigger than the whole. The truth of this balance resides in the collective unconscious—the ultimate team—which according to Jung is "made up essentially of archetypes."[15] Although his definitions of this phenomenon changed subtly, and sometimes not so subtly, throughout his life, its outline remained thus:

> This collective unconscious does not develop individually but is inherited. It consists of pre-existent forms, the archetypes, which can only become conscious secondarily and which give definite form to certain psychic contents.[16]

In *The Avengers* we see the psychic struggle of these autonomous processes, sometimes raging against each other, resembling a single dysfunctional entity whose limbs do not work in unison but sometimes fight side by side to prevent them collectively being swallowed by the unconscious Other. In Marvel's other Hollywood superhero teams that have drawn huge viewing numbers we see similar fiery combinations of characteristics and projections. In the Fantastic Four films the team is family-based: Sue and Reed Richards (the Invisible Woman and Mr. Fantastic) marry, and Sue's brother is the tricksterish Human Torch; the lumpen Thing finds solace with a blind lover. In the X-Men films the mutants band together and pool their bizarre powers. The power of the group that is greater than its parts is explored in other film genres; a notable example is Akira Kurosawa's 1954 *Seven Samurai*, emulated in 1960 by John Sturges's *The Magnificent Seven*.

CONCLUSION

More than any other commentator Jung appreciated the power of collective archetype. Modern cinema with its CGI and all-around sound is perfectly placed to convey that power, particularly through the modern myths that are superheroes. Jung writes:

> The change of character brought about by the uprush of
> collective forces is amazing. A gentle and reasonable being can
> be transformed into a maniac or a savage beast. One is always
> inclined to lay the blame on external circumstances, but
> nothing could explode in us if it had not been there. As a
> matter of fact, we are constantly living on the edge of a
> volcano, and there is, so far as we know, no way of protecting
> ourselves from a possible outburst that will destroy everybody
> within reach. It is certainly a good thing to preach reason and
> common sense, but what if you have a lunatic asylum for an
> audience or a crowd in a collective frenzy? There is not much
> difference between them because the madman and the mob are
> both moved by impersonal, overwhelming forces.[17]

So in the Avengers, as in the other Marvel groups, it is the collective
forces rather than ego-driven solo hero that provide the redeeming
energy for humankind. And with this insight I recall why the solo heroes
of the 1960s DC Comics were so lacking in numinosity and power. In
a postwar, postmodern world in which nuclear apocalypse appeared
to beckon at any moment the anodyne Superman of that time and the
equally uninteresting, and disinterested, Batman could not help. The
grouping that included them was the Justice League of America, but
it had none of the fractious energy of the Avengers in the same way
that boring Batman could not compare, in my young eyes, with the
teenage Peter Parker (Spider-Man), who could not afford a motor
scooter, could never get the girl, and spent his evenings patching his
worn superhero costume.

In recent popular American TV series we see a return to apocalypse
and the meeting of its challenge by teams or groups of people rather
than by overriding, ego-driven individuals. This is the theme of Frank
Darabont's *The Walking Dead* and the Spielberg-produced *Falling
Skies*. British TV also reached back to former horrors to remake *The
Day of the Triffids* as a 2009 miniseries and in 2007 confronted the
specter of millions dying in London in *Flood*. Again it is modern,
electronically advanced cinema technology that heightens the
emotion, perhaps even the numinosity, of the psychic battles played
out on screen. Hockley notes: "Given the power of cinema to awaken
such responses it is curious that academic film theory has paid virtually
no attention to the issue of the emotional relationship that viewers have

with films."[18] Hockley emphasizes the affective power of cinema and recalls that by 1921 Jung was "working towards a view of affect . . . in which both the physiological elements of affect were clearly identified."[19] One can only assume that big screens, surrounding sound, and even 3D in the case of some superhero films (*The Amazing Spider-Man*, 2012, for example) would increase this. Certainly the assembling of the multiple aspects and projections of the individual Avengers into the collective whole produces powerful affect. As Bassil-Morozow asks: "Without a fixed habitus and with so many external influences offering alternative identities (or rather fragments of identities) in its place—TV, newspapers, magazines, advertisements, the shops, the Internet—how can one pinpoint the exact boundary between truth and fiction?"[20] Bassil Morozow continues:

> Frederic Jameson argues "the shift of the dynamics of culture pathology can be characterized as one in which the alienation of the subject is displaced by the fragmentation of the subject." Since the "true" subject, the solid subject, the subject who knew exactly who he was, is dead—what is this fluid thing in his place that is breathing and moving?[21]

As for the inclusion of a "living, breathing" Norse god surely Jung would have enjoyed and even predicted it. As Segal tells us, "the revival of traditional myths might seem a step backward, but it is really a step forward. While the myths here remain traditional ones they are revived as living myths and not merely as literary metaphors."[22] He cites Jung's example of the twentieth-century revival of the worship of Wotan or Odin, Thor's father. Thor's journey to Earth or Midgard across Bifrost, the rainbow bridge, with Mjolnir, his hammer, and his return with Loki is an example of what Campbell calls the crossing of the return threshold:

> The two worlds, the divine and the human, can be pictured only as distinct from each other—different as life and death, as day and night. The hero adventures out of the land we know into darkness; there he accomplishes his adventure, or again is simply lost to us.[23]

Superheroes on screen are magical almost religious figures. Jung's observation can be applied to the gods and superheroes in *The Avengers*:

Western man has sunk to such a low level spiritually that he even
has to deny the apotheosis of untamed and untamable psychic
power—the divinity itself—so that after swallowing evil he may
possess himself of the good as well.[24]

The persona that is Iron Man, the shadow that is the Hulk, the
dark anima of the Black Widow, and the ego-seeking Stark stand with
a displaced hero from the past and another from mythology to resolve
the dark threat facing humanity. In doing so they represent the psychic
struggle every single one of us faces throughout our lives, throughout
our own heroic journey. Stan Lee, the creator of Marvel and the Avengers
and the brand's indisputable *senex*, is ninety years old this December
(2012). Always at the cutting edge of popular myth, he has more than
300,000 twitter followers and always makes Hitchcockian cameo
appearances in Marvel films. In *The Avengers* he fleetingly appears
playing chess. And in wry acknowledgment of the truth that every one
of us is our own collection of striving, autonomous archetypes, the
Manhattan-born Lee observes with a knowing smile: "Superheroes? In
New York? Give me a break."

NOTES

1. Ajit Mookerjee, *Kali: The Feminine Force* (London: Thames and
Hudson, 1988).

2. James Hillman, *Anima: An Anatomy of a Personified Notion*
(Woodstock, NY: Spring Publications, 1985), pp. 115, 116. The quotes
from Jung are from CW 7, § 391, and CW 13, § 62, respectively.

3. C. G. Jung, "Concerning the Archetypes, with Special Reference
to the Anima Concept," in *The Collected Works of C. G. Jung*, vol. 9i,
The Archetypes and the Collective Unconscious (Princeton, NJ: Princeton
University Press, 1959), § 142.

4. William Anderson, *Green Man: The Archetype of Our Oneness with
the Earth*, photographs by Clive Hicks (London: HarperCollins, 1990).

5. William Shakespeare, *A Midsummer Night's Dream*, act 3, scene 2.

6. Robert Workman, "Will *The Avengers* Assemble a Game with
Ubisoft?" retrieved March 8, 2012, from http://www.comicbookresources.
com/?page=article&id=38524; Tom Chatfield, "Videogames Now

Outperform Hollywood Movies," *Guardian,* retrieved March 8, 2012, from http://www.guardian.co.uk/technology/gamesblog/2009/sep/27/videogames-hollywood.

7. C. G. Jung, "On the Nature of the Psyche," in *The Collected Works of C. G. Jung,* vol. 8, *The Structure and Dynamics of the Psyche* (Princeton, NJ: Princeton University Press, 1960), § 410.

8. C. G. Jung, "The Meaning of Psychology for Modern Man," in *The Collected Works of C. G. Jung,* vol. 10, *Civilization in Transition* (Princeton, NJ: Princeton University Press, 1964), § 315.

9. *Ibid.,* § 302.

10. Christopher Hauke, *Jung and the Postmodern: The Interpretation of Realities* (London: Routledge, 2000), p. 70.

11. *Ibid.*

12. Andrew Samuels, "The Return of 'The Individual': A Jungian Arrow Shot to the Heart of Academic Orthodoxy, Our Newest Contribution to Political Liberation," paper delivered at the combined conference of the International Association of Jungian Studies and the International Association of Analytical Psychology, Braga, Portugal, 2012.

13. C. G. Jung, "Conscious, Unconscious, and Individuation," in *The Collected Works of C. G. Jung,* vol. 9i, *The Archetypes and the Collective Unconscious* (Princeton, NJ: Princeton University Press, 1959), § 490.

14. C. G. Jung, *Memories, Dreams, Reflections,* edited by Aniela Jaffé, translated by Richard and Clara Winston (London: Fontana, 1995).

15. C. G. Jung, "The Concept of the Collective Unconscious," in *The Collected Works of C. G. Jung,* vol. 9i, *The Archetypes and the Collective Unconscious* (Princeton, NJ: Princeton University Press, 1959), § 88.

16. *Ibid.,* § 90.

17. C. G. Jung, "Psychology and Religion," in *The Collected Works of C. G. Jung,* vol. 11, *Psychology and Religion* (Princeton, NJ: Princeton University Press, 1958), § 25.

18. Luke Hockley, *Frames of Mind: A Post-Jungian Look at Cinema, Television and Technology* (Bristol, UK: Intellect, 2007), p. 35.

19. *Ibid.,* p. 41.

20. Helena Bassil-Morozow, *The Trickster in Contemporary Film* (Hove, UK: Routledge, 2012), p. 51.

21. *Ibid.*, with citation from Fredric Jameson, *Postmodernism, or The Cultural Logic of Late Capitalism* (London: Verso).

22. Robert A. Segal, *Jung on Mythology* (London: Routledge, 1998), p. 181.

23. Joseph Campbell, *The Hero with a Thousand Faces* (London: Fontana, 1993), p. 217.

24. C. G. Jung, "Psychological Aspects of the Mother Archetype," in *The Collected Works of C. G. Jung,* vol. 9i, *The Archetypes and the Collective Unconscious* (Princeton, NJ: Princeton University Press, 1959), § 190.

PSYCHOPATHOLOGIA PSYCHOANALISTIS

AN ESSAY ON *THE MEANING AND MATRIX OF CHARACTER: AN ARCHETYPAL AND DEVELOPMENTAL APPROACH, SEARCHING FOR THE WELLSPRINGS OF SPIRIT* BY NANCY J. DOUGHERTY AND JACQUELINE J. WEST

RONALD SCHENK

The soul has its own logos, which increases itself.
—Heraclitus

This is a heavy book! In paperback it weighs a full pound according to the scales at my grocer's store . . . but what a meal comes from this "bag"—the best of substantial German (and Jungian) cooking from two *Kellern*: the Enlightenment, with its ordering conceptual categories, large language, and reasoning acumen, and the Romantic, with its feeling for imagery and a transcending dynamic. Let's start with the title, an hors d'oeuvre as entrée in itself—*The Matrix*

Ronald Schenk, Ph.D., is a Jungian analyst practicing, teaching, and writing in Dallas and Houston. He is a past president of the Inter-Regional Society of Jungian Analysts and currently president-elect of the Council of North American Societies of Jungian Analysts. His interests are cultural, as well as clinical, and he is author of *American Soul: A Cultural Narrative*, *The Soul of Beauty: A Psychological Investigation of Appearance*, *Dark Light: The Appearance of Death in Everyday Life*, and *The Sunken Quest, the Wasted Fisher, the Pregnant Fish: Postmodern Reflections on Depth Psychology*.

and Meaning of Character: An Archetypal and Developmental Approach with the reading line *Searching for the Wellsprings of Spirit.*[1] Not one, not two, but three phrases, seventeen words in the voluminous Germanic tradition of titles give us a lot to chew on standing right there at the bookshelf.

The word *matrix* comes from the Latin term for breeding animals and is etymologically related to the word *mater* or "mother." It refers to 1) an enveloping substance within which something else originates, or 2) a mold or die. In other words, a matrix is something encompassing and also man-made. The movie by that title gets the essence of the notion—a matrix is a world where the creator is so unseen that the participants don't know they are living out another's creation. Here the authors intend the word to refer to an ordering system they have devised for categorizing different character structures in such a way that each individual structure can be seen on two different continua: one longitudinal, referring to different relational modes; the other latitudinal, referring to historical time in childhood development.[2]

Meaning as a word carries a dynamic quality, something intended, signified, an end. Literally, it is something carried from one place to another, a crossing over. If "matrix" is fixed, matter, boundary, category, static, "meaning" is movement, spirit, transcendent, multiple, fluid. The authors' alchemical purpose here is to bring mercury to the lead, an enlivening *anima*, Isis to the dead matter Osiris, moisture to dry clinical language and concept, while at the same time giving earth or ground to abstract meaning. Alchemy: "Make the fixed volatile and the volatile fixed."[3]

The authors inform us of the multiple layers embedded in the word *character*. Etymologically, it contains the Greek root "to engrave" as well as the Latin root for "original" or "distinct." From this foundation, the authors see a paradox—that which is essentially engraved serves both a defensive function *and* has an archetypal intention. That which Jungians traditionally refer to in an abstract way, individuation through a "process of transformation," the authors see as occurring *through* a distinct mode of being, a "character structure." "It is through our woundedness, with its archetypal background, that we can access our deepest healing and creative energies."[4] Character is not just psychopathology, but personality—all of us, therapist and patient alike, each individuality "engraved" in character. "When we allow ourselves to see these structures as patterns that underlie our own character, we find that we work with patients in a field of mutuality, in contrast to a field of hierarchical distance in which there is the knower and the known."[5] Here psychological thought is at once both theory of personality and of psychopathology, just as Freud and Jung meant for it to be.

"An Archetypal and Developmental Approach"—so, to reiterate, the authors are alchemically congealing two ways of seeing that have traditionally divided both Freudian from Jungian and, within the Jungian school, symbolic from developmental approaches to the psyche. Archetypal and developmental, transcendent and historical, intentional and regressive—Can't have the warp without the woof, the authors say, and our weaving shows you how.[6] This is Jung's thinking, his nondualistic, unified sense of the psyche—psyche as encompassing spirit and matter, the therapeutic field embracing therapist and patient alike.

The final phrase, *Searching for the Wellsprings of Spirit,* tops this multilayered course of a title with a slice of onion. By making spirit a matter of the wellspring, that is, depth, below the surface, the authors go against the classical notion of spiritual home in the heavens, and they maintain a psychological stance which synthesizes opposites— above and below, spirit and matter. *Memory* is etymologically associated with the well, and thus the overall purpose of the book: "to enliven the body of knowledge about character structures by re-membering the mythological themes that underlie human development."[7]

OVERALL VISION—THE MATRIX

Character has been a staple orientation of traditional psychoanalytic thinking since Freud, whose conceptualization of the term evolved throughout the course of his thinking regarding the development of personality. In psychoanalysis the term refers to the enduring, patterned functioning of an individual, his or her habitual way of thinking, feeling, and acting. From a psychodynamic standpoint, it is the person's customary way of reconciling internal conflict. Character is made up of an integrated constellation of traits which are stable and ego-syntonic, as opposed to the ego-dystonic quality of neurotic symptoms. (It was Freud's struggle with the transference resistance of his patients that led him to orient his focus toward the

workings of the ego and the evolution of character.) It is through
character structure that one gains satisfaction and achievement in life,
but an exaggeration or inflexibility in the structure ultimately causes
psychic pain, making the individual amenable for treatment.

With some exceptions, the authors follow traditional thinking
in distinguishing nine different character structures, "diagnostic
and archetypal images," which they classify in a single "mythopoetic
model."[8] The vertical vector of the model or grid is based on a
developmental view of character, focused on the preoedipal phase
of development, with three subphases drawing the authors'
attention in particular—"primal," "narcissistic," and "pre-neurotic,"
as the authors name them. The horizontal vector consists of three
particular relational patterns the authors find—"withdrawing,"
"seeking," and "antagonistic." It is the authors' opinion that one of
these relational patterns can be seen as predominantly informing
an individual's life, a pattern emerging "from a matrix of factors
including archetypal forces, biological predispositions, and
developmental realities, as well as the element of randomness or
chance—the mysteries of life."[9] Each developmental phase
engenders its own version of the three relational modes, and each
relational mode finds its unique expression within each
developmental phase. From this grid, there emerge nine separate,
but related categories or character structures, each of which has its
healthy and pathological elements and in each of which the authors
find elements which they amplify with images from fairy tales,
mythology, art, poetry, and literature.

Dougherty and West follow certain psychoanalytic and Jungian
clinical traditions in founding their psychological system in the
notion of ego development. The three particular developmental
phases they differentiate—primal, narcissistic, and pre-neurotic—
are described by the authors as "narratives" telling the story of
character structure emerging through the interweaving of age-
specific factors and individual-specific relational patterns. The
authors subscribe to the influence of the dominating concept in
traditional Jungian developmental theory, the "ego-Self axis," a
metaphor depicting the tension between the emergent worldly ego
and the transcendent individual essence, the Self. By Self, the

authors state, they are not referring to a thing or reified structure, but a process, "an objective reality that weaves universal meaning into subjective, personal reality."[10]

Dougherty and West indicate that their primal phase refers to the first eighteen months of life.[11] The task during this phase is for the infant to emerge from a relatively undifferentiated state to one of relative separateness and cohesiveness, the "consolidation of differentiation," ego evolving from Self.[12] The authors hold that relational patterns formed in the primal phase create individual character structures along a continuum ranging from flexible, healthy expansion of the ego to fixed, pathological defense patterns of withdrawal, splitting, and projective identification resulting in the constriction of the ego.

In other words, within each character structure there is a continuum from health to pathology. The defensive nature of the primal phase is seen as a platform upon which to construct the notion of the schizoid character. Following Nancy McWilliams, the authors indicate that "a defense begins as a healthy, creative adaptation and earns the term 'defense' only when it is employed repetitively and inflexibly in the face of an unmanageable threat."[13] In their conceptualization, relational patterns of seeking, withdrawing, and antagonizing may be used adaptively, but may come to be more fixed into a defensive structure depending upon the experienced threat. Thus, early dis-eased personality is based fundamentally on defense formation, leaving little space for emergent capacities for qualities such as joy or aloneness and overwhelming evolving psychomotor structures. "In all three character structures in the primal phase, an underdeveloped ego and subsequent defended character structure impede the purposeful flow of psychic energy along the ego-Self axis," a dynamic which is ultimately in service to the central concern of the primal phase, "a basic struggle for survival."[14] What is pertinent for the authors' overall intention in their emphasis on defense formation in the primal phase is their assertion that defenses reflect archetypal forms. It is these forms they intend to elucidate.

The authors' description of the "narcissistic phase," between eighteen and thirty months, closely follows the thinking of psychoanalyst Heinz Kohut in its emphasis on the presence of "mirroring" as a key element in the child's ability to navigate the evolving space between itself and the parenting figures.

Following object-relations theory, the authors imagine the pre-neurotic stage as the period from two and a half to four years, when the child is extracting its identity from a dyadic foundation but still hasn't attained the Oedipal struggle. In the pre-neurotic phase the defenses of repression, rationalization, undoing, turning against one's self, compartmentalization, and displacement are utilized both adaptively and defensively.

The above three historical developmental stages are seen by the authors as venues for the enactment of three distinct relational patterns, withdrawing, seeking, and antagonistic. The authors follow the work of Francis Tustin in seeing withdrawing as a habitual pulling away from contact with others, while seeking is a customary movement toward relationship.[15] The pathological extremes of these behaviors result in either shell-like or merging patterns respectively. The antagonistic pattern is based on a kind of predatory behavior that can take the extreme of a hostile attitude toward self and others. Each of the three relational patterns finds a home in each of the developmental phases.

Although they are presenting a model of categories for individual identity, the authors also offer cautionary disclaimers regarding the intellectual danger of fitting individuals into categorical boxes. "We encourage you to utilize these concepts symbolically, playfully even. Hold them lightly in your mind."[16] Very good advice for approaching any structured model for psychological life (but somewhat of a challenge for a model of this complexity and intricacy). In addition the authors pointedly emphasize the need for self-diagnosis on the part of clinicians. They recognize the field between analyst and patient as bipolar, intersubjectival, "requir[ing] the analyst to be thoroughly familiar with her own character structure, including her regressive challenges and shadow dynamics."[17] With this sensibility, the notion of matrix now comes to encompass both analyst and patient at once. In sum, the authors' diagnostic intentions are ultimately in service to the ancient tradition of calling out the names of each region of the underworld as a psychological necessity in the exploration of pathological life.

Examples from the Nine Character Structures

Withdrawing Pattern
Schizoid—Little Match Girl

The schizoid character structure derives from the withdrawing relational pattern appearing in the primal phase of development. In other words, the presence of an absence is the touchstone of the schizoid character, and persistence in the face of swirling abandonment is the key for treatment. The authors see the schizoid person in a paradoxical way. On the one hand, she is one who habitually declines to engage with the stimulation of the external world in favor of a superficial level of "archaic and rich imagery" in the inner world. At the same time, at its deeper levels, "the unconscious itself is imaged and experienced as a *void* . . . a vast hollow space . . . uninhabited by any life form."[18] Caught between the threat of the external world and the wasteland of the void that is sensed underneath a life of fantasy, "these patients may suffer pervasive bodily fears of disintegration; fears of vanishing into nothingness, coming apart into thin air, decaying into compost."[19]

In their discussion of the diagnosis and treatment of the schizoid individual, the authors make some bold moves. The first is a warning against the under-diagnosis of schizoid character structures due to several causes, one of which is the intention of the condition itself to remain invisible. In other words, the authors give the condition itself a subjectivity. Second is the warning that therapists themselves, while idealizing inner life, may not have worked through schizoid tendencies in themselves, secretly fear intimacy, and therefore keep their work with patients at a safe distance. The endeavors of these therapists, especially with schizoid patients, while superficially productive, are ultimately ineffective in dealing with core issues.

The authors choose images from the fairy tale related by the Dutch storyteller Hans Christian Andersen, "The Little Match Girl," to reflect their amplification of the schizoid character structure.

> A motherless girl, selling matches on a street in mid-winter, bare of foot and hand, sans sales or food, terrified by a father in a cold home, with the coming of night, sits in the snow, burns all of her wares, and dies in the grip of a fantasy of joining her grandmother in the heavens.

In this story the authors see a parallel to the experience and behavior of the person living under the influence of a schizoid character structure—an individual out of touch with body and feelings, terrified underneath, unable to act in an adaptive way in the world, withdrawing into fantasy without redemption.

The authors' interpretation of this and other fairy tales and myths raises questions about the ego-oriented use of archetypal images in the Jungian collective. Archetypal images represent ways of being, ways of seeing and acting that tend to be similar in certain situations across cultures and throughout the ages. They are universal metaphors indicating in a starkly imagistic way the patterns of how things are in their bare psychological actuality. Each image represents a *world* in which consciousness finds itself. So, we cannot use archetypes to justify our contemporary concerns, nor can archetypal images be judged or pathologized. Archetypes are neither positive nor negative, they simply are. The gods are in the dis-eases, in the theories, not the other way around. Oedipus cannot be diagnosed as having a complex; he is the complex.

In using the image of the little match girl, the authors tend toward pathologizing the archetype. The girl is given a developmental history, assigned inner psychodynamics, and assessed as maladaptive.

> [T]he Little Match Girl does not suffer concerns about shame or guilt, she experiences her existence as constantly threatened. She is deeply withdrawn, paralyzed, and unable to reach out for help. Her lack of connection to others and withdrawal into fantasy cause her to succumb to the cold embraces of death.[20]

From this vantage point, the authors focus on the notion of development as inadequate in terms of the capacity to "take action in the world" or participate in the "challenging and complex realm of embodied, affectively charged human experience and relationships" while "caught in the deadly embrace of . . . fantasy life" and withdrawn into the realm of "mind and image" with its "imaginal richness."[21] The ultimate option is for the "spirit world where a real girl cannot exist."[22]

An archetypalist might say this view is itself caught in a particular orientation—that of the Great Mother—that is not relevant to the actuality of the dynamics in the image. This perspective would see the Mother (and there is no mother in the image) behind the heavily utilized notion of "development." It would see the tale being not about the lack of development or capacity but about the presence of something else—*nigredo* and aloneness—and the pathology, one of identification. Following Jung's sense that all consciousness is a product of fantasy, that is, the everyday world created through an image, this vein of interpretation would hold that it is not that the match girl is "alone in archetypal reality," but rather that she *is* the archetypal reality of aloneness.[23] Her image prefigures the characters of Samuel Beckett in establishing isolation and desolation as a predominant form of being. From this perspective it would not be that the match girl does not reach out for help, but rather that she reaches out when, as with another withdrawing figure, Emily Dickinson, "Death / . . . kindly stopped for me."

The authors utilize the notion of "differentiation" to indicate a process of separation of conscious from unconscious in service of ego development, and the archetypalist might share this term by pointing to the differentiation that can occur within the archetypal image itself. What is helpful from the standpoint of an integrated clinical approach is the authors' ability to see the fairy tale in the various psychoanalytic theories regarding the schizoid condition, as well as their intersubjectival observation that "the *analytic dyad* can be freezing in the midst of plenty, looking at life through a frosted windowpane, without the ability to reach out and ask for warmth."[24]

The Seeking Pattern
Dependent Narcissistic Structure—Ophelia, Mother Holle, Demeter/Persephone

The dependent narcissistic character is especially significant given the cultural overlay of its symptomatology. Who does not want the individual dedicated to hard work serving upon organizational committees and in official capacities year after year, the romantic dedicated to the relationship, or the inspiring teacher? Yet, the authors show us through vivid description of developmental dynamics, archetypal amplification, and case studies how a particular pathos underlies these seemingly attractive behaviors. They make the subtle distinction between the dependent personality disorder and the dependent narcissistic character structure by noting that whereas the former tends to cling out of a need to be taken care of, the latter's underlying intention is to gain the recognizing, approving, loving gaze of other people. "Her concern is more deeply rooted in an inner sense that the source of love and meaning lies in the other."[25] While others experience the person as self-sacrificing, the narcissistic dynamics of idealizing/devaluing others and aggrandizing/diminishing self underlie the desirable behavior. "Whether apparently 'giving' or 'getting,' he is forever . . . insatiably hungry but also psychically impenetrable."[26]

Nevertheless, corresponding archetypal images are illustrative of what the authors are getting at. The Cinderella figure in the Mother Holle story serves with a deeper intention of "the search." Likewise Demeter in her wanderings and Persephone in her underworld retreat are extending their core dimensions. The authors' use of Mary Pipher's interpretation of Ophelia as a dependent character holding "no inner direction . . . her value . . . experienced solely through the approval of her father and Hamlet," however is problematic.[27] Here Pipher is mistakenly placing a contemporary ego-oriented perspective inside a classical dramatic character with universal qualities. Shakespeare's female characters, generally speaking, are strong women in that they clearly know who they are, what they want, what is called for in a larger sense, and how to express themselves in a direct manner. Ophelia's love for her father and brother, and especially for Hamlet, is a selfless love, and her death is a sacrifice reflecting the deep corruption of her environment, specifically in relation to the possibility for authentic love to find a place.

The analytic work in the case of Paul, the courtier, is exceptionally admirable. The study is presented under the overarching warning of the danger of the unknowing analyst falling prey to his or her own narcissistic tendencies by becoming caught in the patient's inflation/deflation, cocreating a mutual world of self-involvement. Here, we get a good sense of the analyst's experience and its reflection of the analytic third world. "[H]e constantly aimed to get something from me, something he then paradoxically could not allow in. It frequently felt like we'd do the same futile exercise over and over. At these moments, it seemed as if our work had become simply another round of his endless sucking. I felt 'used' and discarded."[28] With Cinderella/Mother Holle and Demeter/Persephone in the background, we get a sense of the cutting edge accomplishment of Dougherty and West in bringing new life into the clinical experience through precise diagnosis, archetypal amplification, and close attention to the countertransference.

The Antagonistic Pattern
Psychopathic Character Structure—"The Sea Hare" and the Trickster

The authors start with the contemporary cultural (American?) fascination with psychopathy. Indeed, this is the place to start, and this idea could stand an in-depth scrutiny. As ingrained and pervasive as it is in a capitalistic culture, psychopathy can be considered less a pathology than a way of life. The authors' implication of the media as source ("we are being desensitized and presented with compelling models of violence") lies above a deeper notion that cultural images are actually reflections of the collective psyche in its essence, that is, the media reflects, not determines, who we are.[29]

A thorough review of the literature leads to an encapsulating summary of the condition. "[A] psychopathically structured person is someone who suffered a massive failure of human attachment and, as a result, has been unable to incorporate objects into their inner world. Subsequently this person insists upon and relies on the omnipotent control of others."[30] The hallmark of the psychopath, then, is an inability to relate to others except as external objects to control. The psychopath places his condition of lack at the feet of society as ultimately responsible and acts it out irremediably and unreflectively in a vain attempt at its completion. The ego of the future psychopath in the first nine months of life, unable to overcome stranger anxiety and denied the opportunity for superego development, identifies with aggression itself or the predator, and the budding personality is unable to form attachments to others. A very helpful clinical vignette indicates the pitfalls for the therapist treating psychopathy in a naive manner, unrelated to the anger that psychopathy inevitably evokes in the therapy. A good diagnostic indicator is simply finding oneself not liking a patient and not knowing why, and the authors indicate that the paradoxical key ingredient to treating a psychopath is to have no investment in change.

Dougherty and West are particularly good in this chapter in reviewing countertransference challenges and in describing pitfalls from their own work which elucidate the subjectivity of the analyst entrapped in the web of the psychopathic structure. They carry their sensibility regarding the countertransference over into the archetypal realm by bringing in the fairy tale of the sea hare and by introducing the mythical Trickster into their dialogue. "The Sea Hare" tells the story of a haughty, heavily defended princess who lives on her aggression in the sense that she habitually attracts and then beheads her suitors. Her counterpart is a youngest brother who eventually wins her with the help of various animal/divinities, particularly those of the trickster, shape-shifter mold. The creative stroke by the authors here is to analyze the tale primarily from the standpoint of the analyst as the wooing counterpart to the patient as defended hostile princess. Their emphasis is the necessity of the therapist to constantly be able to delve into his or her own unconscious process in relation to the patient.

With their analysis of the psychopathic character structure, the authors have woven three interrelating strands of their discourse in a highly successful manner—a review of theory to come up with a compact but complete image of the structure and dynamics of the condition, a descriptive narration of a case study focusing on the countertransference, and an elaboration of the countertransference process through an analysis of its archetypal mirror in fairy tale and myth.

Alpha Narcissistic Structure—Princess Thrushbeard, Medea, "Mirror, Mirror, on the Wall"

The touchstone of the alpha narcissistic structure is the desperate need to stay on top while feeling constantly under siege. The alpha narcissist is constantly rejecting and ridiculing while defending through alternate idealizing and devaluing in a never-ending effort to be at the top of the self-created hierarchy. The relevant fairy-tale image is that of the princess in the opening of the tale "King Thrushbeard." A princess, beautiful yet proud, maintains herself by inviting and then rejecting various suitors with accompanying ridicule. Again, while the image itself would seem to hold the meaning as Jung might say, the authors psychoanalyze the tale developmentally, noting the inevitable absence of mother. The mythical amplifications include Medea and her vengeful murder of her own children and vicious chastising of Theseus. A caution: it is not that Medea has alpha narcissistic issues, it is simply that she *is* the image of the condition, as are the devouring Gorgon bitches of Greek mythology.

The authors include a very informative discussion of the role of envy and the work of Melanie Klein, while continuing to call the reader's attention to the distinctions in their matrix. Their discriminating move in the category of narcissism is already vital and original, and here they give us an example of this distinction in relation to envy. "The dependent narcissist tends to agonize over her envious feelings . . . the counter-dependent narcissist denies her envy . . . the alpha narcissistic person acts it out antagonistically."[31] The discussion on envy leads into a more general coverage of theory, focusing on the work of Theodore Reich and his notion of phallic-narcissism and Kernberg's concept of malignant narcissism.

This chapter contains another marvelous description of the transference/countertransference issues in working with patients of this type and the need for accurate assessment and diagnosis in order to avoid a superficial kind of therapy that ultimately colludes with the patient's pathology. The key here is an analytic frame that allows for both the patient's idealizing, devaluing, and annihilating projections onto the analyst and an accompanying regression to the underlying paranoid place.[32] "Regression into paranoia puts a person with an alpha character structure into a position to experience and integrate a . . . potential for vulnerability and anxiety."[33] The vicissitudes of such an analysis are described in acute detail.

> I often felt exhausted, frustrated, and angry. Yet I also sometimes wondered if her terrible suffering was somehow my fault . . . "one's essential identity as a helper is being eradicated" . . . I was afraid to confront Elizabeth . . . afraid to contribute more to her sense of internal devastation, afraid of the hatred she directed towards me, afraid of her intelligent rationalizations, afraid of her acting out. I . . . felt that my hands were tied . . . [but as] I was doing worse, she seemed to be doing somewhat better.[34]

Ultimately the bipolar field of swirling antagonism and feelings of inferiority brought out the judicious fight in the analyst, allowing the therapy to move to a different, but equally difficult phase.

Passive-aggressive character structure—Tar Baby/Trickster
Inevitably in a culture where dominance plays such a strong part, the "other side" finds its expression, and there is no better image of passive aggression than the inevitable tar baby. With this character, the more one aggresses, the less dominant one becomes. The trademark for passive aggression is underlying defeat and inferiority with accompanying envy and underlying rage, all defended with rationalization and denial. While the authors feel that connection is

the overriding goal (hard to be disconnected from the tar baby!), finding the disguised aggression is the primary intention of treatment. Again, theoretical precursors are well covered and the character structure is laid out developmentally with defensively impeding tactics seen as taking over for the more appropriate heroic modes. The Trickster is referenced here developmentally, and the authors follow Jung and Neumann in placing the Trickster as a developmental phenomenon. Again, regression is the key therapeutic factor, "to the archetypal ground of the Great Mother in order to readdress the moment when a confrontation with the Great Mother was avoided and the psyche turned to the trickster."[35]

As with the other chapters on the antagonistic modes of relating, the countertransference process is described remarkably well, with the warning, "the therapist may have to wrestle diligently with her own early wounds in order not to get entrapped by the patient's myriad obstructions, swipes, silences, etc. Effectively *receiving and metabolizing* thoroughly denied aggression is without doubt a sophisticated art."[36]

> [T]hese well-developed intuitions of mine were neither appreciated by nor useful to Paul . . . it was with quiet reserve that I sat with my own frustration . . . (ultimately giving up conscious therapeutic intention) I then took it upon myself to live with this sadness and leave Paul to his individual form of development . . . We need not suppose that this person must develop conscious insight and effective integration of affect . . . Paul's growth happened without insight.[37]

The clinician oriented to the therapeutic craftsmanship of genuine countertransference attunement utters "Hallelujah" at reading this description. It also indicates how the authors have achieved the giving up of their own preconceptions and systems in favor of the actuality of the particular individual experience of the other.

Although this writer sees problems emerging with some of the usage of archetypes, *The Meaning and Matrix of Character* remains a stimulating read for the clinician, and the book invites clinicians to reconsider several notions. Regarding the idea of character: the authors' thesis is that individuation is not an abstract or reified process but occurs through particular structures. As clinicians, they place character within particular structures and give an account of how each structural form may be determined through diagnosis and therapeutically addressed, how the particular psychological space can be animated with archetypal imagery, and how each space fits within a larger nine-part system.

It is important to remember, as the authors do, that in its original sense the "engraving" of character is a unique, *individual* essence which resists all categorization or systemization. Systems, in fact, are not of substance in themselves but artifacts that emerge from archetypal fantasies. The mode of systematizing is an emanation from the archetype of the *senex* with its call for order. The symmetrical system, in its own obsessive-compulsive form, is particularly comforting to consciousness in search of certainty. Systems act as tools of understanding, but in the end, they do not tell us as much about lived phenomena as they inform us of the particular system itself. The authors' matrix is an ordering system that, out of all the qualities that soul represents, is limited in that it sees character in terms of only two, albeit two very important, vectors: relational style and developmental history.

Jung posited another way of knowing in addition to the rational or ordering mode: through image, or *esse in anima*. From this perspective, "image and meaning are identical."[38] In other words, we don't need systems to be logical; each image holds its own logic. "Concepts are coined and negotiable values; images are life."[39] The authors follow Jung in this instance very well in warning us to wear their system "lightly" and in introducing archetypal images from fairy tales and myths as a way of animating or inspiriting the Old Man *senex* of psychological systematization.

The question arises, why is the notion of diagnosis necessary at all? After all, isn't any diagnosis relative, depending on a subjective external impression and saying more about the diagnostician than the patient—take *x* number of professionals and they independently come up with *x* number of diagnoses for any one patient? What is the diagnosis of the diagnostician? And assessment always brings up the problem of reliability and validity. What does it mean, for example, that in this system the Trickster archetype is found to inform several categories of pathology? (this author finds himself clinically certifiable in no fewer than six of the nine diagnostic categories and predominantly at home in all three relational patterns in their dysfunctional mode.)

The response of the alchemical clinician is this: practitioners use methods as tools for "making a move." The word *method* stems from the Greek word *hodos* or road, and the move is one of opening up. Diagnosis, in its best use, is an implement to reveal a beginning condition (etymologically the word means "to discern" or literally "to learn apart") and how the patient is constellated by this condition. In the alchemical mode, the practitioner determines the precise nature of the *prima materia*, and this assessment determines the operations and their order. Dougherty and West right-mindedly stress that neglect of accurate diagnostic assessment leads to naive, superficial, and ultimately destructive therapy. Eventually, however, as indicated in many of the authors' case studies, the designation needs to be left behind in order to let the pathology get to its particular wholeness.

Do we even need to think in terms of pathology? Why not let each form of experience have its own lived life space and address it on its own terms? The original Platonic sensibility has the soul choosing its own life circumstances, its own parents, its own body. From this perspective, what we call trauma is an event waited upon by the soul. Again, the alchemical clinician would respond that pathologizing is a psychological necessity (*ananke*) because the psyche works/plays through *pathos* which at its root means "happening" or "moving."[40] Disorder is central to the psyche's being and process. Yes, the clinician uses system to an extent as a kind of ordering containment, but the clinician's work then becomes essentially an activity in service to the eventfulness and movement of soul which is itself pathological in character. It is pathology which provides a uniquely formed perspective. Jung wrote regarding neurosis,

> We should . . . experience what it means, what it has to teach, what its purpose is. We should even learn to be thankful for it, otherwise . . . [we] miss the opportunity of getting to know ourselves as we really are . . . We do not cure it—it cures us.[41]

In this light, the authors are careful to show how what we call psychopathology is a mythology of our time, the place of the appearance of the gods, providing a creative, identity-forming ground for the soul which is inevitably embedded in mythic image. At the same time, their emphasis on the inclusion of regression, the interpretation of defenses, and reductive analysis as a necessary and vital part of the alchemical clinician's opus in addressing pathology and opening it up to a potential is a welcome reminder for the world of traditional Jungian therapy.

One last caveat: Dougherty and West have a threefold intention—to bring spirit to the corpus of clinical thinking, to give a developmental underlay to the use of archetypal imagery in clinical practice, and to give a characterological context to the notion of individuation. I believe the use of the conventional Jungian concept of ego-Self axis lets them down on all three counts. Jung used the term *self* in myriad ways, but his consistent and predominant sense of the ego-self relationship is that the ego is one of many parts of the self and as such is encompassed by and emerging from the latter, as the mover is the object to the mover as subject. The self is "an a priori existent out of which the ego evolves," essentially distinct from or a "prefiguration" of the ego, "completely outside the personal sphere."[42] The ego provides a "difference of standpoint" but ultimately is a "dark body . . . full of unfathomable complexities . . . [and] as a relatively constant personification of the unconscious itself . . . [becomes] the Schopenhauerian mirror in which the unconscious becomes aware of it own face."[43] The sense here is that ego is best understood as a sort of given, reflecting the luminosities of the unconscious.

The contemporary focus on a connection or axis between Self (or self in its more personal sense) and ego comes out of a long history of metapsychological controversy in the Jungian world regarding the relationship of these concepts. The orientation around an ego-Self axis reverts to an image-diminished form referencing the nineteenth-century physics of mechanics and energy, which itself is oriented toward the certainty of rationality. In describing the dynamics of their character structures with language such as "dialogue with the Self," "break in the ego-Self axis," "progressive development of relationship between the ego and the Self," repairing the "flow of energy along the ego-Self axis," the defensive interruption of "the emergence of a dialogic ego-Self axis," finding "authentic contact with the Self," and "power, charisma, and magic in service of the Self," the authors join a large part of the Jungian collective in jumping over some very complex distinctions and lose the psychological impact they have gained with the vividly concrete imagery they have brought to bear upon psychodynamic thinking. In sum, the rational language of ego-Self axis itself depletes the energy field the narrative in this book has worked hard to establish with the reader.

In Jung's evolved alchemical thinking, the notion of self comes to emphasize the unique particularity of each individual soul where individuation is the "process by which a man becomes the definite unique being he in fact is," "to become what he really is," for "one cannot live from anything except what one is."[44] *Meaning and Matrix* helps us understand how the particularity of this "is-ness" is formed through pathology.

Developmental orientation can be extremely valuable in clinical usage as a means of understanding process as applied to the evolving differentiation of a particular form. The result of this process is the evolved sense of "it is not I who create myself, rather I happen to myself."[45] In this mode, with the help of Dougherty and West we are able to see how the trickster of image throws a wrench in the spokes of the wheel rotating on the ego-Self axis to come to a more psychological way of seeing. Following the alchemical Jung, they have led us to be able to imagine the tar baby *as* the self, its particular, unique experience honored in a hands-on manner through the concrete image which Jung refers to as holding all meaning or even life itself.[46]

The Matrix and Meaning of Character is an excellent reference for the clinical practitioner, especially one in the Jungian school. It teaches diagnostic skills in teasing out characterological problems, emphasizes the ascertaining and addressing of resistance, indicates the importance of conducting "regression in the service of the ego," and provides models for using transference/countertransference.[47] The book has been created with care, the system woven with precision, and, for the most part, each well-considered sentence reveals a craftswoman's hand at work. Interestingly, in reading a piece by two authors, one finds continuous reference to the first person plural somewhat intimidating, as if the papal "we" were co-opting authority. What can a mere "I" say in response? On the other hand, the switch to the first person singular in case reports becomes jarring as well. Who is the "I" here? Staying with the unsettled feeling, a narrator emerges, not either or both of the authors themselves, but a third author encompassing the two. This narrator has produced a labor of love through an obvious love of labor. The love of the work that has emerged through the text is itself lovable and works well upon the reader, as the text takes its place among the foundational works in clinical depth psychology.

NOTES

1. Nancy J. Dougherty and Jacqueline J. West, *The Matrix and Meaning of Character: An Archetypal and Developmental Approach* (New York: Routledge, 2007).

2. Intersubjectival psychoanalyst Thomas Ogden also uses the term *matrix* to indicate the make-up of the psyche in his book *The Matrix of the Mind: Object Relations and the Psychoanalytic Dialogue* (Oxford, UK: Rowman and Littlefield, 1993).

3. C. G. Jung, *Mysterium Coniunctionis,* vol. 14, *The Collected Works of C. G. Jung* (Princeton, NJ: Princeton University Press, 1963), § 685.

4. Dougherty and West, *The Matrix and Meaning of Character,* p. 3.

5. *Ibid.*

6. *Ibid.,* p. 4.

7. *Ibid.,* p. 1.

8. *Ibid.,* p. 4.

9. *Ibid.*

10. *Ibid.,* p. 7.

11. While the authors are generally very good in providing antecedent references (the work of psychoanalysts Wilhelm Reich, Theodore Reich, and Otto Fenichel on character and the Jungians Erich Neumann and Edward Edinger on development are well noted), some of the models by major pioneers in developmental thinking in the classical psychoanalytic world are given less notice. The models of Klein and Mahler are given attention in only footnotes, whereas their thinking provides foundations for many of the distinctions and characterizations of the authors' matrix. Meanwhile, the classic models of developmental and character structures by Freud and Erik Erikson are given no mention.

12. Dougherty and West, *The Matrix and Meaning of Character,* p. 7. Keeping in mind the authors' overall intention of weaving together two strands of the Jungian opus, developmental and archetypal, here we might mention a snag. Following Jung's

Romantic inclinations, the authors' primal phase is depicted as a time when the infant's ego emerges from a merged state, the Self. Acknowledging theological as well as psychological antecedents, the authors see the beginning stage of infancy as one of "unity with the All" or being "at one with the universe." Utilizing idealizing, transcendent images, while at the same time writing in the language of literal certainty, the authors put forth a fantasy of infant consciousness, that infants "perceive reality in numinous, absolute terms" (p. 8), a proposal that can't be validated, thus involving an ontological contradiction. If you are "one with the universe," notions of perception, numinous or otherwise, are irrelevant.

The problems with this sensibility of the Self stem in part from the fact that Jung described the Self from several, at times contradictory, metapsychological stances all related to the tension of Kant's distinction between the knowable and the unknowable. For Jung, the psyche was both personal and transcendent, but exactly how to address this conundrum has created much controversy among Jungians. The authors follow the Romantic sensibility of Erich Neumann (*The Origin and History of Consciousness, The Great Mother, The Child*) and Edward Edinger (*Ego and Archetype*) in postulating the metaphor of an ego-Self axis around which development occurs. While the authors seem to equate the Self with the "All" and see it symbolized as an "unknowable presence," "a god or goddess," or, following Jung, "the archetype of wholeness," they describe the Self in the primal phase as in need of defense "from intolerable internal and/or external threats" (p. 9). To describe the Self in transcendent terms, and at the same time to depict it as vulnerable to internal and external threats of phenomenal life, confuses two mutually exclusive notions of the Self, literalizing a Romantic fantasy. The authors reference Michael Fordham, but Fordham adapted his understanding to a notion of "self" qualitatively distinct from the Romantically based "Self," emphasizing a more personal quality and a closer relationship with the ego. Additionally, infant observation research, as the authors acknowledge in a footnote, speaks against an egoless infant. It is now clear that infants from the first hours of life are able to make differentiations in their environment, indicative of a consciousness not symbiotically merged with a transcendent "All."

13. *Ibid.* p. 9.

14. *Ibid.,* p. 28.

15. Two precursor models for this twofold sensibility toward relationship are Jung's typological system of introversion and extraversion and James Masterson's withdrawing and seeking matrix for borderline behavior.

16. Dougherty and West, *The Matrix and Meaning of Character,* p. 13.

17. *Ibid.*

18. *Ibid.,* p. 27.

19. *Ibid.*

20. *Ibid.,* p. 28.

21. *Ibid., p. 24.*

22. *Ibid.,* p. 42.

23. C. G. Jung, *Psychological Types,* vol. 6, *The Complete Works of C. G. Jung* (Princeton, NJ: Princeton University Press, 1971), § 78; and Dougherty and West, *The Matrix and Meaning of Character,* p. 28. A story by Jack London tells of a similar situation of a lone miner using up his last firewood in the Arctic cold.

24. Dougherty and West, *The Matrix and Meaning of Character,* p. 39; italics added.

25. *Ibid.,* p. 135.

26. *Ibid.,* p. 136.

27. *Ibid.,* p. 134.

28. *Ibid.,* p. 147.

29. *Ibid.,* p. 181.

30. *Ibid.,* p. 186.

31. *Ibid.,* p. 213.

32. Klein's sense of the paranoid position is so important here that a reference in the text would seem to be called for rather than in the endnotes as the authors did.

33. Dougherty and West, *The Matrix and Meaning of Character,* p. 230.

34. *Ibid.,* p. 224.

35. *Ibid.,* p. 244. Note again: the Trickster is relegated to the developmental mode of thinking rather than given a phenomeological ground of its own.

36. *Ibid.*, p. 255; italics added.

37. *Ibid.*, pp. 252–53.

38. C. G. Jung, "On the Nature of the Psyche," in *The Collected Works of C. G. Jung,* vol. 8, *The Structure and Dynamics of the Psyche* (Princeton, NJ: Princeton University Press, 1960), § 402.

39. Jung, *Mysterium Coniunctionis,* § 226.

40. See James Hillman, "Pathologizing," in *Re-Visioning Psychology* (New York: Harper, 1975).

41. C. G. Jung, "The State of Psychotherapy Today," in *The Collected Works of C. G. Jung,* vol. 10, *Civilization in Transition* (Princeton, NJ: Princeton University Press, 1964), § 361.

42. C. G. Jung, "Transformation Symbolism in the Mass," in *The Collected Works of C. G. Jung,* vol. 11, *Psychology and Religion* (Princeton, NJ: Princeton University Press, 1958), § 391; C. G. Jung, *Aion,* vol. 9ii, *The Collected Works of C. G. Jung* (Princeton, NJ: Princeton University Press, 1951), § 57.

43. Jung, *Mysterium Coniunctionis,* §§ 133, 129.

44. C. G. Jung, "The Relations between the Ego and the Unconscious," in *The Collected Works of C. G. Jung,* vol. 7, *Two Essays on Analytical Psychology* (Princeton, NJ: Princeton University Press, 1953), § 267; C. G. Jung, "The Psychology of the Transference," in *The Collected Works of C. G. Jung,* vol. 16, *The Practice of Psychotherapy* (Princeton, NJ: Princeton University Press, 1954), § 407; Jung, *Mysterium Coniunctionis,* § 310.

45. Jung, "Transformation Symbolism in the Mass," § 391.

46. Jung, "On the Nature of the Psyche," § 402; Jung, *Mysterium Coniunctionis,* § 226.

47. The psychoanalyst Ernst Kris coined this term in the early 1950s, but one can see its early predecessor in Jung's imagistic notion of the night sea journey in *Symbols of Transformation.*

AND THE DANCE GOES ON

AN ESSAY ON RON'S ESSAY ON *THE MEANING AND MATRIX OF CHARACTER*

JACQUELINE J. WEST AND NANCY J. DOUGHERTY

R eceiving and digesting Ron's sophisticated essay about our book and then forging a conversation-in-response has not been "a piece of cake." It has been far more like a banquet: he has handed us many observations of our work, each with its own flavor, its own substance, and its own complexity. His attentive endeavor invites, like all full banquets do, the art of the dance. So, here we go.

First and foremost, we sincerely appreciate Ron's extremely careful and acknowledging engagement with our work. It is an honor to be so closely studied and critiqued in the classical sense of both applauded and corrected. We *naturally,* though somewhat shyly, receive his abundant applause with delight. It is after all a treat to hear our work

Jacqueline J. West, Ph.D., has served as the president and director of training for the C. G. Jung Institute of New Mexico. Currently she is a senior analyst in the New Mexico Institute and a training analyst in the Inter-Regional Society of Jungian Analysts. She also currently serves as president of CNASJA, the Council of North American Societies of Jungian Analysts. She practices in Santa Fe, New Mexico.

Nancy Dougherty, M.S.W., is a Jungian analyst with a private practice in Austin, Texas. She is a senior training analyst at the C. G. Jung Institute of Chicago and is the former director of training of the Inter-Regional Society of Jungian Analysts. They are co-authors of *The Matrix and Meaning of Character.*

described as "brilliant," "psychologically acute," "compelling," "marvelous," "vivid," "subtle," etc. It is a pleasure to hear his acknowledgment that we carefully show that psychopathogy is an "identity-forming ground for the soul which is inevitably embedded in mythic image," while we also attend to clinical phenomena "as a necessary and vital part of the alchemical clinician's opus." Along with all that, *unnaturally*, that is, as an *opus contra naturum*, we receive, and actually truly appreciate, his "corrections." These, in turn, we will dance with in the following pages.

In Ron's lively, linguistically sophisticated parsing of the title to our book, he cleverly introduces the fundamental intentions of our work. As he continues in his essay following the basic path of our book, he has included an abundance of honoring remarks interspersed with a number of comments that present challenging and interesting perspectives about particular analyses we offer. We'll roughly follow this pattern in our response: responding to his comments about our introduction first, and then to his considerations about each relational pattern in turn.

CONCERNING RON'S COMMENTS ABOUT OUR INTRODUCTION

The majority of Ron's remarks that in one way or another challenge our work are based in his particular reference points for the terms *ego* and *Self*. His perspective will become clearer as we proceed, but before we respond to his comments one by one, we'd like to clarify how we use these terms.

First and foremost, we use the terms *ego* and *Self* as metaphoric descriptions of dynamics that at best are experienced in relationship to one another. Keeping our focus on the relationship between ego and Self, between human consciousness and the collective unconscious, we see each character structure as an intricate interweaving of *both* ego *and* Self as it is expressed in three archetypal relational patterns. These theoretical perspectives encourage us to hold the tension between the archetypal and developmental perspectives in our field as we describe the dynamic differences of nine mythopoetic character structures.

REGARDING THE EGO

In the text of his essay, Ron observes that in our book we suggest that the task during the primal, earliest phase of development is for the infant to emerge from a relatively undifferentiated state to one of relative separateness and cohesiveness, the "consolidation of differentiation," ego evolving from Self. He then embeds a number of quite challenging comments regarding our proposition in a surprisingly long note (no. 12). Even though these challenges appear as an appendage, this humble positioning does not minimize their weight. Nor does it enable us to proceed without addressing them, given that they are aimed at fundamental aspects of our work.

First, Ron suggests that our comment that refers to "the beginning stage of infancy as one of unity with the 'All'" presents a confounding use of transcendent imagery and literal certainty. In this case, and throughout the book, we *choose* to use what he refers to as "transcendent imagery" while writing about "literal certainty" precisely because our focus is on the relationship between archetypal reality and human embodied life, which is, not incidentally, the core aim of our entire book. Ron notes, "For Jung, the psyche was both personal and transcendent, but exactly how to address this conundrum has created much controversy among Jungians." Indeed it is this controversy, which we see enacted in the tendency to polarize and split the archetypal and developmental positions, that interested and challenged us to work toward a synthesis of the two. With our eye on both/and—not either/or—in the phrase "both personal and transcendent," we have aimed for a synthesis of the human and the archetypal.

Employing a strictly literal interpretation of "the beginning stage of infancy," Ron misses the implicit reference to the archetypal "in the beginning" that is imaged in so many creation myths. Then, overriding our explicit comment that we do understand that a human child is born with nascent consciousness, he argues that our reference to an infant's "perception" is inconsistent and even "irrelevant" given our fantasy that an infant is "in the beginning" egoless—a position, as noted, that we explicitly never assume. Yes, as soon as an infant is an infant, there is a nascent consciousness that can most rudimentarily perceive reality. We see the emergence of consciousness as continuous and our descriptions of the primal phase as beginning in "unity" is a metaphoric way of describing the very beginning step in this earliest developmental process. Holding *both* this archetypal perspective *and* also the awareness of the infant's nascent consciousness, we do describe development as beginning in a state of unity, and our emphasis is on the gradual emergence of a differentiation between ego and Self, between consciousness and the archetypal realms. Again, we are using *ego* metaphorically; we intend it to refer to embodied consciousness as subjective, mindful experience. And we are not positing that this differentiation of consciousness happens literally, biologically in utero, or at the moment of birth, or at some arbitrary midpoint in this phase that we describe as lasting eighteen months. Somewhere, sometime in this span of time, the phenomena of consciousness enters human experience, and its relationship to what lies beyond consciousness impacts our lives profoundly.

Ron's literalization of "the beginning stage of infancy" also seems to lead him to remarks that imply that this "beginning" state describes the entire primal phase of development as we see it. Far from it: we see the differentiation of ego in the primal phase, and throughout life, as being a continuous but distinctly nonlinear process, as we will discuss in our remarks below regarding the borderline character structure. As a human life unfolds, consciousness is subjected to regressions and progressions, to disorder and order, and it emerges in various forms of differentiation. There is not a single moment when it passes from one phase to another. For instance, in our book we say that a person with a hysteric character structure has ventured beyond the world of the mother but not yet onto daddy's lap. Clearly, just as in the differentiation of consciousness in the primal phase, we do not mean this literally; and we are not suggesting that this happens at the beginning of this phase, nor at the end. It happens over and over during a lifetime.

These hefty reflections of Ron's do not stand on their own in this sturdy footnote. He also asserts, in the thick of it all, that our notion of the ego-Self axis follows a Romantic sensibility rooted in Erich Neumann and Edward Edinger. Before we turn to this position, we will, once again, first clarify how we use the terms *Self* and *ego-Self axis.*

REGARDING THE SELF AND THE EGO-SELF AXIS

Throughout our book we refer to the Self as a metaphoric description of the collective unconscious, which we also refer to frequently as "the archetypal realms." Jung often reminds us that while archetypes, in essence, are undifferentiated, they are initially *experienced* as bipolar. In general agreement with this proposition, our use of *Self* refers to the various images, affects, and actions that are manifestations of the innumerable archetypes, each of which is initially experienced as a pair of opposites: balance-imbalance, creation-destruction, organization-disorganization, good-bad, and so on. Within the ongoing relationship between these potentia and consciousness, many differentiated forms of the archetype may appear.

We refer to the relationship between ego and Self, between human consciousness and the archetypes, as the ego-Self axis. This expression was adopted from Jung, via Erich Neumann, by Edward Edinger, who illustrated it with his classic diagram of the sphere of the ego emerging in stages from the larger sphere of the Self. We choose to use this expression *as an image of* the dynamic relationship between consciousness and the collective unconscious. We often refer to this dynamic relationship as a dialogue between the ego and the archetypal realms. The activated tension between consciousness and unconsciousness, enacted in a dialog between ego and Self, and the potential emergence of a synthesis arising from this tension is, in one form or the other, at the heart of our work.

Discussions of this perspective will appear a number of times below as we contend with Ron's various comments about it. At this point, we need to address his comments in note no. 12 about the Romantic spirit within these ideas. In an implicit way, by adopting the language of ego-Self axis we may be seen to have aligned ourselves with Edinger and therefore with a romantic notion of Self. This view, in general, sees the Self, typically represented symbolically as a divine figure or a geometric pattern of wholeness, bringing balance and unity into the world. However, this romantic notion of Self, including its romantic notion of development, do not reflect the working assumptions in our book. Consistently we do not frame our work in terms that express a unipolar value regarding progression toward balance and unity. We do frame it in terms of an emerging development of differentiated wholeness. We see this wholeness as the ongoing process of creation and destruction, clinically akin to what Fordham refers to as assimilation and dissimilation and to what we all experience as exhaling and inhaling—and as life and death, symbolically and literally. Whereas Jung sometimes refers to the Self as the organizing dynamic in the psyche, one that engenders balance, we emphasize that the Self is an archetypal wellspring of potential opposites: balance and imbalance, organization and disorganization, unity and multiplicity. This certainly takes the romance out of our explorations, as we wrestle with any individual's particular life and the evil as well as the good and the multiplicity as well as the unity that inform it. This perspective is that of an alchemical clinician, a perspective that, in his ending remarks, Ron appreciates that we express.

While our emphasis in the book is on the relationship between *both* consciousness *and* the archetypal realms, Ron's emphasis throughout his essay is singularly on the archetype. In the process of discussing his objections to ego psychology, Ron inserts his own particular understanding of archetypes as images. This perspective is consistently reflected in his comments and critiques, and it leads to his emphasizing certain points while virtually ignoring others that are very central to an understanding of our work. This is illustrated in, but not limited to, the minimal attention he devotes to our considerations about defenses.

While Ron nominally acknowledges that defenses in general play a significant role in our work, we want to emphasize that we describe, in detail, how different defenses are employed at *each* phase of development. Furthermore, we carefully examine how defenses may be employed flexibly as an effective adaptation or more rigidly as an entrenched reactive dynamic. We pay close attention to these dynamics because they play a central role in facilitating or disrupting what we see as being of essential value to the psyche, namely, the relationship *between* consciousness and the archetypal realms. So, we *imagine*, for example, that rigid defenses "choke" the ego-Self axis. Meanwhile, we see how flexible and adaptive defenses enable consciousness to be well informed and vibrantly inspired by the archetypal realms. Ron summarizes in his words: "early dis-eased personality is based fundamentally on defense formation." Yes, although our emphasis is on the human reality that we all face stress and experience woundings as we wrestle with the inevitable disappointments and periodic traumas of growing up; and we therefore all naturally form defenses in our struggles to survive. In that sense, the more desperate and rigid the defenses, the more "dis-eased" we are. Likewise, the more we turn toward and loosen our defenses, the more access we gain to joy and aloneness. As we say in numerous ways in our book, we develop and gain access to the eternal wellsprings of life *through* our character structures, not in spite of them.

Ron's particular orientation also appears to limit his understanding of the way we have observed that archetypes become manifest. We commented above that our use of *Self* refers to the various images *and* affects *and* actions that are manifestations of the innumerable archetypes. Ron makes an assumption throughout his essay that archetypes become manifest *as images*. This perspective overlooks the essential differentiation we make between the different manifestations of the collective unconscious. We carefully describe how images, as manifestations of archetypal mind and imagination, inspire the three character structures in the withdrawing relational pattern—but not those in the other two relational patterns. All three character structures in the seeking pattern are infused by embodied affect, fueled by archetypal affect. And action, rooted in archetypal aggression, informs the three character structures in the antagonistic pattern. Ron's understanding that archetypes manifest as images alone is a prevalent attitude in the Jungian world that, in our perspective, reflects our community's bias toward mind and imagination. This bias has implicitly, when not explicitly, minimized an appreciation of and attunement to the formative impact of archetypal affect and aggression upon a significant percentage of our own psyches as well as those of our patients.

Brief examples clarify these points. When we witness a person with a schizoid character structure falling into a blinding fascination with her latest brilliant idea this is a manifestation of underlying archetypal mind and imagination. When we face a person with a borderline character structure erupting in chaotic emotions, these emotions are a manifestation of underlying archetypal affect. When a person with a psychopathic character structure attacks, physically or emotionally, this action is a manifestation of underlying archetypal aggression. In our language it is undifferentiated to refer to each of these as an image, since this favors mind and imagination, leaving affect and action unacknowledged and our capacity for analytic attunement, empathy, and love crippled.

CONCERNING RON'S COMMENTS
ABOUT THE WITHDRAWING CHARACTER STRUCTURES

Following the general path in our book, having wandered in and around the rather abstract territory of theoretical formulations, Ron turns, as we did in our book, to an engagement with the heart of our work, the various character structures of the matrix. First, considering the withdrawing relational pattern, he begins with comments about the schizoid character structure. Following a deft summary of the dynamics we describe, including an acknowledgment that we make the bold move to "give the condition itself a subjectivity," he then points out that in our considerations about the fairy tale "The Little Match Girl," we "tend toward pathologizing the archetype." Noting that we describe her as being withdrawn, paralyzed, and unable to reach out for help, he rightly observes that she is an archetype, not a person. He contends that we should have described her and these behaviors as characteristic of a particular person, differentiated from the archetypal reality portrayed in the story itself.

Ron considers this tendency to personalize the archetype as our seeing through the eyes of developmental psychology. There is an inherent tension between the developmental and archetypal perspectives. The developmental approach attends to embodied human experience, often seen as existing within a literalized time dimension; the archetypal approach insists on a symbolic attitude that deeply values the autonomy and eternality of the archetype. While Ron clearly appreciates the overall intent of our work to forge a synthesis of these two very different orientations, he maintains a vigilant eye on those times we transgress by stumbling into a developmental bias. Yet he himself is clearly subject to what we would consider an analogous transgression by stumbling into an archetypal bias. For example, in his discussion about our personalizing the match girl image, he implicitly resorts to the iconic claim that most of us have heard and wrestled with at one point or the other: "Archetypes have us, not vice versa." There is something compelling but also polarized and one-sided about this challenging claim. In our book we try to hold a bifocal perspective, exploring how archetypes have us *and* how we have them. We imagine that this both/and moment arrives when our human, embodied consciousness is in flexible, dialogic relationship to an archetype, and an ensouled experience, a synthesis, emerges.

Even though occasionally in this extensive project we do personalize an archetypal figure, these exceptions are typically in a context where we feel the symbolic attitude carries deep respect for the autonomy of the archetype. For example, in the passages that follow our description of the little match girl we consider a young patient and, in this context, we are in explicit alignment with Ron's emphasis that these dynamics reflect an archetypal terrain of aloneness and desolation. We also clarify that, from our point of view, it is in the relationship *between* ego-consciousness and this archetypal terrain that a creative human life emerges.

As we began this work, following our sense that there are profound and describable interconnections between archetypal themes and clinical diagnostic language, we discovered that archetypal themes guided and informed our explorations. What we enjoy is the process of roaming through the archetypal realms, engaging with the different forces, landscapes, figures, and stories and relating these experiences to reflections about our lives. We were engaged in a process of *both detecting and creating* a mythopoetic portrait of each character structure.

As we related to various archetypal stories and figures, we noticed that they themselves—their stories, their characteristics, their states of being—quite naturally invited us into several different landscapes: one of cold emptiness, one of crowded hot affect, and one of life and death struggle. We noted that these landscapes were consistently portrayed through mind and imagination, affect, and action, respectively. We then noted that these landscapes were consistently manifested, in human lives, through *relational patterns*. The pattern that emerges within a landscape of cold emptiness is associated with withdrawal; a landscape of hot affect is associated with seeking contact; and a landscape of struggle is associated with antagonism. We then began to recognize that the figures and stories that grouped themselves in any one of the three relational patterns reflected different phases of development. For instance, as just noted, the images that stepped up in the withdrawing pattern tend to feature cold entrapment: but for the schizoid, it's in ice; for the counter-dependent, in glass; for the obsessive-compulsive, in bricks.

In his essay, Ron comments only upon the primal phase of the withdrawing pattern, the schizoid character structure. However, it seems essential to us to include at least brief mention of the stories and dynamics that arise in the subsequent two developmental phases so that as we move forward a consistent experience emerges. While the match girl arrived in the primal phase as an archetypal image of aloneness and desolation, Athena appears in the narcissistic phase as an image of aloofness, encapsulation, success with little personal connection, a certain chilling superiority. This reality resonates well with the felt sense of counter-dependent dynamics employed defensively. However, the complex image of Athena also reflects the presence of civic guidance and counsel that sustains community coherence, beauty, and leadership. These creative energies may appear in the life of a person with healthy narcissism who is capable of employing her defenses flexibly and is therefore more inspired than inflated by this archetypal force.

The image of Apollo enters into our discussions about the obsessive-compulsive character structure that emerges in the pre-neurotic phase. Apollo, like other archetypal figures, expresses numerous attributes that can appear as the archetypal wellspring of an individual life. Apollo's capacity for order, archetypally neither flexible nor rigid, can bring about a civilizing effect; or it can be rigidly employed by the individual and create an insufferable contraction. Employed defensively, Apollo's ever bright light can inspire a rigidly defended person to hold his light as a beacon that allows no shadow. As we point out in the book, it "can ruin things that flourish in twilight or moonlight. Constant sun bakes the earth dry of moisture" (p. 101).

CONCERNING RON'S COMMENTS ABOUT THE SEEKING CHARACTER STRUCTURES

The three character structures that emerge in the seeking relational patterns are borderline, dependent, and hysteric. Archetypal affect is the fuel that pervades these dynamics, and it appears palpably in the psychodynamics of people in this relational pattern as well as in the archetypal images that are related to them.

Ron bypasses our discussion about the borderline character structure but we find it essential to at least briefly review these dynamics, since they embody the underlying forces of this relational pattern. In order to gain a felt sense of these dynamics, it helps to clarify how a person with a borderline character structure differs from someone with a character structure in the withdrawing and antagonistic patterns.

For example, when one is engaged with a person with a borderline character structure, you are virtually never let off the hook. If she turns her back on you, it will be dramatic and emotional: you'll know she's "gone," but you'll sense she is still present. She'll sneak a peak, she'll cough, squirm, move, and sooner than you might expect, she'll turn and either love you emphatically or blow up at you. This is so very different than the silent resolve in the turned back of a person in the withholding pattern, with whom you can sit in silence—turned back or not—and *feel* an impenetrable wall between you. Indeed, the person with a borderline structure may enact repetitive dramas of flailing that may well entail flight and return and flight again. The entire dance is fueled by affect; it is hot and unstable, and it aims to break through any form of boundaries; it aims for contact. This is true for the other structures in this pattern as well, the dependent narcissist structure and the hysteric structure, although the heat may be turned down and the dynamics more subtle.

The emotional eruptions so characteristic of each of the character structures in this pattern do not have the directed intent of destructive or murderous domination that are characteristic of the antagonistic pattern. Furthermore, they do not have the primal trickster's sly aim of one-upmanship nor the sophisticated intent of the alchemical trickster that appear within antagonistic dynamics. While a person in the seeking relational pattern may well be manipulative at times, their game is aimed more at connection— love *or* hate—than for domination.

An apt amplification of the dynamics in the borderline character structure takes us to Dionysus, the god of ecstasy *and* agony, of liberation *and* dismembering destruction, an archetype of intense affect, of wild swings between emotionally laden opposites, of suffering and madness. He is a god who is so enraged when he is spurned, so insistent on contact, that he incites his followers into frenzied murderous rampages of dismemberment. He does not follow this eruption by laying claim to any increase of power, to any domination; he is simply and irrefutably enraged at being disvalued.

Allerleirauh, the maiden in the Grimms' tale of the same name, also appears as an archetypal image of these dynamics, leading us into the woods where we live inside the skins of dead, dismembered animals and experience exposure, self-revelation, being witnessed, and entering relationship. When Allerleirauh arrived in our exploration of borderline dynamics we recognized that, for us, she appears as an archetype of living in emotionally charged danger. She fled her incestuous father, who was set up by a collusive mother; she resorted to hiding, disguising her true self in a highly primal and disfiguring way; she risked repetitive, tentative appearances, each seeking contact, punctuated with disappearances. She *is* the archetype of emotionally charged danger. Furthermore, as described above, these elements in Allerleirauh's story evocatively portray the patterns of psyche we observe in people with a borderline character.

Ron commented earlier, in his discussion about the little match girl, that our work could be seen as guided by the idea that development and the emergence of consciousness are ruled by the archetypal image of the Great Mother and the hero's journey. Our assumptions about development are not centrally tied to, or "caught in" this archetypal dominant. Our eye is on the relationship *between* the ego and the Self, between consciousness and the archetypes. From this perspective, we see the Great Mother/hero theme as an archetypal image that can enter this relationship. When it does, and it *rules*, it overwhelms and inflates consciousness, and the clinical pattern of an inflated, narcissistically defended ego emerges. This inflationary defense is associated with frequently related themes of endless growth, unlimited consumption, greed, and conquest—intrapsychically, interpersonally, and collectively. However there are also moments of development, in some cases, when this archetype appears in a creative, guiding, and flexible manner.

What is clear in our work is that not all change is ruled by this particular archetypal theme. Another archetype of change images development as differentiation. This arises whenever a relatively undifferentiated reality finds its way into relationship with consciousness, and this encounter introduces the experience first of opposites and then of multiplicities. This initiates the possibility of a synthesis that then, as multiplicity-within-unity, becomes the next relatively undifferentiated whole, and so on. The archetypal image of this form of development finds numerous expressions: for instance, the images of the great round, of the many goddesses of life and death, of the Kabbalistic creation story of the breaking of the vessels, etc. It is also at times imaged as assimilation and dissimilation, inhaling and exhaling, life and death—the both/and that occurs again and again.

It is this archetypal image that underlies our explorations into the patterns of individual development that we describe in the book. The character structures emerge from an intricate relationship between the underlying archetypal landscape and an individual's multifactored history of the emergence of consciousness influenced by the adaptive nature of their defenses. This is not a process of linear, once and for all, triumphant development. Stories such as Allerleirauh's, or the various other fairy-tale figures we discuss in the book, do not consistently image the hero's progressive development. Neither do they portray a complete lifetime, or even a single, critical phase in a lifetime. They image a process that an individual engages in over and over as the fabric of his or her life is woven.

Following quite appreciative remarks about our explorations in the chapter on the dependent character structure, Ron inserts a qualification about our brief comments regarding Ophelia as an amplificatory image. Enough said, in general, about his vigilant objection to the moments when we personalize the archetype. However, in this case, it is incumbent upon us to respond to his remark about Shakespeare's female characters and how he sees this as related to Ophelia. Ron suggests that "Shakespeare's female characters, generally speaking, are strong women in that they clearly know who they are, what they want, what is called for in a larger sense, and how to express themselves in a direct manner." While this profile captures the sense of many of Shakespeare's female characters, it certainly does not describe the archetypal essence of each of them. It thus seems to us that this is an odd argument to use as a preface to ground his assertion that Ophelia's love *is* a selfless love, and her death *is* a sacrifice. Ophelia's love could just as well be seen archetypally as an image of *not* knowing what one wants, what is called for, and how to express oneself in a direct manner. Perhaps she is an image of a not-knowing woman. From this perspective, her self-murder is one aspect of the image of her nonpresence. This figure also, as in Ron's perspective, may be "reflecting the deep corruption of her environment, especially in relation to the possibility for authentic love to find a place." (Meanwhile, what is the judgment of "strong" doing here? Is this not an ego perspective? If the judgment is allowed, isn't it possible that not-knowing is its own form of strength?)

Ron's comments ring once again of his challenge that archetypes *have us*, which we addressed in the opening section of this essay. At that point, we noted that we hold a bifocal perspective, exploring how archetypes have us *and* how we have them. This prompts us to consider that a young girl may become inflated by the archetypal force of the Ophelia figure—in either sense of how this archetypal figure is understood. Succumbing to its pull, she may disown her own human value and possibly even embrace death. It also prompts us to consider a very different possibility, namely, that she may be able to forge a sufficiently clear understanding of the dynamics of this archetype that they inform and possibly enrich but do not rule her life. It is the interaction between this archetypal image and our individual consciousness that determines how this story is woven into our ever so real human life.

When one's character structure becomes set in the pre-neurotic phase of the seeking relational pattern, a hysteric character structure emerges. A person with this character structure defends against her true self—and her profound knowing—by disbelieving *in herself*. In this light, the archetype has woven itself into her defenses in such a way that she lives as if she does not know; disbelieving in herself, she presents facile knowledge and/or undoes herself at every turn. When these defenses are entrenched, this person tends to be caught in rounds of convoluted maneuvers that effectively cut her off from the primal wellsprings of affect that could creatively inform her life.

As we describe in the introductory pages of our book, given that both narcissistic and pre-neurotic defenses, in general, support an ego that is relatively more differentiated from the archetypal realms, a person with a character structure in either of these developmental phases may well face the necessity of a regression as a potentially creative process. In this process, she would be challenged by reabsorption into relatively primal, undifferentiated states. This confrontation can initiate a loosening of the rigidity of entrenched defenses and revitalize the psyche.

Meanwhile, it is essential to note that a person whose character structure is rooted in the primal phase, and whose ego is relatively undifferentiated from the archetypal realms, will not find his or her psyche turning toward regression since the only state underlying their tentative differentiation of consciousness leads into psychotic dynamics. In these cases, the archetypal themes of descent that Jungians tend to see as associated with development rarely appear. Rather, we find themes of living in a tomb, cloaked in animal skins, enthroned at the bottom of the ocean, supplemented by images of ascent, as progression.

In our comments just above, we noted that archetypal stories do not necessarily image discrete steps in a linear pattern of development that tell the entire and single story of a lifetime. There are numerous archetypes that tell of processes that occur over and over. Experiences of being intermittently bashed around by the fate cannot be easily rationalized as progression; but they can be understood as meaningful, cyclic regressions.

In this sense, regression can be seen as the essential other side of progression.

Concerning Ron's Comments about the Antagonistic Character Structures

We want to begin this section with a thank you to Ron for his appreciative remarks regarding each chapter in this relational pattern.

He opens his remarks regarding the psychopathic character structure, which emerges in the primal phase of this pattern, with a comment that, indeed, contemporary cultural fascination with psychopathy could stand a deeper scrutiny. This point underscores the concerns we had in mind as we wrote this chapter and as we have been further developing this material. We appreciate that our field in general is turning more and more toward these issues, and we hope that the ideas we have presented in the book will contribute to these endeavors.

In this regard, Ron notes that in our book we speculate that we are being desensitized by the media and its compelling models of violence. He adds that this perspective "lies above a deeper notion that cultural images are reflections of the collective psyche in its essence, that is, the media reflects, not determines, who we are." Here we are once again: our emphasis is not on the deeper notion of the archetypal image alone. Starting from a both/and position, we see cultural images, including the media, as *emerging from interactions* between images that reflect the collective psyche in its essence, which we see as archetypal images, and individual psyche—each reflecting and impacting the other. In this manner, we differentiate cultural images from archetypal images.

Individually, a person with a psychopathic character structure has generally, as an infant, suffered a massive failure of human attachment. This failure arises not only as failure of and with the personal mother, but also as an archetypal experience in which a confrontation with the Great Mother is avoided and the psyche turns to the Trickster as archetypal ground. Subsequently, without the foundational support of a maternal attachment, when faced with the normal dynamics of stranger anxiety, she resorts to identification *with* "the stranger," the archetypal predator, in order to master her anxiety. This interrupts not only the development of a flexible ego but also, essentially, the development of mature conscience. Subsequently this person insists upon and relies on the omnipotent control and domination of others.

When a person in the antagonistic relational pattern enters the narcissistic phase, she turns to defensive maneuvers that reflect her underlying psychopathy. In the formation of an alpha narcissistic character structure, as Ron notes, "the touchstone . . . is the desperate need to stay on top while feeling constantly under siege. The alpha narcissist is constantly rejecting and ridiculing while defending through alternate idealizing and devaluing in a never-ending effort to be at the top of the self-created hierarchy."

Our issue with Ron's comments about this chapter is only that he once again makes the point that we personalize the archetypal images. We must reiterate that we consistently aim toward a bifocal perspective, exploring how archetypes have us *and* how we have them. This both/and moment arrives when our human, embodied consciousness is in flexible, dialogic relationship to an archetype and an ensouled experience, a synthesis, emerges.

It is a treat that in spite of Ron's persistent objections to what he sees as an occasional enmeshment of the archetypal and personal realities, he returns to observations about the strengths of our work. For example, his remarks in this section about our clarification of the different forms of narcissism, seen through our considerations about envy, are particularly appreciated.

In regard to Ron's comments about the very complex and tricky dynamics of the passive-aggressive character structure, we simply join him in his "Hallelujah" about the exploration of the countertransference dynamics we present.

CONCLUDING COMMENTS—RON'S AND OURS

As he concludes his essay, Ron first indulges in yet another statement of his insistence on the value of the image as it is, from his point of view, identical to meaning.

He then moves on to the very interesting and pertinent question that our book explicitly aims to explore: "why is the notion of diagnosis necessary at all?" He answers this question by stating that "in the alchemical mode, the practitioner determines the precise nature of the *prima materia*, and this assessment determines the operations and their order." Indeed, understanding the patient's character structure—as well as our own—helps us in deciding how we might proceed in entering the delicate dance of creating therapeutic attunement. For instance, a different process is involved in ascertaining how much warmth and empathy is useful with a person with a schizoid character structure than how much might work well with a person with a hysteric character structure. A psychopathic patient might see offers of empathy from a therapist as signs of weakness and greet them with devaluation and contempt. As Ron acknowledges in his essay, we explore in our book how neglect of accurate diagnostic assessment can lead to "naive, superficial, and ultimately destructive therapy."

Furthermore, just as a determination of the precise nature of the *prima materia* helps the alchemist to determine the operations and their order, a character structure diagnosis supports the analyst in his or her ongoing interactions with a patient. For example, encouraging a person with a borderline character structure into excessive expressions of archetypal affect may lead him further into an experience of dismemberment, with the aroused energies expressing themselves chaotically in his relationships (including with the therapist), or harshly directed back upon himself. Guiding a person with a schizoid character structure into ever deepening experiences of the archetypal images of mind and imagination could induce her into further withdrawal into the realms of fantasy, leading her out of the nourishment of an interactive life into a terrifyingly cold and lonely emptiness.

Ron further raises the question inherent in our work, "Do we even need to think in terms of pathology?" Again, he answers this question in terms we heartily agree with, as demonstrated throughout our work. He offers these reflections: "pathologizing is a psychological necessity . . . Disorder is central to the psyche's being and process." We see these points amply integrated into our discussions about the essential vitality of primal phase dynamics and of regression, as well as in our central thesis that we transform through our character structures, not in spite of them. We would add, however, that we see character structures along a continuum, ranging from flexible and open to rigid and restrictive. Again, we keep our focus on both/and: regression and progression, life and death, order and disorder, multiplicity and union.

This image of a continuum takes us to the last theoretical point that Ron makes in his concluding remarks: namely that the concept of ego-Self axis is first of all too mechanical and also that it leads us into expressions such as "dialogue with the Self," "flow of energy along the ego-Self axis," and so on, which lessen the impact of the complex work we've presented.

As we have said, we consistently employ the words *ego-Self axis* as a metaphor, not as a noun referring to a literal, concrete object. In this way, it not only conveys but even emphasizes just how deeply consciousness is related to the archetypal realms—for better or for worse, in sickness and in health. Each of the expressions Ron quotes as problematic, we experience as evocative. Seems like the jury is out on this one.

In his truly final comments, Ron expresses puzzlement—perhaps annoyance, though perhaps, as he claims, intimidation—about our use of the pronoun *we* throughout our text. We were pleased and surprised that the metaphor that Ron came up with to describe our collaborative voice is the "papal we." If we dig deep, we might imagine the "royal we" as a more gender-neutral if not a more gender appropriate descriptor, but imagining pontifical vibes emanating from our work is Ron's unique take.

His observation does invite us to comment on our collaborative voice and our collaboration in general. For us, the use of the pronoun *we* expresses a value central to the creation of this work. The concept for this book grew out of our relationship and our growing curiosity, and sometimes delight and sometimes struggle, with our observations about our own, individual characterological differences. We could say that the book "arrived" out of our differences. We quickly recognized that other people in our lives embody yet other interwoven patterns of archetypal and interpersonal dynamics, each with its rich, integral nature. As we explored these, we found ourselves frequently returning to our own differences—as well as to our individual differences with each of the other character structures. As both these dialogues and our relationship deepened, we continued to be amazed at how essentially differently we experienced the world and each other, how differently we came to our interests and observations, how differently we went about relating to others and each other. We noted that our value systems grew out of different roots, although often they were compatible. People who speak with us often remark that they note a marked difference in the ways we express ourselves, in the ways we inhabit our bodies. We sense that the creative tension between these deep differences fueled the dynamic and synthetic quality of our explications of each of the character structures.

We have no trouble in joining Ron in his final comment that "we" have produced a labor of love. And we very, very much appreciate his *seeing* the work—and contributing *his* engaged and careful labor.

BOOK REVIEWS

Stephen J. Foster, *Risky Business: A Jungian View of Environmental Disasters and the Nature Archetype*. Toronto: Inner City Books, 2011.

Robert D. Wagner, Jr., *"Moby-Dick" and the Mythology of Oil: An Admonition for the Petroleum Age*.

REVIEWED BY SUSAN ROWLAND

B oth these books offer valuable and intriguingly related analyses of the environmental crisis from a Jungian perspective. In so doing, *Risky Business*, by Stephen J. Foster, and *"Moby-Dick" and the Mythology of Oil*, by Robert D. Wagner, Jr., also expose fundamental issues within Jungian studies of language and scholarship. For as philosopher Kate Soper has argued, any address to ecological perspectives comes up against historical and cultural complications of the way we use the word *nature* and how far "human nature" is regarded as indigenous to it.[1]

Susan Rowland, Ph.D., is a member of the core faculty at Pacifica Graduate Institute and previously professor of English and Jungian studies at the University of Greenwich, UK. She was a founding member and first chair of the executive committee of the International Association for Jungian Studies 2003–2006. She has published several books on literary theory, gender, and depth psychology, including *Jung: A Feminist Revision* (2002) and *Jung as a Writer* (2005). Her latest book is *The Ecocritical Psyche: Literature, Complexity Evolution, and Jung* (2012), arguing that literary symbols are embodied, biosemiotic, and communicative between human and other.

Soper draws attention to the three broad contexts of the word *nature* as used in English today. In the first place nature is employed in a binary division with culture in a structure of meaning that places humanity and its artifacts *outside* nature. Nature is the nonhuman while culture covers all pertaining to humanity and its products. On the other hand, in phrases such as "the laws of nature" we include such phenomena as gravity which subsumes human culture within the nature of the universe. Gravity is the nature that includes us. Finally, nature is used in an aesthetic sense as that which we value for its intrinsic loveliness and wish to preserve. Here, a city park is protected from development even though it represents *cultivated* nature.

Of course these contested significances have histories in myth and in religious interpretations of it. Moreover, nature regarded mythically continues to embed environmentalism in a debate about the human impact upon the nonhuman world. So while the term "mother nature" reveals the lingering presence of the earth mother goddess who was the origin of all presences on the planet, including the human, she finds modern incarnation in the theory of evolution as progenitor of all life. As prior to division into genders, earth mother also found a new home in the preoedipal (m)other of psychoanalysis and depth psychology.

Binary nature/culture stems from another ancient structure, this one dualistic, which became especially activated in the sky father gods who eventually sponsored monotheism. Distinguished by creating the earth and its inhabitants as separate from the divine, this model of disembodied transcendence was also mapped onto gender difference— it fostered patriarchy and the notion that to be human was to be *other* than nature. Here, culture is regarded as the superior alternative to nature. Inevitably divinely instituted separation was enacted as masculine dominance over the feminine *as* nature, connoting also the material body, sexuality, and death.

Ultimately, as Ann Baring and Jules Cashford have so eloquently shown in *The Myth of the Goddess*, the two diverging mythical orientations to nature are two equally necessary models of consciousness.[2] Earth mother creation myths regard consciousness as based upon connection, embodiment, sexuality, immanence, and what Jung called Eros. By contrast monotheistic myths prioritize consciousness structured through separation, discrimination, differentiation, and transcendence, including Jung's Logos. I have argued elsewhere that fundamental to Jung's treatment of gender and modernity is his intuitive drive to rebalance the creation myths of consciousness.[3] His aim is to remedy the fragility of a modern psyche built on an overemphasis of separation.

The consequences of this mythical diversity surrounding the structural relations of humanity and nature are profound for both the environmental movement and for Jungian studies. Such consequences are also vital for humanity's response to the twenty-first-century climate crisis, as both Stephen J. Foster and Robert D. Wagner, Jr. demonstrate. Evolution, as successor to the earth mother mythical narrative, presupposes that human culture is derived from the processes of creativity that predate and originate human beings. Therefore, if human culture is irreparably harming the planet, then does that (self-)destruction indicate a fault in evolution or in us? Does evolution possess a *telos*, goal, or purpose? Given that species are believed to have perished, even without human intervention, is evolution blind to what we call "environmental disaster"? If so, then maybe human destruction of the planet is yet another interruption of an evolutionary process that will simply proceed after humans have extinguished themselves.

A more hopeful alternative may be one that puts faith in evolution as purposeful. Perhaps humanity and its cultures can be forced into more rapid periods of social and psychical evolution by crisis itself. Here Jungians Foster and Wagner position themselves as relative optimists by positing a process in which deep changes or evolution of consciousness can occur in time to avert catastrophe. Such a faith in a necessarily imminent period of rapid psychic development hopes for a restructuring the Western nations' rapacious consumption of nonhuman nature, a nature still being disastrously treated as infinite resources.

Fascinatingly, both Foster and Wagner, although operating largely within laws of nature that include humans as an intrinsic part of (earth mother) evolution, do not entirely reject the binary structuring of culture/nature that results from the patriarchal interpretation of Genesis. Both books situate the human relationship to nature as one of stewardship, therefore continuing to place human culture as preeminent. Indeed, Wagner draws on the notion of a "second Adam" from rabbinical scholar Joseph Soloveitchik in a rethinking of Genesis to switch from the emphasis on dominion over nature to stewardship.

In a similar mode of weaving together immanence and transcendence of nature, earth mother and sky father, Foster follows Jung into alchemy and the teaching of Gerhard Dorn. Here is a premodern science model of extracting the spirit from matter that Jung explored for its analogy to psychic individuation. Within alchemy symbolism is figured a union or conjunction of genders, followed by resolving soul and body together. These processes lead on to the last stage of uniting with the *anima mundi* or soul of the world. Where Jung emphasized this pathway as a spiritual journey to the greater powers of the self for the individual person, Foster repositions Dorn and alchemy as potentially an ecological model of conscious evolution. It is an ecological alchemy that culminates in a transformation of human relations with nature. It is time to consider his notion of the Nature archetype.

Risky Business begins with a proposition for a Nature archetype, which is "a universal life force that has both physical form (earth, seas, mountains, etc.) and psychological power (it activates both instinctual and spiritual drives)" (p. 10). He is careful to insist that although culture has assigned feminine aspects to define nature, "she" also has masculine properties. Hence his specified Nature archetype is structurally similar to the earth mother goddess with the developmental preoedipal role as the ground of body, life, and vitality in the process of becoming individuated.

Humanity therefore expresses aspects of the Nature archetype, but not all of it. We are called upon to complete our individuation by an embodied psychic union with the *anima mundi*, or world soul. For she (*anima mundi*) is the spiritual animation of Nature (the archetype) in nature, its physical form external to us. In a fascinating and innovative extension of Jungian ideas, Foster builds on Jung's intimations of deep collective processes in the cultural conscious and unconscious. He suggests that just as the individual ego has to expel and repress in order to survive, so Western modernity has constructed itself upon its externalization of unwanted material that it chooses to define as waste. Hence pollution is endemic to modern societies, and there are deep collective psychic resistances to stopping it.

On the other hand, the individual ego is sick if it also does not have a mutually sustaining relationship with the other or unconscious. If repression and externalization go too far, then the instinctual part of the psyche, energized by the Nature archetype, cannot support the ego in a healthy relationship to its other psychic energies, or environment. Collectively, a culture that has overstressed externalization is sickened by the loss of connection to Nature in its physical form as nature. Such a lost bond to physical nature also severs society's collective psyche from the *anima mundi*.

In a further striking innovation, Foster draws on Donald Kalsched's model of the self-care system distorted by early trauma.[4] Kalsched argues that trauma in infancy may cause a split in the nascent self to instate a persecutory relationship that continues to weaken the adult person. The infant neutralizes an unbearable external threat by reconfiguring it as an internal punishing entity. The healing energies of the psyche are stunted by this polarized self: the malignant internalized persecutor seals the ego away from the potentially helpful energies of the psyche. Extending this map of the traumatized psyche to the collective, Foster suggests that Western industrialization caused the traumatic split from the Nature archetype as nature. Such a notion of deep split in the collective psyche works as a helpful explanatory frame for the seeming inability of the Western nations to adequately address the environmental crisis, in particular climate change. Our desire to change lacks vitality because the collective is split off from the vital positive energies of Nature and nature.

To be more precise, if both the individual ego and collective consciousness have been traumatically split from Nature in their histories, they suffer from acute anxiety about survival. Such infantile anxiety reinforces strategies of externalization and pollution even in the face of an instinctual understanding that harming the other is damaging the prospects for survival of both nature and the Nature that includes us. Intriguingly Foster cites the polarization in debates over climate change as evidence of the cultural complex that is the split in the psychic-physical Nature archetype. Denying climate change, he argues, represents a collective resistance engendered by deep trauma over the loss of contact with Nature as nature in the Western nations.

Of course, there are limitations to mapping Jungian psychology onto all kinds of cultural complexities. Describing non-Western nations as needing to be helped through infancy on externalization as pollution by Western environmental specialists has a point, but does leave out the extremely sophisticated ways of working *with* nature that many non-Western nations possessed before exhorted to adopt Western industrial models. An infant-based developmental model is potentially relevant to other cultures *if* they are embarking upon "Western" development.

Whether it is the best epistemological model by which to study other cultures per se is a further debate important to Jungian studies, for it asks us to consider whether Jungian ideas are indigenous to the Western paradigm from which they emerged. Does Jungian-inflected developmental theory work at a cultural level for all societies or only some of them? Foster's book implies a more universal application. Interestingly, Jung did not apply his ideas unquestioningly to non-Western cultural groups. Rather he indicated throughout his work that concepts and theories, like archetypal images themselves, were culturally influenced.

Robert D. Wagner, Jr. uses a combination of Joseph Campbell's theories of myth and Jung's notions of psyche to explore the role of a work of art as a bearer of myth acutely relevant 150 years after the novel's composition.[5] Herman Melville's novel *Moby-Dick* (1851) is explored incisively as a key expression of a myth about oil that is acutely relevant to today's oil industry. Wagner powerfully and successfully tests out one of Jung's lesser-known theories of art: that a symbolic work with deep links to the collective unconscious was teleological, could indicate where the collective was going, and if necessary, as here, carry a warning.

Unsurprisingly then, *"Moby-Dick" and the Mythology of Oil* offers a real connection to Foster's work in *Risky Business*. Indeed one could argue that Wagner uses whales in nature, in the novel, and in mythology as a prime carrier of the Nature archetype for Western culture. Whales, brutally hunted in the nineteenth century for oil, were treated as waste once their valuable liquids had been extracted. Yet scientists today note the sophisticated social interactions of whales and their larger brains and longer evolutionary span than that of humans. They may indeed be as much *anima mundi* Nature as nature!

Moby-Dick, Melville's whale, was a rare creature in being aggressive toward human beings. This particular white whale was responsible for Captain Ahab's severed leg, thereby spurring that man's obsessive pursuit. Based upon an actual nineteenth-century whale known to have rammed and destroyed a whaling vessel, Moby-Dick in turn sinks the ship carrying those determined to kill him. Only Ishmael, the narrator of the novel, survives to tell the story. Wagner points out how unusual was such behavior from the hunted whale. Despite greater strength and maneuverability, whales rarely fought back. Wagner links this restraint to the way whales sometimes allow themselves to be fatally stranded upon beaches. Do whales have a greater individuation into what Foster terms the Nature archetype? Wagner speculates: Might these magnificent gentle creatures sometimes allow themselves to be sacrificed for the greater environment?

Also like Foster, Wagner considers the problem of evolution and human folly in seemingly attacking our own conditions for survival. After a cogent and illuminating analysis of the dynamics of the economy of what he calls "the petroleum age," Wagner invokes Campbell's hero myth as a structure calling for an extremely rapid psychic evolution in the collective. Where once the hero was called, tested, rewarded, and returned in the service of making the ego or sky father consciousness based upon separation, today the hero has to be modern economic culture itself. For now the hero's call is the cry that evokes collective sacrifice and the journey of humankind to its marriage or *coniunctio* with the planet as a living entity.

Ending with an insightful and superbly articulated conclusion, *"Moby-Dick" and the Mythology of Oil* calls for a change in the collective mythos. The book diagnoses the contribution of the petroleum industry to today's environmental crisis as entirely analogous to the story of the novel, *Moby-Dick*. For not only is the contemporary oil industry built along the same terminal lines as the nineteenth-century pursuit of whale oil, but Ahab's self-destructive obsession is shown to be a viable mapping of how the modern West (and the United States in particular) is irrationally driven by the thirst for oil. Here is a nice contrast in the methodologies of the two books, for while Foster prioritizes Jungian psychology as an epistemology, Wagner shows the value of combining compatible structures from Campbell, Jung, literature, and myth.

So Wagner argues that the prevailing mythos of the petroleum age is an obsessive and self-destructive pursuit. He then uses Campbell, principally, to suggest the possibility of reorienting the myth toward a collective rapprochement with the planet (Foster's Nature as nature).

Both books show the potential of Jungian and cognate ideas not only to understand, but also to seek to change dominant conditions and ideologies. Having focused on these remarkable works as contributions to ecology and ecopsychology, I want to end this review by considering *"Moby-Dick" and the Mythology of Oil* as a contribution to the discipline of literary studies. After all, innate to depth psychology as a whole is the question of academic disciplines with their diverse ways of knowing.

Literary studies in the form of university degrees is a surprisingly new discipline since study of literature in the vernacular was only instituted in the academy in the late nineteenth century. It is therefore fascinatingly contemporary to the founding of depth psychology itself. The epistemology of studying literature in one's native language is that it can be a viable ground of knowledge without requiring anything added to it to justify its value. By this definition *"Moby-Dick" and the Mythology of Oil* is a fine addition to literary studies for it demonstrates that the novel can find an epistemological approach that is augmented by Campbell and Jung, yet does not absolutely require these theorists in order to supply such a way of knowing. Wagner shows that the novel works as a quest for knowledge in its own right.

Moreover, unlike many studies of Melville's novel that also offer historical analysis of ideologies of nineteenth-century whaling and of the politics of United States, Wagner's book provides something that so much literary criticism today lacks. *"Moby-Dick" and the Mythology of Oil* provides a way of mapping the novel onto meaning in our twenty-first-century lives. What the thorough grounding in myth theory and depth psychology offers the reader of *"Moby-Dick" and the Mythology of Oil* is a unified vision that provides purpose to literary criticism. It shows that literature is a route to comprehending and transforming the crises of today, not just those of its own time. While Wagner's book lacks sophisticated literary theory, much of which wants to argue for the supreme importance of literature as a diagnosis of culture and power, it has the advantage of offering a vision that unites what cannot be avoided with a way of treating it. It therefore demonstrates the potential of depth psychology to extend the epistemological range of other academic disciplines.

In the last analysis, both *Risky Business* and *"Moby-Dick" and the Mythology of Oil* are significant works because they succeed in showing that today's psychology is ecopsychology. With the encroachment of environmental anxieties into twenty-first-century life from politics to scholarship, from economics to multiculturalism, the arts, and, not least, as indigenous to personal trauma, the psyche is imbued with an other that can no longer be regarded as separate from us. If psychology is ecopsychology, then it must encompass energies beyond those rationally organized in the ego. Therefore psychology as ecopsychology is also depth psychology. *"Moby-Dick" and the Mythology of Oil* argues that the pursuit of petroleum is a tragic mythos as well as what Foster calls "risky business." It will be with the help of such insightful research as the work of Foster and Wagner that we just might, in time, (re)discover our whole selves in Nature by uniting physical nature and human nature.

NOTES

1. K. Soper, "The Idea of Nature," in *The Green Studies Reader: From Romanticism to Ecocriticism*, edited by L. Coupe (London: Routledge, 2000), pp. 123–26.

2. A. Baring and J. Cashford, *The Myth of the Goddess: Evolution of an Image* (New York: Vintage, 1991).

3. Susan Rowland, *C. G. Jung in the Humanities* (New Orleans: Spring Journal Books, 2010), chapter 3.

4. See Donald Kalsched's argument for splitting of the self-care system in an infant; D. Kalsched, *The Inner World of Trauma: Archetypal Defenses of the Personal Spirit* (London: Routledge, 1996).

5. Campbell's theories of myth begin in *The Hero with a Thousand Faces* (Princeton, NJ: Bollingen, 1949).

BOOK REVIEWS

Eva Pattis Zoja, *Sandplay Therapy in Vulnerable Communities: A Jungian Approach*. London: Routledge, 2011.

REVIEWED BY ASTRID BERG

"This book arose out of practical work, and was written with practical work in mind. However, in the course of the experience, a rich theoretical backbone also emerged" (p. 1). This first sentence in the introduction to *Sandplay Therapy in Vulnerable Communities: A Jungian Approach* is a succinct and fitting description of what this book is all about. The method of expressive sandwork or sandplay is a process that rests on the observation and interpretation of images created through objects in a bounded space of sand, usually a sand tray. Much has been written about this method, but this is the first book that looks at applying the technique with children coming from communities that are living in a crisis situation of one form or another in different parts of the world.

Astrid Berg is a psychiatrist as well as a Jungian analyst. She is an associate professor at the University of Cape Town and a senior consultant in the Division of Child and Adolescent Psychiatry at the Red Cross Children's Hospital in Cape Town, where she heads the university's Parent-Infant Mental Health Service. She also holds an honorary position as associate professor extraordinary in the Department of Psychiatry at the University of Stellenbosch. Since 1995, she has been involved in a community in Cape Town where she is in charge of a weekly mother-baby mental health clinic. Her particular interest is in intercultural communication.

Chapter 1 provides a very interesting backdrop to why this approach is important in terms of its social applicability, namely, the fact that the first psychoanalysts were actually acutely aware of the need to be socially relevant, a historical reality that sadly has been overtaken by the more conservative, individually orientated psychoanalysis of modern times, through which it has become a Western science and method. Sandplay is a nonverbal method that employs a universally known medium and uses objects that come from the children's surroundings. As such it goes beyond culture and can thus be utilized in all societies and groups. This book is testimony to this fact. Archetypal motifs and the collective unconscious are helpful constructs that analytical psychology brings to cross-cultural work in general and serves as an anchor point throughout this work.

Sandplay work with children was pioneered by Margaret Lowenfeld and Dora Kalff, with the latter following the Jungian method of child therapy. However, concepts such as the reverie of the therapist and the importance of the third as an observing other are accepted and useful notions in psychoanalysis in general. In this case we have the child interacting or handling the figures in the sand tray, with the observer providing the position of the third—even if not directly spoken about, the very act of observing and taking in and trying to understand is important. It is this process that becomes the container for the child, a container in which links can be made, albeit at a metaphorical and unconscious level.

These processes can only occur if the environmental provision is good enough. What the book emphasizes, and what makes it unique, is the fact that the setting does not have to be a well-equipped playroom with a myriad of carefully displayed figurines. Sandplay can occur in even the barest, the most minimally comfortable contexts, such as in a school near an informal settlement in Johannesburg, South Africa, or in an orphanage in Guangzhou, China. And it is indeed true that those children who need it most in the world have the least access to psychological help. The method described here could provide a way to redress this imbalance. Psychological trauma affects young children irreversibly—it literally alters the architecture of the brain and thus becomes engrained in the child's psyche for the rest of his or her life. However, while the tree trunk may have been damaged, the roots remain intact and can enable a coherent ego to develop (p. 46). Expressive sandplay is one way in which the roots of the traumatized psyche of the child can be freed in order to enable new growth to take place.

In chapters 6 and 10 details of the technique of expressive sandwork are described. The approach is sensible, always bearing in mind what conditions are like in the neediest and most stressed situations. The challenge in psychological work in general is the training of the psychotherapist or counselor. Psychotherapy in the Western sense of the word is not known in many parts of the world, and the question always is whether it is indeed needed or applicable for all people. However, all children play, and it is this universal and natural tendency to portray psychological realities through action that is the basis of this technique. All adults were children once, so they too can play; this enables the method to be readily experienced by trainees and the basic principles can be fairly easily taught. In addition to the knowledge that play is an externalization of the inner world, there is knowing that the process can be trusted—that the psyche will reveal itself in its own way in its own time and that this is what ultimately results in healing.

Chapters 7, 8, and 9 describe expressive sandwork in three different parts of the world: South Africa, China, and Latin America. Admirably, the author herself participated in all these sandplay projects. The many case examples attest to the fact that this book is based on very real experience.

It was gratifying to read that the miniatures used in South Africa were objects familiar to the children or were made from material that was readily available, for example, making human figures from banana leaves or bits of metal. However, in a country as complex as South Africa care has to be taken not to make generalizations or misrepresentations. For example, *sangoma* is the Zulu word for "healer"—a *sangoma* is not a charlatan or one who deals with occult magic, as stated in the book. Criminal, opportunistic, and fake healers abound, as they do in every society, not just in Africa, but sadly they receive more press coverage than the proper *sangomas* do. That these charlatans damage children is without question, but it is not the norm; it is an aberration and strongly condemned by *sangomas*. However, children in South Africa do suffer from the effects of poverty, family disruption, and epidemic illnesses, and doable techniques such as sandplay can offer psychological alleviation from the trauma and toxic stress.

China is a continent with traumas of a different kind. With recorded knowledge going back thousands of years, the intellectual interest, but also the defenses against feelings, must be of a particular kind. For example, the link described between the pictographic writing of the Chinese language and the psyche is striking and may account for why sandplay has spread throughout China so quickly. The accounts of children overcoming the devastating losses and trauma brought about by the 2008 earthquake are moving and inspiring and describe brave little souls in the wake of so much destruction.

Like South Africa, the case examples in Colombia describe how sandwork can be used by children to order and structure their lives where so little of that is provided by the environment. The fatherlessness of these children echoes those in South Africa. Six-year-old Marcelo, who has experienced much neglect and trauma, comes to depict positive scenes, and the comment is made that "Marcelo has hardly experienced any of these things in his outside reality, but in his inner life there is still an unharmed, soothing place that . . . provides an almost magical protection" (p. 157). This is the foundation upon which this work rests.

What stands out and what makes this book particularly practical and useful is its sound theoretical basis: that is, the objective existence of the psyche which reveals itself through play—the more the observer can understand and know this, the more the child will be able to reveal; that the psyche has a natural tendency to heal itself if it can be shared and held in the mind of another person; and that each child's psyche is unique and will constellate at its own individual pace.

Furthermore the book offers practical guidelines: how to set up the space, what objects are needed, how the process is explained. How to talk with parents is done in a sensible way, and the caution not to literalize children's play is equally well phrased and appropriate. Indeed, nothing could be worse than to translate a symbolic reality into a concrete one and act according to the latter. The photographs of the sand trays are helpful, particularly those in color, and give one a sense of immediacy and concrete reality.

This book is highly recommended to all therapists and trainee therapists who wish to work with children, as well as to lay counselors. This method should not to be limited to the Western, so-called developed world where it originated in this form, but needs to be made known globally. The psyches of our children can only benefit.

BOOK REVIEWS

Daniel Joseph Polikoff, *In the Image of Orpheus: Rilke, A Soul History*. Wilmette, IL: Chiron Publications, 2011.

REVIEWED BY PAUL BISHOP

Writing to Ellen Gregori on 3 August 1957, Jung declared that he and Rilke both drew from "the same deep springs," or the collective unconscious. Yet despite his admiration for Rilke—"his high poetic gifts and intuition" and "the lack of modernity" that is "a badge of genuine poetry-craft"—Jung complained that there was something about this man, "half troubadour, half monk," that suggested Rilke didn't have "what it takes to make a man complete: body, weight, shadow." Rilke's "high ethos," his "capacity for negation," and maybe even his "physical frailty" had led him toward "a goal of completeness, but not of perfection"—an intriguing remark. This letter to Gregori, the author of an essay titled "Rilke's Psychological Knowledge in the Light of Jungian Theory" (sadly, never published), concludes with a wish that "somebody could be found who would set the inner and outer

Paul Bishop has written various articles and books on Jungian thought and German culture, particularly the relation of Jung's ideas to key themes in German classicism, Romanticism, and literary modernism. He is professor of German at the University of Glasgow.

data of [Rilke's] life in order and interpret it with the necessary psychological understanding."[1]

Since the time of Jung's letter, there have been no more than a couple of attempts to elaborate an approach to Rilke's works from a Jungian perspective, but the gap in the market is now filled with this study by Daniel Joseph Polikoff, an independent scholar (and a published poet).[2] He offers here an epic account of Rilke's life and works—epic in its extent as in its rhetorical register (which sometimes puts one in mind of Cecil B. de Mille). Inasmuch as it is a "psychobiographical," indeed "psychospiritual" account, it unabashedly conflates Rilke's life and work (pp. 180, 182). According to Siegfried Mandel, "the link between Rilke's biography and poetry is absolute" (quoted on p. 64), and Polikoff agrees: "insofar," he claims, "as Rilke figures as a preeminent poet of the soul, it is crucial to recognize the degree to which the lines of his *artistic* and his *psychological* creativity braid inextricably" (p. 64). In turn, Polikoff reads Rilke's development as an individual and as a poet within two interpretative frameworks—one mythical, one psychological, both deriving from the work of James Hillman.

In *The Myth of Analysis* (1983), Hillman replaced the basis of Freudian psychoanalysis—the myth of Oedipus—with a myth taken from a work by the second-century Latin prose writer Apuleius of Madaura: the fable of Amor (or Cupid or Eros) and Psyche in his *Metamorphoses*, sometimes called *The Golden Ass*. (For his part, Apuleius derived the substance of this myth from an earlier Greek source—or so Fulgentius [*Mythologies*, 3:6] tells us.) Within the Jungian tradition, this work had been, prior to Hillman, the subject of a commentary by Erich Neumann, and it subsequently attracted the attention of Marie-Louise von Franz.[3] (Neumann's account built on previous work by, among others, Rudolf Pagenstecher, Richard Reitzenstein, and Otto Weinrich, as well as J. J. Bachofen;[4] and Neumann, too, highlighted the links between this myth and Rilke's poems.) Using Apuleius's myth as his template, Polikoff undertakes to "identify phases of Rilke's literary and psychospiritual career with distinct phases of the myth of Psyche and Eros" (p. 182), arguing for an audacious correspondence between the four tasks involved in "the enormous work of Psyche's labors" in that myth and the four major works that constitute "the core of Rilke's mature oeuvre" (p. 297), that is, *New Poems* (1907–1908), *The Notebooks of Malte Laurids Brigge* (1910), *Duino Elegies* (written 1912–1922; published 1923), and *Sonnets to Orpheus* (1923).

Simultaneously, however, Polikoff argues at a second level for a further correspondence between these same works and the signature themes of Hillman's *Re-Visioning Psychology* (1975): first, "personifying or imagining things," "a passionate critique of the monotheistic premises of our dominant spiritual culture and the disenchantment of the universe that follows in its wake," used here as "windows" into "the world of Rilke's *New Poems*" (p. 351); second, "pathologizing or falling apart," as defining the "psychodynamic force" driving the writing of *Malte* (p. 375); third, "psychologizing or seeing through," as elaborating a "psychological initiative" in the *Duino Elegies*; and "dehumanizing or soul-making," as helping us construe "the unique soul-initiative" at the heart of the *Sonnets to Orpheus* (p. 600). Thus armed with Apuleius (read through Neumann) in one hand and the works of Hillman in the other, Polikoff sets out to uncover those "archetypal motifs . . . embodied in Rilke's life and . . . his poetic opus, enacted again and again, and in constantly evolving forms" (p. 628). This journey takes us from Rilke's earliest verse, notably *Dreamcrowned* (1896) and *Visions of Christ* (1896–1898), to "the sonnet cycle addressed to the mysterious archetypal source of his own poetic and psychological being, Orpheus" (p. 628).

If, within the mythic structure of Apuleius's fable, Rilke's early lyrics date from the phase *before* Eros and Psyche's initial meeting, and his encounter with Lou von Salomé represents the advent of Eros and ensuing mutual rapture (p. 183), then Rilke's period in Worpswede between 1900 and 1902 is said to constitute an extended engagement with anima (p. 191, cf. p. 215). Above all, his life among the artists (both male and female) of Worpswede brought about "a significant turn in his sense of the character, autonomy, and value of the image" (p. 209), since—or so Jung believed—"the feminine mind is pictorial [*anschaulich*] and symbolic" (p. 210).[5] In the famous lines of Rilke's poem "Turning Point" (1914)—"Learn, inner man, to look on your inner woman, / the one drawn out of / a thousand natures, this / first now attained but / never truly loved form"—Polikoff detects Rilke's "most explicit embrace" of the psychological idea of the anima archetype (p. 483). Following his departure from Worpswede, Rilke's development entered (in alchemical terms) the stage of *mortification* or *nigredo* (p. 235), a dark crisis resolved through his contact in Paris with Rodin between 1902 and 1906 (p. 309). As with the time spent in Worpswede, Polikoff largely follows the conventional view of the biographical significance of this period, but he identifies Rodin with the *senex*, functioning archetypally as a kind of Pan figure, energizing Rilke's writing of his *New Poems* (p. 309).

Polikoff's reading of Rilke's earlier work is informed by the premise that "throughout [his] creative career erotic love played a central part in his life and art" (p. 46), especially his relationship with Lou von Salomé. Following his journey to Florence in spring 1898 and his visits to Russia in 1899 and 1900, Rilke advanced this project in *The Book of Hours* (1905), a work Polikoff reads as "a profoundly religious text" (p. 107). He sets it against a series of background texts: first, Lou von Salomé's "The Basic Forms of Art: A Psychological Study" (1898/1899), and second, the synthesizing overview of Western civilization offered in Richard Tarnas's *Cosmos and Psyche*, in which Tarnas outlines the modern world view as one that is, in Weber's famous expression, *entzaubert* or "disenchanted."[6] In stark contrast, *The Book of Hours* "sets in motion a precise *reversal* of the evolutionary process Tarnas associates with the rise of monotheistic religion" (p. 113), and Polikoff explains how it does this with reference to a third background work, Henry Corbin's study *Creative Imagination in the Sufism of Ibn Arabi*.[7] In this masterful analysis of the great Sufi mystic, Corbin adduced the notion of theophany, or "a revealing of the visible world as . . . the shining forth of a divine essence" (p. 560). Not only does *The Book of Hours* supply "an exemplary instance of what Corbin calls 'creative prayer'" (p. 170), but its first part—*The Book of Monastic Life*—illustrates the link made by Corbin between the process of individuation and "releasing the spiritual person from collective norms" (p. 182).[8]

Back to Apuleius: Psyche, following her meeting with and subsequent separation from Eros, is set a series of four labors by her jealous rival Venus. In the first task, the sorting of a huge pile of mixed grains or seeds, Polikoff discerns an archetypal connection with Rilke's *New Poems*, and what Hillman (in *Re-Visioning Psychology*) calls "personifying or imagining things" (pp. 350–51). Her second task, the gathering of golden wool from the rams of the sun—a myth linked by Neumann to "the destructive power of the masculine" and "the negative masculine death principle" (p. 423)—is associated with the concept of pathologizing, a path into soul for Hillman and for Rilke (in *The Notebooks of Malte Laurids Brigge*) alike (p. 384). In fact, *Malte* was written at around the same time as Freud's famous case study of Dora, *An Analysis of a Case of Hysteria* (1901; published 1905), yet Rilke's novel, Polikoff argues, is the more psychologically radical work, for these *Notebooks* represent "a concentrated reclamation of *memoria* as a primary faculty of soul" (p. 432).

The third task of Psyche, the filling of a crystal flask from a high crag with water from a stream that runs into the River Styx, is associated with Hillman's notion of "psychologizing or seeing through," providing a mythical-psychological perspective on the *Duino Elegies*.[9] But although the *Elegies* bear the name of Duino, they are informed by the Spanish city of Toledo, captured graphically by El Greco in his *View of Toledo* in 1561, an "originating archetypal image" of which they are the "poetic expansion" (p. 591).[10] Noting the tradition of philosophical interpretation in the case of the *Elegies*, Polikoff is less interested in conceptual approaches and more in the resonance found in Rilke's reading material: Goethe, Hölderlin, the Bible, the Qur'an, St. Augustine, and Pedro de Ribadeneira's *Flos Sanctorum* all left a mark. The *Elegies*' "historic force," Polikoff maintains, "can be most truly heard against the sounding board of the traditions represented in these texts, for . . . the *voice* that resounds in these great poems is primarily that of a prophet" (p. 449; see also p. 517). Polikoff notes Rilke's interest in Islam, but he goes further, arguing that "it can hardly be altogether incredible to construe the *Elegies* as an essentially prophetic text, a vessel of revelation" (p. 578). How so?

On the basis of a letter by Rilke to Countess Margot Sizzo on 6 January 1923, Polikoff asserts that "the telos of Rilke's poetry includes . . . some form of recovery or (better) contemporary rebirth of ancient mystery wisdom" (p. 507). At first sight this claim might appear extreme, and Polikoff's reference to the interpretation of the Sphinx by the esotericist Edouard Schuré (1841–1929) in *The Great Initiates* (1889) insufficient to back it up. (One might even push the argument further. Given Rilke's interest in Orpheus, did his work arise from some kind of incubatory experience? Against the backdrop of astrology in Tarnas's *Cosmos and Psyche*, should one consider the zodiacal sign under which Rilke was born?) In fact, however, Polikoff's claim is

based on a consideration of the eminently formal aspect of the *Elegies*,
inasmuch as "the form and substance of the initiatory experience itself"
is "*enacted* in and through language" (p. 509). "The formal secrets of
the elegy," he insists, reside in "how the soul-force engaged in *giving
voice* to suffering may break through numbness, reviving—in the sound-
wave of its trembling vibration—the nascent sense of life and love's
impossible possibilities" (p. 536).

In his 1980 study of the classical German elegy, Theodor
Ziolkowski argued (in the context of Schiller's "Der Spaziergang" and
Goethe's "Euphrosyne") that the function of the elegy—via the
emergence of an elegiac tension, the introduction of a poetic persona,
the elevation of that persona through meditation, and "a timeless state
of entrancement"—is to produce "a higher level of consciousness at
which a resolution is seen as possible" (p. 510).[11] Ziolkowski's "generic
description" offers a "template" to investigate Rilke's "initiatory
poetics"—a shrewd move, which licenses Polikoff's definition of Rilke's
"purificatory poetics" as being "to initiate the individual soul or psyche
into the higher orders of consciousness implicit in its being—*not* so as
to abandon and betray its earthly existence, but so as to *see through* [cf.
Hillman] the appearance of its *purely* transient nature, *reconnecting* both
soul and world to"—as Rilke put it in his letter to Margot Sizzo—
"that 'really sound and full sphere and orb of being'" (p. 514).

The *Elegies* as a whole "repeatedly involve dual notions of ascent
and descent, transcendence and limitation" (p. 538), thereby enacting
alchemical processes of *sublimatio, coagulatio,* and *circulatio*. But if, in
the *Elegies*, the voice we hear is Rilke's—the voice of "the individual
human soul in its relation to the world of spirit" (p. 581) or "the voice
of Psyche, the human soul in its archetypal longing for union with the
Spirit of Love and the fulfillment of Being that union confers" (p.
582)—then in the fourth of Rilke's major works the voice we hear is
entirely different. Related to the *Elegies* as a "little rust-colored sail" is
to a "gigantic white canvas," as Rilke put it in his letter of 13 November
1925 to Witold Hulewicz, the *Sonnets to Orpheus* "effectively begin
where the *Elegies* leave off" (p. 590), and the "poetic voice that
authorizes the opening of the lighter cycle is *not* readily recognizably
'ours'—a human voice—at all" (p. 590).

For Polikoff, the opening poem of the *Sonnets* must be read as "a
classic instance of ekphrastic poetry . . . a poetic rendition of the visual

work of art" (p. 590)—in this case, a drawing by Cima da Conegliano, a postcard reproduction of which Baladine Klossowska purchased for Rilke and attached above his writing desk at Muzot. This Orpheus, "the 'God' to whom the *Sonnets* are addressed," is "not derivative of a Judeo-Christian or Muslim deity, but belongs to that other spiritual tradition not so readily recognizable as 'religion'—the mythological polytheism of the Greeks" (p. 596). Polikoff takes this divine aspect of Orpheus very seriously, albeit in the specific sense that Hillman defines the psychological divine, that is, whereas in traditional religion the gods "are *believed* in," in archetypal psychology they are "*imagined*" (pp. 597, 599).[12]

On the basis of their form, Polikoff places Rilke's *Sonnets* in the cultural-historical context of the Renaissance, an epoch whose essence is captured in Petrarch's account of his ascent of Mount Ventoux in April 1336. At the top of the mountain, with the landscape of French Provence, the Alps, and the Mediterranean before him, Petrarch took out his copy of Augustine's *Confessions* and read a passage from book 10, chapter 8 (a reflection on the power of memory), which spoke to his actual condition: "And men go abroad to wonder at the heights of mountains . . . and yet pass themselves by."[13] (Does the key to the Renaissance, one is tempted to ask, lie in a moment of synchronicity?) On this crucial moment in the development of the Renaissance consciousness Hillman and Tarnas famously take opposing stances. Whereas commentators and translators have traditionally interpreted Petrarch's ascent as signifying the return from God's world or nature to humankind, Hillman sees it as marking "the return to soul."[14] For Tarnas, however, Petrarch's description and his invocation of Augustine suggest the difficulty in abjuring the Christian mindset, the entire event representing "a powerful metaphor for the arduous spiritual ascent to God."[15] In turn, Polikoff focuses on a suggestive phrase in Augustine's reflection on memory: "A wonderful admiration surprises me, and an astonishment seizes me upon this [*multa mihi super hoc oboritur admiratio, stupor adprehendit me*],"[16] juxtaposing it with a line from the *Sonnets* (I:2): "and every wonder that concerned my own being [*und jedes Staunen, das mich selbst betraf*]" (pp. 618–19).

This echo in Rilke's poem of Augustine, via Petrarch, highlights in Polikoff's eyes the position of the *Sonnets* in cultural history as a completion of the Renaissance project: "Soul, Imagination, Anima,

History, Death, Love and Beauty, Logos as the mythopoetic speech of the soul, regard for the Many as well as the One" are "the pillars of Hillman's invisible Renaissance temple," and also "the founding terms of Rilke's poetry" (p. 622). Moreover, to the extent that the *Sonnets* teach, "Even if the reflection in the pool / often blurs before our eyes: / Know the image [*Wisse das Bild*]" (I:9), they undo the damage done— in Hillman's eyes—by the Reformation (p. 623). After all, "the issue of the image" is one to which Rilke's sonnet returns again and again (p. 632; see *Sonnets*, I:6, I:11, I:12, and I:20; on *Sonnets*, II, see pp. 632–39), and the "astonishing accomplishment" of the *Sonnets* lies in Rilke's "transmission of Orphic voice and vision" (p. 671). For Polikoff, the achievement of the *Sonnets* builds on Rilke's earlier work, demonstrating how "the logic of soul-making cannot involve a shirking of human psychology, but rather entails delving so deeply into the archetypal nature of the human soul . . . that one emerges—if graced by the Gods—*truly transformed*" (p. 671).

In the *Sonnets*, the two central myths of Polikoff's study—that is, the tale of Cupid and Psyche and the legend of Orpheus—are interwoven, but surely the respective happy and tragic endings of these stories cannot both be accommodated in Rilke's work? Polikoff believes they can: "if understood from an archetypally psychological perspective, the events of the traditional story (including Orpheus's death and dismemberment) may well be construed as commensurate with—even integral to—[the] ultimate completion of the Orphic mission of restoring soul to the world" (p. 675). This mission is accomplished by the effective integration of these two myths in Rilke's "poetry of soul" through "a fuller imagination of the whole world, and of the ultimate unity of life and death" (p. 675). Thus the "whole thrust" of Rilke's poetry is revealed as being "to open up the excluded middle, the transitional, inherently imaginal domain of love and the soul, the *metaxy* that translates between timeless ideas of spirit and the mutable sphere of material forms" (p. 673; see also pp. xviii, 53). And so "the 'pure transcendence' [*reine Übersteigung*] celebrated in the *Sonnets* introduces, simultaneously, a poetic philosophy of immanence" (p. 674).

* * *

Polikoff's book raises important questions about psychology and aesthetics, about religion and art. He is at his best on those occasions when he brings new intellectual-cultural contexts—sometimes surprising ones—to bear on Rilke's works. For example, he uses *The Golden Treatise of Hermes* and the *Rosarium philosophorum* (one of Jung's favorite alchemical works) as intertexts to the poem "Prayer" ("Gebet") in *The Book of Images* (p. 236). He illuminates the *Elegies* by references to the instruction of *Nous* (or Mind itself) to Hermes Trismegistus in the eleventh text in the *Corpus Hermeticum*, arguing that for Rilke—as for the quasi-mythological Hermes, or as for Plato—"the source of spiritual desolation and despair" lies "not in the order of the universe, but in the darkened vision of the soul trapped in what appears to it as a purely phenomenal reality devoid of deeper meaning" (p. 513; see also pp. 554–55). And he reads Rilke's notion of *Weltinnenraum* or inner world space in terms of other passages from this same discourse. Then again, the central lines of the Ninth Elegy are brought into fruitful conjunction with some telling remarks on the *Emerald Tablet* by Jung in "The Spirit Mercurius," as cited by Edward Edinger (pp. 567–68). On the first line of the very first of the *Sonnets*, "A tree rose up. O pure transcendence!" he brings to bear the philosophical tree illustrated in the sixth plate of the alchemical series *Splendor Solis*, attributed to the legendary figure of Salomon Trismosin, an early teacher of Paracelsus (p. 606).[17] In archetypal terms, these comparisons are as illuminating and insightful as they are fresh and unexpected.

At the same time, Polikoff is acutely aware of the limitations of his chosen mythical-interpretative framework. In his chapter on Worpswede, for example, he notes that it would be "misguided" to try to "make archetypal psychological sense" by "inflexibly 'assigning parts' in the mythic play" to people in Rilke's life—to Paula Becker or Clara Westhoff, for example (p. 204). And, in respect to the fourth (and final) task Venus demands of Psyche, her descent to the underworld with a jar to request of Proserpine a little of her beauty, Polikoff readily concedes that, since he is interested in "not merely thematic resonance, but poetic *enactment* of symbolic content," the "deeper connection" between this task and the *Sonnets* remains "anything but clear" (p. 661). Rather, he argues, the motives of Psyche's last labor—her dramatic descent, her disobedience, and Eros's final rescue—are already present in *Malte* and the *Elegies*, and the *Sonnets* should instead be associated with the three events succeeding that labor and concluding the myth: Eros's rescue of Psyche from the sleep of death, Psyche's apotheosis and marriage in heaven with Eros, and the birth of Pleasure (p. 661). But the strain of making Rilke's poetic texts fit the Procrustean bed of myth is all too evident.

Ultimately, the analysis of Rilke presented in this book—although Polikoff tends to play down this aspect of his account—is best understood against the background of Neoplatonism.[18] (For his part, Apuleius too had Neoplatonist philosophical leanings.) As Polikoff notes, Hillman's work reveals the Neoplatonic "roots" of archetypal psychology (p. 602), being influenced in particular by the Renaissance Neoplatonism of Marsilio Ficino, the goal of whose philosophizing was, as Eugenio Garin put it, "an invitation *to see* with the eyes of the soul, the soul of things . . . so that the whole world may become clearer in the inner light."[19] Common to Neoplatonic philosophy and Renaissance psychology, for instance, is the principle of unity in diversity, and so *Sonnets*, II:15, about a fountain-mouth, can be seen to hark back not just to Rilke's earlier poem, "Roman Fountain" (1906; published 1907), in which he adopted (and adapted) Rodin's "sculptural aesthetics," but to Plotinus, for whom "the fountain figures as a favorite image of the highest divinity—the One or the Good—constantly flowing out of its own center" (p. 651–52; see also pp. 339–43).[20]

This historico-philosophical note is sounded early on, when Polikoff notes that the image of God presented in *The Book of Hours* "controverts both conventional Christianity and the Platonic metaphysics which often . . . supports and blends with it" (p. 118). Further on, he turns to the passage preceding the famous parable of the cave when, in book 6 of *The Republic*, Socrates introduces the analogy of the divided line: a device to explain the relationship, as Plato saw it, between the visible and the intelligible world (p. 498–500).[21] According to this hierarchical arrangement of grades of being, the Ideas are at the top, while "shadows," "reflections," "images of water" are at the bottom—a level Polikoff equates with "the reflection in the pool" (*die Spiegelung im Teich*) of the *Sonnets* (I:9) (p. 502). Thus Rilke's "poetic logic," in effect, "reverses the order of things, putting the mirror(ed) image first, temporally, ontologically, and valuatively" (p. 634). Indeed, drawing on Otto F. Bollnow's suggestion that Rilke operates a kind of "reverse Platonism" (*umgekehrter Platonismus*), Polikoff points to the contrast between Platonic philosophy and depth psychology (pp. 503, 726n775; see also p. 542): whereas Plato's divided line and parable of the cave tell the story of the ascent of the soul via the ladder of reason, Apuleius's tale speaks of *two* protagonists, Psyche and Eros, whose "quest for spiritual consummation" takes the form of "a *dual* motion of ascent and descent" (p. 504).[22] This "sacred marriage (*hieros gamos*) of above and below that achieves both transcendence of *mere* mortality *and* a transformative immanence of spirit in the body of the world soul" (p. 504) can also be found, he believes, in Rilke, whose "mature poetic opus . . . reads as if the whole cosmic scale of being and knowing figured by the divided line were *interiorized within* the human psyche" (p. 505), especially in the case of the *Elegies*, where "the sequence of the whole . . . revolves around the interaction of the *transcending* and *delimiting* or *containing* gestures associated with Eros and Psyche" (p. 528; see also p. 538).

* * *

Although Marina Tsvetaeva once told Rilke, "You are a topography of soul" (p. 582), and although, in his Rodin book, Rilke spoke of "all those ancient secrets which, emerging from the unconscious, like strange river gods, lift their dripping heads from out the wild current of the blood" (p. 336), he nevertheless maintained a deep suspicion of psychoanalysis.[23] Why should this be, when one might argue that he shared much with Jung? A comparison of two passages reveals just one such telling parallel: in the *Sonnets* (II:28), Rilke talks of "the place where the lyre / lifted, resounding—; the unheard of center" [*die Stelle, wo die Leier sich tönend erhob—; die unerhörte Mitte*], while in *Mysterium Coniunctionis* Jung spoke of "the bilateral activity of the point in the centre" [*eine bilaterale Tätigkeit des Mittelpunktes*] (pp. 566–67).[24] Perhaps what, in these abstract terms, these passages are telling us is more evident from two excerpts, cited by Polikoff, from Rilke's Florence diary of 1898, where Rilke wrote that "art" (*die Kunst*) is "the means by which singular, solitary individuals fulfill themselves" [*das Mittel Einzelner, Einsamer, sich selbst zu erfüllen*], and that "beauty is the involuntary gesture in which a personality distills itself" [*die Schönheit ist die unwillkürliche Geste, die einer Persönlichkeit eignet*] (p. 73).[25] But what does this mean in practice?

Now, the message of the story of Psyche and Eros is that the determination *to see* can lead to disaster.[26] In the case of poetic texts, however, this is not true. In this respect, it is unfortunate that a literary theoretical, or even ideological, *parti pris* becomes evident in this study, reflected in an intense dislike of Paul de Man. Polikoff speaks dismissively of "imput[ing] a kind of clever, reflexive 'self-consciousness' to Rilke's 'language' itself," and he rejects de Man as "a purely academic theoretician" (p. 642). One does not have to be an aficionado of the Yale school of deconstruction, or have any kind of postmodernist leanings whatsoever, to sense that there is a missed opportunity here. For while archetypal psychology may be a "theoretical discourse that construes poetry and myth in terms of the logos of the soul" (p. 593), surely the key to Rilke lies precisely in his *logoi*—in his written words. As a result the most useful and revealing moments in this book come when Polikoff pays close attention to the details of Rilke's writing.

For instance, he notes how in "Jewish Cemetery" Rilke, through rhyme, "links *Er* (he) with *leer* (empty, or bare), both in his end rhyme and—doubling the effect—internally ('denn *er* war *leer*'), thus hammering home the annihilating effect of [God's] absence" (p. 33); or how, in the "enigmatic line" from *The Book of Monastic Life* in *The Book of Hours*, "Doch wie ich mich auch in mich selber neige," the verb *sich neigen* "literally means to bend, lean, or incline," thus implying "an act of psychological introspection . . . with a peculiarly active, almost physical gesture" (p. 117); or how, in the opening of the Tenth Elegy, the phrase "klar geschlagenen Hämmern des Herzens," that is, "clear-struck hammers of the heart," suggests "the telltale hammer pulveriz[ing] or pound[ing] the matter of the heart into waves of sound" (p. 545); or how, in the Seventh Elegy, the phrase "die Sterne der Erde," that is, "the stars of the earth," implies "another, higher octave fusion of spiritual and material realities, a conjoining of heaven and earth, eternal being and the world of becoming . . . an incorporation of the eternal order of the cosmos into earthly existence and a consequent illumination and sacralization of the concrete world" (p. 550); or how, in another sonnet (II:13), the line "Sei ein klingendes Glas, das sich im Klang schon zerschlug" foregrounds two major qualities of the sonnet form, musical sound and brevity (p. 646).

Elsewhere, he notes how, in the poem "Apprehension" ("Bangnis") from *The Book of Images*, the phrase "this withered wood" ("diesem

welken Walde"), denoting *faded* or *withered*, contrasts with the wood
that is "klar" and "aufgelöst" in the first of the *Sonnets* (p. 229); or
how, in Rilke's remarks about Toledo his letter to Ellen Delp of 27
October 1915, the word for "appearance," that is, *Erscheinung* or
"shining forth," evokes the idea of theophany (or shining forth of divine
substance) (p. 471); or how the phrase "new arrangements" (*neue
Ordnungen*) in Rilke's letter to Karl and Elisabeth von der Heydt of
25 February 1911 can be linked to the use of the word *Ordnungen* at
the end of the first sentence of the *Elegies* (p. 451).[27] Above all, he
rightly recognizes the signal importance of Rilke's choice of form, the
sonnet, "the shaping power of poetic form" being the means whereby
"the genius of the period [of the Renaissance] pours into the Rilkean
vessel" (p. 613), while in connection with another sonnet (I:8), he
notes how Rilke "employ[s] figurative language as a means of entering
an imaginal realm wherein the poetic present remains intimately linked
to the ancient past," in this case, "an aura of pagan antiquity" (p. 640).

In other words, precisely the transformational element that so
fascinates Polikoff lies in Rilke's use of language, and close attention to
it allows us to see the actual process of transformation that Rilke's art—
or, if one will, his alchemy—can achieve *through poetic art*. There is
nothing inherently mysterious about it at all. And there is a larger debate
to be had here. Polikoff would, I suspect, agree with Charles Taylor
that, for such writers as Rilke (as for Eliot, Pound, Mann, Lawrence,
Joyce, or Proust), the kind of approach to poetry offered by I. A.
Richards—as "a means of arranging the order of our internal lives by
making an harmonious pattern of extremely complex attitudes, once
thought to refer to an external order of metaphysics but now seen to
be a symbolic ordering of our inner lives"—is one that "manifestly will
not do"; rather, "the poet, if he is serious, is pointing to something—
God, the tradition—which he believes to be there for all of us."[28] Is
poetry essentially self-referential or does it refer to something else outside
itself? And, if so, whether this something is God, or whether it is the
tradition—that is the sixty-four-dollar question for Rilke, but it is also
the sixty-four-dollar question for Jung.[29]

In *Sources of the Self*, Rilke serves Charles Taylor as an example of
"an articulation of our farther, stronger intuitions, of the way the
world is not simply an ensemble of objects for our use, but makes
a further claim on us."[30] So it is significant that Polikoff refers to

Lou von Salomé's "psychological aesthetics" (p. 151), cites E. M. Butler's remark about Rilke's "aesthetic religion" (p. 600), and draws on Noel Cobb's equation of archetypal psychology with "aesthetic psychology" (p. 627). For it should lead us to ask: Is Rilke ultimately concerned with religion? Or with art?

One final thought: in this book, St. Augustine emerges as something of the villain of the piece, despite Rilke's long-standing interest in the subtle mind of this scholarly theologian. We are told that chief among the "basic metaphysical terms" underlying Augustine's work is sin (p. 129); that Augustinian Christianity is "suffocating" (p. 621); indeed, that his dualistic understanding of the world is "schizoid" (p. 673). Yet Augustine was right about one thing: when he referred to Apuleius's *Metamorphoses* by the title of *The Golden Ass*, he wanted to draw attention to a significant dimension of this ancient text which, while susceptible to an esoteric reading, is first and foremost—as is evident to anyone who reads it—a *comic* work.[31] So it is especially important, when bringing this text to bear on Rilke, not to overlook the dimension of humor. Rilke himself, as those who knew him recalled, was a complex, ironic, and witty individual. As Carl Jakob Burckhardt wrote to Hugo von Hofmannsthal, Rilke had "an unforgettable laugh"; Jean Rudolf von Salis described his laugh as "a natural, relaxed laugh . . . a manly laugh, without pressure, not forced"; and Rudolf Kassner went to considerable lengths to describe how Rilke used to laugh. This aspect of Rilke's work, so often unappreciated, forms a counterpoint to the unleavened seriousness of Polikoff's discussion. Yet it is wonderfully captured in the photograph of Rilke chosen to grace this book's front cover, which shows the poet during his final years in Switzerland, his face charmingly lit up by a warm smile. "Perfection, it seems to me, would have broken him" was Jung's judgment on Rilke. The challenge remains for us to try to appreciate *how* Rilke achieved perfection in his works.

NOTES

1. C. G. Jung, *Letters*, ed. Gerhard Adler and Aniela Jaffé, trans. R. F. C. Hull (London: Routledge and Kegan Paul, 1973, 1975), 2:381–82.

2. See Helmut Barz, "Das Unbewusste und die Sprache: Symbole bei Rilke" (lecture, C. G. Jung-Gesellschaft, Stuttgart, June 14, 1989); and C. Roelands, "Rilkes 'Neue Gedichte' im Lichte der Archetypenlehre C. G. Jungs: Versuch einer Interpretation," *Neophilologus* 78(1994):599–612.

3. Apuleius, *Amor und Psyche, mit einem Kommentar von Erich Neumann: Ein Beitrag zur seelischen Entwicklung des Weiblichen* (Zürich: Rascher, 1952); Erich Neumann, *Amor and Psyche: The Psychic Development of the Feminine*, trans. Ralph Mannheim (New York: Princeton University Press, 1956); Marie-Louise von Franz, *The Golden Ass of Apuleius: The Liberation of the Feminine in Man* (1970; repr. Boston: Shambhala, 1992).

4. For Bachofen, the story of Psyche traces a development comparable to Goethe's *Faust* (*Versuch über die Gräbersymbolik der Alten* [1859], in *Mutterrecht und Urreligion*, ed. Hans G. Kippenberg (Stuttgart: Kröner, 1984), p. 46).

5. See Jung's letter to Dr. S. of 22 March 1935 (*Letters*, 1:189); cited in Hillman, *Anima: An Anatomy of a Personified Notion* (1985, repr. Putnam, CT: Spring Publications, 2007), p. 68.

6. Richard Tarnas, *Cosmos and Psyche: Intimations of a New World View* (New York: Viking Penguin, 2006).

7. Corbin, *Creative Imagination in the Sufism of Ibn Arabi* (Princeton, NJ: Princeton University Press, 1969).Originally published in French in 1958, this work was based in part on two Eranos lectures given by Corbin in 1955 and 1956.

8. Corbin, *Creative Imagination in the Sufism of Ibn Arabi*, p. 268.

9. According to Hillman, "seeing through" is "a process of deliteralizing and a search for the imaginal in the heart of things by means of ideas" (quoted on p. 533; see James Hillman, *Re-Visioning Psychology* [1976, repr., New York: Harper, 1992], p. 136).

10. For further discussion, see Fatima Naqvi-Peters, "A Turning Point in Rilke's Evolution: The Experience of El Greco," *Germanic Review*, 72(1997):344–62.

11. See also Theodor Ziolkowski, *The Classical German Elegy 1795–1950* (Princeton, NJ: Princeton University Press, 1980), pp. 99–100.

12. See also Hillman, *Re-Visioning Psychology*, p. 169. For further discussion of Orphism in modernism in general and in Rilke in

particular, see Johanna Janina S. Aulich, "Die orphische Weltanschauung der Antike und ihr Erbe bei den Dichtern Nietzsche Hölderlin, Novalis und Rilke" (master's thesis, Simon Fraser University, 1990); Judith E. Bernstock, "Rainer Maria Rilke and the Artist as Transformer," chap. 2 in *Under the Spell of Orpheus: The Persistence of a Myth in Twentieth-Century Art* (Carbondale, IL: Southern Illinois University Press, 1991); and Erika M. Nelson, *Reading Rilke's Orphic Identity* (Berne: Lang, 2005).

13. Augustine, *Confessions*, vol. 2, trans. William Watts (Cambridge, MA: Harvard University Press, 1912), pp. 99–101.

14. Hillman, *Re-Visioning Psychology*, pp. 195–97.

15. Tarnas, *Cosmos and Psyche*, pp. 495–96.

16. Augustine, *Confessions*, pp. 98–99.

17. See Joseph Henderson and Dyane Sherwood, *Transformation of the Psyche* (Hove, UK: Brunner-Routledge, 2003), pp. 67–71. On the *Splendor Solis*, see also Manly P. Hall, *The Secret Teachings of All Ages* (New York: Tarcher/Penguin, 2003), p. 487; and for the relevant image, see www.levity.com/alchemy/splensol.html.

18. Indeed, some have argued that the Orphic tradition feeds into Platonic philosophy; see Algis Uždavinys, *Orpheus and the Roots of Platonism* (London: Matheson Trust, 2011); and Edouard Schuré, "The Initiation of Plato and the Platonic Philosophy," in *Hermes and Plato*, trans. Frederick Rothwell (London: Rider, 1910), pp. 78–90.

19. Eugenio Garin, *Portraits from the Quattrocento*, trans. Victor A. and Elizabeth Velen (New York: Harper and Row, 1972), p. 153; cited in Hillman, *Re-Visioning Psychology*, p. 201.

20. Compare with those passages in the *Enneads* where Plotinus speaks of the "double-act" of the soul; see Ennead V, Tractate 4, § 2 (Plotinus, *The Enneads*, trans. Stephen MacKenna [Harmondsworth: Penguin, 1991], p. 390); and Ennead II, Tractate 9, § 8 (p. 117).

21. *The Republic*, 509d–511e.

22. See Otto F. Bollnow, *Rilke* (1951, repr. Stuttgart: Kohlhammer, 1956), pp. 134–46.

23. See Ernst Pfeiffer, "Rilke und die Psychoanalyse," *Literaturwissenschaftliches Jahrbuch*, 17(1976):247–320; and Peter Dettmering, *Dichtung und Psychoanalyse: Thomas Mann–Rainer Maria Rilke–Richard Wagner* (Munich: Nymphenburger Verlagshandlung, 1969). The role played by Lou von Salomé in mediating psychoanalysis

to Rilke was crucial; see Christiane Wieder, *Die Psychoanalytikerin Lou Andreas-Salomé: Ihr Werk im Spannungsfeld zwischen Sigmund Freud und Rainer Maria Rilke* (Göttingen: Vandenhoeck und Ruprecht, 2011).

24. C. G. Jung, *Mysterium Coniunctionis,* vol. 14, *The Collected Works of C. G. Jung* (Princeton, NJ: Princeton University Press, 1970), § 296.

25. Rainer Maria Rilke, *Das Florenzer Tagebuch*, ed. Ruth Sieber-Rilke and Carl Sieber (Frankfurt am Main: Insel, 1994), pp. 27, 23.

26. See Joris-Karl Huysmans, *La Cathédrale* [1898], chap. 8 in *Le Roman de Durtal* (Paris: Bartillat, 1999), p. 815.

27. See Rainer Maria Rilke, *Die Briefe an Karl und Elisabeth von der Heydt, 1905–1922*, ed. Ingeborg Schnack and Renate Scharffenberg (Frankfurt am Main: Insel, 1986), p. 173; compare with his remark about "a kind of order and new life" (*eine Art Ordnung und neues Leben*) in his letter to Alexander von Thurn und Taxis of 28 February 1911 (*Briefe aus den Jahren 1907 bis 1914*, ed. Ruth Sieber-Rilke and Carl Sieber [Leipzig: Insel, 1939], p. 126).

28. Charles Taylor, *Sources of the Self: The Making of the Modern Identity* (Cambridge, UK: Cambridge University Press, 1989), pp. 491–92 (citing Stephen Spender, *The Struggle of the Modern* [London: Hamish Hamilton, 1963], p. 17). For an alternative view, see Richard Rorty, "Taylor on Truth," in *Philosophy in the Age of Pluralism: The Philosophy of Charles Taylor in Question*, ed. James Tully and Daniel M. Weinstock (Cambridge, UK: Cambridge University Press, 1994), pp. 20–33.

29. Taylor goes on to say that the poet can only give us this something as "refracted through his own sensibility," and "we cannot just detach the nugget of transcendent truth; it is inseparably embedded in the work," hence "the continuing relevance of the Romantic doctrine of the symbol" (*Sources of the Self*, p. 492).

30. Taylor, *The Sources of the Self*, p. 513; cf. pp. 346, 428–29, 482, 501–02.

31. *The City of God*, XVIII:18:2, trans. Henry Bettenson, ed. David Knowles (Harmondsworth: Penguin, 1972), p. 782. Elsewhere in this work Augustine engages extensively with Apuleius's theory of daimons (see book IX *passim*).

BOOK REVIEWS

Barbara Hannah, *The Animus: The Spirit of Inner Truth in Women*, 2 volumes. Wilmette, IL: Chiron Publications, 2011.

REVIEWED BY PRISCILLA MURR

The Redeeming Power of Love

I t was 1928. Barbara Hannah was in Paris pursuing her interest in painting. Her longtime fiancé, Sir John, had finally asked her to make a decision: either marry him and start a family or set him free to find someone else. In telling this story Hannah spoke of how upset she was, how difficult it seemed to make a decision. Tossing and turning in bed that night, she was startled when the room filled with light. She sat up and saw Jesus standing there. He said: "What do you want to do more than anything else in your life?" Hannah said: "I gave an answer that I never expected, I had never thought of. I said: 'I want to help other people.' 'Then,' Jesus replied, 'do not marry Sir John!'" More than forty years later, she gave her

Priscilla Murr is a Jungian analyst in private practice in Austin, Texas. She studied at the Jung Institute in Zürich where she graduated in 1985. She also earned a Ph.D. at the University of Zürich while living there. She is interested in Native American art and manifestations of the unconscious.

characteristic laugh: "Thank God I said no! My life would have been nothing but horses. I couldn't have stood it."

Having made her decision, however, she found herself at loose ends in Paris, not knowing what to do with her life when she happened upon the only article of Jung's that had been translated into English: "Women in Europe." "I knew immediately that I had to meet this man Jung. I was in Zürich two months later," she said.

Jung's article confronts modern women with the issue of the animus, that is, a woman's relation to her inner masculine energy or mind. Jung raised some very important questions for the modern woman (questions that are equally relevant to women today): What is a woman's relationship to her own inner masculine? Will this relationship dominate her life with collective, unrelated opinions, cutting her off from intimacy and relationships, keep her from the spontaneous flow of life? Or will it be a source of growth and inspiration, advancing her creative potential and expanding her spiritual awareness of life?

In the lectures Hannah gave on the subject of the animus, published here for the first time in *The Animus: The Spirit of Inner Truth in Women*, she shows how Jung's questions were the basis for her lifelong exploration of the nature of woman's mind.

As I experienced Hannah in my more than ten years of analysis with her, the animus question, which is also the question of our relationship to the unconscious and what position it will take in our lives, was central to her life. The animus, as she experienced it in her own life and in that of her patients, was Hannah's life work.

These two volumes from Chiron Publications, which David Eldred and Emmanuel Kennedy-Xypolitas compiled from the notes Hannah left behind, include lectures that span most of her creative life from 1948 to 1971. They fill an enormous gap in the record of Hannah's work because they are in many ways the most important statement of her work with the animus, the clearest and the most useful in terms of working with oneself and with one's clients. Her books—*Striving Towards Wholeness* (1971), *Jung, His Life and Work* (1976), and *Encounters with the Soul: Active Imagination as Developed by C. G. Jung* (1981)—cover different material. These two volumes represent a tremendous act of love by the editors; the articles are amazingly clear and faithful to Hannah's style. Without the dedication of these two editors, this body of knowledge would have been completely lost.

The first lectures in volume 1 present her lifelong work on the animus. She opens the first lecture with a practical recognition of the need for some realistic applications of Jung's theory, in order to help people understand how they can use these ideas in down-to-earth, real-life situations. Having just survived the horror of World War II, she was very aware of the destructive potential of unconsciousness and, in particular, a woman's lack of consciousness when it applies to her masculine energy. One felt a certain urgency in her understanding of her work on the animus. She frequently repeated Jung's admonition that the more people who can stand the tension of opposites, the greater the chance that the world might just escape destruction by the atom bomb (see vol. 1, p. 81; vol. 2, p. 8). She frequently repeated this statement.

She truly believed that the more women (and men, also!) could free themselves from possession by the animus/unconscious, the greater the chance there was for the world to survive, made possible through redemption and growth in consciousness—one individual at a time. Thus, these lectures reflect not only her very down-to-earth practical suggestions on how to understand the animus and find a way out of possession by its archetypal energy, but how this work related to worldwide concerns and can have impact on all of humanity.

Reading these lectures makes me feel as if I've just walked up Lindenbergstrasse, opened the front door (Dr. von Franz has kicked her door shut at the risk of being disturbed by me), and followed Hannah step by step up to her office to sit in her well-worn chairs amidst the books of a lifetime of study and devotion to Jung. To be in this room was to be in the center of the individuation process. The very sentence structure of these published lectures brings her voice alive, her sense of humor and her willingness to laugh at herself. I can hear her voice rising off the page with sentences like: "It is only fair to say that all of Jungian psychology in this paper naturally comes from Jung and is 'begged, borrowed or stolen'" (vol. 1, p. 4). She would be laughing at that joke. As well as the implicit humility to claim nothing unfairly as her own, her words would voice her deep belief in Jung and his work, her fidelity to his opus.

One of the first words I learned from Hannah was *Auseinandersetzung,* a word that defines her view of the work and her attitude to her relation to the unconscious and the animus: to become conscious of the animus, to find the difference between his values and our own personal values, and to find a way to integrate what is important in the unconscious while always maintaining one's human/ego standpoint. To achieve this, we must "have it out" with the unconscious, struggle to hold our position while simultaneously listening to the position of the unconscious, just as we do with people we relate to (vol. 1, p. 19). In working with the animus we need to view him as another person, separate from our ego and with frequently different goals for our life. Learning to hear this inner voice, finding a way to control its negative influence on us, and finding the way for this energy to become helpful to us are the main issues in these lectures.

Jung's challenge to modern European women became Barbara Hannah's personal life challenge: to become conscious of the inner masculine energy. She recognized the need to integrate this energy into consciousness as well as the dangers inherent in this process. She relied on Jung's definition of the masculine as knowing what you want and doing what you need to do to achieve it (vol. 1, p. 3). This goal-oriented attitude differs from women's natural Eros function, which is a more process-oriented attitude to life, based on our instincts and following what she called the spontaneous flow of life. Careful to point out the differences between the anima, the feminine soul of men, and the animus, the masculine mind of women, she points out the greater difficulty women have in seeing the animus. The fact that in our culture God is usually seen as masculine further complicates becoming aware of the animus.

In "The Problem of Contact with the Animus," Hannah begins with the problem of animus possession, that is, possession by what she refers to as "substituting opinions" or "opinionating substitutes." By preventing us from valuing our own opinions, the animus can replace them with collective thoughts that may have some validity but which are not relevant to our present life situation. By believing the animus and not standing by our feelings, we become cut off from reality. An example which Hannah uses is the case of the demon possession of the sixteenth-century nun Jeanne Fery. Finally exorcised, Jeanne's experience can be seen as an example of how the animus can distort our lives. Jeanne had accepted the animus's offer of help at the age of four, allowing this "demon" to protect her from the pain of her father's beatings. Her commitment to the demons grew until she was finally totally possessed, and she came to the attention of her convent and the archbishop.

The turning point in her exorcism, her path toward healing, came when she threw herself at the feet of the archbishop, acknowledging her feelings for him. Then the Self appeared, in the form of Mary Magdalene.

Without the help of the Self, women cannot find their own truth, cannot stand against the power of the animus, and cannot establish a valuable relationship with him. A woman's best defense against the negative animus is for her to reach out to people she cares for, listen to her heart, and find her true feelings. Mary Magdalene came to help Jeanne in her struggle; an image of the Self, she helped Jeanne find her own feelings.

How often women respond to this advice with "But I don't know what I want!" Knowing the difference between our animus-driven ideas and our true feelings is difficult. The negative and possessive animus can give us a sense of false security by telling us that we have the truth, that all doubt is vanquished and we know where we're going because we have the absolute truth. But truth is one-sided. Jung calls it stagnation and death (vol. 1, p. 25). In contrast, doubt has us withstanding the tension of opposites, keeping both sides conscious. When the ego can maintain her (his) firm position in this reality of doubt and questioning, the animus is forced into the unconscious, away from our ego life, and can then help the transcendent function to occur, help the ego find the deep image which unites the opposites and lets life flow again.

Hannah was one of the most intensely alive people I have ever known. She was totally open to everything, nonjudgmental and deeply curious, interested. I remember being slightly shocked when this nice English lady recommended I read Carlos Castaneda's book on Don Juan, the Yaqui shaman. It was a book that came out of the drug culture of the sixties, but she could see past the superficial drug issues to the true encounter with the unconscious. She valued this depth in whatever form it came.

She could be this open-minded because not only had she met her shadow squarely and honestly, she had found her own feminine values whereby her animus was able to stay in his proper position, helping the ego relate to the Self and to the unconscious. She described her own process of coming to understand when she was in the animus and not listening to her own feelings:

> there was a certain eros reaction . . . perhaps a feeling of frustration, of unreality, of not having my feet on the earth, of being out of relation with my surroundings. Whenever the animus spoke or thought, I then had a feeling of it not being my "own" voice or thinking. . . . I had the beginning of a form with which I could approach the unconscious. (vol.1, p. 121)

We are most vulnerable to the negative aspects of the unconscious when we don't take responsibility for our shadow. In the fairy tale "The Goose Girl" (vol. 1, pp. 41–49), we see how the princess's excessive humility and refusal to claim her rightful authority empowers the shadow and leaves the Goose Girl a victim of the animus, living far beneath her proper status. Whenever we permit a vacuum in our outer life by ignoring responsibility for the shadow or giving up on our feelings, the animus flows into that space with his opinions and so-called facts. This negativity continues as long as we refuse the hard work of confronting him. Once we refuse to allow his negativity to dominate us, he can return to his true role of helping us connect with our inner truth.

What I value most in what I received from Hannah, which she underlines on nearly every page of these two volumes, is that the individuation process is an ongoing, daily commitment to finding one's inner truth, to sacrificing ego desires that get in the way of living life more meaningfully, of constantly learning from the unconscious to find what is relevant for our lives. The gift for me in that is a sense that my life has meaning and a purpose. She would frequently say, "But of course your life has a purpose. There is a reason you were born." At that time my animus didn't really let me believe that.

To read the lecture "Animus and Eros" is to experience the simple clarity and thoughtfulness of Hannah's mind. In addition to a profound discussion of Eros, it also contains an explication of one of the very complicated and arcane alchemical passages by Philalethia in *Mysterium*

Coniunctionis. She showed her trust in and devotion to meaning, the *"true living spirit* which generates life according to its own laws," not blinded by collective (i.e., negative animus) assumptions (vol. l, p. 74, in a quote from Jung's *Mysterium Coniunctionis*). In particular she investigated the power of Eros, the energy that is required to bring about a union of opposites and to restore a "fructifying interest" in life (vol. l, p. 92).

The other aspect of this passage that is significant for me is Hannah's own process in writing this lecture. She was a feeling type, thus thinking was her inferior function. She was most aware that the individuation process only began when one took responsibility for the inferior function. She once said of Toni Wolff, Jung's close friend and analyst: "Toni had the worst sensation function of anyone I ever knew. But once she had learned something she never forgot it and always used it."

It is evident in this lecture that Hannah took equal responsibility for her inferior function. While remaining in her feeling function, in particular her feelings for Jung, she managed to connect with her thinking-type animus in a way that enriches both the feeling and the thinking. She said that Eros without Logos is meaningless. The simple brilliance of her depth of feeling for Jung gives her an understanding that allows her to interpret this complicated text in a way that both respects the complexity of Jung's thinking while making it more accessible. This is the end result of very deep and difficult psychological work she did on herself, work developing her trust in her Eros and searching for the transcendent. She ended the lecture with an admonition to women: if women can keep "the animus still and themselves quiet until, remaining in that stillness, they are able to hear the voice of God, or the Self, for here we shall find that the unconscious is able to approach us when it wishes" (vol. l, p. 96). If, in that stillness, Eros can transform the relationship between the conscious and the unconscious, then, quoting Jung, "there is a good chance of one being able to say something really worth while" (*ibid.*).

In the lecture series entitled "The Animus Problem in Modern Women," Hannah introduces the notion of the animus cocoon, an expressive image that conveys the notion of how the animus's "opinionating substitutes" can cut a woman off from life, isolating her in the imaginal security she finds in these animus notions.

As negative as the animus can be, Hannah also realized that the defenses a person chooses are often essential for his or her life, as Jeanne Fery's relations to the animus had provided her protection as a child. She added with reference to the animus cocoon that "if this is accepted and realized, the web yet turns out to have been a cocoon in which the chrysalis of the woman's spirit can hatch out or transform into a winged being" (vol. l, p. 97). Animus-possessed women are often very creative, have a special creative destiny. Jeanne Fery became a nun, a position that gave her greater scope for development, beyond that which her mother had envisioned for her in making her a dressmaker. Sarah, the daughter in the Book of Tobit, is described as being "wise, steadfast, and honorable" (vol. 2, p. 348), absolutely not an ordinary girl with virtues that she would need for her recovery.

Given that her lifework was dedicated to the animus and women's creative capacities, it is fairly obvious that Hannah was interested in the work of creative women. Lectures in both volumes deal with several women authors, a study of whose works takes us deeper into an understanding of the animus. As usual her main focus was on the animus, not forgetting that the animus is always difficult to perceive and only rarely depicted as such in literature. Emily Bronte's Heathcliff is one of the rare examples of the animus appearing as a character in a novel. However, instead of looking for a character in the novel who represents the animus, Hannah introduced the notion of finding the *spiritus rector,* the author's masculine guiding principle, the value system implicit in the work, the author's *Weltanschauung.*

Thus, we don't look to Mr. Darcy in *Pride and Prejudice* to see a picture of Jane Austen's animus. Mr. Darcy is a woman's fantasy of a rather unreal man who lives the Eros most women would love to find in a man. On closer examination of Jane Austen's *spiritus rector,* we find humor, her incredible social realism, and a certain narrowness of vision. We see that same realism, humor, and narrowness in Mr. Bennet, Elizabeth's father, who plays a rather minor role in the novel but who carries Jane Austen's animus.

The lectures in volume 2 focus more deeply on historical and literary examples of women's confrontation with the animus. Jeanne Fery's fascinating story of demon possession and exorcism is explored in greater and deeper detail. The editors point out that the more modern advances in psychology would present this as a case of dissociative identity disorder (vol. 2, p. 51). Nonetheless, Hannah's discussion of the case is remarkably relevant for today's women and therapists.

The last lecture in volume 2 is "The Religious Function of the Animus in the Book of Tobit." I have a personal connection to this lecture as I actually attended it in 1971, my first semester in Zürich. It was at that lecture also that I became Hannah's analysand. I had dreamed of her and after class I asked her if she would work with me: "Oh, no!" came her sharp reply, "I am too old and not taking new clients." I was disappointed but we kept on chatting. I don't remember how the conversation developed, but I happened to mention that I had brought my cat with me from Los Angeles. Again, that sharp British accent: "You brought you cat! Now why would you do that?" Feeling like a total idiot, my father had been right, I shouldn't have wasted time and money on just a cat, I stammered out the only answer I knew: "She's my cat. I love her, what else would I do with her?" "Well," Hannah replied, "if you are that sort of person, I will work with you!" She loved animals tremendously and valued that love in other people. There is another aspect to her reply: she valued Eros. For her, the most valuable quality I could have, and one she always looked for in our work, was my capacity for love. Love was the center of her life, and she felt it should be the center of all of life.

There's a sentence in the lecture on Tobit that seems to me to be the perfect summing up of these two volumes as well as describing Hannah's life: "The way par excellence to transform the animus from the opinionating demon into a creative mind is a devotion to life, a complete acceptance of its reality, and the sacrifice of all illusion about it" (vol. 2, p. 348). That sentence describes all that she gave me and what I believe she lived her life by. She ends her biography of Jung while she stands at Jung's grave in Küsnacht: "And this is how I still feel toward this life which was lived so fully and that we were privileged to know: a profound and boundless gratitude." I feel a similar gratitude to her for what she helped me find within myself: a deeper and more profound relationship to life and reality. She gave with such openness and generosity.

There is a final synchronicity that I would like to share. Hannah was always so committed to women's creativity. This is apparent throughout the books in her constant study of other women's work, not only the authors she studies and analyzes but also the colleagues, the students and peers she frequently referenced in the books. On the very day that I finally took the financial risk of joining a practice in Austin, I received from Hannah's estate her drawing of an elephant which she had made in 1927 at the Rome zoo. I had always loved that drawing and when Hannah realized that I wanted it to hang in my office when I was an analyst, she promised it to me. I always think of her when I look at the drawing and feel its presence as her blessing on my practice.

THE SECRET OF ERANOS

RICCARDO BERNARDINI

> Especially towards the middle of the autumn, the Calcutta nights
> grew incredibly beautiful. There's nothing I could compare them
> with, for their air blended the melancholy of the Mediterranean
> night and the sounds of the Nordic one with the feeling of
> dissolution into non-being, stirred in your soul by the night of
> the Oriental seas, and the strong vegetal fragrances that greet you
> the moment you enter the heart of India. For me, those nights
> were quickened by some magic that I could not possibly resist.
> —Mircea Eliade, *Nights at Serampore*[1]

I f I were to replace Calcutta with Ascona, Switzerland, I could easily
borrow these lovely words from Mircea Eliade's *Nights at Serampore*
to describe my encounter with Eranos—a place that would come
to play an intricate part in my future and the place where I first became
acquainted with the teachings of Carl Gustav Jung.

It has been a few years since I first stood before the grand doors of
Casa Eranos located on the shores of Lake Maggiore in Ascona. Back
then, I was a senior in college in psychology, gathering material for

Riccardo Bernardini, Ph.D., Psy.D., serves as scientific advisor at the Eranos
Foundation in Ascona, Switzerland. He previously taught, as adjunct professor of analytical
psychology and educational psychology, at the University of Turin. He has published,
among other books, *Jung a Eranos. Il progetto della psicologia complessa* (FrancoAngeli,
2011), now being translated into English. He serves as coeditor of the *Eranos Yearbooks*,
the *Eranos Series*, and the Jungiana section of *Spring: A Journal of Archetype and Culture*.

my graduation thesis. It was a mild July afternoon, graced by the lingering freshness of the morning's rainstorm. Leaving behind Ascona's vivacious tourism district, fueled by the summer charm of Lake Maggiore, I walked for a few kilometers beside the cantonal way that runs along the shore to Moscia. With a reverential attitude, almost fearful, I passed through the small wooden gate that leads to the luxurious Eranos garden. Descending the steep stone stairs, I wandered along the small paths, stopping to admire an Indian statue, almost entirely covered in greenery.[2] As I stood on the shore that afternoon, it was easy to imagine Jung jumping into the calm water of Lake Maggiore, perhaps in the company of a lady who is said to have waited for him each morning at a quarter to seven. She used to say that swimming by Jung's side gave her "the feeling of swimming into the collective unconscious."[3]

I had landed at Eranos on Hetty Rogantini-de Beauclair's recommendation. She was a historical witness to Monte Verità,[4] another enchanted *topos* near Eranos that had come to life during my Swiss pilgrimage, a pilgrimage begun through the suggestion of a dream I had and which would also bring me, during the summer, to other symbolical places in Switzerland, such as Montagnola, Küsnacht, Dornach, and Stein. I don't remember exactly what I was discussing with Rudolf Ritsema, the renowned *I Ching* scholar, to whom I had been introduced by the house servant who welcomed me at the door of Casa Eranos. Maybe, while we were sipping the Chinese tea served to us in the semidarkness of his office, we were talking about the graduation thesis that I had decided to dedicate myself to, encouraged by the enthusiast support of my dissertation advisor who had agreed to mentor me during this research project. I left Eranos with a signed copy of Ritsema's translation of the *I Ching* with an inscription that, every now and then, I still read again with a certain nostalgia.[5]

I was a regular visitor to Casa Eranos in the coming months. Often, I'd stay late into the night, conversing with guests on the terrace of Casa Gabriella, the oldest building on the Eranos property. It was on such a day that I asked Ritsema which books, other than those of the annual *Eranos Yearbooks*, could help me get closer to the essence of Eranos. At first, he had no answer for me—his opinion seemed to be that no one book could live up to such a task. Maybe, he offered, it could prove useful to acquaint myself with the theoretical bases of traditional Chinese medicine, perhaps starting with the work that Manfred Porkert developed at Eranos.[6] Sensing my disappointment, he thought for a moment, then rose and, hardly leaning on his walking stick, headed for his library shelves. He came back with a tiny book, saying: "Here you are. This is maybe the most important book to Eranos. Do you know it?" He was holding a German edition of *Nights at Serampore*. I was baffled: how could such a small novel, and on top of it, one of Eliade's lesser-known works, speak to the Eranos phenomenon? How could this small book even begin to explain the complex and unique outlook on the human sciences to be found here?

However, I was deeply impressed by the novel, to say the least. In particular, I always found particularly captivating the scene of the meeting between the protagonist, the young Eliade, and Swami Shivananda, one of the greatest yoga masters of the twentieth century. Eliade speaks to Shivananda about an extraordinary experience he had in Serampore, near Calcutta, where he felt himself "outside of time," that is, brought from the present to a time several hundred years ago. Shivananda then shows Eliade how, in Tantrism, not only can the future be modified, but, by getting rid of spatial-temporal categories, the past can be changed as well. The idea Eliade presents is of a future and a past that meet and possibly interact. The description of a similar interaction can be found in Eliade's *Youth Without Youth*, when thunder strikes and releases its frightening power.[7] There is reason to believe that Eliade took these ideas seriously; for, as Ritsema explained to me, Eliade indeed became anxious anytime a thunderstorm rolled in above Lake Maggiore. Still, I wondered what *Nights at Serampore*, Chinese medicine, and Eranos had in common. I posed this question to Ritsema, and he replied: "The existence of different levels of reality (*l'existence de différents niveaux de réalité*)." I pondered the meaning of this statement for a long time. In fact, it was still lingering in my mind a few nights later during an impromptu dinner party. A friend who had accompanied me pulled me aside after dinner to ask if I knew about a book she'd found by chance, while browsing Casa Gabriella's library that afternoon. She didn't need to tell me the title—I recognized *Nights at Serampore* immediately when she pulled it from her purse.

Jung, at that time, was for me still lingering in the background among other scholars I was studying. During that lonely winter—later becoming a *Spring, Summer, Fall, Winter . . . and Spring*—spent at Casa Gabriella, I started asking myself what role the "nocturne production" (the narrative production) of Romanian scholar Mircea Eliade played in Eranos's imagination.[8] Ritsema later concluded that *two* of Eliade's novels contained immediate reference to Eranos. On the one hand, we have *Nights at Serampore* (*Nopti la Serampore*, 1940), which in addition to being a simplification of yogic shamanism, seems to be explaining the relativity of time and the possibility of bringing distant events into the present. On the other hand, there is *The Secret of Doctor Honigberger* (*Secretul doctorului Honigberger*, 1940), wherein Eliade sheds light on the matter of the individual's disappearance and the possible direct experience of nirvana. Together, they are the *"deux longues nouvelles 'yogiques,'"* as Eliade referred to them.[9] When *The Periplus of the Eranos Archetype* (Ritsema's unpublished spiritual "testament") was discussed, Ritsema told me that Eliade authorized him to include these two novels at the end of his work.

The Jungian turn in my research came not long after when I ran into a letter, dated March 13, 1974, that Ritsema wrote to Eliade about another one of his novels, *The Old Man and the Bureaucrats [Pe Strada Mântuleasa]*, (1968):

> The juxtaposition and interpenetration of "reality" and "myth," of two different levels of experience, has . . . the value of a model. . . . So far I knew that you had the gift of telling myths in a way that makes them transparent. But *The Old Man and the Bureaucrats* goes beyond the art of a myth's storyteller: it's the creation of a double experience. I can see the model of the purpose toward which the post-Jungian psychotherapy needs to aim: make the man able, or rather conscious, of his daily life on different levels [*rendre l'homme capable, c'est-à-dire conscient, de sa vie quotidienne sur différents plans*].

The direction to follow was hinted at; the path to follow was traced: Eranos, in light of Jungian psychology, and Jungian psychology, in light of Eranos.

However, I still had no clue how far this path would take me—that it would lead me to so much more than just a graduation thesis. But, despite my ignorance of my ultimate destination, I stayed the course, through my specializations and doctorates, under the patient guidance of several masters and with the trust of the Eranos Foundation itself. The systematic collecting of literature and mostly unpublished textual, photographic, and iconographic documentation to which I dedicated myself afterward made it clear to me that there weren't any existing studies that were able to provide an exhaustive image of the Eranos's phenomenon.[10] The notable exception was, of course, Hans Thomas Hakl's *Der verborgene Geist von Eranos* (2001), now finally available in English as *Eranos: An Alternative Intellectual History of the Twentieth Century*—it was at that time newly released and was brought to my attention by Annemarie Äschbach.[11]

I felt strongly that a new study should be conducted of another series of works that, for different reasons, would never see the light of day, would never be published and well known. Such works intrigued me for that very reason—for their elusive and "mysterious" quality. The works I decided to focus on included the *The Periplus of the Eranos Archetype* by Rudolf Ritsema, mentioned above, and *Eranos in seiner Geschichte* by Gerhard Wehr, a study with a historical tone that, although set to be released around 1996–1997, never came out, probably because it didn't meet Ritsema's approval.[12] Another unreleased work that caught my eye was *L'Œuvre d'Eranos et Vie d'Olga Froebe-Kapteyn* by Catherine Ritsema-Gris, a historical and biographical document that, because of the author's advanced illness, was never completed. Another noteworthy work in this group is *Die Geschichte von Eranos* by Olga Fröbe-Kapteyn, which the Eranos's founder composed between 1952 and 1958. According to Fröbe-Kapteyn, and probably under Jung's inspiration, this fragmentary typescript was meant to become a draft of a history of Eranos from the point of view of its promoter's inner experience.

Exploring the territories of Jung's theoretical contribution at Eranos, I thus realized how these were also the boundaries of an open epistemological horizon which allowed for the growth of Jung's complex psychology. Retracing Jung's intellectual itinerary through twenty years of conferences at Eranos, I came to recognize how this was also a path revealing hermeneutic possibilities of complex psychology. Finding again pioneer initiatives' traces promoted by Jung during his involvement with Eranos, it became clear to me how these could be viewed as the footsteps of part of a wide cultural afterthought program

pursued though the study of complex psychology: this was evidenced
especially by the Eranos Archive for Research in Symbolism project—
in which, through photographic reproductions, thousands of symbolic
images were collected, consisting of various samples from oriental and
occidental religious imagery to those of alchemy, folklore, mythology,
general arts, and "archetypical" representations from the contemporary
era. All of these, along with long-term research work, performed and
collected under the constant encouragement of Jung, were collected
into archives and libraries all around the world in the 1930s and 1940s
by Olga Fröbe-Kapteyn.[13]

   I came to the conclusion that releasing a study of Eranos
phenomenon while omitting its main characters' inner vicissitudes—
starting with Olga Fröbe-Kapteyn and continuing with those
scholars who, with Jung, formed at different times its inner circle,
as well as those pupils, such as Alwina (Alwine) von Keller and
Emma Hélène von Pelet-Narbonne, who worked and spent most of
their life at Eranos—would lead me to miss a fundamental aspect
of Eranos, and perhaps the most important one.[14] That is to say, I
glimpsed the possibility of uncovering a "secret" history of Eranos,
made from the echoes left by those who had taken part in its
adventure—on a spiritual, intellectual, and human level, all at the same
time. All those countless novels, dreams, visions, and imaginations,
which seemed to re-echo to the *fils secrets et ténus qui ont été tissés par le
Genio loci ignoto,* as recalled by Catherine Ritsema-Gris, appeared to
be defining themselves as precious elements, hardening and
crystallizing right beneath the surface, waiting to be found. And once
I started to dig and came upon them, I found them to be pieces of a
puzzle that together formed a text, a fabric, which is irreducibly
narrative, strongly lived and, even more real and thick with meaning
than anything to be found on the surface. Indeed, it's not by chance
that speaking of the "secret" side of Eranos should bring us to the topic
of music—a history retraced, that is to say, by echoes, assonances, and
resonances—for the Greek word *eranos* ("banquet") has as its palindrome
a Latin and Italian word, *sonare* ("sounding").[15]

   It is finally to that small novel recommended by Ritsema, *Nights
at Serampore,* that I must return to find the proper words to describe
my first encounter with Eranos—and thus, with Jung. For within that
singular tale, as within the hallowed halls of Casa Eranos, exists a story

in which thousands of folds of the past seem to forewarn the future, while the future seems to be yet revisiting the past. Borrowing Eliade's words once more, and now replacing the Ganges with Lake Maggiore, I can sum up the Eranos experience:

> I don't remember what happened then. When I woke up, the next day, in my *kutiar*, the sun was high in the sky, and the green waters of the Ganges seemed to me gentle beyond words, incomparably clear and soothing.[16]

NOTES

1. Mircea Eliade, *Two Strange Tales* (1986; reprinted Boston: Shambhala, 2001), p. 4.

2. I would find out later this had been donated to Olga Fröbe-Kapteyn, Eranos's founder, by the rich baron Eduard von der Heydt, owner of Monte Verità since the mid-1920s (see Riccardo Bernardini, *Jung a Eranos. Il progetto della psicologia complessa* [Milano: FrancoAngeli, 2011], p. 174).

3. Mircea Eliade, *Giornale* (Torino: Boringhieri, 1976), p. 136.

4. Yvonne Bölt and Gian Pietro Milani, eds., *Dal Monte Verità di Ascona . . . a Berzona in Onsernone: Hetty De Beauclair racconta il meraviglioso mondo della sua infanzia* (Losone: Serodine, 2004).

5. Rudolf Ritsema and Shantena Augusto Sabbadini, eds., *Eranos I Ching. Il Libro della Versatilità. Testi oracolari con concordanze* (Como: Red, 1996), published in English as *The Original I Ching Oracle— The Pure and Complete Texts with Concordance, Translated under the Auspices of the Eranos Foundation* (London: Watkins, 2005).

6. Manfred Porkert, *Fünf Eranos-Vorträge 1979–1987* (Dinkelscherben: Phainon Editions and Media GmbH/Acta Medicinae Sinensis, 1998).

7. Mircea Eliade, *Youth Without Youth* (Chicago: University of Chicago Press, 2007).

8. Kim Ki-duk, *Spring, Summer, Fall, Winter . . . and Spring*, Sony Pictures Classics, 2003; Mircea Eliade, letter to Károly Kerényi dated November 29, 1949, quoted in Natale Spineto, *Mircea Eliade storico delle religioni. Con la corrispondenza inedita Mircea Eliade-Károly Kerényi* (Brescia: Morcelliana, 2006), pp. 250f.

9. Mircea Eliade, letter to Károly Kerényi dated November 15, 1949, quoted in Spineto, *Mircea Eliade storico delle religioni*, pp. 245f.

10. Several still unknown photographs were published, e.g., in Gian Piero Quaglino, Augusto Romano, and Riccardo Bernardini, *Carl Gustav Jung a Eranos 1933–1952* (Turin: Antigone, 2007). A huge amount of unpublished documentary material appeared later in Bernardini, *Jung a Eranos*, now being translated into English. With the support of the Eranos Foundation and licensed by the Foundation of the Works of C. G. Jung, more specific articles, e.g., on Jung's unpublished Eranos seminar on Opicinus de Canistris, appeared in the last four years: see, e.g., Gian Piero Quaglino, Augusto Romano, and Riccardo Bernardini, "Opicinus de Canistris: Some Notes from Jung's Unpublished Eranos Seminar on the Medieval *Codex Palatinus Latinus 1993*," *Journal of Analytical Psychology* 55(3, 2010):398–422; Riccardo Bernardini, Gian Piero Quaglino, and Augusto Romano, "A Visit Paid to Jung by Alwine von Keller," *Journal of Analytical Psychology* 56(2, 2011):232–254; Riccardo Bernardini, "*Amor spiritualis, amor carnalis*: Notes on Jung's Treatment of Love from an Eranos Seminar on Opicinus de Canistris," *Eranos Yearbook* 70(2009–2011): 339–371; Riccardo Bernardini, "Hillman a Eranos," *Anima* (2012), pp. 47–93; and Riccardo Bernardini, Gian Piero Quaglino, and Augusto Romano, "Further Studies on Jung's Eranos Seminar on Opicinus de Canistris," in *Journal of Analytical Psychology* 58(2, 2013). Other studies, based on documents belonging to the Eranos archives, will be featured in the Jungiana section in upcoming issues of *Spring: A Journal of Archetype and Culture*, in agreement with the Eranos Foundation in a program of recovery, preservation, and valorization of its archival estate (see Riccardo Bernardini, "Prospettive di ricerca storica in psicologia analitica," in *Tempo d'analisi. Paradigmi junghiani comparati* 1(0, 2012,) pp. 151–175).

11. Hans Thomas Hakl, *Eranos: An Alternative Intellectual History of the Twentieth Century* (Montreal: McGill Queens University Press, 2012).

12. In Gerhard Wehr, *Jean Gebser, Individuelle Transformation vor dem Horizont eines neuen Bewusstseins* (Petersberg: Via Nova,1996), p. 273.

13. Bernardini, *Jung a Eranos*, chap. 3.

14. Bernardini, Quaglino, and Romano, "A Visit Paid to Jung by Alwine von Keller." Emma Hélène von Pelet-Narbonne's analytic diaries (1935–1964), in particular, are now being studied and edited by Riccardo Bernardini, in agreement with the Eranos Foundation, in preparation for publication by Spring Journal Books.

15. Bernardini, *Jung a Eranos*, p. 56; and Riccardo Bernardini, "Il segreto di Eranos," *Anima* (2011), pp. 91–98.

16. Eliade, *Two Strange Tales*, p. 60.

Celebrating the 75th Anniversary of Jung's Bailey Island Lectures

In the fall of 2011, a special event organized by the Jung Center of Maine was held to celebrate the 75th anniversary of Jung's Bailey Island lectures, in which Jung explored the dreams of a young scientist, now known to us as the physicist Wolfgang Pauli.

Jung was invited to Bailey Island, Maine by Drs. Beatrice Hinkle, Esther Harding, Kristine Mann, and Eleanor Bertine. The latter three of these dynamic women had private practices in New York City and summered on Bailey Island. They had close ties to Zürich through their work and analysis with Jung, helped to found the Analytical Psychology Club of New York, and in 1941 created this journal, establishing *Spring* as the oldest Jungian psychology journal in the world.

Spring is delighted to have the opportunity to publish three papers that were presented at the 2011 event honoring the 75th anniversary of Jung's Bailey Island lectures. This issue features the following article about Dr. Esther Harding (1888-1971) written by psychologist and Jungian analyst Polly Armstrong.

Articles about Dr. Kristine Mann (1873-1945) by Vassar professor and Jungian analyst Beth Darlington and about Dr. Eleanor Bertine (1887-1967) by Chris Beach, a Jungian analyst in Maine, will appear in upcoming volumes of *Spring*.

THE DICHOTOMY OF
M. ESTHER HARDING

POLLY ARMSTRONG

W hen I was asked to speak about the life of Esther Harding at the seventy-fifth anniversary of Jung's seminar on Bailey's Island, Maine, it was specifically requested that this not be some theoretical speech but rather informative and creative and that I speak from my own heart. This was a welcome and timely invitation for me since I now live in Maine not far from Bailey's Island and recently had heart surgery, so I have been very focused on Maine's strikingly beautiful natural environment and its powerful impact on the human heart.

To begin our journey into the world of Esther Harding, it will help first to ground ourselves by envisioning Bailey's Island's physical ambiance, where Esther Harding, Eleanor Bertine, and Kristine Mann shed the pressures of New York City and spent three months each

Polly Armstrong, Ph.D., is a licensed clinical psychologist and Jungian analyst trained in New York, with a private practice in Washington, D.C. for over 30 years until her retirement, when she moved to the coast of Maine. She was president of the Washington Society for Jungian Psychology and director of education for the Jungian Analysts of the Greater Washington Area. She earned graduate degrees from Columbia University and the University of Maryland, has taught psychology and education, and has conducted organizational development workshops throughout the United States for the National Training Laboratories.

summer. Even today the narrow remote island jutting out into the Atlantic Ocean plunges the human senses, acclimated to the energetic stimulation of urban life, into a veritable feast of imaginal and visceral delight. At the beginning of the twentieth century, it was even more dramatically isolated and accessible only by boat for the intrepid few willing to make the voyage. In the 1920s, there were only a handful of small cottages on the entire island, few people, and utter silence except for the wind, an occasional cry of seagulls, and the rhythm of the crashing surf. Bailey's Island is less than three miles long, and in those early days it was pristine and unspoiled by civilization. Vast unbroken sky and brisk, clean, salty air blew off the dark ocean that fell over the distant horizon. Towering pungent pine trees and windswept blueberry bushes clutched the high edges of rugged granite cliffs that made up much of the island.

Today, driving along the only paved road which hugs the spine of the island, past the quaint white clapboard library where Jung gave his seminar, past the Trident House on the hill above the library overlooking the open ocean where, in earlier years, all three women lived and saw analysands, you come to the summer home of Esther Harding. Driving down the long dirt driveway at Inner Ledges, you are immediately overtaken by tall dark pine trees pressing in on both sides of the road. But as the forest begins to thin, you suddenly realize you have emerged out onto a small private peninsula jutting out high over the ocean. Harding's charming two-story fieldstone home sits solidly facing the sea. It includes several inviting places to gather including an old fashioned swing and Adirondack chairs on the front porch overlooking the open ocean, several comfortable, overstuffed chairs around a large stone fireplace in the generous living room, and a warm spacious kitchen with its own spectacular view of the sea. Her home perches on top of massive granite cliffs that plunge straight down on two sides to the crashing surf thirty feet below. It is breathtakingly beautiful and utterly private, completely isolated from the outside world. It is here that Esther rested and refueled her soul, did a lot of her thinking, and wrote some of her most important books. This simple, numinous space on this remote island deeply influenced the life of Esther Harding.

In thinking about how to offer a glimpse of her life, I decided that my goal would be to try to bring to life Esther Harding the person,

Esther Harding the woman who was drawn to this remote island off the coast of Maine each summer. I really wanted to create a more intimate picture, to tell a personal story that genuinely offers insight into who she was behind her professional persona. What I discovered is that her public reputation was dramatically different from her very private personal self. We might even say this is a story of the contrast between the professional New York Esther Harding and the personal Bailey's Island Esther Harding.

For years at the New York Institute during my own analytic training, I really didn't pay much attention to Esther Harding, the person. I was too busy reading her books and digesting her ideas. I regularly walked past her large, very dignified, rather imposing photograph hanging high on the wall in the bookstore. I often heard her referred to as one of the "important" Jungians of historical significance. But as I began to develop this talk, I discovered that there is very little personal information available about her anywhere. No biographies have been written about her. She left no autobiography and only smatterings of personal references are scattered through the Jungian literature. So I decided to interview people who directly or indirectly knew her, gathering their comments, memories, and personal experiences. I read *Quadrant's* memorial issue dedicated to the life of Esther Harding and listened to her dignified English voice, which was recorded during a formal interview toward the end of her life. I was surprised at the number of Jungians who still carry personal experiences, memories, and feelings about Esther Harding. Her colleagues, analysands, spouses of analysands, and other Jungians who directly or indirectly knew of her all had their stories and readily shared them with me.

But, much to my dismay, I began to hear some pretty jarring opinions about her. "She was a stern, tough tyrant who frightened people with her aloof, harsh judgmental style." "She was a stiff, British grande dame who ran the whole show with an iron fist." According to some, she was highly opinionated and her powerful presence was palpable wherever she went. Like Jung in Zürich, she too had a special chair reserved at the front of the auditorium. One person said that when Esther Harding strode into the auditorium accompanied by her retinue of devoted followers, it was like she "created a wake behind her and immediately was in command of the whole room." She would often stand up in the middle of someone's presentation and loudly object to what they were saying and correct them. Nervous presenters learned to glance cautiously in her direction to see if she was nodding approvingly or was about to attack. Her followers also watched her every move and followed suit. If Dr. Harding attacked, they also attacked the hapless presenter. So apparently her influence in Jungian circles was quite formidable. And she had favorites! Woe to those not in this category. Apparently, she could be quite harsh and rejecting of those who were not in her favor. According to one of her analysands, Edward Edinger was her all-time favorite, and she ultimately asked him to be the executor of her will. Edinger also inherited a treasure trove of her valuable personal papers, which incidentally are currently at the center of a contentious debate about how to preserve them. I attempted to get access to these papers for my preparation of this talk but was told that they are strictly under lock and key in a bank vault somewhere. As someone in New York kiddingly said to me, Esther Harding is still very much alive and still causing controversy in the Jungian community.

After hearing all of these stories, I was rather stunned and uncomfortable with what I was discovering. Frankly, I wasn't sure I should even share this side of her. However, slowly, as the complex picture of who she was began to expand, my own initial prejudice and discomfort quickly dissipated. In short, I opened my own heart and my mind as I began to better understand the private Esther Harding. And I want to share some of my insights with you here.

Before I begin, I want to clarify two terms. When I say *feminine*, it is the feminine principle of relatedness—intuitive, receptive feelings in both women and men. And because we are focusing on these particular women of Bailey's Island, it quickly became apparent to me that it would be impossible not to address the patriarchal challenges these women experienced. When I refer to *patriarchy*, I am not exclusively referring to men, although males have traditionally tended to claim this role of power and dominance in our society more than females. By patriarchy, I mean dominance over others and abuse of power by men and women alike.

As I have already acknowledged, I have had to struggle with my own negative judgments about Esther Harding. But the more I learned about her personal history and the better I understood the historical context of women at the end of the nineteenth century and beginning of the twentieth century, the more quickly my negative attitude dissipated. My admiration has grown, and today I feel nothing but respect and gratitude for this complex and extraordinary woman.

Because analytical psychology is primarily about the pursuit of inner transformation, I wrongly assumed there was little need to address the social context surrounding Esther Harding's life. However, I quickly found myself forced to examine carefully the many historical, political, and cultural forces that made her who she was. In retrospect, it makes me smile because, in her day, she was highly ambivalent about the collective, which she considered potentially dangerous and almost irrelevant to Jung's intrapsychic work of individuation. She was even adamantly opposed to group therapy of any kind. However, I found the historical and cultural context essential for understanding Esther Harding as a person. I began to explore questions like these:

1. What was it like being raised a female child in Shropshire, England, at the end of the nineteenth century?
2. How did that unique English cultural context influence the development of young Esther's psyche?
3. What specific British and American political pressures influenced who she later became?
4. How did her birth order and having many sisters and no brothers affect her psychological development?
5. Why was she driven to leave England and become so professionally successful in America when most women of her generation on both sides of the Atlantic never ventured much beyond family, hearth, and home?

Esther was born into a middle-class family in Shropshire, England, in 1888. Shropshire, located in western central England, shares a border with Wales. Because of frequent border disputes and military conflict in that area since earliest medieval times, thirty-two of England's 186 castles are scattered throughout Shropshire. It has been considered a place of turmoil but also of abundant natural resources, rivers, vast forests and agricultural land, and plentiful in minerals. And importantly, it is considered to be the birthplace of the Industrial Revolution. Incidentally, Esther once said, "If you don't understand that I am Shropshire all the way through, you don't understand me at all."

Esther was the fourth of six sisters. Her father, whom she adored and idolized, was a dental surgeon. Unfortunately, Esther's relationship with her mother, a homemaker, was always problematic, and they were never close.

I find it intriguing and relevant that all three women of Bailey's Island—Esther Harding, Eleanor Bertine, and Kristine Mann—fit the following description: all three were father's daughters and experienced a negative, difficult relationship with their mothers; all were exceptionally intelligent and ambitious well beyond the turn-of-the-century dreams and expectations of the average woman; all three challenged the prevailing norms of the times; they never married or had children; and they all became medical doctors in an era when that was socially unacceptable and extremely difficult for women to do. So who were these exceptional women who chose to live in New York City during the winter months and Bailey's Island, Maine, every summer for all of their adult lives?

Apparently, Esther was deeply lonely, an isolated unhappy girl, a loner homeschooled by a governess until she was eleven. Unlike her popular older sisters, she had almost no sustained friendships during her entire childhood. This continued to be true well into her early thirties. She reported that the only boy she ever loved was her five-year-old cousin, and she was devastated when he moved away. The few other childhood friendships she attempted with female peers were similarly short-lived. They all seemed to disappear, leaving her isolated and lonely. A highly intelligent girl with a difficult and distant relationship with her mother, she resorted to hiding in her bedroom, burying herself in books and dreaming of becoming a missionary like her older sister.

After graduating from high school in Shropshire, she did indeed begin to pursue her dream by attending the London School of Medicine for Women. For her internship, she went to the Royal Infirmary in London, which was the only place that accepted women interns. She was one of nine students and a real oddity in 1914, when the pervasive societal expectations for women were to marry a man and raise children.

London was a dark, forbidding, harsh environment for the lonely girl from Shropshire. It was at the height of the British Empire's imperial power abroad and the era of Dickens's child labor, with terrible working conditions for the lower classes. Everywhere the Industrial Revolution was transforming British society. The constant demeaning and cruel insults she experienced simply for being a "lady doctor" made those years exceptionally grueling and difficult for young Esther. One of the few things I was able to find that indicated any pleasure in her painful life was a description of how, on occasion, very late at night after a long day's work, she would join other medical students to listen to the haunting rhythms of Spanish guitar.

When the announcement was made of the first London performance of Stravinsky's *The Rite of Spring*, Esther had very little money, but she saved for weeks to buy one cheap seat high in the gallery. Apparently, this music "swept over and through her with stirring force." She said later,

> I knew that I was listening to a statement from a new world. High in the gallery that night I knew that the Victorian age was over. Those rhythms were from another world—another level of human experience that the Victorian had guarded himself from. Stravinsky helped me to see the validity of that other world which had so fascinated me and which was so alien to my whole upbringing.

Those insightful and revealing words point to her deeply passionate heart and intelligent soul which understood and felt so much at such a young age.

In 1914, because the onset of World War I had taken most of the men, immediately after she graduated she was given total responsibility for running one of the hospitals near London during the war. She was twenty-six years old! Imagine the heavy responsibilities and internal pressures she must have been experiencing. During this time of professional success but deep loneliness and personal crisis, she was fortuitously given a copy of Carl Jung's "The Psychology of the Unconscious." Being verbally abused, emotionally isolated, and overburdened with so much excruciatingly hard work, she was indeed confronting a major psychological crisis. It was this article that led her to Zürich to start analysis with Jung right after the war in 1919. While working with him, she had the following dream:

I was floundering helplessly in the open sea and had almost lost hope when Jung appears in a large, sturdy ship in the guise of Noah, offers me his hand, and helps me aboard.

As Edinger later said, Esther's encounter with Jung was indeed decisive and life-saving. She was immediately enthralled by Jung and his theory. Indeed, she was one of the first to recognize how revolutionary Jung's psychological discoveries really were. She enthusiastically went back to England and was instrumental in forming the London Psychoanalytic Club dedicated to studying Jung's ideas.

It was there, at the age of thirty-two, that she met and fell in love with another Jungian student and enthusiast, Eleanor Bertine. They instantly recognized a soul mate in each other, someone who finally understood them, was excited by the same things they were, someone they could talk to about their mutual enthusiasm for Jung's ideas. Almost immediately, they began discussing living together. That Christmas, Esther traveled to New York where Eleanor lived, to discuss whether she would move to New York or Eleanor would move to London. With the possibility of starting an analytical training group in New York along with Kristine Mann and Beatrice Hinkle, Esther decided to leave her native England behind and move to New York to be with Eleanor and to begin their life together. When throwing the I Ching, Esther frequently got the Wanderer, which helped her accept this emotionally painful rupture and once again strike out toward challenging new frontiers. But this time she was not alone.

In those early years in New York, she and Eleanor lived together in an apartment on Morningside Park where they saw analysands in the bedroom of their apartment. The three women of Bailey's Island, along with Beatrice Hinkle, together established a small Jungian Institute in an apartment on the lower east side. Later, Esther was instrumental in helping to create the Analytical Psychology Club as well as the C. G. Jung Foundation, where she frequently lectured and presented some of her newest ideas. Seventy-five years later, these organizations are still in existence today. I found it moving to discover that she personally bequeathed approximately one million dollars of her own money to ensure the continuation of these organizations she loved and worked so hard to establish.

Esther and Eleanor often gave delightful dinner parties at their Morningside apartment, a coveted invitation for the lucky ones who were invited. They were highly stimulating and enjoyable evenings filled with wonderful conversation and excellent food prepared by the two women. This suggests quite a different side of Esther than the lonely, grim persona of her London years. I have come to believe that this is when she began to truly come alive, intellectually and emotionally. And, I would also respectfully hypothesize, probably physically as well. The reality that she was a lesbian is usually discreetly sidestepped in most Jungian circles. But I believe at this point in history, when American laws are finally beginning to recognize the legitimacy of homosexual couples, it is also time to acknowledge and respect Esther's important and deeply intimate relationship with Eleanor Bertine. Their relationship was not only intellectually fulfilling for Esther but also emotionally lifesaving and transformative as well. At long last, she had found another human being who fully met her on every level despite the rampant homophobia of the times. As you may know, the lesbian subculture has been grossly misunderstood, overly sensationalized, and shrouded in mystery for years. She had to have known that she was not well understood by most people. Here is another demonstration of the tremendous grit, courage, and inner strength Esther had to live with deep authenticity in a society that not only did not understand her but harshly condemned who she was.

It is interesting to me that it was Jung himself who encouraged their liaison. Yet I learned that Esther was not part of Jung's inner circle in Zürich despite her importance in America. She was not even one of his favorites and was considered by some a "slightly neglected daughter of Jung." Apparently, Jung was rather repelled by her aggressive feminism. But she remained one of Jung's loyal followers to the end of her long life. Her books and lectures as much as anything were some of the most important factors that first helped to widely disseminate Jung's ideas to the general public here in the United States.

I want to consider briefly three different ways I used to deepen my understanding that Esther the person was much more than her intellectually aloof public persona.

The first and most obvious piece of evidence I have just mentioned—her very private and rewarding life with Eleanor Bertine. From the time she partnered with Eleanor, she seemed to finally hit her stride and emotionally blossom. Of course, she was highly discreet and maintained her very proper, dignified British persona for analysands and the general public. But I have come to believe that privately she was finally loved and deeply fulfilled.

Surprisingly, their sexual orientation was common knowledge among New York analysands at the Institute. The fact that there were prominent analysts who were publicly recognized as lesbians in the patriarchal society of the early 1920s is itself rather remarkable considering the deep and pervasive cultural prejudice against homosexuality at that time. In the 1920s, women were still considered by most men and women alike to be inferior, weaker, and less intelligent, second-class citizens who were legally allowed to vote in elections only recently, in 1920. Emotions and intuition, the realm of the feminine, were considered inferior to rational thought, allegedly the realm of the masculine. Racism and homophobia were rampant in America. Public lynchings were still common in the south, and most homosexuals were totally closeted and terrified of being discovered. If exposed, they stood to lose their jobs, their friends, and their connections to their families, and they were often physically attacked and even killed. Yet here were two prominent Jungians defying these powerful cultural norms, and thriving. I find it remarkable that Esther mustered the fierce courage to live such a socially unacceptable lifestyle in full view of those who could have condemned her. I can only believe it was possible because of her powerful inner strength and her own passionate soul which refused to succumb to the tremendous pressures of a patriarchal society where standards of behavior were defined and strictly enforced.

The second reason for my belief in her intense passion is the inner awakening she must have experienced doing the research for her seminal and groundbreaking book, *Women's Mysteries: Ancient and Modern*. In a patriarchal world dominated by men who wrote history primarily about other men, I can only imagine what it must have been like for twenty-seven-year-old Esther, Jung's seminar student, to discover that females actually had their own important historical and mythological underpinnings. Almost no one, including Jung, had that perspective toward human history at that time. Men dominated politics, industry, medicine, finance, indeed most of the public arena, almost exclusively and were the head of household at home as well, but Esther's book dramatically ripped the lid off these old assumptions, suggesting a whole new cultural orientation for men and women alike. Her discovery had to have deeply excited and emboldened her own personal sense of herself as a woman.

Today, women's prominent roles in society are taken for granted, but in 1935, when *Women's Mysteries* was first published, it was revolutionary. Her research findings startled Jung and electrified the eager reading public, who placed her book on the national best-selling list for an extended period of time. Her book is considered by many to be the forerunner of Robert Graves's profoundly influential classic, *The White Goddess*. And it is still in print seventy-six years later. I personally enjoyed imagining what must have been stirring in her young woman's soul as she began to open these doors, one by one, into an obscure, ancient world of feminine history no modern person had ever comprehensively compiled in one place before. Few realize that this original research done by the young girl from Shropshire was one of the very first documents that instigated the future women's movement. Obviously, her work has had a far-reaching impact on our culture. I believe that what started out as her intellectual research into the symbolic meaning of the crescent ended up facilitating a shift in feminine and masculine consciousness that is still reverberating throughout our culture up to the present day. And I don't believe any woman could have remained intellectually detached when the archetypal feminine ground of her own psyche was being metamorphosed by her own hand.

A third reason why I am hypothesizing that Esther was privately a deeply passionate soul full of feelings is her courageous willingness to write the introduction to a provocative book called *Dreaming in Red*, by Nor Hall and Linda Fierz-David. It is a fairly obscure but marvelously juicy, thought-provoking book about a secret initiation hall for women discovered in the ruins of Pompeii in 1910. It is referred to as "the red room" because of its highly sensual, Dionysian, blood red walls dramatically lined with powerfully mysterious women's imagery of childbirth, intimacy, stillbirths, spiritual evolution, and so on. Esther was so personally fascinated by this red room that she traveled from New York to Pompeii, Italy, to see it for herself. Respectable, middle-class Roman women would go there in secrecy to experience intense and life-transformative Dionysian rituals. Esther clearly understood the importance and value of this alternative reality, which was condemned by rational patriarchal Roman society as pagan, provocatively irrational, and even dangerous.

Here are some words from her introduction to *Dreaming in Red*. I invite you to listen carefully to her words as a way of potentially offering deeper insight into her own private inner life. She writes:

> Fierz-David's discussion of the hidden and mysterious happenings represented by the pictures in the Villa makes this danger abundantly clear. Her description of what the emotional impact of the ritual must have been on the self-contained and dignified women entering into the ritual way is most impressive and moving. The ritual entails an *inner happening* that enables the woman to realize her own deepest sexual and erotic potentialities. But, as it is, she emerges again chastened and cleansed—born again, as a twice-born. And, interestingly enough, from here on she is no longer alone in the conscious dignity and self-possession of the first scene but is received almost as a child into the company of initiated, that is, of mature women, now her sisters. The self-contained, self-sufficient woman of the first scene has become one of the sisterhood of women who do not need to assert their value or themselves, either. Their value is obvious; they are among the wise ones, simple, natural, at one with themselves, whose inner dignity needs no advertisement.

When I first read *Dreaming in Red*, I again asked myself: What possessed this allegedly "cold," British woman to write an introduction to such a book? Upon further reflection, I now believe she could have been speaking about a quest toward her own personal psychic initiation, her own wisdom and dignity and sense of belonging to her own sisterhood experience with the three Jungian women of Bailey's Island.

Part of my motivation to articulate the personal side of Esther is that I now believe it was here on Bailey's Island in Maine that she could finally be free to be her most complete feminine self—relaxed, creative, passionate, even playful, knowing she was fully embraced by the natural world of Gaia. I believe she was emotionally nourished by the raw, powerful, archetypal forces unleashed around her: the towering pines dancing with the ocean winds, the rhythmic, haunting call of the sea crashing against the ancient granite rocks, and the dense, cold, heavy fog that sometimes enveloped the entire island for a week at a time.

Known by the locals on Bailey's Island as the "lady doctors" or "those women," Esther, Eleanor, and Kristine were not distracted or consumed by the usual demands on women in those times—caring for children, promoting their husbands' careers, and feeding their families. They were totally free to think, to sit on their front porch for hours drinking "whiskey with a splash of water" (Esther's choice), laughing a lot, and talking deeply with friends and each other. I have wondered if Esther would have been able to reach such depths of understanding about the human psyche if she had not had the intense privacy and emotional nourishment that the natural sanctuary of Bailey's Island offered. I have also wondered if the power and privacy of the island may have become a kind of "red room" for all three of these women, a private sanctuary where they could freely explore the depths of their own feminine souls.

I had the delightful opportunity to talk at length with one of Esther's favorites, one of the lucky analysands who was regularly invited to Bailey's Island each summer to be analyzed. After hearing so much that was negative about her personality, it was a relief and a pleasant surprise to hear his glowing report. His enthusiastic comments conjured up warm memories and delight at being asked to talk about Esther so many years after her death. He said, "She was wonderful, very alive and engaging." At the time, he was a young, inexperienced New York investment banker but during their third analytic session, she emphatically stated, "You *must* go to medical school and you *must* become a Jungian analyst!!! First you must deliver physical babies and then you can deliver psychic babies." For him, it was like "coming home" to work with her. "She was a spiritual mother for me." But he readily admitted that she was also very rigid and opinionated. She once stomped her foot at him and said, "That's impertinent. If you do that, you won't be an analyst." But later, she also said, "Be true to what is moving you."

According to this analysand, it was a wonderful experience to be invited to Bailey's Island. You would walk into her house and hear the low drone of voices upstairs in her bedroom where she saw her analysands. A jigsaw puzzle was spread out downstairs in her living room where you waited your turn. When the session was finished, Esther would make lunch for him, and they would have a very friendly chat. Apparently, she often asked him to do "manly" chores, like stack wood for her. One charming personal bit she told him was that, when tense, her therapy was to get down on her hands and knees and scrub the kitchen floor. Once when sitting together listening to a talk by Joseph Wheelwright, she leaned over and said to her analysand, "I loved Wheelwright's speech but I didn't understand a word of it. Did you?"

* * *

In 1977, at the age of eighty-three, Esther was the last of the three women still alive. She had had a minor heart attack and cataract surgery. Her eyesight was failing, and she was old and frail. But she was determined to take one final trip she had always wanted to make—to Greece. She said, "This trip will be a spiritual quest for me." So, shrunken and frail, dressed in her very wide, very black wraparound sunglasses and a ridiculously awful looking black hat that protected her failing eyesight, she and her friend William Kennedy began a six-week trip to Greece. They stopped in Zürich where, for the first time, she was finally able to visit Jung's tower at Bollingen and also spent time with Marie-Louise von Franz, Barbara Hannah, and others. She then went on to Greece where, Kennedy reported, she mostly sat quietly, drawn deeply into herself, absorbing the meaning of ancient places like Delphi and Eleusis. She admitted that she had never before felt such spontaneous and genuine joy in a collective atmosphere. Kennedy later reported that the themes she spoke about the most were of relationship, sacrifice, and rebirth—especially on the role of women and the changes taking place in the feminine psyche in the West.

On the way home, after six wonderful days with her family in Shropshire, which she had not seen in ten years, she returned to a hotel at the London airport for her flight back to New York the following morning. Kennedy reported that she was in good spirits. In their conversation at dinner that evening, Kennedy said something about being irresponsible, and she said to him, with a sparkle in her eye, "Let's go into the lounge and sit for awhile and talk irresponsibly. I love to talk irresponsibly sometimes, don't you?" She also said, "It's been a wonderful trip and now we're home safe." That night, Esther died peacefully in her sleep.

I want to close with a quote from the introduction of her book, *Psychic Energy: Its Source and Its Transformation*, because I believe she is expressing here why Bailey's Island was so pivotal in the lives of these three Jungian analysts. In the summer of 1948, she wrote from her home on Bailey's Island:

> This book was conceived during the war years, amid the din of a world cataclysm. Yet day by day I sat at my desk in utter solitude and peace, with nothing to disturb my quiet but the call of the gulls and the sound of the Atlantic breaking eternally on the rocks below my window.

SOURCES

Maggie Anthony. *Jung's Circle of Women: The Valkyries* (1990). York Beach, ME: Nicolas-Hays, 1999.

Thomas B. Kirsch. *The Jungians: A Comparative and Historical Perspective*. London: Routledge Press, 2001.

Linda Fierz-David and Nor Hall. *Dreaming in Red: "Reading the Women's Dionysian Initiation Chamber in Pompeii" and "Those Women."* Putnum, CT: Spring Publications, 2005.

Genevieve W. Foster. *The World Was Flooded with Light*. Pittsburgh, PA: University of Pittsburgh Press, 1985.

M. Esther Harding. *Psychic Energy: Its Source and Its Transformation*. Princeton, NJ: Princeton University Press, 1948.

M. Esther Harding. *Women's Mysteries: Ancient and Modern* (1935). Boston: Shambhala, 1971.

Quadrant: Journal of the C. G. Jung Foundation for Analytical Psychology, number 11 (Autumn 1971). Memorial issue to M. Esther Harding.

Samuel Van Culin and Margaret Barker. Interview with M. Esther Harding, April 27, 1969. New York: Jung Library Archives.

Spring
A Journal of Archetype and Culture

Spring: A Journal of Archetype and Culture, founded in 1942, is the oldest Jungian psychology journal in the world. Published twice a year, each issue explores from the perspective of depth psychology a theme of contemporary relevance and contains articles as well as book and film reviews. Contributors include Jungian analysts, scholars from a wide variety of disciplines, and cultural commentators.

Upcoming Issues of Spring Journal

VOLUME 89 — SPRING 2013
Buddhism and Depth Psychology
Refining the Encounter
Guest Editor: Polly Young Eisendrath, Ph.D., Jungian analyst, author, and editor (with Shoji Muramoto) of *Awakening and Insight: Zen Buddhism and Psychotherapy*

VOLUME 90 — FALL 2013
Jung and India
Guest Editors: Al Collins, Sanskrit scholar and psychologist, and Elaine Molchanov, Jungian analyst

Subscribe to Spring Journal!

2 issues (1 year) *within United States* ($40.00)
2 issues (1 year) *foreign airmail* ($65.00)
4 issues (2 years) *within United States* ($70.00)
4 issues (2 years) *foreign airmail* ($115.00)

To order, please visit our online store at:
www.springjournalandbooks.com

Spring Journal, Inc.
627 Ursulines Street, #7 New Orleans, LA 70116 Tel: (504) 524-5117

The 8th Jungian Odyssey

Annual Conference & Retreat

ECHOES OF SILENCE
Listening to Soul, Self, Other

David Whyte, Poet
Lionel Corbett, Jungian Analyst
and Friends & Faculty
of ISAPZURICH

June 15 – 22, 2013
Kartause Ittingen
Thurgau, Switzerland

The former Carthusian monastery, founded 1150

ISAPZURICH
INTERNATIONAL SCHOOL OF
ANALYTICAL PSYCHOLOGY ZURICH
AGAP POSTGRADUATE JUNGIAN TRAINING

www.isapzurich.com
info@jungianodyssey.ch

Photo by Memori, Übersicht über die ehemalige Klosteranlage von Osten,
© Memori, 2011, from http://commons.wikime dia.org/w/ index.php?
title=File:Kartause_Ittingen_1.tif &page=1 (accessed 19 April 2012).